FORGOTTEN FORTRESS

Fort Millard Fillmore
and Antebellum New Mexico
1851 - 1862

Richard Wadsworth

Yucca Tree Press

First printing: December 2002

Wadsworth, Richard
    FORGOTTEN FORTRESS: Fort Millard Fillmore and Antebellum New Mexico, 1851-1862
        1. Southwest United States - History.   2. New Mexico - Frontier History.   3. New Mexico - Indian Wars.   4. Indian Wars - New Mexico.   5. U.S. Civil War, 1861-1865 - New Mexico.   6. Fort Fillmore, New Mexico.
        I. Richard Wadsworth.   II. Title

Library of Congress Control Number: 2002102682
ISBN: 1-881325-57-1

Printed in Canada

CONTENTS

LIST OF ILLUSTRATIONS

ACKNOWLEDGMENTS

I would like to thank the members of the Doña Ana County Historical Society for supporting this study with advice and direction and the Museum of New Mexico for allowing me to view their collection of Fort Fillmore artifacts. There are so many people who have contributed information and/or access to artifacts which came from Fort Fillmore. Special among these are Dr. Edward Staski, New Mexico State University, who provided all available information on the 1986-87 NMSU Excavation at Fort Fillmore. Special help along the way was provided by Tom Leachman, Paul Russell, Terry Humble, William Kupke, James Kuethe, F. William Kuethe, Jr., David O'Bannon, Paul and Mary Taylor, Sally Meeks, Dr. Glenna Dean, Karl Laumbach, Rose Apodaca, Carolina Carbajal, Nermina Paz, Bob Hart, and Ken Davis. Special thanks to Karl Laumbach, John Smith, Leroy Grizzel, Steven Grizzel, Russell Schneider, and John Saige of the Friends of Fort Selden Group for a very special day in October 2000 at the Fort Fillmore Cemetery. I don't think any of us will forget what we saw.

John Salopek and Charlotte Priestley, landowners on whose property Fort Fillmore and the Fort Fillmore Cemetery lie, are to be thanked for allowing the author access to the historic sites and for allowing members of special groups to wander the grounds and create some special memories for the author. Special thanks to John Salopek for preserving the Fort Fillmore area for the future. Special thanks to Charlotte Priestley for going above and beyond the call for historic preservation and allowing the author so much special access in order to prove that an occupied Fort Fillmore Cemetery existed.

The Geronimo Springs Museum in Truth or Consequences, New Mexico must be singled out for special appreciation, for allowing the author access to the Fort Craig collection of artifacts and for providing a home for the Tom Leachman Collection of Fort Fillmore reconstructed china, as well as for gathering military artifacts from many different collections in order to save that part of New Mexico's past for the future.

Finally, I want to give special thanks to Anthony Romero of Santa Clara, New Mexico who, with modest help from the author, was able to find the Bonneville Depot on the Gila River, and who also made available for viewing such important historical sites as Fort Daniel Webster, Fort Joseph Rodman West, Fort McLane at Apache Teju, and others.

Richard Wadsworth
October 2002
Truth or Consequences, New Mexico

INTRODUCTION TO THE ANTEBELLUM U.S. ARMY IN NEW MEXICO

September 23, 1851 - The Beginning

The road was already old. It had seen the passing of many carts, the trampling of untold feet over the centuries since the first cuts in the desert ground were made which told of its establishment. Had the road been able to tell its tale, the column of men now passing along its uneven dusty brown surface would have been remarkable only in the sameness of their dress and in the evenness of the cadence their feet made as they marched along.

The steady clop, clop, clopping of horses' hooves, the rattle and bang of metal meeting metal, the rumbling cadence of drums, the shuffling sounds made by moving feet, announced their coming. A few horses and their riders led the column, with many men following on foot behind, the van made up of mule or ox-drawn wagons trailing off toward the south. At the very front, one man rode alone as he turned eastward off the road onto near virgin desert soil, spoiled only recently by the arrival of others dressed similarly, who waited in formation to welcome him and the column he led.

The leading rider was Dixon Stansbury Miles, a name of importance to this story. Dixon Miles was, at that time, the newly appointed lieutenant colonel of the U.S. Army's 3[d] Infantry Regiment, a portion of which would soon be making the same turn in the road.

Miles, at that time forty-seven years of age and an army veteran of twenty-seven years service, was the commander of the regiment in fact, but not in name. The actual commander of the 3[d] Infantry Regiment on that date, September 23, 1851, was Colonel James

Many. Colonel Many was in New Orleans, and had been there since 1843. James Many, appointed commander of the 3[d] Infantry in 1834, had not been with his regiment during the recently ended Mexican War, a war in which the 3[d] saw much bloody action. Colonel Many was a relic of a United States Army custom: There was no retirement system at this time. James Many, desperately ill for years, held on to his position by right of occupancy. He could hold his colonelcy until he died, or resigned—1851 was his fifty-third year in the Army.[1]

In a letter to General N. Hickman in November 1852, Dixon Miles gave his opinion of old colonels hanging onto their rank until they died, even though they could no longer serve their regiment:

> ... You ask my prospect of promotion. Since I have been a Lieut. Col. I have run up with unprecedented rapidity having risen four files in 18 months—three are still between me and a Colonelcy —two of these will be overslaughed or ought to be—as they can't see, eat, walk, ride, set or hear themselves fart . There are three Colonels, old as that oldest inhabitant, and perhaps will die some time in the 19th Century. They ought to have gone to their happy rest twenty years ago. My prospect of promotion is fair, for I may be a full Col. now. I may be in six months, but almost certain in two years to come. I live in hope.[2]

Dixon Miles was barely acquainted with the officers and men in his new command. He had been appointed to the position only on April 15, 1851, while still serving with the 5th Infantry Regiment at Fort Leavenworth, Kansas Territory. At that time the head-quarters of the 3[d] was in Santa Fe, New Mexico Territory. In order to reach his new command Miles traveled, by his estimate, twelve hundred miles. His journey from Fort Leavenworth to the Post Opposite Paso del Norte, Texas, started on July 24, 1851 and ended on September 15, 1851, a total of fifty-four days. He rode his horse, George, for all but one hundred miles of that trip. Miles was accompanied by sixteen recruits for his regiment. He tried briefly traveling with a wagon train for safety reasons but found that method of travel too slow.[3]

This was not Miles's first time at the new fort site. After arriving at Santa Fe from Fort Leavenworth he gathered some head-quarters personnel together and set out on the Camino Real, or Royal Road, a name derived from the road's ancient Spanish origins. Miles journeyed south to take command of some 3[d] Infantry Regiment companies which were clustered in the region across the Rio Grande River from the Mexican town of Paso del Norte (modern Juárez). Since 1849, troops, principally a battalion of the 3[d] Infantry Regiment, had been stationed at Coons's Ranch near the river crossing to Paso del Norte and on a river island to the south containing the villages of Socorro and San Elizario. The journey from Santa Fe to Coons's Ranch was over three hundred miles of hot and desert—dusty, largely uninhabited, country. Miles arrived on September 15 and imme-diately turned to the business at hand. He had orders to muster the battalion and move it upriver some forty miles to a new fort site, the first fort to be built in southern New Mexico Territory.[4]

Miles's orders were transmitted personally by Colonel Edwin Vose Sumner, newly named commander of the 9th Military Depart-ment, a vast domain which encompassed all of what is now New Mexico, Arizona, parts of Colorado and Nevada, and also included the westernmost section of the state of Texas. Sumner had his orders from higher headquarters. He was to cut costs in the 9th Department by any means necessary. One of the first moves was to remove the headquarters of the 3[d] Infantry from its quarters at Santa Fe to a new fort site far downriver.

There was not a single settlement for miles, but, nonetheless, this spot in the middle of a seemingly endless desert terrain had been care-fully selected. Although not yet anything but a military camp and tent city, the new fort site already had a name. Fort Fillmore was named for President Millard Fillmore, the man who had much to do with creating the New Mexico Territory on which the fort was to stand.

A few other horsemen, the adjutant and senior staff, probably accompanied Miles at the front of the infantry column; these included Assistant Surgeon John F. Hammond, and Brevet-Captain and 1st Lieutenant Barnard E. Bee, the regimental adjutant.

Dixon Stansbury Miles
Courtesy: National Archives, Washington, D.C.

Two majors were allowed in an infantry regiment at that time, as specified in the United States Army Regulations of 1847. Neither were with Miles on September 21, but they should be mentioned. One was Major Electus Backus, the senior field grade officer, on detached service in northern New Mexico. The other was Major Gouveneur Morris, then at El Paso but soon to be at Fort Fillmore. Lieutenant Colonel Miles, Major Backus, and Major Morris were West Point classmates, and there appears to have been friction between them. One critical point of contention was that Miles was promoted to lieutenant colonel ahead of Morris and Backus, both of whom had at one time been senior to Miles in rank and time in grade. The difference was Dixon Miles's brevet to the rank of lieutenant colonel for bravery during the Mexican War. By virtue of that brevet, a military concept that will be examined here in some detail, Miles was senior when the new permanent lieutenant colonel position came open in the 3^d Infantry Regiment.[5]

Once the 3^d Infantry staff passed into the fort area, the next most likely regimental members to appear would have been the enlisted men carrying the two silken colors (flags) that infantry regiments of the period carried in the field when the regimental commander sallied forth. One of these would have been a national flag, with the name of the regiment embroidered in silver on the center stripe. The 3^d Infantry Regiment may not have had an up-to-date flag with the proper number of stars, thirty-one, since California's admission was very recent and acquisition and transport processes very slow. The other color, the regimental flag, was medium blue in background, with the arms of the United States embroidered in silk in the center. On a scroll beneath the national eagle, which was part of the arms, the name of the regiment was embroidered. The singular characteristic of these infantry colors was that they were huge, both being six feet six inches fly, and six feet deep on the pike. In addition, yellow fringe ran around the edges of each. They could be furled on the march if a wind came up, as it would be difficult for the men carrying such large flags to hold them.[6]

As the bearers passed into what would be the regiment's new home at Fort Fillmore, they had the colors unfurled and flying.

Perhaps the regimental band played as they followed the colors. The 3ᵈ Infantry Band was with Miles on September 23 as his letter of October 9, 1851, attests. Given that Fort Fillmore was to be an infantry regimental headquarters with attached troops and staff, the regimental band would also have made the move. Records have not been located describing the makeup or instruments the band brought with them, but we can say something about the band's possible size. The 1860 census indicates the 3ᵈ Infantry Band was composed of a principal musician and thirteen other members. In 1851 the 3ᵈ Infantry staff had sixteen enlisted men, including the sergeant major and quartermaster sergeant. Most or all of the rest must have comprised the band.[7]

In addition, each company of infantry had one fifer and one drummer assigned. When an infantry company was in barracks or on the road these fifers and drummers kept the cadence, sounded assembly and the long roll, and announced other calls to duty. These individuals would have been with the infantry main force as it followed the band into the new fort site.

Lieutenant Colonel Miles had only one infantry company with him on the journey up from El Paso, although additional troops were expected. That was Company 'K,' 3ᵈ Infantry, commanded by Brevet-Major and Captain Israel Bush Richardson, an 1841 West Point graduate.

An infantry company in September 1851 was supposed to be composed of three officers and seventy-eight rank and file. Rarely were the companies ever at full strength. Men were discharged, some deserted, a few died. More often the reduced strength was caused by men being on detached service—escorting wagon trains and important travelers, farming, doing construction, or even out on campaign against the Indians.

Replacements came to New Mexico in batches, whenever they could be gathered together back East and transported from places like Jefferson Barracks, Missouri, Fort Leavenworth, Kansas Territory, or even up from San Antonio, Texas. Miles brought only a small group, sixteen soldiers, when he came to the New Mexico Territory. More often large groups of recruits arrived at the 9ᵗʰ Department headquarters at Santa Fe under officer escort, there to be distributed to companies on an as-needed basis.

Rarely were the allocated three officers on duty with their company at any time. In the case of Company 'K,' they were led by the actual company commander, Brevet-Major Israel Richardson. Richardson served during the recently ended Mexican War, where he earned two brevets (to the ranks of captain and major) for gallantry at the Battles of Contreras, Churubusco, and Chapultepec. Richardson had been promoted to the Regular Army rank of captain only recently, on March 5, 1851. Because of his brevet awards in the war with Mexico, he could be addressed as major when on detached service. The brevet to major helped at promotion time also. Richardson served at Fort Fillmore as a captain, rather than in his brevet rank, for which he was paid a bonus. When he was moved to Fort Daniel Webster at a later date, he was there acting in the grade of brevet-major, commanding the fort.[8]

The infantry company was followed into the fort by wagons carrying tents, equipment, extra weapons, food, tools, and sundry supplies that a regiment establishing a new fort in the middle of a vast desert might need. They had not brought everything. The 3d Infantry's quartermaster, Captain Andrew Bowman, stayed at Coons's Ranch across from Paso del Norte with a large amount of government property, to be removed later or sold to the local community.

The arrival of the 3d Infantry Regiment staff and one company of infantry at the site of Fort Fillmore has been depicted as somewhat formal. The reason for this is that one other unit, a mounted company of United States dragoons, was already at the site waiting for Miles to arrive. Because of their presence, Miles probably made a formal entrance with band playing and drums beating. There might also have been officials from the communities of Doña Ana and Las Cruces. A new fort in a place where there were so few people must have been a grand occasion.

Company 'H,' 1st United States Dragoon Regiment, commanded by Brevet-Captain and 1st Lieutenant, Abraham Buford, arrived at the Fort Fillmore site earlier. Company 'H' had been resident at the small village of Doña Ana, some twelve miles north, since late 1849, the first American military unit stationed south of the Jornada del Muerto.

Brevet-Captain Buford was an 1841 West Point graduate. He had served on the western frontier ever since, coming to Company

'H' at Doña Ana earlier in 1851. Buford received a brevet to the rank of captain during the Mexican War for gallantry during the Battle of Buena Vista in Mexico. He was commanding in that brevet rank at Fort Fillmore.[9] Buford, no doubt, had his company of dragoons mounted and as smartly arrayed as possible in anticipation of the arrival of Lieutenant Colonel Miles and his 3[d] Infantry staff.[9]

The headquarters of the 1st Dragoons was at that time at Fort Leavenworth, Kansas Territory. Dragoon companies, scattered among many posts in the New Mexico Territory and elsewhere, served as the quick reaction force of their day. The Indians, at least the ones who raided the local Mexican farmers, were most often mounted and only a mounted force could catch them. Hence, Fort Fillmore usually had one mounted company of horsemen, sometimes two.

Before briefly viewing the surrounding communities, we will examine the fort grounds as the officers first saw them in 1851. The land upon which the dragoons camped, and into which the 3[d] Infantry arrived, was a sea of sand, scrubby grasses, and mesquite, but was not without the touches of civilization. Miles said of the site on his earlier pass-by:

> There is no comparison but that Major Morris has selected the best and only eligible site for building on, an occupancy by troops, on the whole road from this to Dona Ana. The site of the fort is on a gently inclined plain, having sandy, gravelly soil, with a sufficiency of good tillable land in front. The old acequias running up to the base of the fort, and cottonwood so much more abundant than at the place of that name.[10]

Miles's comments on the acequia provide an important insight. Man-made irrigation systems, moving river water to where it was needed to grow crops, came right up to where the fort was to be constructed. These tell of a growing farm economy, not a desert wilderness. It is true that toward the east and the Organ Mountains all was desert plant and mesquite. But to the west and north for some distance was a fertile valley, well irrigated, and already gaining in population before the fort was built.

The Rio Grande lay less than one-half mile from the fort. Across that river the land belonged to Mexico. The Mexican town of Mesilla, lying some six miles northwest of the Fort Fillmore site, was created in March 1850 by Mexican farmers from Doña Ana who preferred living under Mexican rule. Led by Rafael Ruelas, by 1851 the colonists had quickly established a thriving town with a significant population. For some reason, the people of Mesilla were counted in the 1850 U.S. census. This was probably because the permanent boundary had not yet been firmly fixed in that region. In December 1850, there were two thousand inhabitants living in Mesilla. That alone shows that Fort Fillmore was not in a vast wilderness far from civilization, as some historical accounts suggest.

On the American side of the river, along the road to Santa Fe that Fort Fillmore would help guard, were the villages of Doña Ana and Las Cruces. Doña Ana was established in January 1844 by a band of Mexican colonists led by Pablo Melendrez. Melendrez, a farmer and merchant, was the Alcalde of Doña Ana when Company 'H,' 1st Dragoons, was stationed there.

Even with the loss of so many families to the Mesilla colony after the American occupation, the 1850 census shows one thousand persons living in or near Doña Ana. Las Cruces, which was destined to outgrow both towns, was surveyed in 1849 by Captain Delos Sackett. Sacket laid out the town site at the request of Pablo Melendrez, who, satisfied to live under American rule, wanted to move more colonists south to take advantage of the irrigable land in that direction. By December 1852, American census takers reported a Las Cruces population numbering five hundred.[11]

If a map drawn by Captain John Pope in 1853-54 is in any way indicative of the situation in 1851, the Mesilla Valley was already a vast crop-growing region, rich in corn, beans, and a variety of other crops, when Lieutenant Colonel Miles brought the 3d Infantry to their new home. The military, although planning to grow their own crops, eventually learned they had to rely on the inhabitants of the Mesilla Valley for much of their sustenance, animal fodder, and technological skill. Soldiers were soldiers, not farmers, as time would certainly tell.

Introduction - Notes

1. Francis B. Heitman. *Historical Register and Dictionary of the United States Army, From Its Organization, September 29, 1789, to March 2, 1903, Volume I.* (Washington, D.C.: Genealogical Publishing Co. Inc., 1994), Biography of Colonel James Many. (Hereafter cited as Heitman, name of officer referenced.)

2. Dixon Stansbury Miles to General N. Hickman, November 15, 1852. This letter was included in the unpublished private correspondence of Colonel Dixon Stansbury Miles, acquired from Mr. Bill Kuethe, Glen Burnie, Maryland. Mr. Kuethe provided letters and envelopes with this correspondence. Photographs of the envelopes containing the letters show the earliest American postal system in New Mexico and West Texas in operation. Post offices include Santa Fe, Socorro (New Mexico) and Fronteras (Texas), not El Paso, Magoffinsville, San Elizario, Post Opposite El Paso, etc. A post office at Fronteras was a major surprise. Miles first used the Santa Fe mail route north and across the plains, later turning to the Texas route through the El Paso region (Fronteras) as being faster. (Hereafter cited as Kuethe Correspondence.)

3. Dixon Stansbury Miles to Sarah Ann Briscoe Miles, wife, September 16, 1861, Kuethe correspondence. This letter was mailed from El Paso (Post Opposite Paso del Norte) and may have gone through the Santa Fe Post Office. No envelope is extant.

4. Miles to Buell, September 16, 1851, *National Archives: Letters Received, 9th Military District, Department of New Mexico, 1849-1853, Record Group M1102, Roll #4.* (Hereafter cited as M1102, Roll #.)

5. Heitman, Dixon Miles.

6. War Department, *General Regulations for the Army of the United States - 1847.* (Washington, D.C.: J. & G.S. Gideon, 1847), p. 215. (Hereafter cited as *1847 General Regulations.*)

7. United States Government, 1850 and 1860 National Census, New Mexico Territory, Santa Fe.

8. Heitman, Israel Bush Richardson.

9. Heitman, Abraham Buford.

10. Miles to Assistant Adjutant General, Santa Fe, September 16, 1851, M1102, Roll 4.

11. United States Government Census, 1850 - Doña Ana, Mesilla, Las Cruces.

1

PRE-FORT FILLMORE MILITARY PRESENCE

The first Regular Army unit to arrive in southern New Mexico south of the Jornada del Muerto, was Company 'H,' 1st United States Dragoon Regiment. That unit arrived in the village of Doña Ana in January 1849, under the temporary command of Brevet-Major and Captain Delos Sackett. Sackett was not the true commander of Company 'H,' but he remained in command as the only officer available until the unit's actual commander, Brevet-Major Enoch Steen, arrived in July 1849. Doña Ana was then the only village between the large Mexican town of Paso del Norte, which lay some fifty miles away to the south on the other side of the Rio Grande, and the village of Socorro at the north end of the Jornada del Muerto. Jornada del Muerto (Journey of Death) was an arid stretch of desert some ninety miles long where the Camino Real established by the Spaniards, moved away from the river's vital sustenance due to impassable wagon terrain along that section of the river. While on duty in Doña Ana, Brevet-Major Sackett laid out a second small farming village to the south of Doña Ana which was to be called Las Cruces. Sackett performed this duty at the request of the Alcalde of Doña Ana, Don Pablo Melendrez.

There was no United States military garrison near the Mexican town of Paso del Norte until October 1849, when several companies of the 3^d Infantry Regiment, commanded by Brevet-Major and Captain Jefferson Van Horne, arrived from their former posts in Texas. One company was stationed on an island in the middle of the Rio Grande, on which were situated the small communities of

San Elizario, Ysleta, and Socorro. At a former Mexican presidio, or fort, at San Elizario, one 3^d Infantry company found a home. Three other companies were stationed at a rented site on property owned by Franklin Coons. Van Horne established the 3^d Infantry Regiment headquarters there. The post at Coons's Ranch, or Paso del Norte, or Franklin, or El Paso, as it was sometimes called, was located where the Convention Center now stands in today's El Paso, Texas. The purpose of the post was to show the American flag to the large Mexican town just across the river; a secondary purpose was to protect commerce moving along the Camino Real into Mexico.

Brevet-Major Van Horne commanded at Coons's Ranch by virtue of his brevet rank and in the pay grade of major. He was actually an army captain of almost twenty-four years service. A West Point graduate, class of 1827, Van Horne received a brevet to the rank of 'honorary' major in August 1847 for bravery during the Battle of Churubusco in Mexico. Because of this recognition Brevet-Major and Captain Jefferson Van Horne commanded four infantry companies—two battalions in that day—with corresponding responsibility. The near doubling of the number of men Van Horne had to clothe and feed gave a dedicated and meticulous officer like himself headaches other officers might not have felt as intensely. The powers that be at Santa Fe and Austin, who provided his charges with clothing and provisions, had concerns of their own. The increase in the numbers of soldiers in infantry companies, lately mandated by the U.S. Congress, brought administrative, logistical, and commissary problems, straining the ox- and mule-drawn wagon system which bore the burden of such changes. Early 1851 saw this system breaking down. Questions arising from the resulting stress received much attention at the highest command levels of the army.

Staff officers, including the General-in-Chief himself, Major-General Winfield Scott, in his offices in New York City, dealt with issues far more vast than whether Brevet-Major Van Horne, out on the edge of the frontier, had sufficient clothing for his infantrymen. There were new posts to be founded, roads to be laid, land surveys to be conducted, California-bound immigrants to be protected,

Indian problems to be solved, and more. Due to the many problems arising in the newly conquered territories in the west, with the best of efforts it would be years, even decades, before any final solutions came about. Until then, the watchwords were experiment and go forward. Many proposals and plans attempted to solve some of these problems. For instance, in relation to the questions raised by Van Horne, the debaters argued over whether the problem of increased mouths to feed and clothe could be solved by having the soldiers grow their own food, thereby allowing the creaking supply system to find some relief.

Brevet-Major Van Horne had little inkling of the debates that were to bring sweeping changes to his command and to the region. Besides clothing and feeding problems, he had other concerns. The Mexican-American national boundary was in flux as the result of the American victory. A far-reaching border survey was being conducted by a Boundary Commission under the dual leadership of a presidential appointee, John Bartlett, assisted by Mexican government representatives. This effort was winding down locally in early 1851, although part of the commission survey party was still working in the region. The 3ᵈ Infantry supported that effort by providing protection for the survey parties using escort troops. On January 9, 1851, Company 'A,' 3ᵈ Infantry, left Coons's Ranch for the Santa Rita Copper mines in the Mimbres River region near present-day Silver City and an old Spanish fortress there which the Bartlett Commission soon renamed Cantonment Dawson.[1]

The border region was plagued with thefts, mostly the result of Mescalero Apaches coming down from their mountain homes to steal stock, but also from American and Mexican bandits out for the same goods. Early in January, James Magoffin, one of the leading citizens of the small and widely separated colonies on the American side of the border, reported the loss of twenty-two mules from his fortified compound, which he had named Magoffinsville. Another citizen, a Mr. White, who established a community to the west of Coons's Ranch which he called Fronteras, reported all of his cattle stolen. On January 13, thieves again struck Magoffin's compound, stealing another twenty-five mules. Brevet-Major Van Horne fumed at his inability to do anything about this situation. Moccasin tracks were found but anybody could wear moccasins. Unless the post at San Elizario or his headquarters at Coons's Ranch was directly attacked, Van Horne's infantry were relatively helpless. By the time the foot soldiers reached the scene of the depredation, the thieves were long gone. Pursuit against horse-mounted foes was ludicrous.[2]

Van Horne was not averse to mounting his infantry on mules if that had been possible. In fact, during 1850, he had done so at least once when Apaches temporarily held California-bound immigrants captive. He simply did not always have the animals available; when he had them, he used them.

The nearest mounted unit on which Brevet-Major Van Horne could call was some fifty miles away at Doña Ana. By early 1851, Captain Oliver Shepherd commanded that post with Company 'B,' 3[d] Infantry and Company 'H,' 1st Dragoons, in residence. Company 'H,' being mounted, was the rapid reaction force of its day for all of New Mexico south of the Jornada del Muerto. Of course, the process of sending couriers to Doña Ana to see if the dragoons were available was almost as slow as sending the infantry after the thieves. By the time the horse soldiers could be ordered out, the trail was very cold.

In theory, Brevet-Major Van Horne's command should have been assigned to the Department of Texas, which at that time was called the 8th Military Department. New Mexico was the 9th Military Department until 1854. San Elizario, Socorro, Ysleta, Fronteras, and Coons's Ranch were located within the accepted boundaries of the state of Texas. The problem was that if Van Horne received his orders from the 8th Department commander in San Antonio, he would not be able to call upon the dragoon company in Doña Ana for assistance. That company was under the control of the 9th Department commander. The Army was strict on honoring departmental boundaries and spheres of influence. The Army command in New York City eventually decided to consider the entire region across from the Mexican town of Paso del Norte to be a functioning part of the 9th Department. This decision was never fully accepted by the 8th Department commander; arguments for changing the status of the region continued throughout the 1850s.

For a brief period in 1850 the entire New Mexico Territory east of the Rio Grande almost became part of Texas. The Compromise of 1850 ended claims made by Texas, and Texas received a financial settlement. Regardless of what transpired, the issue of which military department should control the infantry companies at El Paso was still an open one. On January 14, 1851, Governor Sam Houston of Texas, in a letter to Secretary of War Charles M. Conrad, asked once again that the El Paso area be brought under the control of the 8th Military Department (Texas); Houston expressed a concern that the western tip of Texas might be detached one day if New Mexico Territory continued to retain nominal military control over the region. Secretary Conrad refused Houston's request.[3]

Indian raids were not the only trouble in the El Paso area early in 1851. Members of the United States-Mexico Boundary Commission soon traveled to the Santa Rita Copper Mines, escorted by Company 'A,' 3d Infantry. Before leaving, an incident occurred at their camp near the village of Socorro, which was not far from the army post at San Elizario. Van Horne reported the murder of two teamsters working with the commission, and that the lives of the commissioners had been threatened. He ordered Captain William Brooke Johns, commanding Company 'C' at Coons's Ranch, to take a sergeant, a corporal, and nine men to Socorro to "preserve order and protect the property." Before they arrived, the perpetrators of the murders had been tried and hung on the authority of the boundary commissioner.[4]

Brevet-Major Van Horne was quite curt when he notified the 9th Department concerning this incident. The affair was the result of a dance held at San Elizario. One of the commission employees, a man named Clarke, was stabbed to death in a drunken brawl by three of the rowdy teamsters who had accompanied the Boundary Commis-sion from San Antonio. Dr. C.L. Sonnichsen in his book, *Pass of the North*, comments that murder was not viewed as such a serious criminal act in that day as it is today. In fact, the accused murderers, William Craig, Marcus Butler, and John Wade seemed surprised when they were charged and brought to trial. They may have gotten away with it, save for the fact that the deceased was an employee of the boundary commission; the law was quite clear about what should happen in such a case. The three were tried and hung, a fourth man having made his escape.[5]

In New York City, Washington, and Santa Fe, where the highest-ranking officers weighed the military problems associated with the new far-flung territories, cost-conscious minds were in the majority. They looked at Doña Ana, San Elizario, Fronteras, and Coons's Ranch, often by then called Paso del Norte or Post Opposite El Paso, or simply El Paso, and asked how they might cut costs. Wouldn't it be better if the United States government did not have to rent building space, but leased land on which soldiers might build and maintain their own quarters? Also, might the soldiers not better serve the nation through providing themselves with their own foodstuffs, and in the bargain save the United States government hard-to-get money that might be better used elsewhere? Where might such productive and cost-effective sites be found within the Territory of New Mexico, and who would be the best serving officer to bring such changes to fruition? Those questions soon came to the forefront.

While Brevet-Major Van Horne worried about bandits, Indians, and clothing in El Paso, crucial command decisions were finalized. On March 1 he pulled the infantry guard back from Socorro, Texas to Coons's Ranch because the situation there had stabilized. The hangings did their work. The final felon, Alexander Young, was captured in Carrizal, Mexico and returned to Socorro, Texas. During the arrest of Mr. Young, five dragoon deserters were also apprehended and brought back. These errant soldiers had deserted from the dragoon company at Socorro, New Mexico, above the Jornada del Muerto. Brevet-Major Van Horne ordered their return to that post.[6]

During the years 1849-50, when the great expansion was beginning to take place in California, New Mexico Territory (including Arizona at that time), Oregon (by agreement with Great Britain), etc, the cost of supporting the army units serving in the seven pre-expansion military departments was $2,413,580.74. The cost of the four new departments, including New Mexico's 9th Military Department, was an astronomical $7,444,261.26—three times as much. Costs had to be cut.[7] In addition, in the case of New Mexico, someone familiar with the necessity of making those cuts, and with the power to do what was necessary, had to be sent there to do it. Colonel John Munroe had been the head of the 9th Military Department since receiving official orders on May 26, 1849. He was replaced by a man who would alter the 9th Department so drastically that the former commander would hardly have recognized it a year later. That man was Brevet-Colonel Edwin Vose Sumner.

Edwin Sumner was a career Regular Army officer of a class fast becoming a rarity in 1851—high-ranking officers who were not West Point graduates. Sumner was born on January 30, 1797, making him fifty-four years of age when he was given the New Mexico command. He had been appointed a 2[d] lieutenant of the 2[d] Infantry Regiment from New York on March 3, 1819, forty-two years before. Serving in various infantry assignments through-out the 1820s and early 1830s, Sumner volunteered for service with the 1st Dragoon Regiment on March 4, 1833, when that regiment was founded. There had been no horse soldiers in the United States Army since 1815 and the end of the war with the British. Congress believed the expense of cavalry formations too great for the nation to bear. But, as the American forward thrust burst onto the Great Plains, and infantry formations encountered the well-mounted Indians of that region, cavalry was quickly seen to be a necessity. Captain Sumner served with his regiment into the Mexican War, being promoted to the rank of major, one of two field grade officer ranks in that regiment, on June 30, 1846. That promotion was quickly followed by two brevets, to lieutenant colonel on September 8, 1847, for bravery at the Battle of Molino del Rey, and then to full brevet-colonel on July 13, 1848. Thus he came to command in New Mexico with a high, but brevet, rank. No matter, there was a job to do, and Edwin Vose Sumner was definitely the man to do it. What did this proud officer think upon taking command of the huge New Mexico Territory, when most other department commanders were generals, while he was still a lieutenant colonel, although having a brevet one grade higher?[8]

On March 3, 1851, John C. Calhoun became governor of the New Mexico Territory. Calhoun was a friend of then President of the United States, Millard Fillmore. He did not get along with Colonel Munroe, Sumner's predecessor, which is perhaps another reason why Colonel Munroe was replaced. The question of military versus civilian authority in the territory was a point of great contention—a problem which the new military commander found reason to exacerbate rather than solve.

California-bound emigrants moved in significant numbers through the region in 1851. Although no longer new, gold fever among Americans was still at a heightened pitch. As a result, one of the problems the military in southern New Mexico Territory faced was desertion among the troops, some of whom probably enlisted to get a free trip to a point nearer the gold fields. Deserters, when caught, could be punished in a number of ways, including having to make up the time they were gone by extended enlistment, or sometimes being branded with a 'D' and discharged. General Order No. 21 of the year 1851, issued in April by the Adjutant General's Office in Washington, addressed punishments for deserters. General-in-Chief Scott had learned of these unusual punishments which he judged excessively cruel. Scott stated that deserters might be confined, with or without ball and chain. They could be flogged with whips, and either discharged or reprimanded and sent back to duty. They could be made to work at hard labor under guard and forfeit pay and allowances. They could not be tortured.[9]

By late March, Washington finalized decisions regarding decreasing costs in the West. The adjutant general of the Army, Colonel Roger Jones, gave Brevet-Colonel Edwin Vose Sumner his marching orders. Life among the military in New Mexico Territory was about to change radically. Jones was very specific:

The General-In-Chief directs that you proceed to New Mexico without unnecessary delay. You will, according to the provisions of General Order No. 49, of 1849, (which see) to the command thereof. There is reason to believe that the stations occupied by the troops in the 9th Department, are not the best for the protection of the frontier against the inroads of the Indians. Accordingly, as the responsible commander in that quarter, you will use a sound discretion in making such changes, as becoming acquainted with the country, you may deem necessary and proper. By authority of the secretary of war, on assuming command of Department No. 9, you will consider yourself on duty according to your brevet rank.

Instructions have been given to send to Santa Fe 342 recruits for the 3d Infantry and the two companies, 2d Artillery, serving in the Department. And orders have been issued for 300 recruits for the nine companies of dragoons, there on duty, making six hundred and forty-two in all. You will give all necessary orders for their march from Fort Leavenworth, and in the meantime, under the instructions of Bvt. Brig. General Clarke, commanding 6th Department, you will commence the arrangements for equipping these troops for the march. General Clarke has received instructions respecting pushing forward the recruits as far as Fort Leavenworth.[10]

Adjutant-General Jones did not use the word 'cost' when referring to the need to change the distribution of the troops. Perhaps he realized that if a copy of this order regarding costs reached the 9th Department it might raise concerns among the owners of property currently being leased by the Army. Many of the ways of doing Army business in southern New Mexico were about to change, impacting the profits certain businessmen made from government contracts and rentals.

A major Indian raid occurred near Coons's Ranch in late March 1851, about the time Sumner was appointed. Brevet-Major Van Horne reported that Indians killed a number of Mexican teamsters on the road to Carrizal in Chihuahua. These men were escorting a corn train belonging to Juan Ponce de Leon, a noted El Paso area trader. These same Indians then came up to Paso del Norte and killed two more Mexican farmers. Van Horne put his troops on alert, although he had no mounted force with which to pursue the perpetrators. In addition to problems with Indians, Brevet-Major Van Horne spoke out in early April about a group of bandits that seemed to be the notable Comancheros of Texas. These individuals he called "piratical interloping traders." They bought horses and mules from Indians along the border near San Elizario, knowing that these same Indians murdered Mexican citizens to get those animals. Van Horne said gaining proof in order to try these Americans for their crimes would be difficult since many Americans in the region seemed to be involved in the traffic.[11]

It was at about the time of these raids that the government and the Mescalero Apaches signed their first treaty. This treaty was formalized during a meeting between the Governor of New Mexico Territory, James J. Calhoun, who was also Superintendent of Indian Affairs, Brevet-Colonel John Munroe, who still commanded the 9th Military Department, and several leaders of the sub-tribe of Apaches called Mescaleros, who resided on the east side of the Rio Grande. In return for not raiding American and Mexican communities, the Apaches were granted the right to approach the settlements and roads for trading purposes, as well as to receive implements of farming and gifts at the discretion of the American government. Neither side held to the agreement.[12]

Surprisingly, nothing was directly stated in the treaty about supplying food to the Apaches, the central reason for most Apache raids. The Spanish colonial administration's recognition that peace with the Apaches could be gained only by feeding them was not directly addressed. One surmises that the Americans believed in the early days that the Apaches would willingly become farmers if they were provided with the tools and taught how to grow crops.

Colonel Sumner traveled from the East over the Santa Fe Trail. Because his arrival in Santa Fe was to bring major changes to military life, Governor Calhoun moved quickly to provide New Mexico with a working territorial government designed to challenge military authority. The old state assembly was rendered null and void following the declaration of the United States Congress that New Mexico would be a United States territory. Governor Calhoun called for an election of representatives to a new legislature. Voters in the eight districts elected thirteen senators and twenty-six representatives to a legislative body scheduled to meet for the first time on June 3, 1851. Calhoun saw the most pressing problems as education, Indian attacks, and the general isolation of the new territory from the centers of United States power. In fact, as far as education was concerned, the 1851 census states that out of a population of 56,984, seven of every eight people were illiterate.[13]

In the last few days before Colonel Sumner's arrival in June, an incident at Doña Ana emphasized the lack of a social safety net for the military then serving in New Mexico. If an accident happened which disabled a soldier serving on the frontier, there was little concern shown by the government as to his future. First Sergeant Theodore Bird of Company 'H,' 1st Dragoons, had been the 1st sergeant for several months when he maimed his hand in a freak accident while he was off duty. Thereafter, Bird was unable to fully utilize that hand and could no longer ride his horse. Brevet-Major Shepherd was careful to mention the fact that the accident happened off duty. That allowed the army to discharge Bird without any kind of recompense. In fact, Brevet-Captain Abraham Buford, the commander of Company 'H,' permitted Bird to resign his 1st sergeant's rank for that of private, on the condition that he be given an immediate furlough. Shepherd asked the Colonel commanding the 9th Department to meet with Bird and allow him to proceed to his home, where he still had an eighty-four-year-old father living. He would then be considered discharged.[14]

Nineteenth century societies, like many today, did not allow for the care of individuals who went down on one knee, so to speak. If there was no family, then God help them, for nobody else did. Had the accident happened on duty, Sergeant Bird may have been allowed to live the rest of his life at a soldier's home set up for that purpose, one of which existed in Washington, D.C.

The man taking over the 9th Military Department had little concern over whether his enlisted, mostly immigrant, force were fully satisfied with their lot. Colonel Sumner had a department to reorganize, and he was just about to get started.

NOTES - Chapter 1

1. Van Horne to McLaws, January 12, 1851, M1102, Roll 3.

2. Van Horne to McLaws, January 14, 1851, M1102, Roll 3.

3. Houston to Conrad, January 14, 1851, M1102, Roll 3.

4. Van Horne to McLaws, February 1, 1851, M1102, Roll 3.

5. C.L. Sonnichsen. *Pass of the North*. (El Paso: Texas Western Press, 1968), pp.137, 138.

6. Van Horne to McLaws, March 1, 1851, M1102, Roll 3.

7. Robert W. Frazer, *New Mexico in 1850*. (Norman: University of Oklahoma Press, 1968), pp.57-63.

8. Heitman, Edwin Vose Sumner.

9. Adjutant General's Office, *General Order No. 21 of 1851, April 3*. Washington D.C., M1102, Roll 3.

10. Jones to Sumner, March 29, 1851, M1102, Roll 3.

11. Van Horne to McLaws, April 1, 1851, M1102, Roll 3.

12. The treaty signed in April 1851 between Governor Calhoun, Colonel Munroe and the Mescalero was only the first of many. In effect, what the treaty did was allow the United States Army to hunt down any and all Apaches who came near the American and Mexican settlements without permission. No Mescalero was safe from a fired round sent his/her way by a United States soldier. This treaty, in effect, codified into law the principle that was already being carried out in practice.

13. Robert W. Larson, *New Mexico's Quest for Statehood*. (Albuquerque: The University of New Mexico Press, 1968), p. 65.

14. Shepherd to McLaws, June 1, 1851, M1102, Roll 3.

2

SUMNER TAKES COMMAND

The new commander of the Department of New Mexico was sometimes called 'Bull Head,' a nickname acquired during the recent war with Mexico; a musket ball glanced off his head and left him uninjured. Brevet-Colonel Edwin Vose Sumner arrived at Santa Fe on July 19, 1851 and wasted no time in making sweeping changes as to how Army units were structured and housed in New Mexico Territory, all with the permission of the War Department in Washington.

Edwin Sumner is often portrayed as a strong moralist who sought to get the troops away from the vice and depravity available in the towns. There were other equally important reasons for the changes he made. The first involved expenditures associated with keeping troops billeted in towns. Another part of the rationale involved making the forts self-sufficient though farming. Sumner believed troops manning the forts could sustain themselves. The troops could farm and raise stock, as well as perform their missions as soldiers, thus providing a cost benefit to the nation.

Brevet-Colonel Sumner's mark on New Mexico Territory affected all commanders who followed him. Before September 1851 the troops were stationed in villages and towns, where they rented suitable quarters and were situated to protect the major population centers. Pre-Sumner garrisons were stationed at Rayado, Taos, Abiquiu, Santa Fe, Las Vegas, Albuquerque, Cebolletta, Socorro, Doña Ana, Coons's Ranch, and San Elizario. Most were well-established infantry posts, with a mission of area defense.

Military force layouts at the close of Brevet-Colonel Sumner's tour of duty show an entirely different distribution. Except for

Santa Fe and Albuquerque, the alteration was total. For the first time the word 'fort' appeared in New Mexico Territorial history. Soon the designations Fort Fillmore, Fort Conrad, Fort Union, Fort Webster, Fort Defiance, Fort Massachusetts (Colorado), and Camp Vigilance—all established well away from the towns— became familiar to many in the Territory. These were the legacy of Edwin Vose Sumner.

Major Electus Backus was one of two field-grade officers serving in the 3^d Infantry Regiment as members of the staff. By June 1851, and before Brevet-Colonel Sumner arrived to take command of the 9th Military Department, Major Backus took brief command at El Paso. Backus's decisions later aided Sumner in his final choices for the Department's reorganization. Major Backus arrived in June via the southern route from San Antonio, traveling as part of a large government wagon train bringing supplies for the Bartlett Boundary Commission. Upon his arrival in the El Paso area he relieved Brevet-Major Van Horne and sent Van Horne, with Company 'E,' to San Elizario, transferring Captain William Brook Johns and Company 'C' to Coons's Ranch.[1]

Backus knew that part of his mission to New Mexico was to evaluate where costs might be cut in territorial operations. Order No. 1, of 1851, from the Adjutant General's Office in Washington, urged experimentation with farming projects by the soldiers. This was to include construction of their own living quarters on building sites suitable to the evaluation of the experiment. On July 12, not long after his arrival, Backus made a preliminary assessment of the El Paso region for that purpose. His opinion, relating to the suitability of continuing to garrison military forces opposite the Mexican town of Paso del Norte, had far-reaching consequences for the people of that region. His entire evaluation, driven by economic concerns, no doubt pleased the cost-cutters in Washington. He thought expenses were too great at Paso del Norte. However, nowhere did Major Backus show any concern for the mission of protecting the people and property on the American side of the Rio Grande. Troops, customs employees, and expenditures alone concerned him.[2]

Electus Backus did not seem to be concerned about the Apache threat either. He never mentioned it in making recommendations. Apache lands lay all around, spreading through what became the state of Arizona and to the Texas borders on the east side of the Rio Grande. There were four principal bands within what is today known as the Chiricahua group. The easternmost of these, the Eastern Chiricahuas, became familiar to Fort Fillmore troops by location names, such as Mimbres, Copper Mines, Warm Springs, Mogollons, and Gilas. These Apaches lived mostly in the mountain ranges west of the Rio Grande—the Cuchillo, Black Range, Mogollon, Pinos Altos, Burro, and Florida Mountains. Although nominally all of the Chiricahua bands fell under the potential influence of the 1850s U.S. Army, most, in reality, remained outside that influence. The Eastern Chiricahua were the closest, and hence were most impacted.

A second Apache sub-tribe east of the Rio Grande caused most of the early problems. Fort Fillmore was established at the western edge of lands claimed by the Mescalero tribe. The Mescaleros raided near the Rio Grande communities Fort Fillmore would directly influence, including Doña Ana, Las Cruces, Fronteras, San Elizario, El Paso, and Mesilla.

The decision to create Fort Fillmore as the first combined arms fort in the heart of Apacheria must have been made with the realization that the Apaches were not a people easy to dominate or intimidate. Early in the Spanish era, Franciscan monks tried, with little success, to convert the Apaches. One reason for this lack of success was that the Apaches were mainly a mountain-based, nomadic people. They did not build permanent settlements like the Pueblo people, nor did they farm to a great extent or raise flocks like the Navajo. They were, when necessary, a raider people who chose to live off what they might take from others at times when they could not feed themselves. All other tribes were their enemies and, to the Mescalero, the Spaniards, the Mexicans, and the Americans were simply other tribes.

By August 1, 1851, Major Backus, having made his recommendations on moving the troops out of El Paso, was in the

Navajo country serving with Brevet-Colonel Sumner's first campaign in that region. Brevet-Major Van Horne returned briefly to command at El Paso, only to be replaced by Major Gouveneur Morris, the second field grade officer of the 3[d] Infantry Regiment. Sumner sent Major Morris to finalize the movement of the troops to their new location.

The first of the new military bases, Fort Union, established in July northeast of the town of Las Vegas, served as Sumner's headquarters. By August word had spread to the civilian community near Paso del Norte that Sumner was making changes to the old arrangement between the civilians and the military in New Mexico. Franklin Coons pleaded with the Army not to move the soldiers out of the El Paso district. On August 4 Sumner received a petition outlining the basics of how important the region was and how badly the local American citizenry needed protection. Such notable pioneers as Hugh Stevenson, Charles Ogden, Simeon Hart, James Magoffin and C.W. White signed the petition. Had these gentlemen been willing to give the government free and usable land for a fort, Sumner might have situated Fort Fillmore closer to El Paso. Their basic recommendation was that the present quarters of the troops be retained, a possibility Sumner wasn't about to consider, given the expenditures there.[3]

Magoffin, a prominent American trader, owned a fortified point to the east of Coons's Ranch called Magoffinsville. At the time he signed the petition, Magoffin also wrote to Sumner and offered a deal on land he owned if the army agreed to remain at El Paso. Magoffin offered to sell the government a tract of 320 acres, all of what might have been his fortified site of Magoffinsville, with improvements, for the sum of $15,000, or he would rent the property for $1500 per annum. He did not understand the nature of Sumner's mandate. Sumner wanted free land, or land that could be leased for the most nominal of costs.[4]

Although Hugh Stevenson signed the petition appealing to Brevet-Colonel Sumner to keep the troops at El Paso, he may even then have been thinking of his mining interests in the Organ Mountains and how they might benefit by a military presence in that region. It was Stevenson's land on which Fort Fillmore was eventually situated, and at a very nominal cost.

August 17 was a key day for decision making. On that day Brevet-Colonel Sumner sent several letters having to do with the shifting of troops in southern New Mexico Territory. At this point the decision to move the troops had been finalized, although the location for a fort had not yet been confirmed. Sumner responded formally to James Magoffin's proposal for land on which to build a fort near El Paso. He indicated that he had already made his decision and, although it was not fully in Magoffin's favor, the El Paso pioneer could have an impact. The post would be located somewhere between Doña Ana and El Paso. Sumner let it be known that economics, and only economics, were driving his decisions. He offered to establish a guard outpost of twenty soldiers at Magoffinsville, if Magoffin allowed free rent.[5]

Also on August 17, while addressing the concerns of the merchants in El Paso, Sumner issued orders to Major Morris to prepare to move to a new site before winter prevented the erection of suitable quarters. Apparently, Sumner was convinced that the move would be made to a location known as the 'Cottonwoods,' a site believed to have been somewhere near modern-day Canutillo, Texas. Based on Morris's recommendation, that site was later dropped. Sumner informed Morris:

> ... You will receive the order of today establishing a new post for your headquarters. I wish you to carry this order into effect as rapidly as possible, in order that your command may be comfortably quartered before winter. If there is timber on the ground suitable for log buildings, I wish you to erect such, as they will be quicker built, and much cheaper. If there is not you will have to use adobes. I leave the plan of your fort entirely to yourself, not doubting but it will be suitable in all respects.
>
> It will be called Fort Fillmore. I do not expect that you can finish your work this fall, but that you will be comfortably sheltered, and next year you can finish your buildings, and at the same time carry on agricultural experiments. I will send you seed and implements of all kinds.

I expect that Mr. Magoffin will furnish quarters for use of the guards at his place, without rents. And I wish you to find some person a little below Dona Ana, who will do the same. If not, the guard cannot be left there.[6]

We don't know precisely why the name Fort Fillmore was selected although there were a number of obvious possibilities. Millard Fillmore was the current President. He had a strong impact on events in New Mexico through influencing the Compromise of 1850 that created a New Mexico Territory free from concerns over Texan land claims. In addition, a 3^d Infantry camp at San Antonio was named for Millard Fillmore. Major Backus was stationed there before arriving at El Paso. Brevet-Colonel Sumner may have been given the name before he left Washington for Santa Fe. This letter was the first indication of the name. Of additional interest is the mention of stationing small military guard units at both Magoffinsville and Doña Ana, if the local merchants wished to pay for their upkeep. This appears to have been an attempt to offset complaints coming from the local citizenry of both communities. After all, not only were some of the more affluent citizens losing their rental customers but, once the move was made, the Apaches could be expected to visit the unprotected communities in force.

Benjamin Franklin Coons, who would lose his lucrative rent contract when the infantry departed, made a final attempt to keep them at his ranch through an appeal to Colonel Sumner on August 26, 1851. Coons upped the ante, offering the land on which the troops were then stationed free of rent for one year. In addition he offered to give a large parcel of ground for construction of barracks, storehouses, etc., adjoining the current land, including a farming lot of 250 acres, the latter parcel to be selected by the commanding officer. This property would be free of rents to the government for the term of twenty years. After twenty years the land was to revert back to Coons's ownership or that of his heirs. This is exactly what the military wanted. Had he made this offer earlier, Brevet-Colonel Sumner might have considered it. No matter, the wheels of change were moving, orders had been issued; the military was no longer in a position to reconsider, even though they had not yet picked the final site. In any case, El Paso was no longer a consideration.[7]

Gouverneur Morris took pen in hand on August 27, 1851, to give voice to objections concerning the 'Cottonwood' site for the new Fort Fillmore. Morris believed the Coons offer should be considered, and then turned to the subject of the Cottonwoods site and how unsuitable he believed that site to be for the location of the future fort. Morris noted:

> ... The inclosed proposition from Mr. B. F. Coons, proprietor of the land opposite the Mexican town of El Paso, has been made to me, and from the many and real advantages which this proposition offers to the government, I respectfully transmit it to the Col. Commanding the Department for his approval and adoption.
>
> I am authorized by Mr. Coons to state to the Commanding Officer of the Department, that should he accept of this proposal, all rents for storehouses and quarters will cease from today, and that the public stores of every description at this post together with the troops, will be stored and quartered <u>free of expense</u> to the government.
>
> The advantages of this position, over all others between Dona Ana and El Paso are, that it is central in the valley, possesses the best site upon which to establish a garrison, whilst it is the key on opening of the great thoroughfare to the State of Chihuahua, and the City of Mexico; it protects the interests of our own citizens and gives to Mexico, to a great degree, that protection guaranteed by the treaty of Guadelupe Hidalgo; the acequias to irrigate the land in question are made, and no expense on that account will be necessary; and the land appears to be as fertile, if not more so, than any other which could be selected between this place and Dona Ana. And as favorable as far as it goes to carry out the interest of Genl Order No. 1 of 1851, as relates to farms, etc.
>
> I have examined the site of the "Cottonwood" for a post, and find from personal inspection, and information derived from the old inhabitants of the country, that that situation has the following objections.

The whole country from Dona Ana to the Pass is subject to overflow, and although no place designated in Dept. Order No. 27 for a garrison is perhaps on the highest and best ground which can be obtained, yet I am by no means certain that it is not subject to the same objections. The communication from, to, and by, this place is liable to be obstructed from the effects of overflow and there are through the whole extent, numerous crevasses or arroyos which conduct the water at high stages. Over the ground in rear (which gradually lies lower than that near the river) rendering it useless for cultivation, and probably unhealthy. As the land just above the Cottonwood is lower for many miles than at that place, an acequia from four to six miles in length will have to be constructed to irrigate the soil; and lastly every portion and parcel of the soil is so perfectly saturated with saline matter, called by the Mexicans "Tequez-quite" and "salitre" that I doubt whether it can be rendered suitable for cultivation.

I wish the Commanding Officer of the Department distinctly to understand that in forwarding this proposition and my remarks thereon, I <u>am not</u> delaying the execution of Dept. Order No. 27. I have examined the ground selected, the most eligible site; not deeming myself confined in that selection to the exact place known as the "Cottonwood". The force at my disposal will be entirely employed, getting out timber, and making adobes, which materials can be used at the "Cottonwood" or at the position opposite El Paso.

It is proper for me to observe that from the best information I have been able to obtain by conversation with the cura of El Paso, and citizens who pretend to hold Spanish grants or titles on the river, that there are no grants covering the lands designated in Order No. 27, Head Quarters of the Department, and that the land, to use their own expression, is "Congress Land".[8]

This letter from Major Morris probably finished the Cottonwoods as the future site of Fort Fillmore. Morris was simply trying to do a good job with his negative comments about that property. Coons's land may have been the most desirable site, for exactly the reasons Major Morris stated. The region was the commercial and emigrant crossroads to Mexico, Santa Fe, Austin, and California. The farming experiments could easily be conducted there. Transportation was available. The decision seemed obvious. That Brevet-Colonel

Sumner did not accept the Coons offer might have come from secondary considerations. Several sources speak of Brevet-Colonel Sumner having a problem with the towns' immoral impact on his soldiers. He is reported to have said, upon assuming command of the 9th Department, that his "first step was to break up the post at Santa Fe, that sink of vice and extravagance." He may have held a similar opinion with respect to the vices of Paso del Norte, just across the river from his troops.

Aside from vice, other factors may have entered into Sumner's calculations. There was the work of the Bartlett Commission to consider, as well as the growing importance of the Mesilla Valley as a farming community. The safety of the Bartlett Commission, with its surveyors and their valuable instruments, was of high political import. Placing Fort Fillmore nearer that work made the Bartlett Commission parties easier to reach. Colonel Sumner, having a finite number of troops, may have split the difference for political reasons. Shortly after Fort Fillmore was founded, a second fort, Fort Daniel Webster, was erected near the Santa Rita Copper Mines. That fort was controlled and supplied from Fort Fillmore, as were the guard troops left at El Paso. Had the troops been at El Paso, assistance for the Bartlett Commission, the Mesilla Valley, and the mines would have been difficult to provide. .

At Magoffinsville in late August, James Magoffin and several others, apprized of Coons's offer, recommended that Sumner adopt it. He believed the one year free rent offer would allow the Department commander time to make a proper decision, hopefully one satisfactory to the citizens on both sides of the Rio Grande. Magoffin added a postscript to this letter in which he reported receiving information from the Bartlett Commission that most of the mules belonging to the Commission and to Craig's Company 'A' had been stolen. Buford's Company 'H' was sent out from Doña Ana in response. Magoffin added, "Those damd [sic] Indians will have to be badly whipped before we can ever live at peace & no mistake." He also requested that, if El Paso be the Fort Fillmore location (he did not know the name), Major Backus be brought back as commander.[9]

In making this last request, James Magoffin was out of line. The military was jealous of the prerogatives of command, and especially of who was to command. We do not know if Sumner resented Magoffin's effrontery in recommending Backus over Morris. The Colonel was more concerned over the fact that El Paso was part of Texas. If Sumner put a fort in Texas, there was danger that the authorities would one day recognize the 8th Military Department's (Texas) claim to have authority there. The Cottonwoods site, although not as satisfactory as Coons's Ranch, was over the territorial border in New Mexico, at least so Sumner originally thought. No reference has been found to confirm that Sumner considered the Texas-New Mexico ramifications as part of his decision-making process, but, knowing the jealousies of command, he probably did. Sumner was a brevet-colonel. The Department of Texas was commanded by Brevet-Major General David Twiggs, who even then was extending his line of forts closer to the El Paso area.

Although the El Paso area civilians did not know it, the decision as to who would command the new post had long since been made. On August 26, Lieutenant Colonel Dixon Stansbury Miles, only recently appointed to command the 3d Infantry Regiment, arrived at Santa Fe. Miles was soon be on his way south to take command at the new Fort Fillmore, wherever it was located.

Major Morris recommended a site some miles upriver from the Cottonwoods as being more suitable for the new fort. Although lying over forty miles from El Paso, Morris's recommendation was acceptable to Sumner, provided Lieutenant Colonel Miles approved. Miles visited the new fort site while on his way to El Paso, as the land lay next to the road on which he was traveling. Miles did not reach El Paso before September 15, 1851. At that time he responded to Morris's recommendation in a letter to the 9th Department:

> ... I have the honor to report that I arrived at this station on yesterday. I find that San Elizario has not yet been abandoned, owing to the want of transportation. There being but one wagon team here that could be used for that object. I brought with me from Fort Leavenworth three teams, but nearly broken down, that will be used to bring up the stores from that station. The

number of loads supposed to be there, amounts to about forty, or fifty, and as wagons can make a trip only in two days, it will take twenty days to withdraw the stores from that point. As these four wagons have to be depended on, in transporting the supplies and stores to the site of the new Fort [Fillmore] the delay will be most injurious to the health of the troops by exposure to the inclemency of the weather before they can be placed under cover. Under these circumstances I have not hesitated in directing teams to be hired at a moderate price to haul at once all the stores from San Elizario which will leave me then at liberty to immediately remove the troops and necessary supplies to Fort Fillmore.

As I came down from Dona Anna [sic] I carefully examined the site selected by Maj. Morris of the new Fort, & also Cottonwood. There is no comparison, but that Maj. Morris has selected the best and only eligible site for building on, and occupancy by troops; on the whole road from this to Dona Ana. The site of the Fort is on a gently inclined plain having sandy gravelly soil, with a sufficiency of good tillable land in front. The old azequias [sic] running up to the base of the Fort, and cotton wood so much more abundant than at the place of that name, that I think it must be the place that you intended the Fort should be located at. From my own observation I concur fully with Major Morris in all the objections he has enumerated in his letter to you under date of the 27 ultimo, against the site of Cotton Wood, with this in addition. The site of Cotton Wood, is now well understood to be within the State of Texas and under location of dead right claims by Col. Howard of that State and Bvt. Lt. Col. Johnson, Top. Eng. If this is true and I have every reason to believe so, a location of the Fort there, will involve the government without their concurrence, in an unknown expense hereafter, that never could be justified by any supposed eligibility of the site—another objection. The land from never having the appearance been tilled, no azequias [sic] around it, would lead to the influence [sic] it is not arable and therefore useless for our farming purposes. I camped on the night of the 15th instant at Cottonwood. The lower part of it, and the best portion, where a squatter had already taken possession. The ground was dry, the grass green and the shade of a few old large cottonwood trees gave it a pretty appearance and an inviting one as a resting place. Soon after my tents were pitched, a rainstorm came, and poured in torrents for two or three hours. The scene was immediately changed to a broad sheet of water standing all over this position to several inches and I then discovered there was no drainage and no position for the location of a Fort.

The absence of Bvt. Captain Bowman, Regt. Quarter Master, who is accountable for the immense quantity of commissary and Quarter Master supplies at this station, embarrasses me greatly; to protect him, I shall leave here in command Major Morris with a small detachment keeping an accurate account of all tools and supplies received at Fort Fillmore which will be required at that post.

Bvt. Major and Capt. Van Horn [sic], with his Co, E. 3rd Inf., has been ordered to the mountains by Maj. Morris about twelve miles east of Brasito, the selected site of Fort Fillmore, to get pine lumber for the fort. From report he is progressing rapidly and doubtless will soon have a sufficiency when his company will be withdrawn.[10]

In this letter are all of the true reasons for Fort Fillmore being founded where it was. Cost and expenses for the maintenance of the troops was the first and most important factor. Farming by the troops in an attempt to make them entirely self-sufficient was the second reason. The acequias were already built up to the site of the new Fort Fillmore. In effect, some of the land was therefore ready for farming. The third reason was that the Cottonwoods site was simply a poor location for the fort. The land could be flooded, farming was doubtful, and the location was believed to be in Texas rather than in the Territory of New Mexico.

Miles did not wait for Sumner's final concurrence on the Morris recommendation. On September 18, 1851, Major Morris finalized the lease agreement with Hugh Stevenson, the El Paso area rancher and miner who owned the land on which Fort Fillmore was to be situated. During the trip from Santa Fe, Miles set Brevet-Captain Buford to work moving his troops into tents on the new site, and that before the lease was even finalized. On that same day Major Morris briefly provided the particulars of the lease to the 9th Department, stating the lease would last for twenty years at a cost of ten cents annually paid to the lessor. The military had indeed reduced their costs to a dime per annum. The fort area was about a mile square.[11]

Miles notified the 9th Department on September 18 that "by tomorrow night all the stores at San Elizario will be removed, when I shall immediately commence the removal of troops and stores to Fort Fillmore." There was one problem—an over-abundance of quartermaster and commissary material at the Coons Ranch garrison. Much appeared to be damaged beyond use, with the surplus commissary goods in an advanced state of spoilage. The quartermaster officer, Brevet-Captain Andrew Bowman, being absent, Miles stated he was leaving Major Morris behind at Coons's Ranch to handle the initial preparations for disposal of this property, at least until Bowman returned.[12]

As Miles readied his command to march north, Brevet-Captain Abraham Buford, at Doña Ana, was already locating some of his company in tents at Fort Fillmore. There are indications that troops were living at Fort Fillmore as early as September 15, 1851, although the official founding of the post was on September 23, following the arrival of Miles and his staff.

NOTES - Chapter 2

1. Backus to McLaws, July 1, 1851, M1102, Roll 4.
2. Backus to McLaws, July 12, 1851, M1102, Roll 4.
3. Petition, various El Paso area citizens to Brevet-Colonel Sumner, August 4, 1851, M1102, Roll 4.
4. Magoffin to Sumner, August 6, 1851, M1102, Roll 4.
5. Sumner to Magoffin, August 17, 1851, *National Archives Microfilm: Letters Sent by 9th Military District, Department of New Mexico, Group M1012.* (Hereafter cited as M1102. Roll 1.)
6. Sumner to Morris, August 17, 1851, M1012, Roll 1.
7. Coons to Sumner, August 26, 1851, M1102, Roll 4.
8. Morris to Sumner, August 27, 1851, M1102, Roll 4.
9. Magoffin to Sumner, August 28, 1851, M1102, Roll 4.
10. Miles to Buell, September 16, 1851, M1102, Roll 4.
11. Morris to Buell, September 18, 1851, M1102, Roll 4.
12. Miles to Buell, September 18, 1851, M1102, Roll 4.

Lieutenant Colonel Dixon
Stansbury Miles, 1804-1862.

Sarah Ann Briscoe Miles,
1812-1875.

Photos Courtesy: Bill Kuethe Collection.

3

THE FIRST FOUR MONTHS

The founding date for Fort Fillmore is generally believed to be September 23, when the new commanding officer, Lieutenant-Colonel Dixon Stansbury Miles, arrived with his staff and Company 'K' of the 3[d] Infantry Regiment. In fact, the actual establishment date could have been as early as September 15, the date on which Brevet-Captain Abraham Buford's Company 'H,' 1st Dragoon Regiment, moved out of Doña Ana to establish a temporary tent camp on the selected Fort Fillmore land.

Lieutenant Colonel Miles described in a letter to the 9th Military Department on September 26 what happened after the troops arrived. In this letter we not only learn of the establishment date, but also of the arrival of a second infantry company under Brevet-Major Jefferson Van Horne. As might be expected, the men were very busy. Miles noted:

> I have the honor to report that I arrived at this position with the Head Quarters 3d. Inf & Bvt. Maj. Richardson, Co. K, on the 23rd Inst., where I found Bvt. Cpt. Buford comdg. H Co. 1st Drags encamped. Bvt. Maj Van Horn, Comdg. E Co. 3d. Inf., arrived with his company from a pinery on yesterday, completing the number of companies designated for the garrison of the post.
>
> Every officer, soldier and animal at the post is fully employed in arranging our camp & store houses, receiving stores, etc. to enable me at once to commence building.
>
> As there is not a sufficiency of timber near here, to erect log buildings, and it is too late in the season to make adobes, I shall

build Jacal houses as being the soonest made, with the least destruction or consumption of timber.

I hope by the 1st proximo that all the stores at Dona Ana will have been removed, so as to stop any rental there, also by that date, the removal of stores at El Paso, permitting a concentration of them; to materially diminish the expences [sic] at that place.[1]

Two infantry companies and one dragoon company were engaged in constructing their winter living quarters, and moving and storing supplies. The first thing on Colonel Miles's mind was expenditures; he had not misinterpreted Colonel Sumner's order to cut costs everywhere and in every way. This brief letter is fortunately not the only correspondence we have from the first days of the fort. Miles wrote to his wife on October 9, telling her of his first days in a totally different fashion, free from the official tone he used with the Department adjutant. Miles recounted the hardships he and his troops endured far from the civilized amenities which she had available back in Baltimore. He wrote:

... On the next day, 23d Sept. the anniversary of the battle of Monterrey, I reached this place and established this fort—It is a beautiful situation, is all I can say of it. Our nearest neighbors live at Cruces 12 miles off; of course we have no marketing and it is hard living on commissary alone. Sometimes I get onions but that is all, and sometimes, peaches, grapes and pears which we have to eat to keep off the scurvy—as I have had some symptoms of it. I greatly dread that disease. It, neurology and old age are the only causes of death here ... I am living as all the command, in tents. I have two wall tents pitched opposite each other with an interval, a fly covering the interval; something like a double log cabin which you have seen, one is for my bed and the other my parlor. I have another, at a little distance, for my dining room, and then Patrick [Miles's Irish servant] has two common tents, one to sleep in and the other for a store room, besides a bower to cook under. Which answers very well just now, there being no rain at this season of the year. My tents have floors and are as comfortable as tents can be—but still they are tents and the nights being cold are uncomfortable. I have caught a cold and have an attack of neurology in the muscles of my breast which annoys me very much. Until today I have been wearing my cotton undershirts. This morning I put on my flannel under ones and I think my heart is better.

Col. Sumner the commander of this Department has issued an order, that no officer should draw from the commissary more than one ration for himself and one for every person in his family. As we have nothing else to live on, it is hard work to make it last. For instance one candle and a bar of soap is a ration for a whole month. 4 lbs of coffee and 8 lbs of sugar is all allowed for a month. The flour and pork is sufficient, but a gill of salt and gill of vinegar is not. I don't know how Patrick and I will make out. You will be amazed when I tell you the price of a ration per month at this place is Eighteen Dollars—but it is true—how the subalterns [junior officers and possibly non-commissioned officers] can live I cannot tell, particularly those having wives and children and there are a few only (thank fortune) so situated. The ladies, poor things, get along badly and suffer much. The regulations give them but one tent, or rather half of one and this is their bedroom, parlor and dining room. Close quarters that, but such is the case.[2]

Dixon Miles was the senior military officer in New Mexico Territory south of Santa Fe. In this letter he portrays himself as being totally at the whim of Army regulations and Brevet-Colonel Edwin Vose Sumner. The former controlled most of his daily activities and prerogatives. The latter assigned his strategic missions. Miles had little latitude in his actions. Even though the Lieutenant Colonel was at Fort Fillmore with only an Irish servant as part of his household, he was directed by regulations to have more and larger quarters than any of those men under him. One can only imagine the conditions which married enlisted men, often with families, endured during this early period.

The construction of more sturdy quarters began immediately. Large stands of sturdy, tall, yet narrow, brushwood grew along the Rio Grande. The abundance of such material led to a quick decision to use it for building the first structures, called 'Jacals,' as Miles referred to in his letter. *Webster's New World Dictionary* defines a jacal as "a hut in Mexico and the Southwest, with walls of close-set wooden stakes plastered with mud and roofed with straw, rushes, etc." Using this river-bottom material, and digging the poles into the soft sand perhaps three feet, a structure six to nine feet tall could be erected in a hurry. River bottom mud, mixed with a little sand and rushes was then used as a crude plaster. In 1853, Colonel Joseph Mansfield, on his inspection of Fort Fillmore, indicated that many of these jacal-type buildings were still standing and in daily use.

What knowledge the troops didn't have concerning the building of such structures was provided through the hiring of native Mexican laborers. Though not listed as being present at Fort Fillmore in the month of September 1851, these local experts —hired at the rate of 75 cents per man per day and rations—were on duty from October onward.[3]

In the October 9 letter, Miles informed his wife that one house, his own, was under construction, the first to be built of substantial materials other than poles from the river bottom. Although he did not use the word adobe, Miles was obviously speaking of a far more substantial structure than a jacal. He noted:

> ... I am building as fast as I can, my quarters are nearly completed. On the front I have two 20 foot square rooms having an interval of 12 feet between. To the rear runs from these rooms two others, on each side, the first 18 ft by 14 ft. The two back ones 14 ft. square, one of these, for a kitchen, the other for servants—so I have a parlour of 20 ft. square, a dining room 18 by 16, a sleeping room 20 ft. square and a spare room for strangers 18 by 14 ft. The house is built this way, suppose you look west as the front [Miles included a tiny drawing of the structure at this point]. Altho I have built this fine house I do not expect to occupy it, but anticipate a removal to Fort Conrad at Valverde, where as yet Maj. Howe who is commanding has built no house. So I may be in a tent all winter, which is quite severe here and there—owing to our elevation about 4500 feet above the sea, the snow falls here two and three feet I am told.[4]

Miles spoke of two separate structures with an interval between, a space that may have been later filled by other construction. Until the Miles letter of October 9 surfaced, there was no knowledge of

Fort Fillmore in 1854. *Courtesy: Rio Grande Historical Collection, N.M.S.U.*

which building on officers' row housed the commander. His drawing of this unusual separated structure made site identification possible at last. In 1852, Brevet-Captain Abraham Buford completed a map of the Fort Fillmore site which has generally been considered to be a conjectural view of what was intended to be constructed rather than what was actually constructed. It is true that Buford's map shows seven officer's quarters rather than the six that are known to have been built. It is also known that there is a space where a seventh building may have been intended but was never constructed. Since no archeological excavation has occurred in that area, we may never know for sure if a seventh building was started. No matter, in the center of Buford's view of officers' row is a building exactly as Miles described in his letter to his wife. There were two small rectangular buildings separated by an interval with what Miles call a "piazza" in the space between.

The 3^d Infantry and mounted companies had many problems building living quarters and providing themselves with sustenance. The officers also had time to consider the tremendous job they were about to undertake, being the only United States military force present in all of southern New Mexico. Fort Fillmore, in 1851, was responsible for protecting an enormous territory, one filled with a variety of potential problems and perils. This vast area, which ran from the Texas border to the California border, could not by any means all be protected by the Fort Fillmore garrison. For example, if there was trouble in the mining region at Santa Rita, a dragoon company took three to four days getting there, an infantry company even longer. The situation was equally bad if they had to pursue Mescalero raiders back into the Sierra Blanca region.

The Indians were the wild card in a cultural and social mix that promised interesting, if not always solvable, problems for the future. Did Miles and his soldiers know they were building Fort Fillmore on the boundary line between two branches of the Apache nation? Had they yet made that distinction, or were all Apaches believed to be the same? Perhaps the officers never saw beyond their own national interests. After all, to them, there were no

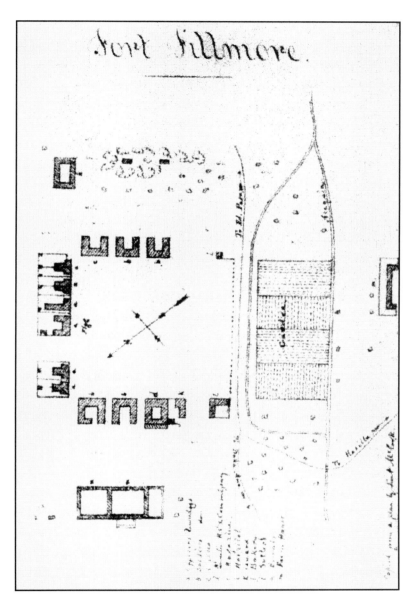

Fort Fillmore map from Colonel Joseph Mansfield's
1853 Inspection Report.

Apache lands, only the new American territory they were sent to protect. Fort Fillmore stood on the east side of the Rio Grande River, which put the fort squarely in the lands of the Mescalero Apache Tribe, bands of which roamed from the Pecos River to north of the Jornada and south into Texas and Mexico. To the United States military, the Apaches were more a nuisance than a threat. This is proven in that the soldiers didn't bother to wall their fort, leaving it wide open to any visitor or enemy that happened by. The Apaches were viewed more precisely as thieves, not threats– hardly a Hollywood version of events.

It was to the west where the strongest Indian problem would arise. On the west side of the Rio Grande, up to and just across the modern Arizona-New Mexico border, lived the Chiricahua Apache bands which Fort Fillmore soldiers referred to as Mimbres, Gila, Mogollon, Coyotero, White Mountain, or Warm Springs. More distant, in what became the state of Arizona, was the terrible spectre of Cochise. He and other leaders threatened the safety of any wagon train sent to Fort Fillmore from the west, and or of travelers and supplies going west to California. The main road to the California gold fields split near Fort Fillmore, one route going north to Santa Fe and the other going west past the Santa Rita mines, so there was always the safety of emigrants traveling on the roads to consider.

Fort Fillmore, although still in its infancy, was a very large army post in the making. As many as three companies of infantry and two of cavalry were present at a time when most United States Army military installations struggled along as one- or two-company posts. Also present was a sizable regimental staff belonging to the 3^d Infantry, many of whom arrived with Lieutenant-Colonel Miles.

Although he was acting regimental commander, Miles did not exercise full control over the 3^d Infantry companies then serving at other posts around the territory. For instance, Company 'B,' 3^d Infantry manning Fort Conrad, operated completely outside Miles's control, and 'B' was the closest unit to him. This was the result of an order issued by the Adjutant General's Office in Washington directing that the commanders of the companies of the 3^d Infantry in New Mexico be assumed to be on detached service. Thus, each company officer was responsible for all his actions when not under the direct command of Miles at Fort Fillmore.

As to the rest of the 3^d Infantry staff, two other officers besides Miles were present at Fort Fillmore that September. The first was Assistant Surgeon John Fox Hammond, a medical doctor and the man responsible for the health of all military forces in the Fort Fillmore area of control. The other was Miles's adjutant, Brevet-Captain Barnard E. Bee.

The senior enlisted man serving with the 3^d Infantry staff was an unknown regimental sergeant major. As part of his duties he kept records, reports, and orders coming into the regiment. He was, in his senior position, also responsible for receiving and maintaining the records brought forward by the company first sergeants and preparing the monthly returns for the regimental commander's signature, in accordance with the instructions of the adjutant.

The next most senior non-commissioned officer serving at Fort Fillmore, absent at Paso del Norte in the month of September, was the quartermaster sergeant. As a staff member, he was responsible to the adjutant for reporting all deficiencies and needs of the regiment for clothing, commissary, etc. Brevet-Captain Bowman, as both quartermaster and commissary officer of the 3^d Infantry Regiment, depended on this sergeant for accomplishing and carrying out his orders. Men were detailed to duty with the quartermaster and commissary from the companies.

The 3^d Infantry Regiment had two principal musicians who were responsible for field music and for the regimental band. These men and the band members were also a part of the staff. In September 1851, fourteen privates were listed in the monthly returns as members of the staff and band.

While Fort Fillmore was a blessing to growth in the Mesilla Valley, the opposite was true for the farms and ranches at San Elizario, Ysleta, Socorro, Coons's Ranch, Magoffinsville, and others. Lonely Fort Fillmore, in the desert forty miles from El Paso del Norte, twelve miles from Doña Ana, and at an impossible distance from the Indian tribes who raided in the area, became a bone of contention for those who needed that protection. Raids on El Paso, San Elizario, and Doña Ana had increased significantly once the town garrisons were withdrawn.

As with all major decisions, good and bad came out of those made by Colonel Sumner. As to the secondary consideration of the availability of the various forms of vice, those practicing it simply packed up and came as near as possible to the forts. Most certainly the small villages that the soldiers' visited, Santo Tomás, Mesilla, and Las Cruces, did not remain free of such attractions; if the soldiers could walk to the vice, no doubt they did so.

In startling contrast to the complaints for support made by settlers in the El Paso region, Brevet-Colonel Sumner initially felt there were more troops in New Mexico than were needed. His reason is interesting. He believed if American troops shielded and protected the majority Mexican population, they would become debased. In effect, he wanted the dragoons sent elsewhere so that a newly raised Mexican militia would eventually take over all military duties in the territory and United States troops could be withdrawn.[5]

The mention of a Mexican volunteer force opens another subject related to the Fort Fillmore garrison. Many replacement troops brought into the territory from the East were immigrants with no ties of loyalty to their new country, but there were no attempts to enlist soldiers from among the loyal Mexican population into the Regular Army. Many male residents would have happily accepted army pay, which was often more than they could earn locally. One reason local recruits were not accepted into Regular Army formations was the current belief among major European colonial powers that a locally recruited garrison might not fire on a rebellious populace if ordered to do so. Hence, soldiers from another area or, in the case of European colonialists, another colony, were brought in as the garrison. No doubt the same idea operated within the American Army of the 1850s.

Local Hispanics and Anglos served in the militia, or as spies (the title for Army scouts throughout the 1850s), guides, packers, etc. In fact, the army in the field could hardly function without these people, which included members of Indian tribes serving as scouts. If the war was against the Apaches, Navajo and Pueblo scouts were sought; vice versa when the Navajo were the enemy. There seemed to be no dearth of volunteers. There were many occasions for such employment, as the Apaches continued to act outside of what both Mexicans and Americans considered tolerable civilized behavior.

In October 1851, while the Fort Fillmore garrison settled in, building and learning the requirements of southern New Mexico farming. Mexican Army troops from Sonora operated against the nearby Apaches. A Sonoran army led by José María Flores moved into the Chiricahua Mountains southwest of Fort Fillmore, in land that eventually became part of the Gadsden Purchase agreement, but was then still recognized as part of Mexico. The Mexican Army campaign did not approach Mesilla, but news of the action must have reached the little village. This was the third Sonoran campaign of 1851. Three hundred men, divided into two units, were involved. They burned a ranchería at Carretas and killed four warriors. Flores, taking part of his group, moved up north into the Gila country, east into the Burro Mountains (near Silver City), into an area which eventually became well known to Fort Fillmore troops. This Flores expedition may have been part of the reason Fort Daniel Webster was established so quickly in January of the following year.[6]

While the Sonoran army was engaged in mortal combat with their Apache enemies, scant miles away Fort Fillmore remained at peace. The command changed very little during October 1851. The staff did not change at all. The aggregate for Company 'H,' 1st Dragoons rose from fifty men in September to a grand total of seventy in October. Twenty-six recruits from Fort Union arrived to reinforce the company. Six members of Company 'H' were discharged from the army in October, accounting for the aggregate increase of twenty men. These twenty-six dragoon recruits brought with them to Fort Fillmore an additional eighteen horses, which brought the total number of animals at the post, in serviceable condition, to sixty-one.[7]

Companies 'E' and 'K,' 3[d] Infantry, also saw slight increases in their aggregate numbers for the month of October. Transfers and recruits brought the total numbers for the two companies from one hundred fifty-two to one hundred sixty-five. Of these, one hundred and twenty were available at Fort Fillmore proper, the rest being on detached service or leave. For the first time in the short history of the fort, one man deserted. Although desertion is often stated as being endemic in the army of this period, the number of desertions at Fort Fillmore never seemed to be very high. There were only one or two a month in the worst of times.[8]

Post records for October also indicated a continued need to hire Mexican laborers to assist in the construction of fort buildings, contrary to Lieutenant Colonel Miles's statement that they would be needed for only a short time. There is no mention whether these Mexican workers came from Las Cruces, Doña Ana, Mesilla, or nearby independent farms. People lived close by because Miles indicated that the acequias, which were going to be extended to provide the farm at Fort Fillmore with water, ran right up to the edge of the fort property.

Private Sylvester Matson, Company 'K,' 3[d] Infantry, began a diary on November 1, 1851, while at Fort Fillmore. Matson had enlisted in Chicago, Illinois, on December 14, 1850, and was sent to New Mexico as an infantryman. His insights into life as an enlisted man at Fort Fillmore, and later at Fort Daniel Webster, are helpful in understanding the non-officer side of military life at that time. Matson's infantry company was commanded by Brevet-Major and Captain Israel Bush Richardson. Matson reported November 1, 1851, to be "a beautiful day with a clear sky and birds singing sweetly everywhere around me." He added that, although the day was bright, he found it to be gloomy. A Mexican woman working at the fort had been pressed back into slavery (Matson used that exact word) as a peon when her owner came to the fort and demanded she be given over to him as his property. Peonage was a form of economic slavery, about which Private Matson seemed very well informed. He added that the Mexican taking her would, "charge her what he pleases for the supplies he furnishes her, food of the plainest kind and clothing of the coarsest texture, and he will see that the sum he charges her exceeds the credit to which she will be entitled, and so the poor woman will have to toil and slave until death relieves her and gives her rest." Those thoughts, and thoughts of his home in Ohio, made the sunny day dreary.[9]

Lieutenant Colonel Miles commented on an approaching court-martial in a letter to his wife dated November 13, 1851. A court-martial meant travel. He dreaded the journey to Fort Conrad, since he had been ill the previous month and had not fully recovered his strength. With the Jornada del Muerto between the Fort Fillmore command and their higher headquarters, a journey was not to be taken lightly. Miles noted:

> ... On the 7th of last month I was taken with an ague & fever, then with a neurology in all the muscles of my breast and back, then with torpidity of the liver and inflammation of the kidneys, afterwards with inflammation of the lungs, having a dry hacking cough. More than once I thought my time had come, as I became so weak I could not get my legs out of bed. Here I lay day after day, night after night, solitary and alone, suffering the most intense agonies. Oh how hard a time I have had. Happily my strong constitution carried me through and I am now perfectly restored except in strength, which I am gaining fast.
>
> On the 10th of next month I have to be at Fort Conrad (Valverde) as President of a general court martial, and I dread the passage of the awful Jornada, or desert of 100 miles, without wood or water. It is now covered with snow and will be worse on 10th of next month—but I have to go and by wrapping up warm no doubt will get through as the others along.[10]

Another and more tragic first in Fort Fillmore history occurred on November 12, 1851. Private Martin Butler, a member of Brevet-Major Van Horne's Company 'E,' became the first recorded death at the fort. We know very little about Private Butler save for the fact that he enlisted on November 20, 1849, in Harrisburg, Penn-sylvania. We can surmise that he was an American citizen, given the fact that he enlisted in Pennsylvania, rather than a German, Irish, or English immigrant straight off the boat in New York.[11]

Chances are Martin, like other recruits, was first taken to either Carlisle Barracks, Pennsylvania or Newport Barracks, Kentucky, then transported down the Mississippi River to Jefferson Barracks, Missouri. At some point somebody decided that Martin would make a fine infantryman for the 3[d] Infantry Regiment in West Texas. He probably traveled downriver to New Orleans, a major army command center at that time, and then on to San Antonio. There, an officer heading west transported Martin to Brevet-Major Van Horne's battalion at El Paso. That trip took several weeks to several months, depending upon whether Martin marched up from San Antonio with other recruits or helped escort one of the supply wagon trains, notorious for being very slow. Life was not dull at El Paso when Martin served there. Across the Rio Grande River from his station at Coons's Ranch (in the heart of what is now downtown El Paso) was the large Mexican town of Paso del Norte. No doubt Martin visited that town and tasted its varied delights a number of times between 1850 and 1851. He may also have participated in the pursuit of Apache Indians who raided along the river. There were even instances when Brevet-Major Van Horne sent infantrymen mounted on mules in pursuit of the Indians; by 1850 the army was well aware that slow-moving infantry were no match for the mounted Apaches.

Martin was transferred, as a part of a command shakeup in July 1851, to the Rio Grande island on which the town of San Elizario was located. When Major Electus Backus took temporary command of the 3[d] Infantry Battalion, before the arrival of Lieutenant Colonel Miles, protocol dictated that the former commander be moved. Brevet-Major Van Horne, who reverted to his company command at that time, was transferred to San Elizario with all of Company 'E.' Martin Butler was serving there when the orders came to move to the new Fort Fillmore.

One can only wonder what Martin thought of his new home after arriving from timber-cutting duty in the mountains to the east. There was not much to see but a tent city among the sand dunes. Activity there was for sure. Temporary housing, other than tents, was under construction. Water details moved back and forth to the river bringing water for the troops—a duty infantrymen such as Butler performed. Private Butler was not privy to Lieutenant Colonel Miles's thoughts, but he may have noted the intense interest the Fort Fillmore commander paid to the water courses west of the post. Rumors must have been rife concerning the importance of the upcoming farming experiment.

Miles mentioned Martin Butler's death in his November 13 letter, the day after Butler died. although he did not mention the soldier by name. Miles said:

> I as well as the troops here are yet living in tents. For the last week it has been rainy, sleety and snowy, cold and damp. I thought more than once I would have frozen to death. One of my soldiers did die from the extreme change of the weather.[12]

Did Martin Butler freeze to death in his tent at Fort Fillmore, or did he die of complications from pneumonia or a similar problem? We do not know. The lieutenant colonel did not know it yet but a second soldier, Private Francis Clemens, died the next day. It is possible both boys froze to death. Storms of incredible ferocity and cold are not unknown in the desert.

Private Martin Butler's death may have led to choosing the location of the Fort Fillmore Cemetery just south of the post near the Camino Real. Miles made no mention as to the funeral arrangements. A site may have already been preselected, given the fact that a cemetery would seem a natural part of fort planning.

On November 13, 1851, the first conflict between Fort Fillmore soldiers and the surrounding Apaches took place. A messenger arrived from Robledo Campground, where Fort Selden would years later be established, that Apaches were raiding in that vicinity. Brevet-Captain Buford, and Company 'H,' 1st Dragoons, numbering at that time fifty-eight men and one officer, left Fort Fillmore in pursuit. Private Matson reported he was allowed to go out on this chase even though he was an infantryman. His diary entry is partially confirmed by the Fort Fillmore Post Records for November: that twenty-seven dragoons and fourteen infantrymen took the campaign trail against the Apaches that month. Buford's command followed the raiders all that day and the next, coming upon the body of a murdered man who had been scalped. The dragoons trailed their prey to a crossing on the Rio Grande, with Mexico on the other side. Unable to cross the river, they returned to Fort Fillmore empty handed.[13]

Brevet-Colonel Edmund Vose Sumner visited Fort Fillmore on November 24, 1851. No doubt one topic of discussion was a letter Sumner wrote on November 20 to the General-in-Chief of the Army, Winfield Scott, then at New York City. Three distinct cultures, Mexican, Indian, and American, operated independently in the New Mexico of the 1850s, and were often at odds with each other, as were the U.S. Army and the New Mexico Territorial government. The situation was exacerbated by an incident involving the Governor of the Territory and his use of Mexican militia against Navajos in the region of the new Fort Defiance. Sumner informed Scott:

> ... I regret to trouble the General-In-Chief with a voluminous correspondence with Governor Calhoun. I have endeavored to avoid these differences as much as possible, but in this case it is so important to prevent any Mexican marauding parties from harassing the Indian country, that I was obliged to enter this discussion.
>
> This predatory war has been carried out for two hundred years, between the Mexicans and Indians, quite time enough to prove, that unless some change is made the war will be interminable. They steal women and children, and cattle, from each other, and in fact carry on the war, in all respects, like two Indian nations.
>
> This system of warfare will interfere very much with my measures, and indeed do away with all the advantages, that I confidently expect to reap from the establishment of Fort Defiance. This large post is in the very midst of the Indians, and it will harass them so much, that they will gladly make peace, and keep quiet, provided they find that this post can protect as

well as punish. They have already shown a disposition to enter into a treaty, and have sent a message to the government that they would come to Santa Fe for that purpose.

I would respectfully request that explicit orders may be sent, by the proper authorities, to Gov. Calhoun, to abstain from sending any parties of Mexicans into the Indian country, and that he should confine himself strictly to defensive measures, in this country occupied by the forces of the United States Army.[14]

Territorial Governor Calhoun had sent New Mexican militia units into the Navajo country in response to raids conducted against the citizens of the territory. Colonel Sumner was unable to prevent Calhoun from doing so, thereby jeopardizing his efforts to control the Navajo Nation through the army garrison at Fort Defiance. This open conflict between the cultures, the interminable war Sumner mentions, would not be resolved until the Navajo were finally brought to submission during the American Civil War. No doubt Sumner wanted to confer with Miles as to his views on the situation between the Mexican population and the Apaches in the Fort Fillmore region. After conferring with Miles and inspecting the Fort Fillmore garrison, Sumner continued south to assess the situation at Magoffinsville, where a small contingent of troops and quartermaster personnel still worked.

After two months, Lieutenant Colonel Miles began to appreciate the problems with soldiers being both soldiers and farmers. The farming experiment was dear to the heart of Brevet-Colonel Sumner, and probably of many others up the chain of command. Miles faced the potential failure of the experiment by pleading soldierly ignorance of the technology needed to succeed at farming. In late November, Miles brought certain absolute costs to the attention of the thrifty commanding officer of the 9th Department, saying:

> To cultivate with success in this valley, on an extensive scale, requires the employment of suitable persons acquainted with the cultivation practiced in this section of country. It is useless and waste of labor and seeds and material to attempt the culture of land here, on the system used within the United States. The making and management of acequias, all important to the

raising of any vegetable or grain, together with the time and manner of planting, is only understood by those raised in this country. I therefore request authority to hire an overseer and ten Mexicans for the object of farming at this place.

As a farm is to be commenced at this place, the expense of opening the same will involve a much greater outlay than any year in future. I will as nearly as I can, state this expense, and also the amount of produce I expect to raise, estimating the sale of such at St, Louis prices; the most unfair for this country that could be devised; as the prices of every thing here range over 100 per cent above those of St. Louis.

The hire of an overseer I presume I can get for $40. per month, employed six months - $300.

Ten Mexicans at fifty cents per day, employed 25 days in the month for six months - $750.

Rations for the same - $80.

100 oxen or 50 yoke to run twenty plows at $60 per yoke - $3000.

The plows, hoes, harrows, rakes, grain and seeds. I suppose already purchased - and the employment of soldiers in ploughing, planting and gathering in the crop, to cost nothing additional.

Total Expense - $3830.

I propose to cultivate 300 acres of corn providing at least 9000 bushels - $4050.

100 tons of fodder at $20 per ton - $2000.

500 bushels of beans at $3.00 per bushel - $1500.

If furnished with 20 bushels of barley to sow 15 acres producing 80 bushels at 50 cents per bushel - $600.

9 bushels of oats on nine acres producing 80 bushels to the acre a200 bushels at 20 cents per bushel - $162.

Pumpkins sufficient to feed horses and cows all winter -

Cost of articles raised at St. Louis prices - $8312.[15]

This is a truly calculated letter. First, Miles stated that his troops did not have the special qualifications necessary to create a working farm at Fort Fillmore on their own. The primary ingredient in the farming experiment—a self-sufficiency without costs to the government —could not be reasonably attained. Miles wanted an overseer and ten Mexican laborers, working personnel who were used to the environment and the needs of the land. After listing costs for oxen,

Miles included a total cost figure that must have staggered Sumner. The outlay Miles estimates would not be the zero amount desired. Instead, costs were expected to be closer to $3,850 per year.

Not all the news was bad. If everything went exactly as planned, the farm would be a working entity, with free soldier labor doing the planting, tending, and harvesting. The pumpkins, corn, fodder, beans, and oats the farm was intended to produce were valued, at very high St. Louis prices, at $8,312.

Miles was priming Sumner to expect the failure of the farming experiment if outside workers could not be hired and if soldiers were not made available as free labor to do all the work. Soldiers were required to perform daily soldierly duties. If there were no Indian problems, and if the demand as escorts, necessary military transfers, and a myriad other detached service duties did not arise, the farm experiment might have had a chance. But this was the frontier and Fort Fillmore was in the very heart of Apachería. Brevet-Colonel Sumner's grand experiment in altering the duties of his soldiery had to fail.

December 3, 1851, was an important day at the post. Sumner directed Miles to make a close examination of the corn being fed the horses of his command. Spoiled corn was blamed for the death of two horses and for making other horses and mules at Fort Union sick. Miles was to examine his supply "and what is unfit for issue, condemned and sold." More pleasant news also arrived. Miles received authorization to hire a foreman and ten Mexican laborers to open the farm. The expense for their hire was not to exceed $175 per month; their wages were to be taken from the funds of the Assistant Commissary Bowman and charged as farm expenses. This was a tacit admission that the farming experiment, as initially proposed, was a failure.[16]

President Millard Fillmore addressed the Senate and House of Representatives late in 1851, saying:

> By the Treaty of Guadalupe Hidalgo we are bound to protect the Territory of Mexico against the incursions of the savage tribes within our border with equal diligence and energy

as if the same were made within our territory or against our citizens. I have endeavored to comply as far as possible with this provision of the treaty. Orders have been given to the officers commanding on that frontier to consider the Mexican territory and its inhabitants as equally with our own entitled to their protection, and to make all their plans and arrangements with a view to the attainment of this object. Instructions have also been given to the Indian commissioners and agents among these tribes in all treaties to make the clauses designed for the protection of our own citizens apply also to those of Mexico. I have no reason to doubt that these instructions have been fully carried into effect; nevertheless, it is probable that in spite of all our efforts some of the neighboring States of Mexico may have suffered, as our own have, from depredations by the Indians.

To the difficulties of defending our own territory, as above mentioned, are super added, in defending that of Mexico, those that arise from its remoteness, from the fact that we have no right to station our troops within her limits and that there is no efficient military force on the Mexican side to cooperate with our own. So long as this shall continue to be the case the number and activity of our troops will rather increase than diminish the evil, as the Indians will naturally turn toward that country where they encounter the least resistance. Yet these troops are necessary to subdue them and to compel them to make and observe treaties. Until this shall have been done neither country will enjoy any security from their attacks.[17]

This speech heightened expectations among the Fort Fillmore command that they would be coming to the aid of Santo Tomás and Mesilla, which at the time were completely without protection from Mexico.

Sumner visited Fort Fillmore again in early December, detailing activities to be conducted along the then-Mexican border west of the fort. Miles was ordered to establish a sub-post, Fort Daniel Webster, near the Santa Rita Copper Mines. All support, including troops, was to be provided from his Fort Fillmore command. Major Morris, Miles's second in command and still at El Paso, was ordered to take command at Fort Webster and to depart from Fort Fillmore before the end of December, health permitting. Sumner later warned Morris:

... As soon as the train arrives at El Paso, take your supplies to Fort Webster, if your health will permit. I wish you to proceed immediately to that post, taking with you Bvt. Maj. Richardson's Company 'K,' 3rd Infantry. On your arrival there you will take possession of the quarters vacated by Bvt. Lieut. Col. Craig, and immediately make such repairs, as will make them habitable for the winter. If the Apache Indians should express a desire for peace, let them understand, distinctly, that they must pledge themselves to abstain, at once, from all depredations upon the Mexicans before any truce can be granted. If they will do this propose to them to meet the Governor and myself at Fort Conrad, as early as possible, to enter into a definite treaty of peace.

The Company of Dragoons belonging to your post, will not be sent out before spring. You are authorized to keep two of the wagons belonging to the train that moves your command and 52 oxen and draft and beef cattle.[18]

On the morning of December 14, forty-four mules and three horses belonging to a government wagon train hauling lumber from the Organs were stolen. For the first time Mescaleros from the Sierra Blanca region were mentioned in Fort Fillmore correspondence. Brevet-Captain Abraham Buford mentioned this when he filed his after-action report, detailing the reprisal foray which began on the morning of December 15. Buford stated:

I have the honor to report, that on the morning of the 15th Inst. at Reveille, I proceeded with all the effective men of 'H' Co. Drags in pursuit of a party of Indians that had stampeded and run off 44 mules and 3 horses of a government train of seven wagons engaged in transporting lumber from the east of the Organos Mountains to this post.

I arrived at the camp from which the mules were run off, early in the morning, a distance of about forty miles from this post. I soon got on the trail of the stolen mules and horses and followed it until dark: when I could follow it no longer, I bivouacked my men for the night. On the following morning at day-light, I was in the saddle, and followed the trail until about eight or nine O'clock in the morning when directly east of the San Nicholas Spring, the trail turned and evidently ran across the Jornada between the chain of the Organos Mountains and that of the Sacramento and White Mountains. After getting on this Jornada and satisfying myself that the mules and horses had been taken to the White Mountains, I saw at once it was of no use for me with the command I had to follow this trail any longer; for it was evident that my only chance was to overtake the Indians before they reached the Sacramento or White Mountains, and this I saw at once was impossible as they were then more than twenty-four hours ahead of me, and they could travel night and day. And I could follow only by day-light. Again I had only twenty men in the saddle with me, and I may say all of them save three or four, raw recruits that I have never had an opportunity to drill or instruct in the least in consequence of the building of quarters at Fort Fillmore.

With such a command as this I knew it would be folly in the extreme to enter the Mountains with the view of carrying on war against the Indians.

The attack on this train was made about eight or nine O'clock in the morning of the 14th inst. in which Ankle of 'H' Co 1st Drags was severely wounded receiving three arrows in his body. His sabre belt alone saved his life.[19]

Private Silvester Matson gave the only known description of a Fort Fillmore Christmas when he wrote of celebrating December 25, 1851, while on guard duty. After duty he ate a good Christmas dinner at the Company 'E' mess. Matson was not a member of Company 'E,' but was permitted to eat Christmas dinner with them for a reason that he did not specify. The probable reason was that Company 'K,' Matson's company, was preparing to leave the fort for the Santa Rita Copper Mines and may have been in the throes of preparations for that event.[20]

On December 29, in the bitter cold of winter, Brevet-Major Richardson led Company 'K,' 3d Infantry, out of Fort Fillmore and onto the road to the Santa Rita Copper Mines and the establishment of Fort Daniel Webster. Richardson was accompanied by his second in command, 2d Lieutenant Laurens O'Bannon, and sixty-seven rank and file infantrymen of Company 'K,' as well as a wagon train with a dragoon escort carrying his supplies and equipment. Richardson did not have to construct a fort at Daniel Webster as was being done at Fort Fillmore. He was to occupy buildings vacated by the Bartlett Boundary Commission, which was then at San Diego, California, its job of boundary survey completed.[21]

Company 'K' marched only five miles the first day, encamping at a point Private Matson called the big bend of the Rio Grande. Private Matson wrote of traveling only as far as Las Cruces the next day, having a good dinner, and the opportunity to watch a number of chicken fights, as well as attending a fandango, or Mexican dance. Company 'K' camped at Las Cruces for several days into the new year. They may have been picking up the wagons and animals that were to accompany them to Fort Daniel Webster.[22]

In December 1851, Company 'E' was still commanded by Brevet-Major Jefferson Van Horne, the only officer present with the company. The NCO staff, at least those not on detached service, numbered two sergeants and one corporal. Two musicians were on duty, one drummer and one fifer. Seventeen of the privates of the company were on special duty within the fort itself. Three men were sick in hospital and an additional thirty-two were available for regular duties as assigned. Sixteen enlisted men were on detached service outside the fort. One recruit arrived from the general depot (perhaps Fort Union). Ten more recruits were required to bring the company strength up from the current seventy-four to the eighty-four allocated by Congress.[23]

The year 1851 ended with Fort Fillmore still very much in the throes of settling into its new role. Permanent quarters were still a long way off; the farming experiment was being contracted out. Fort Daniel Webster must now be supported from dwindling Fort Fillmore assets. Brevet-Colonel Sumner's appetite for accomplishing many goals was whetted, but the available resources were simply not there.

NOTES - Chapter 3

1. Miles to Buell, September 26, 1951, M1102, Roll 4.
2. Dixon Miles to Sarah Ann Miles, October 9, 1951, Kuethe Correspondence.
3. Fort Fillmore Post Returns, October 1851.
4. Dixon Miles to Sarah Ann Miles, October 9, 1851, Kuethe Correspondence.

5. Sumner to Jones, October 31, 1851, M1012, Roll 1.

6. Edwin Sweeney, *Cochise,* pp. 88, 89.

7. Fort Fillmore Post Returns, October 1851.

8. Ibid.

9. *The Journal of Arizona History,* Volume 31, Number 4, Dinges,Bruce J, Editor-in-Chief, et al. "With the Third Infantry in New Mexico, 1851-1853: The Lost Diary of Private Sylvester W. Matson." (Phoenix: The Arizona Historical Society, 1990), p. 355. (Hereafter cited as The Matson Diary.)

10. Dixon Miles to Sarah Ann Miles, November 13, 1851, Kuethe Correspondence.

11. Martin Butler's basic history was taken from an unpublished letter found at the Museum of New Mexico in 1998 by the author. The letter was dated June 12, 1996, written by Dr. John Wilson, the archaeologist who conducted the 1966 excavation at Fort Fillmore. The letter included the names and statistics of all soldiers' names found up to that time by Dr. Wilson. Most, or all, are believed buried in the Fort Fillmore cemetery.

12. Dixon Miles to Sarah Ann Miles, November 13, 1851, Kuethe Correspondence.

13. The Matson Diary, p. 356.

14. Sumner to Jones, November 20, 1851, M1012, Roll 1.

15. Miles to McFerran, November 29, 1851, M1012, Roll 4.

16. McFerran to Miles, December 3, 1851, M1012, Roll 4.

17. The speech by President Millard Fillmore was included in a compendium of presidential speeches gathered by James D. Richardson, titled, *Messages and Papers of the Presidents.*

18. Sumner to Morris, December 5, 1851, M1012, Roll 1.

19. Buford to Assistant Adjutant General, Santa Fe, December 20, 1851, M1102, Roll 4.

20. The Matson Diary, pp. 358, 359.

21. Buford to McFerran, December 29, 1851, M1012, Roll 4.

22. The Matson Diary, p. 358.

23. Fort Fillmore Post Returns, December 1851.

4

1852 · GROWING PAINS

The command at Fort Fillmore might have solved the Indian raiding problem by adopting a military technique once advocated by the Spaniards in that part of New Mexico. The Spaniards had similar problems with the Indians, especially the Mescalero, who were continually raiding Paso del Norte and the surrounding region. Two Spanish choices were to take the fight to the enemy warriors, and their families, or simply react to Indian attacks through pursuit of the perpetrators after crimes were committed. The American choices were the same. An alternate Spanish colonial practice, when implemented properly and followed with care, was quite successful—feed the Apaches, thereby rendering them harmless through lack of a need to raid. The founding of Fort Millard Fillmore and its outpost at Fort Daniel Webster saw all three of these methods tried in a very short time.[1]

Private Sylvester Matson reported that Company 'K' left Las Cruces early on the morning of January 3, 1852, and marched approximately seven miles to the town of Doña Ana. They left there on January 4 and marched fifteen miles to what Matson called "Santiago." San Diego Crossing was a point on the river (south of Hatch) where most of the oxen and mule trains crossed the Rio Grande to the western bank. The company halted there for several days. To keep the troops busy, Brevet-Major Richardson unlimbered a brass mountain howitzer and held firing practice, sending several shells into the mountains to the great excitement of the natives.[2]

While Company 'K' slowly trudged toward the famed Chief Mangas Coloradas's Apache lands, Doña Ana County, the southern New Mexico county in which Fort Fillmore was to be situated, was being established. This action was taken on January 6, 1852, by the 2d Legislative Assembly. The Village of Doña Ana was designated as the initial county seat.[3]

Company 'K' traveled thirteen miles to the Rancho del Santa Barbara on January 13. Santa Barbara consisted of a small hacienda with a dozen huts and a mixed population of Mexican and Indian origins. Santa Barbara houses were constructed of the same mud and stick ingredients then being used to build the first accommodations at Fort Fillmore. On January 20, after a march of several days, they reached the Mimbres River and, on January 21, 1852, Company 'K' arrived at its new home at the Santa Rita Copper Mines. They took up station at the old Spanish presidio (fort), a triangular-shaped structure built of adobe, with an open court inside the enclosure.[4]

Troubles with the Indians began on January 22, 1852, when some one hundred Apaches approached the fort. The troops were drum-rolled to arms immediately. A squaw walked out alone from among her people and, waving an old white shirt attached to a pole as a flag of truce, approached the wary soldiers. She was met by Richardson, O'Bannon, and an interpreter. The squaw said the Apaches wanted a treaty of peace with the soldiers. Brevet-Major Richardson told her to go back to her leaders and tell them that he would treat with them. She returned to the band where a 'pow-wow' soon began, according to Private Matson. Two male leaders came forward, the rest of the Indians remaining out of range. One of these was the very tall Mangas Coloradas and the other was Ponce. Matson reported that Richardson told the Chiefs to 'vamoose,' warning them not to be prowling around the vicinity or the soldiers would make trouble for them. The Apaches left, insulted. When it appeared that the tribe was stirred up and perhaps ready to fight, Richardson ordered them fired upon with small arms and the brass twelve-pounder mountain howitzer. Several Indians fell, and the rest fled. Two wounded squaws were captured.[5]

The attack on the Apaches caused Richardson to increase his vigilance and to quickly strengthen his fortifications. The brevet-major erected a platform on which to mount the brass howitzer, where it could be aimed over the wall of the fort. At about eleven o'clock on the morning of January 26, Company 'K' was brought to arms once again by the long drum roll. According to Private Matson, the post had a large herd of cattle and oxen, used in hauling provisions from Fort Fillmore. The herders fled to the fort, saying Apaches had attacked them and driven off some of the cattle. Most of this herd were valuable oxen and much needed for the Fort Fillmore farming experiment. There was a sharp fight between about fifty Apaches and the troops. The attack was so brief that the mountain howitzer was not brought into action. The Apaches escaped with several oxen and the bodies of their dead. During the engagement, two soldiers, Sergeant Bernard O'Dougherty and Private John Croty, were killed. Sergeant Nicholas Wade, captured by the Apaches during the battle, was feared dead, perhaps by torture. Wade's mutilated body was later found not far from the fort.[6] The news of this Apache raid arrived at Fort Fillmore in early February from Fort Daniel Webster. Colonel Miles indicated to the 9th Department that if he could not replace the oxen, he would have to forestall the farming experiment, a critical cornerstone of Sumner's cut-costs-in-every-way philosophy. Without the oxen, Miles could not cultivate.

Brevet-Captain Abraham Buford, with a section of Company 'H,' 1st Dragoons, left Fort Fillmore in early February to scout the Jornada del Muerto. He returned to Fort Fillmore on February 6, having journeyed to the Point of Rocks, a known Camino Real camping ground and favored attack point of the Apaches. No Indians were seen, nor were any signs of them encountered.[7]

Company 'E' of the 2d Regiment of Dragoons arrived from Fort Conrad on February 9. This mounted company was under the command of 2d Lieutenant Nathan George Evans, a West Point officer, Class of 1848. When Company 'E' arrived, there were three sergeants, four corporals, two buglers, and fifty-nine privates, in addition to Evans. Nathan Evans had an illustrious career. He transferred to the 2[d] Cavalry Regiment in 1855, a unit known for the number of future Confederate generals in its ranks. Robert E. Lee, Joseph E. Johnston, and Robert Ransom, all noted Confederate general officers, also served with that regiment, as did Edwin Vose Sumner after he left the 9th Department. Among his many accomplishments, Evans became a Confederate brigadier general of cavalry, and was given the thanks of the Confederate Congress and a gold medal after the Battle of Balls Bluff.[8]

On February 12, Miles reported a rumor that the mail party from San Antonio had been slaughtered some ninety miles south of El Paso and across from the Mexican military colony of Guadalupe. Five American bodies were reportedly found, the wagons burned, and letters and papers strewn in every direction. What was singular about the incident was that the pocket watches of the mail carriers had been broken against rocks. All except one man had been shot by two ball-holes through the body. One man had been shot in the head. Miles sent Brevet-Captain Buford and soldiers from Company 'H' to El Paso in a useless attempt to find the attackers. Buford was soon back.[9]

At Fort Daniel Webster on February 12, Private Sylvester Matson reported that an express arrived from Fort Fillmore with his pay. He received twelve dollars, and the express rider got twenty-six dollars for carrying the funds from Fort Fillmore, a truly hazardous duty.[11]

Soldiers of the 3[d] Infantry were scattered on detached service all over the 9th Department and Miles made a concerted effort to send them back to their correct units. Most companies being under strength, post commanders were reluctant to release any warm bodies. The total strength at Fort Fillmore increased over January. Miles had two hundred and thirteen men at the post, including nineteen on the staff, forty-three in Company 'H,' 1st Dragoons, seventy-two in Company 'E,' 2[d] Dragoons, the latter an increase over the first arrival, and seventy-two infantrymen of Company 'E,' 3[d] Infantry. The two dragoon companies had only fifty-two serviceable animals between them, an additional thirty-four being broken down.[11]

In 1852 the Republic of Mexico lay just a mile or so west of Fort Fillmore across the Rio Grande. Relations were seldom good with the Mexicans, although now both sides of the river depended upon one another for survival. The little town of Mesilla, still nothing but a farming village, was started in early 1850 as a result of a segment of the Mexican farming population not wanting to be included in the American nation. On February 15, 1852, Lieutenant Colonel Miles was accused by an angry Mexican government of stealing Mexican wood. Miles responded in turn. He noted that who was cutting wood on whose side of the Rio Grande was hardly worth mentioning, there being sufficient wood for all. Miles believed the little tempest was the result of Mexico being a nation which seemed "inclined on every and the most trifling occasion to demand remuneration of our government under the slightest pretexts for trespass." Usable trees were not plentiful along the banks of the bounteous Rio Grande, despite of Miles's assertions that there were enough for all. It was a constant source of friction between the Mexican and American communities all along the river.[12]

Three days later, an Apache raid occurred near the village of Fronteras on the Texas border, near White's Ranch, about thirty-five miles south of Fort Fillmore. There were six clearly identifiable populated sites on the American side of the river up to Las Cruces. These were White's Ranch (Fronteras), McClelland's Ranch, Cotton-wood camp site, Fort Fillmore, Tortugas Pueblo, and Las Cruces. The Camino Real ran through each and was called the Big Road by some in the Fort Fillmore command. On the other side of the river were three Mexican towns, Los Amoles, Santo Tomás and Mesilla. Miles ordered out the dragoons from both Buford's and Evans's com-panies. The dragoons making the scout crossed the border into Mexico to chase the Apaches. By the time they arrived in the area where the depredation had occurred, the Apache raiders were long gone.

Another, and far more bloody, clash with Apaches occurred on February 21, 1852, when the mail party from Santa Fe was attacked at the Point of Rocks on the Jornada del Muerto. Miles described this incident:

> As Sergt. B. Dougherty with his party and mail was within four miles of the Point of Rocks, he was attacked by about thirty Indians on yesterday. The evidence of a citizen and eye witness to the affair, gives the sergt and party much credit for their coolness and bravery. He whipt [sic] the Indians off, killing one and wounding two. He had a man killed—Pvt. Collins of D. Co. 2d Drags.—as he was getting out of the wagon, and two wounded, an Infantry soldier and a citizen by the name of Craddock. One or two of the mail mules were wounded. To get his wounded [care] the sergt. returned last night to Dona Ana.
>
> A party of twenty drags left here immediately (after reveille) under Bvt. Capt. Bee, 3rd Inf. who volunteered for the service, to conduct the mail to Fort Conrad and fight all Indians he may meet with.
>
> I am convinced no party of ten men can now travel across the Jornada in safety, and I shall until otherwise directed send for the future 20 men with the mail.
>
> Capt. Bee, from Ft. Conrad, will give you more particular information of this affair, as it is the first time of any of their attacks that this so completely failed. They [sthe Apaches] got nothing which may be attributed to the escort being afoot. Had they been Dragoons, as undisciplined as the men and horses are, half would have been killed and all the mules and horses lost.[13]

Lieutenant Colonel Miles had a negative opinion about the capabilities of the dragoon soldiers (drags he called them) at his post. He found them ill-disciplined in both arms drill and horse training. Miles praised the 3ᵈ Infantrymen who fought off the attack with the pride of an infantry officer in his command. During this period there was a concern as to the capability of the dragoon arm to function as expected. Dragoon companies could not keep officers with the units in any numbers greater than one, and for long periods no officers were available to command in some companies. The enlisted men's discipline and cohesion were affected, especially when it is remembered that each dragoon unit in the New Mexico Territory acted independently of regimental command.

1

2

3

4

Military buttons found during Fort Fillmore excavations:
(1) Infantry officer's button - Mexican War era;
(2) Overcoat button - Mexican War era;
(3) Dragoon officer's button;
(4) Rare circa 1854 blank shield enlisted button.
Courtesy: Geronimo Springs Museum.

Colonel James B. Many, Commanding Officer of the 3ᵈ Infantry Regiment, although not with the Regiment at any time at Fort Fillmore, died in New Orleans on February 3, 1852. The command at Fort Fillmore did not receive news of his passing until February 23. By that time a new commander, Colonel Thomas Staniford, had already been selected. Staniford had served in the United States Army for forty years. He was a life long infantry officer, serving at various times with the old 11ᵗʰ Infantry during the War of 1812-15, then with the 6ᵗʰ, 2ᵈ and 8ᵗʰ Infantry Regiments, before being made Colonel of the 3ᵈ Infantry Regiment on Many's death. Staniford once received the unusual brevet of having served ten years in one rank. He was also breveted for valor at Palo Alto and Resaca de la Palma during the Mexican War. Like James Many, Thomas Staniford never reported to take active command of the 3ᵈ Infantry at Fort Fillmore.[14]

Major W.H. Emory of the Topographical Engineers was at Fort Fillmore in late February. Emory, who still had survey work to do in the region, was very concerned about the Indian problems then occurring near Fort Fillmore and Fort Daniel Webster. Emory wrote to Colonel Sumner requesting an additional infantry escort to be provided his survey party. He also requested additional ammunition and weapons from Fort Fillmore stocks. Miles was not about to fill Emory's request for an additional infantry company, Fort Fillmore having only Brevet-Major Van Horne's Company 'E.' Nor was he likely to hand over forty rifles. Miles provided neither.[15]

Second Lieutenant Nathan Evans left Fort Fillmore for Fort Webster on March 15 with Company 'E,' 2ᵈ Dragoons. His unit's total strength was two sergeants, four corporals and fifty-seven privates, including a farrier. As Evans made slow progress toward Fort Webster, his future commanding officer, Major Gouveneur Morris, raised a number of issues concerning an expedition led by a Major Howe out of Fort Conrad:

> ... I have the honor to inform the Colonel Commanding the Dept. that the command under Maj. Howe, 2nd Dragoons, arrived at this post, on or about the 28th ult. and left on a scout against the Apaches on the 1st Inst. Returned to this place from said scout

on the 12th Inst. His expedition this far has been a total failure. I am well informed that he did not go over twenty or twenty five miles from this place, and never saw an Indian during the period he was about. We cannot however state that there are none in the country, for on his march to this place his command was fired upon by the Indians and his guide severely wounded.[16]

Lieutenant Colonel Miles received word that the Mexican General Angel Trías, from Chihuahua, also on an expedition against the Apaches, was rumored to be heading for the region of the Gila. Miles knew Brevet-Major Howe and his dragoons were campaigning there, and commented that "Howe's campaign may be fortunately timed and successful" if the two forces were to combine. General Trías, of whom we will hear again on another matter related to Fort Fillmore, was accompanied by an unusual band of men that had come to Mexico as the result of another war. The war between the United States and the Seminole Nation in Florida had been a savage one, lasting years. When it finally ended some Seminole tribesmen, especially those of mixed Seminole-Negro blood, moved to Mexico to serve the Chihuahuan government in its problems with the Apaches. Lieutenant Colonel Miles was informed that Chief Wild Cat, a Seminole Chief and leader of a mixed band of one hundred Seminoles and former Negro slaves, accompanied General Trías as scouts during the Gila campaign. Despite the presence of so formidable a pursuing force, the Apaches eluded them.[17]

Miles showed gaps in his knowledge about the Apaches when he reported to Captain McFerran in a letter dated April 10, 1852, that the Apaches had abandoned the Gila River region and moved to the Sacramento Mountains, obviously confused by the fact there was more than one Apache band in the region he was to protect. Miles also reported that a local man named Grandjean, who was leading a wagon train returning to Santa Fe from Chihuahua, was attacked by Indians near Corralitos, Mexico. Granjean and at least two other men were wounded. The battle lasted some sixty hours and included fires set by the Indians to smoke the party out of their defensive positions. Eight Indians were supposedly killed and a number wounded.[18]

On May 12, Miles reported that the smoke house at Fort Fillmore was about completed and soon the bacon, then under canvas at Fort Fillmore, would be hanging in storage. Miles said a Captain Bowen (Andrew Bowman), Army commissary, informed him that much of the bacon was destined for forts above Fort Fillmore, such as Fort Conrad. The present day was none too soon to move any excess bacon north, as the weather was still cool. When the hot weather came the bacon would have to be taken from its wrappings and placed in smokehouses for protection.[19]

In the middle of May, Fort Daniel Webster almost experienced a disaster. The Rio Grande rose to flood level, probably due to spring runoff far to the north. Miles had no way of communicating with Fort Webster nor of crossing the river to the Mexican side, short of traveling south and crossing near El Paso. There was as yet no river ferry to take horses and wagons across the river. Miles could not get to Mesilla and he could not send a courier to Fort Webster to tell Morris why his supplies and mail were delayed. Since Miles could not get a forage train to Fort Webster from Fort Fillmore by the shorter route, he hired James Magoffin in El Paso to cross there with a train and travel on the Mexican side up to Mesilla. There an escort from Fort Webster met the wagon train. The tenuous link between Fort Webster and the army supply system was tested to the maximum.[20]

Territorial Governor Calhoun, in poor health and possibly exhausted from trying to solve the often unsolvable problems of the New Mexico Territory, planned to return to the East in May. The stories say he was so ill and in such low spirits that he took his own coffin along on the trip, not expecting to reach the East alive. Somewhere on the plains of Kansas, Governor John C. Calhoun indeed breathed his last. President Fillmore appointed William Carr Lane, a man then in his sixties, as Territorial Governor to replace Calhoun.[21]

As events at Fort Fillmore and the surrounding region went from bad to worse—floods, troubles with Mexico, etc.—other problems for Colonel Miles were taking shape at Fort Daniel Webster. Major Morris decided that the current location of the fort was unsuitable. He explained:

... I would respectfully represent to the Colonel Commanding the Dept. that the garrison at this place be removed to some eligible situation on the Rio Mimbres for the following reasons.

The original and sole object of establishing a Fort at this place was to give protection to persons engaged [in] working the Copper Mines, but since the exploitation of the mines has been abandoned, the necessity for a military garrison just at this particular spot no longer exists.

The Apaches live near and frequent the Valley of the Mimbres, more than they do at this place: That valley is well adapted for cultivation and settlement, the country being open, and being covered by inaccessible mountains on one side, renders stock more secure and less liable to be captured by the Indians than here.

The lines of communication to either Fort Fillmore and Conrad would be greatly reduced in distance and the worst part of the road avoided. It will also have the advantage of being nearer the Indian Country than the present post is. Moreover, the benefits arising from having land to cultivate, good grazing and an abundant supply of healthy water, are sufficient inducements in my opinion to authorize the removal of this post. I will add, that most of the work which has been done at this place, (such as sending doors, windows and getting out [?] can be removed and used in the construction of the quarters at the new post. Besides, the quarters here are insufficient and not yet finished. They will require about as much labor to put them in a proper condition for the accommodation of troops as it would to build new barracks. It has been mentioned to me, that this Fort is private property, and it would seem to be poor policy to improve the property and after which to have to pay rent for it.

I intend to go day after tomorrow to make a reconnaissance of the Mimbres for the object of reporting upon the best position to establish a military post. I will be gone two or three days and will give you the result of any observations.[22]

On June 16, Major Morris reported the visit of Apache Chief Cuchillo Negro. This chief's Territory is often given as north of the copper mines region, which was in the territory of Mangas Coloradas's band. Cuchillo Negro was to be slain by United States soldiers in 1857, during the Bonneville Expedition. Morris wrote to Sumner, noting:

... I have the honor to inform the Colonel Commanding the Dept. that on the 1st Inst. Cuchillo Negro, an Apache Chief, accompanied by about fifty men, and a few women came into the camp on the Mimbres, expressing friendship, and desired to have a talk with the Commandant of the fort; immediately on being informed of their presence on the Mimbres, I repaired thither, taking with me Lieut. Evans, and a small command. On the morning of the 2nd Inst. the Indians sought, and had a parley with us; the Chief Cuchillo Negro, said that he and his people came in for the purpose of making peace with the government of the United States, that they had lived all their lives on and about the Mimbres, and wished to be on terms of friendship with the whites. I asked him whether it was the wish of all the Apaches to make peace. I told him, that the United States would not enter into any treaty of peace with one portion of the Apaches and be at war with the rest: That if he, with some of his men would go with us to the fort, I should then believe he was sincere. He accordingly did so, and whilst there [sent a] dispatch runner to Mangas Colorado, and the other principal Chiefs to come here and hold a council with the Commanding Officer on the subject; he said that most of the Chiefs were some distance off, and scattered over the country and it would take nine or ten days before he could communicate with them, and give them time to come in; on the 15th Inst. Ponce, the second Chief of the nation, Josecito, Ituna [sic] and Cuchillo Negro came to the fort with a large number [of] warriors. Ponce said that it was the wish of all the Apaches to make a permanent treaty of peace with the United States. I replied that I could not conclude the terms of a treaty with them, but would take them to Santa Fe where they could arrange the business in person with the proper authorities. He said it would take about three weeks to send to Mangas Colorado, Delgadito, and other Chiefs and principal men and get them to come here. So soon as I am able to contact all the Chiefs and principle men will proceed with them to Dept. Head Quarters, and if I am not interfered with by subordinate Agents of the Indian Dept. or irresponsible traders, trust I shall be able to conduct this business to the satisfaction of the Colonel Commanding.[23]

Major Morris made peace contacts with some of the leading Apache leaders of the period. His reference to "subordinate Agents of the Indian Dept." indicates there may already have been trouble between the Indian Department and the Army, although as yet there were no Indian Agents or an agency in the Fort Webster area.

Changes were coming, at least to the hostile situation then operative between the soldiers and the Apache bands surrounding Fort Daniel Webster. On July 1 the first peace treaty between the Mimbres bands of the Apache and the American government was signed in Santa Fe. Celebrations at Fort Webster followed the signing of the peace treaty. Private Sylvester Matson reported that the Indians got very drunk on the liquor supplied to them by 2^d Lieutenant Nathan Evans. Evans had the most to gain from the treaty, in that now his dragoon horses would not be stolen by the Indians, at least in such large numbers as had formerly been the case.[24]

Brevet-Captain Bowman, the quartermaster officer for Fort Fillmore, Magoffinsville, and Fort Webster, examined the stores at Fort Fillmore in June 1852 and reported a small surplus of 32.7 pounds of salt meat, 6.3 pounds of hard bread, and 1.3 pounds of beans. There were deficiencies of varying degree in flour, rice, coffee, brown sugar, regular sugar, vinegar, candles, soap, and salt. Bowman also reminded Brevet-Colonel Sumner that during his visit to Fort Union, he had indicated that the store of pork (bacon) at Fort Fillmore was old and much was close to spoilage. Bacon was the basic foodstuff at military posts and Fort Fillmore was not scheduled to be re-supplied until August 1853. Bowman indicated the current salt pork on hand would be spoiled from age by that time. One other critical commodity was also specifically mentioned: The post was very low on candles and expected to be out of them within a month. Since candles lit the fort buildings inside at night, the situation bordered on the critical. When Sumner visited Fort Fillmore, Bowman had reported a sufficiency of candles but during a subsequent robbery, ten boxes of candles had been stolen. This theft had caused the critical shortage.[25]

Brevet-Captain Abraham Buford left Fort Fillmore for the East and recruiting duty on July 11, 1852. Brevet-Major Enoch Steen, the actual Company 'H' commander, replaced him in command. Steen was a familiar figure in southern New Mexico, having been a very aggressive military leader at Doña Ana in 1849 and 1850.

July saw other changes in the Fort Fillmore command structure. Brevet-Major Jefferson Van Horne, the longest-serving officer in southern New Mexico, was ordered East to serve a tour as an army recruiter. Van Horne eventually returned to New Mexico, serving at the future Fort Stanton and other places before dying in New Mexico on September 28, 1857, at the age of fifty-five. Captain Bowman, recently promoted, also left the post for other duties.[26]

One arriving officer did not replace any of the three departing men. He was Major Benjamin W. Brice, and his arrival must have made the troops very happy. Brice was paymaster for southern New Mexico, including Forts Fillmore, Conrad, and Webster, as well as all of the small detached units in the area. Brice was forty-six years of age in 1852, having graduated from West Point with the Class of 1829. He was to rise in the Pay Department to the rank of brevet-major general-paymaster during the Civil War, retiring from the Army in 1872 at the age of sixty-six, as a full brigadier general-paymaster. He served a long tour of duty at Fort Fillmore as the regional paymaster for southern New Mexico.[27]

When Major Enoch Steen arrived from Fort Leavenworth, Kansas Territory, to take command of Company 'H,' 1st Dragoons on July 30, 1852, he returned to a weak and badly rundown unit. The Fort Fillmore Post Returns for July 1852 show only thirty-seven dragoons available for duty, to include four sergeants, two corporals, two buglers, and twenty-nine privates. The situation with the horses was almost as bad. Of the twenty-seven cavalry horses then at Fort Fillmore, ten were unfit for use. Frequent desertions from the dragoon detachment at Magoffinsville—no less than seven in the month of July—accounted for the Company 'H' situation. These deserters crossed into Mexico and lived openly in Paso del Norte. Their stolen horses, arms and equipment were the price of their protection in Mexico.[28]

On July 19, two peons working outside Las Cruces discovered three Indian ponies tied in a cornfield near the town. They also found three empty long guns. During the same night a man and a woman, sleeping outside, were shot and wounded by arrows. The next morning, mounted Mexican militia took the trail of the Indians, and caught them when they reached a gorge in the mountains to the east of Fort Fillmore. One Indian was killed in the ensuing fight. Locals were not enlisted in the Regular Army, but were encouraged to form militia companies which served as auxiliaries in times of trouble.[29]

On July 21 at Fort Webster, Private Matson recorded that an Indian named Poncita, probably the brother of the Apache Chief Ponce, arrived at Fort Webster. With Poncita were several warriors and a number of widowed squaws. The latter had cut off their scalp locks in mourning. The women's husbands had been killed in battle with a squadron of Mexican lancers. These Apaches came to Fort Webster seeking the protection of the American soldiers, as per Mangas Coloradas's agreement with the military at Santa Fe earlier in July. When that party arrived, other Indians under Ponce, Cuchillo Negro, Delgadito, and Ocita, with their warriors, left. Apparently, they intended to go to Mexico to take their revenge for the deaths of the women's husbands. The Apaches usually sought to take revenge. This may be why the American Army chose a similar strategy of massive reaction to the killing of an officer or soldier; the Apaches understood such a response and came to fear it.[30]

On July 23 Chief Mangas Coloradas arrived at Fort Daniel Webster and announced that he had made a treaty with Brevet-Colonel Sumner. Mangas was dressed in the uniform of a Mexican general of artillery with an epaulette missing from one shoulder. Private Sylvester Matson believed it was the coat of some Mexican officer slain by the Apache leader. The Mexican Government had a $10,000 reward out for Mangas, dead or alive. Mangas also spoke fluent Spanish. To show that he could hold his people to a peace treaty, Mangas brought forth an Apache warrior who had been disfigured by having his nose and ears cut off. This man had killed a Mexican without permission, and had paid this horrible price.[31]

By the end of July it was known that the farming experiment at Fort Fillmore had failed. The reasons were explained in a plaintive letter from Miles to Sumner. The blame, according to Miles, fell partly on the nature of the desert terrain, and partly on the fact that such work was better suited to Mexicans than to American soldiers.

The soldiers could not, and would not, be farmers and soldiers at the same time. This is clear from the reports Miles had sent previously. He could barely mount guard because most of his infantry was in the fields trying to grow their own food, and doing a bad job of that. The flooding of the still-wild Rio Grande was a surprise, washing away much of the work the soldiers had done. He indicated they could not free the land from the water, and spent much time "leg deep in mud." The farm continued in operation at Fort Fillmore for an undetermined period of time, but under civilian contract and not operated by the soldiers.[32]

The first post office in Doña Ana County and in all of southern New Mexico Territory was established at Fort Fillmore on August 6, 1852. George Hayward, the Fort Fillmore Post Sutler, became the first postmaster, and the office was in the sutler's store at the northwest edge of the fort. The second post office in Doña Ana County was established at the town of Doña Ana on January 5, 1854, almost one-and-a-half years after the Fort Fillmore Post Office. The postmaster at Doña Ana was P.M. Thompson, the man who turned the Fort Fillmore farming project into a success with local, rather than soldier, labor. Las Cruces followed only days after Doña Ana, when the post office was established there under the care of Mr. Benjamin F. Read. The spelling of the Las Cruces office was 'Las Cruzces' or 'Las Cruzees.' Mesilla, although a populous community in the early 1850s, was not an American town until 1855 and did not have a United States Post Office until January 21, 1858, when the U.S. Post Office named Charles A. Hoppin to the position of first postmaster there. Officially known as La Mesilla, the post office has always been called simply Mesilla.[33]

The new assistant quartermaster officer of the 3[d] Infantry Regiment, replacing Brevet-Captain Bowman, arrived at Fort Fillmore on August 10, 1852. He was 1st Lieutenant John Courts McFerran, the 9th Military Department adjutant until he assumed the Fort Fillmore job. McFerran was an 1843 graduate of the United States

Military Academy and was commissioned in the 3[d] Infantry. McFerran had a natural bent for quartermaster duties, filling his first role of that type with the 3[d] Infantry during the War with Mexico. He filled other quartermaster posts, including the job at Fort Fillmore, until he became Chief of Quarter Master, Department of New Mexico, during the American Civil War. By the end of the Civil War, McFerran was promoted to brigadier general for meritorious service during the war.[34]

Judge Hoppin, an influential El Paso pioneer, reported that on the morning of August 12 a party of approximately eighteen Apaches descended upon the El Paso region and ran off twenty-seven mules and horses. The Apaches stole the animals at a point near Magoffinsville, taking the stock toward the west where they were observed crossing the Camino Real near White's Ranch at Fronteras. The Indians then moved up river about five or six miles from White's Ranch, crossing the Rio Grande at that point and disappearing in the direction of the copper mines. Judge Hoppin suspected the animals would be offered for sale at Fort Webster. Hoppin appealed to Miles at Fort Fillmore for help, adding that soldiers at Fort Webster might be offered the animals in trade.[35] An Apache raid on a ranch or farm in daytime was a rare event in early Fort Fillmore correspondence; Apaches almost invariably used stealth and the darkness of night to steal stock, fighting only if they were opposed by herders or other farm hands. The eighteen Apaches made no attempt to massacre the local residents, however, being content only to steal the animals.

Brevet-1st Lieutenant John Darragh Wilkins, the officer in command of the small detachment at Magoffinsville, reported officially to Lieutenant Colonel Miles concerning the Apache raid on August 12. Henry Skillman rode into the midst of the Apache raiders as they were stealing the stock and recognized Delgadito, a well-known Apache Chief, as their leader. A Mr. Hubbel, Judge Hoppin's partner, was prepared to go to Fort Webster to see if he could find the animals there. It was rumored at Fort Fillmore that Major Morris bought two of the mules from Delgadito. Miles confirmed the purchase of the animals but stated that Morris himself had not purchased them, only authorizing the post sutler to do so. Miles's informant from Fort Webster stated that Brevet-Major Richardson, Company 'K,' 3ᵈ Infantry, may also have bought some of the stolen animals.[36]

Fort Fillmore received reinforcements on September 6, 1852, when Company 'C,' 3ᵈ Infantry, commanded by 2ᵈ Lieutenant William Dennison Whipple, finally arrived. Company 'C' consisted of Whipple, four sergeants, three corporals, two musicians—a fifer and a drummer—and seventy-one privates. 2ᵈ Lieutenant Whipple was serving in his first Army assignment, having graduated from West Point in June 1851. The actual com-manding officer of Company 'C,' who would have been a captain, was not listed in the returns. The other officer listed as part of Company 'C' was 1st Lieutenant John C. McFerran—on detached service from the company, functioning as post quartermaster and commissary officer.[37]

On September 7 Fort Fillmore received further reinforce-ments, as Company 'K' of the 2ᵈ Dragoons arrived at the post. Company 'K' came from Fort Conrad with no officers. Four sergeants, four corporals, one bugler, one blacksmith and forty-eight privates rode on only thirty-five horses. Company 'K's' absent commander was to become one of the American Civil War's most famous general officers. He was 1ˢᵗ Lieutenant Alfred Pleasanton; however, he never served at Fort Fillmore with his company. The enlisted men of Company 'K,' having no officer, were placed under the command of Brevet-Major Enoch Steen, whose Company 'H,' 1ˢᵗ Dragoons, was still at the post in a depleted condition. Together these two weak companies became one full-strength dragoon company.[38]

Two hundred and seventy head of cattle arrived at Fort Fillmore on September 8. One hundred and sixty-five were sent on to Fort Union with the cattle herder, a Mr. Mitchell. Lieutenant McFerran stated in a letter to the 9ᵗʰ Department that Colonel Miles had him search the post for soldiers honest and caring enough to be herders. He found none among the complement. The soldiers were too busy building and repairing post structures, among other military duties. Miles then ordered McFerran to hire Mexican herders at fifty cents per cow per month, with the herders responsible for any losses not caused by natural death or Indians. Also, the cattle were not expected and there were no corrals in which to keep them at the post. Lieutenant McFerran held strong negative opinions with respect to the potential for carelessness among the soldiers, should they have been assigned to guarding the cattle; also McFerran believed the Mexicans made excellent thieves. It was better by far to have the thieves guard the herd for pay than have them steal the cattle. McFerran actually preferred that the cattle be sold and not tended at Fort Fillmore at all. He believed it was better to contract for meat than to have soldiers attempt to raise their own meat.[39]

A most important event took place at the Santa Rita Copper Mines when, on September 9, 1852, the entire command began its move twelve miles down the road from the old Spanish fortress to a new location on the Mimbres River. The name, Fort Daniel Webster, was retained for the new log structure post which would remain in use for the rest of 1852 and most of 1853. Fort Fillmore remained responsible for supplying the new post.

Territorial Governor William Carr Lane arrived in Santa Fe on September 9 and was welcomed by his political party and by the citizenry. Lane also received a military salute, although not one sanctioned by the 9th Department Commander, Colonel Sumner. Brevet-Lieutenant Colonel Horace Brooks so angered Sumner with his simple act of courtesy that Sumner reprimanded him for his actions. Brevet-Colonel Sumner, in Governor Calhoun's absence, had acted as both military commander and governor of the territory. The war between military and civilian authorities that had begun with Governor Calhoun and Colonel Munroe continued. only now the names were changed to Lane and Sumner. One source stated that Sumner chose to haul down the national flag that Stephen Watts Kearny had raised over Santa Fe in 1846. When Lane requested a flag to replace it, Sumner said he was not authorized to furnish the governor with government supplies. From that insult on, relations deteriorated.[40]

The new Fort Webster on the Mimbres immediately experienced a series of cattle, horse, and oxen thefts at the hands of unknown thieves. The peace treaty with the Apaches had been signed on July 12; on July 25, someone stole fifteen head of beef cattle; on the 28th, a number of oxen belonging to Lieutenant O'Bannon were taken. These were followed by the theft of several mules belong-ing to a local citizen. Soon thereafter, more mules belonging to Lieutenant Evans were stolen. In all of these 'attacks,' the Indian perpetrators never harmed humans. Major Morris, in describing the Indian lifestyle, said they led an "indolent and improvident mode of life, and with the scarcity of game in their country, they have not the means of living and depend on what they can steal to exist."[41]

Toward the end of September Boundary Commissioner Bartlett, Dr. Webb, Mr. H. Jacobs, and ten soldiers, accompanied by Colonel Langberg, commander of the Mexican Army at Paso del Norte, set off for Fort Fillmore. Bartlett wanted to visit both Fort Fillmore and Mesilla. He estimated that Mesilla had about 1,900 people at that time, only about twenty of whom were Americans. The Boundary Commissioner described Fort Fillmore as a fort with simple buildings constructed in the 'jacal' style. This meant that most of the post buildings were still crude structures, the perma-nent adobe buildings not yet having been erected.[42]

Bartlett mentioned the presence of four American women at Fort Fillmore. He also stated they might have been the only 'American' women between San Antonio and the Pacific Coast. At least one was the wife of 2[d] Lieutenant Wilkins. Miles's wife was still in Baltimore, and Brevet-Major Steen's wife had died at Fort Leaven-worth in 1849. Bartlett reported only that they were members of officers' families. In September 1852, other officers present were Major Benjamin W. Brice, the paymaster for the region; Brevet-Captain Barnard Bee, post adjutant and single; 1st Lieutenant John McFerran; and 2[d] Lieutenant William Whipple, 3[d] Infantry.[43]

Major Gouveneur Morris's initial enthusiasm for the new site of Fort Daniel Webster on the Mimbres River had diminished by early October. Morris reported Nathan Evans's dragoon company was in miserable condition. The horses were broken down and had not been furnished with corn for a long time. Morris reluctantly asked that the dragoons be withdrawn and replaced by an infantry company. In fact, only twenty horses remained in serviceable condition. The rest were either broken down or had been stolen by the artful Indians. The major requested that, if the dragoon company was removed, he be furnished with six or eight horses with which to herd the cattle near the post.[44]

One wonders about the soldiers in the commands at Fort Fillmore and Fort Webster. At times there appears to have been little or no control over them and their discipline. Obviously, given the number of stolen animals and the prevalence of theft and desertion, somebody was not doing their job. Morris indicated that most of his discipline problems were with Nathan Evans's Dragoon Company 'E.' The command had two privates of dragoons and one infantryman desert on September 8, a corporal and three privates of dragoons on the 9th. These men took with them the best remaining animals on the post, both horses and mules. The high desertion rate was blamed on California-bound emigrants who frequently passed Fort Webster on their way to the beckoning gold fields. Morris sent a column of infantry after the mounted deserters, having few decent horses in Evans's company left to pursue them. The deserters were not found.[45]

In mid-October, Lieutenant Colonel Miles received word from Don Pablo Melendrez at Doña Ana that an Apache man and woman had asked for permission to visit Fort Fillmore to talk about peace. Miles seems to be unfamiliar with the name Mescalero, for he referred to the couple as Sacramento Mountain Indians. Miles responded that he would accept a visit by the whole tribe on November 10 at the fort. This is the first recorded visit of friendly Apaches to Fort Fillmore. The visit did take place and talks were held. Miles notified Colonel Sumner of the outcome immediately, saying:

> ... On the day I wrote to you last, I had an interview with two Apache (Muscaleros [sic]) men and one woman. Their object

in coming here, was to ascertain, if we were at peace, or would make one. I tried to explain, that the peace you made extended throughout the country: but that, if they would go out and bring the principal warriors and Chiefs in, at next new month (11th of Novb.) that it was possible you would be here yourself and would fully explain to them, that your treaty was one of peace to all. And so long as they observed it, by refraining from stealing and killing, they would be treated friendly, by Whites and Mexicans.

I gave them a few presents and some rations and started them to the Sacramento Mountains apparently pleased and satisfied. These Indians assured me that their tribe was afraid of the Gila Apaches, who recently had killed one of their Chiefs. This was new to me. I ever thought they acted harmoniously with each other nor had I ever heard they were at war.

A few days since, as a wagon with dry goods was coming up from Paso for Mr. Lucas it was attacked by four mounted men, painted and dressed as Indians. The goods were rifles in part only. A citizen had his trunk rob'd. The driver escaped, nor was an attempt made to injure him. There are many circumstances in this robbery would lead to the suspicion it was done by Mexicans and Americans. I think myself there is not a doubt of it, and it is so generally believed done here by every one. The country is full of strolling vagabond Americans. No one knows where they come from or how they got here and how they support themselves.

I have my command a good deal cut up just now. One party with Lt. Wilkins in the pinery hauling down vigas [sic], another with Lt. Wilson, escorting a train to Fort Webster, and tomorrow another will be about escorting the mail.

I have heard lately from Ft. Webster that the men are deserting in squads, and have taken away several mules. I have the California Fever in my command and I fear every night a platoon will break. After pay day some always desert, the facility of escape is so great at this place that its next to an impossibility of catching one.

Should I hear of any news by the mail from El Paso I will inform you.[47]

American and Mexican bandits, dressed like Indians, raided along the old Camino Real just south of Fort Fillmore. This letter details a problem current for years along the New Mexico frontier. The beckoning California gold fields, coupled with the presence of a great number of "vagabond Americans" as Miles called them, had the worst effect upon the men at Fort Webster and at Fort Fillmore. Fort Webster, closer to California, had a greater problem, although Miles feared a similar outpouring of deserters from his post.

Company 'K,' 2[d] Dragoons, departed Fort Fillmore for Fort Conrad on November 19 without the 1st Dragoon's commanding officer, Lieutenant Wilson. He stayed at the fort awaiting an assignment with Company 'G,' 1st Dragoons, at Los Lunas. Company 'K' left Private John B. Montague at Fort Fillmore, where he died shortly after their departure. On November 20, 1852, Company 'H,' 1st Dragoons, under Brevet-Major Enoch Steen, departed Fort Fillmore for Fort Webster. Company 'H' had only thirty-five men on departure, not having received recruits since Major Steen's arrival.[47]

Franklin Pierce was elected to replace Millard Fillmore as President of the United States on November 23, 1852, defeating the Whig candidate, General Winfield Scott. Figural pipe heads in the shape of the actual heads and faces of Presidents Fillmore and Pierce were filled with tobacco and smoked in this period at Fort Fillmore. More Pierce heads than Fillmore heads were found in refuse dumps. No such figural pipes for James Buchanan or Abraham Lincoln, the next two presidents, were noted. Also present were pipe heads in the shape of Andrew Jackson, Henry Clay, and George Washington.

Major Enoch Steen was designated commanding officer of Fort Webster soon after his arrival there, replacing Major Gouveneur Morris on November 25, 1852. Company 'D,' 2[d] Dragoons, departed Fort Conrad on November 27 to take up station at Fort Fillmore. The Company Commander, Brevet-Major and Captain Graham, was on detached service and not with the company. Company 'D' was commanded by 2[d] Lieutenant Beverly Holcombe Robertson. Brevet-Major Israel Richardson, commanding

President Millard Fillmore

President Franklin Pierce

Man With Turban

Man With Fez

Figural smoking pipes found at Fort Fillmore
Courtesy: The Author

Company 'K,' 3ᵈ Infantry, left Fort Daniel Webster for Fort Millard Fillmore as part of a change of duty station move.[48]

As the month of November closed, Fort Fillmore was garrisoned by Companies 'C' and 'E' of the 3ᵈ Infantry, a total of 158 soldiers. Private Sylvester Matson was back at Fort Fillmore on December 6, 1852, for a second tour of duty. He reported five soldiers, accused of mutiny, in chains at the post. In the same diary entry Matson reported the arrival of an escort from Chihuahua, bringing the murderer of a Sergeant Graves and his family back to Doña Ana. This "party of citizens" escorted the murderer to Doña Ana, but promised to return him to Chihuahua if he were found innocent. Matson called the murderer a "horrible looking villain." The posse had him manacled hand and foot. The man wore Graves's trousers, rode Graves's horse, and even had his rifle and overcoat when captured.[49] Punishment for the murderer was administered at Doña Ana in early December. 'Judge Lynch' was at work in the town, as the murderer of former dragoon Sergeant Graves and his family was tried, convicted, and sentenced. The murderer was hung for the crime. The citizens allowed the body to swing on a limb all night to remind others of his kind what they would face for such a crime.[50]

Assistant Surgeon Charles Sutherland arrived at Fort Fillmore in early December from Fort Webster, with Company 'K,' to be the medical officer at the 3ᵈ Infantry Regimental Headquarters. Sutherland had been only recently (1852) been appointed an assistant surgeon of the Army. Fort Fillmore was his first major assignment after leaving his home state of Pennsylvania. Charles Sutherland served forty years in the army and retired as a brigadier general-surgeon in 1893.[51]

Private Sylvester Matson spent part of the Christmas holiday at Fort Fillmore reading Nathaniel Parker Willis's book, "Dashes Of Life" (*Dashes at Life with a Free Pencil*). It may have been part of the Fort Fillmore Post Library, which is known to have existed. Private Matson reported on an officers' soiree held at Fort Fillmore that night, the first known mention of such an event at the fort. Soirees meant dancing, and dancing indicated the presence of at least some females. Were they wives, or were they local senoritas, as hinted by Matson?[52]

The end of 1852 at Fort Fillmore saw the post occupied by part or all of three companies—Companies 'C' and 'E' of the 3[d] Infantry were still part of the command. Second Lt. William Whipple commanded Company 'C' while 1st Lieutenant John Wilkins commanded Company 'E.' Company 'K,' 3[d] Infantry, which had been at Fort Webster, returned to Fort Fillmore on December 7, 1852. Brevet-Major and Captain Israel Richardson still commanded Company 'K.' The arrival of Company 'K' brought the number of infantrymen at the post to two hundred thirty-two. Added to this were nineteen members of the staff and band, and fifty-nine dragoons from Company 'D,' 2[d] Dragoons, some of whom were on detached service at Magoffinsville, Texas, where 2[d] Lieutenant Beverly Holcombe Robertson commanded. There were twenty-six other persons temporarily at the post, making the total three hundred and thirty-six. Most of the temporary men were from Company 'A,' 3[d] Infantry, the unit assigned to protect the members of the Boundary Commission. In addition to the soldiers, Company 'D' recorded the presence of forty serviceable dragoon horses. Fort Daniel Webster was commanded by Major Enoch Steen of Company 'H,' 1st Dragoons. With Company 'K's' departure, there was no longer an infantry component at the post along the Mimbres.[53]

NOTES - Chapter 4

1. Alfred Barnaby Thomas, *Forgotten Frontiers: A Study of the Spanish Indian Policy of Don Juan de Anza, Governor of New Mexico, 1777-1787.* (Norman: University of Oklahoma Press, 1932), pp. 185, 186.

2. The Matson Diary, p. 358.

3. *La Posta*, Volume 2 #4, July/Aug. 1970, p 2.

4. The Matson Diary, p. 361.

5. Ibid., p. 363.

6. Ibid., p. 364, 365.

7. Miles for McFerran, February 9, 1852, M1102, Roll 4.

8. Ezra J. Warner, *Generals in Gray: Lives of the Confederate Army Commanders.* (Baton Rouge: Louisiana State University Press, 1959), p. 84. (Hereafter cited as Ezra J. Warner, *Generals in Gray.*)

9. Miles to McFerran, February 12, 1852, M1102, Roll 4.

10. The Matson Diary, February 12, 1852, p. 366.

11. Fort Fillmore Post Returns, February 1852.

12. Miles to McFerran, February 15, 1852, M1102, Roll 4.

13. Miles to McFerran, February 21, 1852, M1102, Roll 4.

14. Heitman, Thomas Staniford.

15. Emory to Sumner, February 27, 1852, M1102, Roll 4.

16. Morris to McFerran, March 16, 1852, M1102, Roll 5.

17. Miles to McFerran, March 19, 1852, M1102, Roll 5.

18. Miles to McFerran, April 10, 1852, M1102, Roll 5.

19. Miles to McFerran, May 12, 1852, M1102, Roll 5.

20. Miles to McFerran, May 19, 1852, M1102, Roll 5.

21. Robert W. Larson, *New Mexico's Quest for Statehood,* pp. 75, 76.

22. Morris to McFerran, May 31, 1852, M1102, Roll 5.

23. Morris to McFerran, June 16, 1852, M1102, Roll 5.

24. The Matson Diary, p. 374.

25. Bowman to McFerran, June 19, 1852, M1102, Roll 5.

26. Fort Fillmore Post Returns, July 1852.

27. Heitman, Benjamin Brice.

28. Fort Fillmore Post Records, July 1852.

29. Miles to Assistant Adjutant General, Santa Fe, July 19, 1852, M1102, Roll 5.

30. The Matson Diary, p. 375.

31. Ibid., 376.

32. Miles to Assistant Adjutant General, Santa Fe, August 1,1852, M1102, Roll 5.

33. *La Posta*, Vol II, #4 July/Aug. 1970, pp. 2-5.

34. Heitman, John Courts McFerran.

35. Hoppin to Miles, August 15, 1852, M1102, Roll 5.

36. Miles to 9th Department Adjutant, August 16, 1852, M1102, Roll 5.

37. Fort Fillmore Post Records, September 1852.

38. Miles to Assistant Adjutant General, Santa Fe, September 7, 1852, M1102, Roll 5.

39. McFerran to Bee, September 9, 1852, M1012, Roll 1.

40. Robert W. Larson, *New Mexico's Quest for Statehood,* p 76.

41. Morris to Assistant Adjutant General, 9th Department, September 19, 1852, M1102, Roll 5.

42. John R. Bartlett, *Personal Narrative of Explorations and Incidents in Texas, New Mexico, California, etc., Vol. II.* (Chicago: The Rio Grande Press, Inc., 1965), pp. 281-292.

43. Ibid.

44. Morris to Assistant Adjutant General, 9th Department, October 12, 1852, M1102, Roll 5.

45. Ibid.

46. Miles to Sumner, October 19, 1852, M1102, Roll 5.

47. Fort Fillmore Post Returns, November 1852.

48. Fort Daniel Webster Post Returns, November 1852.

49. The Matson Diary, pp. 378, 379.

50. The Matson Diary, p. 379.

51. Heitman, Charles Sutherland.

52. The Matson Diary, p. 379.

53. This information combines data from the Post returns of December 1852, from Fort Millard Fillmore and Fort Daniel Webster.

5

1853 · TROUBLES WITH MEXICO

Second Lieutenant Beverly Holcombe Robertson, a Southerner who became a well-regarded Confederate cavalry general during the Civil War, commanded the twenty-man detachment at Magoffinsville, Texas in early 1853. Although over forty miles south of the fort, he was still considered part of the Fort Fillmore command. Although he had no power to effect decisions in such matters, Robertson was urged by Simeon Hart, owner of Hart's flour mill, to ask his commanders for additional troops. Robertson's small detachment could protect Magoffinsville from Indian raiders. Hart pleaded, in the name of the Mexican citizens in the outlying area, that their entreaties be considered as well.[1]

South of Magoffinsville, across the border in Mexico, the political situation in the State of Chihuahua was deteriorating, as pro- and anti-Santa Anna forces battled over who would control that defeated nation. In early January, small groups of Mexican officials, led by the military commander of the town of Paso del Norte, Colonel Emilio Langberg, crossed the border and sought refuge in Magoffinsville. Langberg, a guest at Fort Fillmore at the time of the Bartlett visit, surrendered his small command to Robertson. Colonel Langberg was a member of a political faction which favored the return to power of the former dictator Antonio Lopez de Santa Anna.[2]

Lieutenant Colonel Miles was familiar with the situation to the south, but did not care how or with what means the Mexicans settled their internal problems. His concern was the participation of

Brevet-Captain Barnard E. Bee,
future Confederate general
Courtesy: Bill Kuethe Collection

Mexicans living on the American side of the border. Miles issued a written proclamation which was distributed in the villages of Franklin, San Elizario, Socorro, Ysleta, and Magoffinsville, as well as outlying ranches, ordering United States citizens to stay out of the fighting.[3]

On January 9, 1853, Brevet-Captain Barnard E. Bee left Fort Fillmore for San Elizario to observe the situation along the border. A wagon train owned by Mr. White at Fronteras, with which 2[d] Lieutenant O'Bannon was traveling, was confiscated in Mexico on a charge of hauling stolen goods. The same courier reported that the people of Paso del Norte were in a state of great excitement due to the fear that Mexican troops loyal to Santa Anna were about to descend upon their town.[4]

By January 14 the situation in the south was calmer. The revolution in the State of Chihuahua proved to be little more than a tempest in a teapot, at least as it impacted the troops and command at Fort Fillmore. General Angel Trías's forces easily took control at Paso del Norte in the name of President Santa Anna. Lieutenant Colonel Miles was furious, however, about a rumor circulating in the El Paso region that he had favored General Trías. It was not good for an American leader to take either side in a Mexican political battle. The wounds of the Mexican War were still unhealed.

On January 18 Brevet-Captain Bee interviewed the alcaldes of the three towns on the river island. They said people living there had no thought of supporting either side during the Mexican Revolution. Most poor Mexicans seemed to welcome Santa Anna back to power in Mexico, but very few believed Santa Anna would march to that part of the country and cause trouble for the Americans.[5]

The impact of the Mexican troubles was felt in the Mesilla Valley also. Refugees from Chihuahua caused problems for Don Pablo Melendrez, the Alcalde of Doña Ana. 'Ladrones' (thieves) from Chihuahua walked the streets of Doña Ana at night, singing praises to Santa Anna's victories and glories. Miles sent word to Don Pablo to jail every 'Ladron' he found. If Melendrez could not manage them, Miles promised to send a military force to the town to assist him in quelling any disturbance.[6]

Second Lieutenant Robertson, commanding Company 'D,' reported in, without fail, for muster at Fort Fillmore with his twenty dragoons on the last day of every month. Miles ordered this done while the troops were stationed at Magoffinsville, so separate records would not need to be kept. As soon as his men were inspected Robertson rode back to Magoffinsville. Watchful Apaches must have noted this routine. Robertson had just returned to Magoffinsville on February 3 when he was informed of an incident that happened while he was away at Fort Fillmore for muster. He reported to Miles:

> ... I have the honor to state for the information of the Col. Comdg. Fort Fillmore that during my absence from this station at your post <u>fourteen (14)</u> <u>mules</u> and <u>one (1)</u> <u>bell-mare</u>, the property of Juan Perea of New Mexico, were stolen by the Apache Indians.
>
> I started to Fort Fillmore on the morning of the 29th of Jany. with my command, and the depredation was committed on the night of the same day. This induced me to believe that the depredators were Mexicans who had been advised relative to my movements, and in order to satisfy myself on this subject, I left this post yesterday morning with the greater part of my detachment, and followed the trail of these animals about twenty miles. From its direction I soon became convinced that they were Indians belonging to the Tribe of White Mountain Apaches, and that they were travelling directly towards the "Willow Spring" from which the road goes through the "Canon del Perro" [Dog Canyon] straight to the White Mountains.
>
> The stock was stampeded off about five or six miles distant from Magoffinsville, where they were in the habit of grazing every day, and as information of the fact was immediately brought in, I have little doubt that the Indians who were only three in number, and <u>dismounted</u>, could have easily been overtaken, had I been present at the time. They attempted to cross the Solidad Mountains near "Sierra Colorada," but were so closely pursued by the Mexican herders, that they were compelled to strike at once for their country.
>
> A pair of moccassins [sic], which I found on their trail, is another proof of their being Mezcal [Mescalero].[7]

The mention of Cañon del Perro [Dog Canyon] and Soledad Pass tell of the traditional routes the Mescalero Apaches used in raiding in the El Paso region and in the Mesilla Valley. Another Mescalero Apache raiding and trading route was over the mountains by way of San Nicholas and San Augustine Springs near the present-day White Sands Missile Range, and down into the area of Doña Ana and Las Cruces.

Peaceful Apaches came to Doña Ana to trade and camped near the town in comparative safety. On February 5, 1853, Don Pablo Melendrez wrote Miles concerning the murder of Apaches by Mexican citizens from Mesilla. This was the first event of this kind in Fort Fillmore's history, but it would certainly not be the last. On February 3 an undetermined number of Mexicans crossed the river from Mesilla with murder on their minds. Supposedly, as first reported, fourteen or fifteen Apaches had been slain in their campground near the village. Miles sent an angry reply to Alcalde Melendrez, showing his frustration at those he called "bad people," noting:

> ... It is with great regret I learnt of the outrageous conduct of the bad people of Mesilla in killing the Indians near Dona Ana. I foresee that it will involve innocent people of our country in much trouble, as the Indians cannot, or will not hereafter, draw the distinction between the people of Mexico who are guilty and our inhabitants, in the vengeance they will surely endeavor to take. You have done all you could and your course is satisfactory.
>
> Send by all means the delegation to the Indians, and let them know that our inhabitants observe the peace made with them, and further, that you will confine any of the Mesilla people you can catch for the infraction of our law & territory; for the outrage they have committed; and this I advise you to do, if you know them. I can do nothing, it is a civil case and as such, you must deal with it before the United States court. — Whatever you do, I will support you.[8]

Since the crime occurred inside the jurisdiction of the village of Doña Ana, Miles's options were limited. On February 6, he dispatched a letter to the Alcalde of Mesilla concerning the Apache Indian deaths at Doña Ana. Miles had by this time received full details and reported them to the 9th Department Commander, stating:

> ... I received last night a communication from Don Pablo Melendrez, Prefect of the county of Dona Anna [Doña Ana], announcing to me that some twenty men, hailing from Mesilla, had killed a party of fourteen or fifteen Apache Indians, in the neighborhood of Dona Anna and within the territory of the United States. You must be aware, that this is a gross trespass on the soil of the United States and cannot be for a moment overlooked, nor permitted. These Indians came into Dona Anna in the security of Treaty stipulations of peace, have been for some months past, quietly residing at San Nicholas Spring and so far as I have learned, not committed a single depredation on any one. This act of the Mesilla people, reopens the war with this Tribe and they surely will take their revenge—on probably innocent people, who had no participation in the murder of their companions.
>
> The Treaty of Guadelupe Hidalgo stipulates that the Indians within the United States shall be controlled by that Government from committing depredations on that property, or inhabitants of Mexico, but this cannot be effected, if the citizens of the latter Government will not adhere to the Treaties of peace made by the United States with the Indians bordering on the boundary; and if the Mexican authorities do not instantly repress the disposition of their people to individual redress for wrongs done them by the Indians and if such a feeling prevails among your inhabitants, the efforts of the officers of the United States Government to keep the Indians at peace, will ever be attended with vast expense and vexation and [?] and I request you will make this, my determination known; that hereafter, I will apprehend and turn over to the civil authorities for prosecution, every resident Mexican armed body, found within the limits of the United States territory, seeking, killing or pillaging Indians; as being contrary to the laws enacted by the Congress of the United States.[9]

On February 8, the situation changed. The information was wrong, at least initially. Rather than fifteen or twenty dead

Mescaleros, Miles found that only one woman had been killed. She was an important Indian female, a relative to either a Mescalero chief or head man. Melendrez convinced a very dissatisfied Indian delegation that Mexicans from Mexico were the only people involved. No citizens of Mexico were arrested for the attack.[10]

On February 14 Private Sylvester Matson gave insight into the only St. Valentine's Day celebration ever reported from Fort Fillmore. The troops were paraded to celebrate the birthday of 1st Lieutenant John McFerran's daughter. Matson reported that Mexican Colonel Langberg was at Fort Fillmore with a party of lancers and they participated in a full-dress parade in honor of John McFerran's little girl. Private Matson referred to her as Señorita McFerran.[11]

Following the killing of the Apache woman at Doña Ana, Miles invited the revenge-minded Apaches to Fort Fillmore for talks. On February 16, accompanied by Don Pablo Melendrez, some came. Miles quickly informed Sumner about what happened:

> ... I take pleasure to inform you that I had a visit on yesterday from nine Apache Indians of the band of the murdered woman. They were brought here by Don Pablo Melendrez. They seemed to be fully aware that the murderers were ladrones (thieves) from Mesilla, and assured me of their desire to be at peace.
>
> The new government of Mexico has sent to this section of the country, three commissioners to settle and regulate affairs, with absolute power to displace persons, make, or unmake all laws and regulations. Day before yesterday they arrived here on a visit to me, and assured me of their great desire to cultivate an amicable feeling with our authorities—have censured the people of Mesilla for their conduct and ordered them to make reparation to the Indians. Just before the arrival of the Indians they left me for that town, and I thought it would have a good effect for the Indians to visit and have a talk with them. Don Pablo accompanied them and I followed in the course of the afternoon. The result was satisfactory, as all Mesilla seemed to vie with each other in making them presents. They left there, as they said, perfectly satisfied and buried the hatchet. Nor would they think again of their murdered woman.

These Indians are in a most destitute condition. They have nothing to eat, nor clothing to cover their nakedness. Necessity will force them to steal if the government does not furnish them some means to live on. I gave them some fresh beef and corn, which seemed to be the only subsistence they desired. They promised to visit me again soon and that their Chiefs will come in, so soon as they return from hunting.[12]

On February 22 the post celebrated Washington's birthday with a concert by the 3[d] Infantry Regimental Band. They played patriotic songs. The monthly mail from Santa Fe, the only mail they received at this time, via Fort Conrad, arrived the morning of February 23, 1853. No doubt the arrival of the monthly mail was an occasion of some import to everyone at the post.[13]

As Miles mustered his command on the last day of February, events at 9th Department headquarters in Santa Fe would potentially embroil Miles and Fort Fillmore in a second international incident, one which could provoke a war with Mexico. On March 3, Brevet-Colonel Sumner alerted Miles about a request by New Mexico Territorial Governor William Clark Lane for a military escort to the Mexican town of Mesilla. Miles was warned to be wary of such a request and to deny it in Sumner's name.

> ... I have received a letter from the governor asking that a company of horse, a piece of artillery and a flag, from your post, should be placed at his disposal for a week, if he should think it proper to call for them. I have replied to him that it was necessary that he should inform me for what purpose he wanted these troops, before I could answer his application. I supposed, of course, that he wanted them for the Indian country, but to my great surprise I learn since I arrived here today that it is not for the Indian Country that he wants them. I can, therefore, only suppose, that he intends making some demonstration upon the Mexicans. You will please refuse on my authority to furnish any troops for any such purpose, and farther, I enjoin it upon you not to permit any U.S. troops whatever to invade any part of Mexico, or what has hitherto been considered Mexico, until you receive orders from myself or some higher military authorities.

The Adjt. Genl. has been informed that an order can be sent to me from Washington in fifteen days, and I do not choose to anticipate the government in a matter of this kind, more especially as it is a case that does not require immediate action. You will please furnish the governor with a safe escort to Fort Webster if he requires it.[14]

Miles was ordered to refuse Governor Lane United States troops to do with as he wanted. This letter must have been a surprise as, at the moment, there was no disagreement with the Mexican government. Any troops accompanying the governor into Mesilla would have been in violation of Mexican sovereignty. However, the worst was yet to come. Governor Lane soon appeared on the Fort Fillmore parade ground, assured of his power as the senior state official and ready to conquer new lands across the river. Miles was ready for him.

On March 6, Brevet-Major Steen at Fort Webster sent word to the Fort Fillmore command that Indians were all around that post seeking food, and Steen attempted to feed them. This situation led, in the fall of 1853, to the first active measures taken by Indian agents in the region to feed the Apaches and keep them peaceful. An Indian agency was established, first at Fort Webster, then at Doña Ana, and eventually at the newly created Fort Thorn.[15]

Meanwhile, on March 13, 1853, New Mexico Governor Dr. William Clark Lane, still in Santa Fe and acting on Anglo-American concerns about the heavy influx of Mexican people into the Mesilla Valley, officially notified the Mexican government that he was taking over the disputed territory surrounding the village of Mesilla, even though the final boundary survey was still in progress. The text of the governor's incendiary proclamation was as follows:

... I, William Carr Lane, Governor of the Territory of New Mexico, (upon my own official responsibility, and without orders from the cabinet in Washington,) do hereby, in behalf of the U.S., re-take possession of the said disputed Territory, to be held provisionally by the U.S., until the question of Boundary shall be determined by the U.S. and the Mexican Republic.[16]

Upon receiving the American governor's proclamation, President Santa Ana in Mexico City ordered the governor of Chihuahua to send troops to the Mesilla Valley. For the second time in a year, war was possible between Mexico and the United States.

Governor Lane arrived at Fort Fillmore on March 10, departing the next day for Paso del Norte to meet with Mexican representatives and present his demands that Santo Tomás and Mesilla be given over to the Americans. Second Lieutenant Alley, escorting Governor Lane, reported to Lieutenant Colonel Miles with further instructions from Brevet-Colonel Sumner, ordering Miles to deny Lane the use of United States troops in any venture toward Mesilla. Before the Governor left for the south, Miles firmly told Lane that any request for military support would be denied. Lane was furious, but unable to win Miles over to his cause. He stormed off to Paso del Norte to bring his demands before the Mexican government.

Two companies of Mexican lancers were hurriedly sent to Mesilla, causing rumors of war to pass among the Fort Fillmore garrison. The Mexican response to Lane's demand that Mesilla be annexed to the United States was contained in a long document directed to the Territorial governor's attention by representatives of the governor of Chihuahua. In that document, the Mexican representatives stated that annexing Mesilla to the United States would break the Treaty of Guadalupe Hidalgo. The representatives pointed out that the line agreed to by the two governments placed Mesilla in Mexico, and that the State of Chihuahua had legally taken possession of that town, under the 5th Article of the treaty. Governor Lane replied that the State of Chihuahua had made no attempt to protect the citizens of Mesilla from Indian depredations. The Mexican government responded that Mesilla's title had been in dispute until the Bartlett Commission had done its work. Now, with Mesilla in Mexican Territory, remedies to correct the problems would be taken. They denied

Lane's right to claim Mesilla and the surrounding region for the United States.[17]

Returning on March 19 from Paso del Norte, Governor Lane did not visit Miles, but sought his assigned quarters to dictate a letter. Lane made it known that he was aware, as Miles should be, that the military was subordinate to the civil authorities and his orders should be obeyed for an escort of troops to take him to Mesilla. Miles ignored the written request as he had the verbal. The Governor left the next day for Fort Daniel Webster by an alternate route through the San Diego Crossing.[18]

Miles wrote the Western Division commander in New Orleans, Ethan Allen Hitchcock, concerning the tempest raised by Governor Lane's letter. He warned Hitchcock that the Mexicans had massed some three or four hundred soldiers at Mesilla and word had come that perhaps as many as one thousand more were being sent from Chihuahua. Miles pointed out that Governor Lane obviously would attempt to discredit the United States Army in the matter, and included Governor Lane's letter so stating. Brevet-Brigadier General Hitchcock had once been the commander of the 3^d Infantry Regiment during the Mexican War, a fact Miles used in reminding the commanding general of the readiness of his command to oppose any and all aggression. Miles proudly noted, "the Third Regiment of Infantry stationed here, is the same Regiment in material, equipment and discipline that he [Hitchcock] led so often to victory in the late war with Mexico."[19]

Miles also wrote Brevet-Colonel Sumner, providing his best intelligence concerning the potential for hostilities with the Mexican force in Mesilla, stating:

> ... The minds of the Mexican people are wrought up to the highest pitch and increasing. The Mexican authorities are exerting every nerve to arm and equip soldiers, incurring heavy expenses (I think unnecessarily) in the expectation of an immediate conflict with the United States. The Town of Mesilla is garrisoned by three or four hundred soldiers. Large guards, the Mexicans at night, station at the crossings over the Rio Grande from Las Cruces and this place—almost all intercourse

has ceased between the inhabitants of the two sides of the river. We are deprived of obtaining marketable produce. Nor will they [Mexicans] but with reluctance sell us beef cattle—has forbid Mr. Grandjean from taking corn from there to fulfil his contract with the Indian Dept. at Fort Webster. Videttes and picketts are placed on the sand hills on the different roads centering in Mesilla, in the day time, and whenever any one crosses from this side, the inlaying pickets are turned out and stand under arms during his stay. This state of things is disquieting and annoying and cannot last much longer without a collision in some shape or other. For I suppose their troops are not under the best or strictest discipline and formed of the lowest vagabond cast. Wherever they could be seized—not caring what they do, or whether the two countries are involved in war or not. Besides, I am informed there are 1200 more soldiers expected soon from Chi-hua-hua, formed no doubt out of the same class as those here, perhaps, being from a large city, with worse habits and morals. It is under these circumstances I deem it proper to stay this excitement if possible and let matters settle down to the hitherto peaceful quietness usual to this valley.

I have been cautious in not commenting on the acts of the Governor compromising the Government, and hope my communication will effect a reconciliation of the inhabitants, and re-establish the former amicable relations, that has ever existed here.[20]

Mexican troops patrolled the streets of Mesilla and guarded the entrances and exits, but Miles chose not to challenge them or create an incident, preferring to allow the Mexicans to let off steam as long as no harm came to United States citizens. If the United States troops at Fort Fillmore were dependent on the Mexican farmers and merchants for much of their sustenance the Mexicans were as dependent, in desperate need of the commerce to sustain their own economy. Miles displayed wisdom in not forcing the matter to an undesired conclusion. In fact, so mildly did he view the threat from Mesilla, and his attempts to defuse it, that the commander of the 3[d] Infantry Regiment chose to leave the post on an extended journey to Albuquerque on March 24.

First Lieutenant John C. McFerran had become post commander at Fort Fillmore in Miles's absence. Miles was concerned about

Sumner's order to not support Governor Lane with troops in the forced takeover of Mesilla. While Lane was still en route to Fort Webster, Miles chose to travel and speak with Sumner, perhaps to work out their position if questioned by a higher authority.

McFerran had fifty-eight dragoons with only twenty service-able horses, and two hundred and twenty-four infantrymen from Companies 'C,' 'E,' and 'K' to defend the post. The embers of the smoldering fire Governor Lane had lit flared anew once more on April 6 when Bennett Riddles, Consul of the United States at Chihuahua City, arrived at Fort Fillmore with messages for Brevet-Colonel Sumner. General Trías, marching from Chihuahua City toward Paso del Norte, intended to bring a force to Mesilla to counter any invasion plans by Governor Lane. Consul Riddle desperately wanted to speak with Sumner, and departed from Fort Fillmore for Fort Conrad on the morning of April 7. Lieutenant McFerran provided an escort over the Jornada del Muerto. McFerran did not anticipate any difficulty from Trías's forces, but was prepared to take action in any eventuality.[21]

Second Lieutenant Beverly Holcombe Robertson departed Fort Fillmore on April 23 for Fort Leavenworth, Kansas Territory, leaving no officer in charge of Company 'D,' 2[d] Dragoons, at Fort Fillmore, or in charge of the detachment at Magoffinsville. Poor Company 'D.' Poor dragoons. Their record at Fort Fillmore was at best unfortunate, mainly due to the lack of proper leadership in the dragoon companies. Save for Enoch Steen, then at Fort Daniel Webster, there was rarely even an officer of Captain's rank on hand. Now Company 'D' was abandoned to its fate. Over the many months that the company remained at Fort Fillmore it never again had an officer of its regiment in command.[22]

The situation in Mesilla remained quiet through late April. Miles returned from his meeting with Sumner to face problems as serious, if not as interesting as the Mesilla situation. Beef was scarce, the price for a single cow rising to as high as forty dollars, and very few head were to be had in the Mesilla Valley. The soldiers at Fort Fillmore subsisted on mutton, which 1st Lieutenant McFerran purchased in the now-quiet Mesilla marketplace for five dollars per head. A herd of one hundred cattle was located at the 3ᵈ Infantry post at Fort Conrad. The beef was desperately needed, but the river was up, meaning the San Diego Crossing was impossible to ford and there was no ferry at the crossing to ship the cattle. When the river was not up, the cattle were herded along its bank to the San Diego Crossing (near Hatch), forded there from the western bank to the eastern, and then driven down through Doña Ana and Las Cruces to Fort Fillmore. With the river up, the only alternative was to ford the river at Fort Conrad, and drive the cattle through the Jornada del Muerto, where the only available water was at the Ojo del Muerto Springs. Miles chose this latter route. In order to decrease losses in the herd, the cattle were driven only at night, rested one day at the spring, and then driven at night again toward Fort Fillmore.[23]

Unexpected orders arrived from Albuquerque in early May directing the transfer of the headquarters of the 3ᵈ Infantry Regiment from Fort Fillmore to Albuquerque. The transfer included Lieutenant Colonel Miles, his staff, and the band. It did not include any of the companies of the 3ᵈ Infantry then at Fort Fillmore. Brevet-Colonel Sumner officially notified Miles that, as he was going on leave of absence for four months, he wanted Miles to move the headquarters of the 3ᵈ Infantry Regiment temporarily to Albuquerque, arriving by May 23 or May 24, 1853. Miles was to take command of the 9ᵗʰ Department in Sumner's absence.[24]

When James Magoffin was at Fort Fillmore, Miles asked to be notified when General Angel Trías and his troops arrived at Paso del Norte. General Trías did not arrive until the 24th of April, and Magoffin duly notified Miles of the event. There were many Mexican troops at Paso del Norte during this period, but they were not being moved upriver to threaten Fort Fillmore directly. According to James Magoffin, a single Mexican Army company was to be sent to Mesilla.[25]

Judge Ankrim, James Magoffin's friend on the American side of the river, added a few troops to General Trías's command when he wrote to Colonel Miles on the 25th. Ankrim estimated not less that eight hundred and perhaps as many as a thousand troops had come in with General Trías. Ankrim feared that outlaws among those troops might cross the river and create problems on the American side. Ankrim also asked that Lieutenant Colonel Miles visit Franklin and Magoffinsville in the near future. He pointed out that Mexican troops were not well disciplined nor were their needs met by their officers.[26]

An extract from a letter sent by Judge Hoppin in Paso del Norte to White's Ranch detailed an anti-American speech General Trías supposedly gave to his troops on April 28, 1853. A copy of this extract was sent to Fort Fillmore for Miles's perusal.

> ... It is said that Gen. Trias made a speech to his soldiers in El Paso yesterday in which he told them, that he had neither gold nor silver for them. That it was with great difficulty that he could obtain the beans and corn which he issued to them daily but that if they remained true to him, victory would be theirs, and they would triumph over their enemies. That if any one desired to leave him, he could do so, and go to those who had gold and silver. This speech was received with shouts of Viva la Republica, viva El General Trias, muerte a los Americanos (Death to the Americans).[27]

Despite the hate rhetoric, the great upheaval in southern New Mexico created by Governor Lane was brought to a peaceful conclusion through the action of Lieutenant Colonel Miles, who journeyed south to Paso del Norte to meet with the bellicose Mexican general. Miles informed Trías of his orders not to support the governor's annexation plan. Miles even got Trías to agree to visit Fort Fillmore in the near future, hopefully before Miles was to leave for Albuquerque with his staff.[28]

General Trías visited Fort Fillmore as promised on May 16. He was accompanied by Colonel Langberg, the Paso del Norte military commander, one surgeon, one captain, two lieutenants, and a bodyguard of twenty-five Mexican lancers. Sylvester Matson reported that when Trías arrived at Fort Fillmore "... all of the troops, horse, foot and dragoons, were turned out, paraded, and there was a grand review." Matson supposed this parade had the intention of impressing Trías that "our garrison was strong and well armed." The review was held in a blinding dust and sand storm, so dense that one could not see halfway across the Fort Fillmore parade ground.[29]

On May 21 Dixon Miles, accompanied by his adjutant, Brevet-Captain Bee, the 1st sergeant, quartermaster sergeant, principal musician, and members of the band, left for Albuquerque to serve as 9th Department commander. Brevet-Major Israel Richardson was placed in charge at Fort Fillmore. Major Brice, the southern New Mexico paymaster, Assistant Surgeon Sutherland, 1st Lieutenant McFerran (Quartermaster and Commissary), Brevet-1st Lt. Wilkins (Company 'E') and 2d Lieutenant Whipple (Company 'C') remained to garrison Fort Fillmore. Company 'D,' 2d Dragoons, was placed under McFerran's command.[30]

Brevet-Colonel Sumner was not merely going on leave from his post with the 9th Department, as he at first believed. His replacement was selected before Sumner left for the East. Brevet-Brigadier General and Colonel John Garland was already on his way to New Mexico by the middle of May, even as Miles took the command. Perhaps the bad blood between Sumner and Lane played a part in Sumner's removal.

Richardson's stint as commander of Fort Fillmore didn't last long. On July 1, his Company 'K,' eighty-eight men strong, took the road north, returning once more for duty at Fort Webster on the Mimbres. 1st Lieutenant McFerran took command of the fort. By July 5, Richardson's company had arrived at Cook's Springs, exhausted by their walk across a very hot and dry desert. On their arrival at the springs the soldiers encountered a Mormon wagon train. The Mormons were celebrating some occasion and the night air was filled with the sounds of their fiddling and dancing. The soldiers were too tired to 'trip the light fantastic' with them, although the Mormon women urged them to do so. These invitations made the Mormon men angry; trouble appeared to be brewing with the soldiers. Before a flashpoint was reached, Richardson marched the soldiers away from the spring. The already weary men trekked across the mountains until 3 a.m., when they arrived at the Mimbres River. A quick journey upriver to Fort Webster followed the next day.[31]

On July 8, 1853, Private Matson reported seeing four girls who had been captured by Delgadito the younger's band. The Mexican town of Guadalupe had invited the Indians to a peace conference many years before. The inhabitants planned to kill the Indians through a ruse in which the Indians were invited into the local church, then massacred. The massacre happened, and many of the chiefs were killed. The citizens thought this lesson would keep the Apaches away, but the Apache people rarely forgot or forgave an injury. Years later, when many of the people of Guadalupe had for-gotten the former incident, the Apaches struck and destroyed the town. The four girls Matson saw were captured in that slaughter. Major Enoch Steen, commanding Fort Daniel Webster, rescued them. One was in terrible condition, and stayed in the fort hospital for some time. Matson reported that both the church where the massacre occurred and the town itself were now nothing but ashes and rubbish.[32]

Brevet-Brigadier General John Garland assumed command of the 9th Military Department at Albuquerque in August 1853, freeing the 3[d] Infantry regimental staff and band to return to Fort Fillmore. Lieutenant Colonel Miles and his adjutant Barnard E. Bee went on leave of absence for the East following Garland's arrival. Miles and Bee had not been on leave since arriving together in southern New Mexico in August 1851, almost two years before.

Miles's replacement at Fort Fillmore, 1st Lieutenant John McFerran, believed the road north to Fort Conrad was safe to travel most of the time, with little threat from the Indians, unlike the case in early 1852. The mail route from San Antonio was not so safe. On August 7 a Mr. Rhine wrote to McFerran of a terrible massacre of men near a place called Thorn's Wells. Rhine, leading a wagon train of supplies from San Antonio by way of Hueco Tanks, had his train attacked by an estimated one hundred Apaches, who drove off twenty-seven horses and mules. Thirteen of the train's men pursued the Indians but were in the end ambushed and surrounded near Thorn's Wells, said to be about forty miles from where the wagon train was attacked. Only one of the pursuers escaped to tell the tale. The bodies of the massacred were left where they fell.[33]

McFerran decided to respond with force. First Lieutenant John Wilkins, commanding Company 'E,' 3^d Infantry, put on a different hat and took over Company 'D,' 2^d Dragoons, then at Fort Fillmore without an officer. Wilkins left the post on August 9 and by August 20 was back at Fort Fillmore, having failed to find any bodies. Wilkins claimed the Rhine party was apathetic as to the fate of their comrades, and that he could get no cooperation from the men of the party in recovering the bodies. McFerran decided to take no further action in the matter, since the attitude of the Rhine party was not conducive to cooperation. In addition, Wilkins was unable to accurately ascertain, without their help, where the massacre took place.

Instead of hunting for the bodies, McFerran recommended that two companies be detached to conduct a campaign into the White and Sacramento Mountains to punish any and all Indians found. He wanted one party to move out from Fort Fillmore and one from Fort Conrad, both to converge on the area and cut off any Indian retreat. Another old Spanish tactic when dealing with the Apaches was to strike at the families of the warriors, who were easier to catch and whose loss was more disruptive than a simple battle against warriors. The army moved slowly in the early 1850s, however, and any action against the Mescalero could not be anticipated before the end of 1853.[34]

Major Electus Backus arrived at Fort Fillmore on August 30 from Albuquerque with the headquarters and band of the 3^d Infantry Regiment. Backus was the senior officer in the 3^d after Miles. He brought with him a number of officers, one of whom was 1st Lieutenant William H. Wood. Wood was to command Company 'A,' 3^d Infantry, many of whose members were already at the post, listed as temporarily on duty there. Detachments from Company 'A' had been responsible for guarding the former Boundary Commission on its mission. Now the parts were being reassembled into a whole at Fort Fillmore. Also arriving at this time with Major Backus were Captain William B. Johns, commanding officer of Company 'C,' 3^d Infantry, who would replace William Dennison Whipple. Johns was accompanied by an officer of his company, 2[d] Lieutenant Charles Henry Rundell, an 1852 graduate of West Point only recently arrived in the Territory.[35]

In August 1853, Colonel Joseph Fenno Mansfield, the Army's Inspector General, began his inspection of the 9th Military Department, counting 798 captains, lieutenants, and enlisted men on the company rolls of the 3[d] Infantry, the principal foot unit in the Territory. That averaged almost eighty soldiers per company, just six short of what was allocated for the regiment. On further examination, Colonel Mansfield trimmed that figure to sixty-one per company because of losses due to detached service and recruiting duties, etc.[36]

The newly arrived 9th Department Commander, Brevet-Brigadier General John Garland, was notified by the Headquarters of the Army that a post would soon be established opposite Paso del Norte, and garrisoned by a new regiment out of Texas, the 8th Infantry Regiment. Garland was ordered to adopt the necessary measures for establishing the post and supplying the troops. Brevet-Colonel Sumner's old problem of El Paso County being in Texas was solved by the army high command stating that, "... though within the limits of the 8th Department, to be under your command."[37]

Colonel Mansfield arrived at Fort Daniel Webster to inspect that post on October 10, 1853. He did not like what he found. The post was too far from where it should be situated. The Inspector General reported:

> ... Fort Webster is in latitude 33 degrees on the River Mimbres about 14 miles east of the [Santa Rita] copper mines. It was commenced in October, 1852, under the command of Major G. Morris of the 3rd Infantry, but in November, Brevet Major E. Steen of the 1st Dragoons was in command. Grazing, hay and wood are abundant here, and the soil on the bottom lands good. It is among the Apache Indians, and dependent for supplies on Fort Fillmore, 135 miles [distant] and Fort Conrad, 150 miles [away]. The distance however to Fort Fillmore via the Jornada where the road forks at Cooks Spring, and in dry seasons 50 miles without water, is 30 miles less. This route strikes the Rio Grande del Norte opposite Dona Ana at the commencement of

the cultivation in the Mesilla Valley, and it is usual to pass through the village of Mesilla and cross the river directly over to Fort Fillmore. This road is very good with some minor exceptions. The buildings of this post are made of logs and mud and quite indifferent and not sufficient for the command as one company and the sick were in tents.

The old post at the copper mines has nothing at all to recommend it, and was judiciously abandoned. All posts through an Indian country should be placed on or near the great thoroughfares where aid and protection can be had by the traveller in case of necessity. Such positions would be equally convenient to overawe the Indians, and their depredations and murders would sooner come to the knowledge of the troops there stationed, and therefore protection or assistance [would be] readily afforded. My opinion is that this post is not properly located, that it should be on the Gila River, on the route travelled by the traders to California, and thus form one in a chain of posts that must eventually be extended across [to] the Pacific, and that the present post should be given up to the Indian Agent, J. M. Smith, who resides here, and encouragement given to these Indians thereby to settle permanently where they can be reached.[38]

Joseph Mansfield's inspection party left Fort Daniel Webster for Fort Fillmore on October 13. This was to be the last stop on his inspection tour of the posts in the 9th Department. He then continued down the Rio Grande to visit the communities there in order to determine whether a military post was truly necessary opposite Paso del Norte, as was being projected. The Inspector General then turned west, where, in 1854, he inspected the military posts of California, Washington, and Oregon.[39]

The trip down the Mimbres to Cook's Spring and on to Fort Fillmore took only five days, Mansfield and party arriving at the post on October 17. They remained at Fort Fillmore until October 28. At the time of Colonel Mansfield's inspection of Fort Fillmore, most of the old mud and stick framework buildings had been replaced with adobe structures. One description of life in a mid-nineteenth century frontier post was included in *The Soldiers,* one of the Time-Life series on the old West. The Time-Life author stated:

The amenities of a typical early frontier post were minimal. Officers occupied private quarters [there were six officers' buildings on the east side of Fort Fillmore], usually a row of small houses where each officer had from two to four rooms, but enlisted men were crammed into barracks where rows of bunks or cots stood head-in to walls ... . Candles provided flickering gleams of light, and a round iron stove [parts of such stoves were found in the Fort Fillmore excavation of 1966] offered a tiny circle of warmth in an all enveloping atmosphere of draft and chill.[40]

Colonel Mansfield was displeased that the Fort Fillmore command had wasted so much time and effort in building post structures and in establishing a farm. These had, according to the Inspector-General, hindered their military efficiency. The post did pass his inspection, receiving a commendation for its neatness and appearance, as well as the discipline of the post troops. Mansfield departed, making no major recommendations for changes to the post routine.

Inspector General Mansfield's recommendation relative to Fort Daniel Webster was accepted by the Department. On November 7, Order No. 16 directed that the post at Fort Webster be broken up and the command moved to a new fort, on a site to be selected, near Santa Barbara, a small community near present day Hatch, on the Rio Grande. The grand experiment which began in January 1851 was coming to an end. No doubt the Fort Fillmore command breathed a sigh of relief, especially 1st Lieutenant McFerran, the quartermaster officer. Fort Daniel Webster was not the only southern New Mexico fort that was to be closed and the garrison moved. The abandonment of Fort Conrad (which had also been recommended by Mansfield) and the construction of a new post some eight miles south of the old site was another development.[41]

On November 6, 1853, Apache leader Cuentas Azules was murdered near Doña Ana by a Don Pedro Borule. Borule claimed the Apache had stolen one of his horses. In fact, Cuentas Azules and fifteen of his followers had approached Fort Fillmore, where he had purchased a horse from one of the dragoon's soldiers. This could not have been a government horse; private animals were allowed to be owned by soldiers, and this one had indeed earlier been purchased from Borule. Borule traveled to Doña Ana, found the Apache in a drunken state and clubbed him to death. At this time Mesilla, where Borule lived, was not under U.S. jurisdiction. Borule was tried one year later and was acquitted of any wrong doing in the incident. The 1850s were not a time when Mexicans or Americans were punished for savagery against an Apache.[42]

Brevet-Brigadier General John Garland visited Fort Fillmore and the El Paso region in late December 1853. Garland arrived at Magoffinsville on December 20 and found that all needful preparations had been made for the arrival of the 8th Infantry companies, expected there in early January. Garland selected Magoffinsville as the fort site because quarters and storehouses for equipment were already available there.[43]

As of December 11, revenge was planned for an old massacre. The entire Mescalero Apache tribe was supposed to pay in blood for the massacre of the Rhine party in August at Thorn's Wells. The commands at Fort Fillmore and at Fort Conrad were ordered to field a force to be gathered at Doña Ana, and to then proceed to the White Mountains before the first day of the new year.

On Christmas Day 1853, Company 'D,' 2[d] Dragoons, some fifty-nine rank and file strong, left Fort Fillmore for Doña Ana to take part in the expedition against the Mescalero. The officer in com-mand was 2[d] Lieutenant Robert Ransom, a later Confederate general officer who, in 1853, was an officer in the 1st Regiment of Dragoons. Ransom was sent to Fort Fillmore to take charge of Company 'D,' which had no officers. As was typical with the small military retribution raids of this period, the forces used were not sufficient and the troops came home empty handed. The Mescalero, informed well in advance of an arrival of the army in their territory, simply went south to Mexico until the situation cooled.[44]

The new post at Santa Barbara, the replacement for Fort Webster, was active by late December 1853, although yet unnamed.

Brevet-Major Israel Richardson was in command there, with Company 'K,' 3ᵈ Infantry, the only unit. The new post was later called Fort Thorn, after Captain Herman Thorn, 2ᵈ U.S. Infantry, who drowned in the Colorado River on October 16, 1849.[45]

As a final gesture to the passing of 1853, President Franklin Pierce, desirous of settling the southern boundary question with Mexico, despatched James Gadsden of South Carolina to Mexico to see if he couldn't come to a monetary settlement for the disputed lands across the Rio Grande from Fort Fillmore. Gadsden's skillful diplomacy succeeded where Governor William Carr Lane's heavy-handed attempt had failed. On December 30, 1853, a treaty was drawn up which transfered what would be called the Gadsden Purchase to the United States for the sum of ten million dollars. The transfer included both Mesilla and the growing town of Tucson.[46]

NOTES - Chapter 5

1. Hart to Robertson, January 6, 1853, M1102, Roll 5.
2. The Matson Diary, p. 381.
3. Miles to Sturgis, January 7, 1853, M1102, Roll 5.
4. The Matson Diary, p. 381.
5. Bee to Miles, January 18, 1853, M1102, Roll 5.
6. Miles to Sturges, January 18, 1853, M1102, Roll 5.
7. Robertson to Bee, February 4, 1853, M1102, Roll 5.
8. Miles to Melendrez, February 5, 1853, M1102, Roll 5.
9. Miles to the Alcalde of Mesilla, February 6, 1853, M1102, Roll 5.
10. Miles to Sturges, February 8, 1853, M1102, Roll 5.
11. The Matson Diary, pp. 381, 382.
12. Miles to Sturges, February 17, 1853, M1102, Roll 5.
13. The Matson Diary, p. 382.
14. Sumner to Miles, March 3, 1852, M1012, Roll 1.
15. Miles to Sumner, March 6, 1853, M1102, Roll 6.
16. Robert W. Larson, *New Mexico's Quest for Statehood*, pp. 80, 81.
17. Antonio Jaques and Tomas Zuloaga to Lane, March 19, 1853, M1102, Roll 6.
18. Lane to Miles, March 19, 1853, M1102, Roll 6.
19. Miles to Hitchcock, March 20, 1853, M1102, Roll 6.

20. Miles to Sumner, March 21, 1853, M1102, Roll 6.

21. McFerran to Sturges, April 6, 1853, M1102, Roll 6.

22. Fort Fillmore Post Returns, April 30, 1853.

23. Miles to Sturgis, April 24, 1853, M1102, Roll 6.

24. Sumner to Miles, April 25, 1853, M1012, Roll 1.

25. Magoffin to Miles, April 25, 1853, M1102, Roll 6.

26. Ankrim to Miles, April 25, 1853, M1102, Roll 6.

27. Hoppin to White, April 28, 1853, M1102, Roll 6.

28. Miles to Sumner, May 12, 1853, M1102, Roll 6.

29. The Matson Diary, 386.

30. Fort Fillmore Post Returns, May 1853.

31. The Matson Diary, p. 388-390.

32. Ibid., 391, 392.

33. Rhine to McFerran, August 7, 1853, M1102, Roll 6.

34. Wilkins to McFerran, August 11, 1853, M1102, Roll 6.

35. Fort Fillmore Post Returns, August 1853.

36. Gregory J.W. Urwin, *The United States Infantry* (New York: Sterling Publishing Co., Inc., 1991), p. 78. (Hereafter cited as Urwin, *U.S. Infantry.*)

37. Thomas to Garland, September 14, 1853, M1102, Roll 6.

38. Joseph F. Mansfield *Mansfield in the Condition of the Western Forts, 1853-54,* edited by Robert W. Frazer. (Norman: University of Oklahoma Press, 1963), pp. 25, 26.

39. Ibid. p. 223.

40. Ezra Bowen, editor, et al. *The Soldiers* (Alexandria: Time-Life Books, 1975), p. 57.

41. Dan L. Thrapp, *Encyclopedia of Frontier Biography.* 3 vols. (Lincoln & London: Univ. of Nebraska Press in association with Arthur H. Clark Co., Spokane Washington, 1988), p. 353. (Hereafter cited as Thrapp, *Encyclopedia.*)

42. Nichols to Chandler, December 7, 1853, M1102, Roll 6.

43. Garland to Thomas, December 24, 1853, M1012, Roll 1.

44. Ibid.

45. Fort Thorn Post Returns, December 1853.

46. Robert W. Larson, *New Mexico's Quest for Statehood*, pp. 81, 82.

6

1854 - CONTROLLING THE ENVIRONMENT

United States military power in southern New Mexico increased measurably in 1854. Since 1850, United States Army officers had been seeking permission to mass forces against the Apache peoples to punish them for their depredations. In January 1854 the first attempts at such massing of forces took place. Units from Fort Conrad (soon to be Fort Craig) and Fort Fillmore were in the lands of the Mescalero Apaches taking revenge upon that people for murders committed east of the El Paso settlements. The troops returned to post by mid-January, without success in finding Apaches, but the mission was a warning for the future.

The first month of 1854 found Major Electus Backus in command of the 3^d Infantry Regiment staff and band at Fort Fillmore, along with Companies 'C,' 'E,' and 'A,' 3^d Infantry and 'D,' 2^d Dragoons. Other officers at the post included: Major B.W. Brice, paymaster for southern New Mexico; Assistant Surgeon Charles Sutherland; 1st Lieutenant John C. McFerran, quartermaster and commissary officer for the post; and 1st Lieutenant William H. Wood, as temporary 3^d Infantry Regimental adjutant in Bee's absence. Captain William Brooke Johns commanded 'C' Company 'C', 3^d Infantry, with 2^d Lieutenant William Dennison Whipple serving as his second in command. Second Lieutenant Richard Vanderhorst Bonneau commanded Company 'A,' 3^d Infantry. Second Lieutenant Junius Daniel commanded Company 'E,' with 2^d Lieutenant Alexander McDowell McCook serving as his second in command. Second Lieutenant Robert Ransom commanded Company 'D,' 2[d] Dragoons, in the absence of the normal complement of Company 'D' officers.[1]

Brevet-Colonel Alexander and his 8th Infantry command arrived at Magoffinsville on January 11, effectively establishing Fort Bliss and providing the protection El Paso area residents had demanded since the establishment of Fort Fillmore three years earlier. This move increased Fort Fillmore's capability to slow or stop Apache depredations.

One of the more interesting questions about Fort Fillmore in this period revolves around the absence of all assigned officers from Company 'D,' 2[d] Dragoons. In January 1854 Company 'D' was under the temporary command of 2[d] Lieutenant Ransom. Second Lieutenant Beverly Robertson had commanded the company before he was sent to Fort Leavenworth for court martial duty. Robertson was supposed to return to Fort Fillmore by January; but he never reported for duty. In an angry letter from the Headquarters of the Army in New York City we find the lieutenant had been remiss in his duties—staying in a Washington D.C. hotel while his company was abandoned at Fort Fillmore. The still officer-less Company 'D,' 2[d] Dragoons, left for duty at Fort Union on April 9, 1854.

There was little improvement in efficiency until the companies in New Mexico were fully staffed with officers. This situation did not improve markedly throughout the 1850s. During Fort Fillmore's span of active use, the officer situation was rarely satisfactory. An order in March 1854, from the Adjutant General's Office in Washington, stated that due to the dearth of officers serving their regiments in the Department of New Mexico, some of the many on detached service or leave were ordered back to their units. These included Fort Fillmore officers Abraham Buford, Beverly Robertson, Gouveneur Morris, Barnard Bee, and Nathan Evans. Dixon Miles, on leave since September 1853, was ordered to go out with the recruits in the spring.[2]

Another order sent a strong infantry force from Fort Fillmore and Fort Bliss to pursue and punish the Mescalero Apaches. The order arrived at Fort Fillmore in early April. Major Backus immediately asked Brevet-Colonel Alexander at Fort Bliss for two companies to send on the expedition. One of the South's most famous Civil War generals, George Edward Pickett, made his single documented appearance at Fort Fillmore in overall command of the two infantry companies, 'I' and 'K' of the 8th Infantry. Pickett left El Paso on the evening of April 9, headed north. On arrival at Fort Fillmore, his force was joined with Company 'C,' 3d Infantry, under Captain Johns. Their destination was supposed to be the Sacramento Mountains.[3]

On April 14, Captain William Brooke Johns, in overall command of the three-company force, marched out of Fort Fillmore heading south rather than east. Company 'C' consisted of fifty men and two officers, Captain Johns and 2d Lieutenant Whipple. Company 'I,' 8th Infantry, under Brevet-Captain George Pickett, had forty-three men. The other 8th Infantry company had thirty-nine men. Johns and Pickett returned to Fort Bliss, as other events trumped the original mission against the Mescaleros in the Sacramento Mountains. Apaches had struck the San Antonio-El Paso wagon route. A cattle drive out of San Antonio headed toward California was attacked at Eagle Springs by sixty to eighty Indians. Two men were killed and 176 cattle driven off toward the Guadalupe Mountains. Rumor said some one hundred and ten Indians had joined the drive, expressing friendship. Some of these later attacked the cowboys working the cattle. The leaders were said to be Peña, Solidita, and Marcos, known Mescalero leaders.[4]

On May 8, 1854, Governor David Meriwether received notice that Dr. Michael Steck had been appointed by President Franklin Pierce to the office of Indian Agent for southern New Mexico, replacing James M. Smith, now deceased. Dr. Steck was ordered to take the oath of office, to post a bond in the sum of $10,000 with the Department of Indian Affairs, and then to report to Governor Meriwether in Santa Fe. Although the Apache peoples had no idea of Steck's coming, he would be the single man in the 1850s in southern New Mexico to become their friend and benefactor. That peace of a kind endured between the Apaches and the Americans through much of the 1850s was often due to his efforts. Steck established at Fort Thorn the first effective Indian Agency in southern New Mexico, serving the basic needs of both the Mescalero Apaches and the bands living on the west side of the Rio Grande.[5]

By May 11, Captain Johns was back at Fort Fillmore with Company 'C.' The three companies had marched all the way to the Guadalupe Mountains on the route to what is now the Carlsbad Caverns, but found no Indians. There was one milestone to the mission: this was the first time Fort Fillmore and Fort Bliss troops combined for an operation. The mission was also further proof that infantry alone could not effectively chase a fast-moving Apache force. All the Apaches had to do was keep out of the infantrymen's way—the most common tactic they employed throughout the entire period of the Indian Wars. The time was not yet right in 1854, and the numbers not sufficient, to catch and bring the Apaches to bay. A mix of horse soldiers and infantry, coupled with a supply depot where the men didn't need to move and slaughter their food on the road was needed.

Horse soldiers returned to Fort Fillmore a few days after Captain Johns led his dusty infantrymen back to the post. First Lieutenant Samuel Davis Sturgis, commanding Enoch Steen's old Company 'H,' 1st Dragoons, arrived on May 17. Sturgis, formerly the adjutant of the 9th Military Department, was on leave in the East when he received orders to bring recruits to New Mexico. Sturgis's career at Fort Fillmore was unremarkable, but typical of an officer serving at a frontier post at that time. He became a general officer on the northern side during the American Civil War. Despite those major accomplishments, Samuel Davis Sturgis's name is more familiar in American military history for being the officer who actually commanded the 7th Cavalry Regiment while George Armstrong Custer took the regiment into the field. Sturgis was given a desk job managing the acquisition of cavalry horses in St. Louis while Custer rode to final glory with Sturges's regiment.

Colonel Sturgis took the massacre of his regiment at Little Big Horn in 1876 very badly, as one might expect. He had a double reason. First, were the losses among the troops and of the prestige of the regiment. Second, Colonel Sturgis's son, who had just graduated from West Point, had pleaded with his father for a posting with the 7th Cavalry. Relenting, Sturgis sent his boy to serve under Custer, only to have him die at the Little Big Horn. The body was never recovered from the battlefield.[6]

The month of June was a busy time for raiding Apache bands. Mescalero Chief Gomez, whose band lived in and raided from the Davis Mountains in Texas, was attacking along the San Antonio-El Paso Road. The American military still did not discriminate well between the separate Apache bands. Gomez had nominal contact with his brethren in the Sierra Blanca region and those Indians took part of the blame for his raids, even though they may have known nothing about them. As a result of the raids, Brevet-Brigadier General Garland, wanting to launch a major offensive against the Mescalero, was beginning to see the wisdom of establishing a fort near Sierra Blanca.

The Apaches to the west of Fort Fillmore were busy in June as well. Delgadito and Costales penetrated into Sonora, raiding at Alamos. The raiders re-crossed a border into lands that soon came under United States control as per the Gadsden Purchase agreement. For a brief period the purchase of the land by the United States benefited the Apache raiders, since Mexican troops no longer pursued north of the new border. Until American troops were stationed in the Gadsden Purchase in some numbers, there was only Fort Fillmore to bar the way, and that fort was simply too far away to prevent any raids. Colonel Mansfield's recommendation that Fort Daniel Webster be moved to the Gila River was the right decision, but his advice was not immediately followed.

On June 18, two companies of the 3d Infantry, 'A' and 'E,' left Fort Fillmore for another extended campaign against the Mescalero. Company 'A' was commanded by 1st Lieutenant James Noble Ward, assisted by Brevet-2d Lieutenant Richard Bonneau. Company 'E' was commanded by 2d Lieutenant Junius Daniel, assisted by Brevet-2d Lieutenant Alexander McDowell McCook. They were not to return to the post until August 15. This was the second time in 1854 that infantry went forth alone on a mission which, at best, should have been given to a combined arms force. The use of the infantry rather than dragoons was not explained in official channels. Company 'H,' 1st Dragoons, had been at the post since May 17. One reason may have been that the dragoon horses, always a concern as to their health and strength, had become reduced to only twenty-seven usable animals.[7]

On June 29, 1854, the United States Senate ratified the terms of the Gadsden Purchase, completing the process begun earlier through the signing of the treaty by the Mexican government. All that was left to do was to pay ten million dollars and hold a transfer ceremony at Mesilla. That process took another year to complete.

Dr. Michael Steck, President Pierce's new appointment as Indian Agent in southern New Mexico, arrived at the village of Doña Ana on July 6, 1854. In a letter to Governor Meriwether, Dr. Steck appeared disgusted by what he found. He refused to sign a receipt for any of the Doña Ana Agency property, which he said only included an old musket, a worn out saddle, and a couple of other items abpit which he wrote, "none of the articles are worth the paper it would require to write the [receipts] upon." Dr. Steck mentioned that Apache Chief Ponce, who headed a Mimbres band, had been killed during a drunken scuffle with other Apaches. As to the Doña Ana location for Apache Agency, Dr. Steck indicated he was immediately moving the agency to Fort Thorn.[8]

Companies 'A' and 'E' returned to Fort Fillmore from their campaign against the Mescalero on August 15, 1854. That campaign had lasted for almost two months, with little result other than chasing scattering small bands that successfully evaded the marching soldiers. There were no casualties among the troops during this operation, or among the Indians.

Dr. Steck, using the term "Apache Agency Fort Thorn" for the first time in correspondence on August 22, reported his return to the Agency after visiting the Apache bands camped near the abandoned site of Fort Daniel Webster on the Mimbres. The Apaches were friendly and received him with what appeared to be happiness. Agent Steck stated he was unable to meet with any of the main chiefs and believed that they may have been deliberately avoiding him. He found the chiefs believed a military campaign was about to be launched against them from Fort Fillmore and Fort Thorn, and that Steck and the two men with him were spies. Steck advocated the policy of teaching the Apaches to feed themselves. He indicated that the Apache farming practices were minimal and what was growing was very poorly tended, possibly because of a lack of working implements and someone to encourage them.[9]

Major Electus Backus left Fort Fillmore to serve a tour as a recruiting officer in the East on August 25. Lieutenant Colonel Dixon Miles was expected to take over the command. Miles was still on the road bringing a group of recruits into the Territory as Backus was leaving.[10]

Down at Fort Bliss, Captain James Longstreet and Brevet-Captain George Pickett, both of whom became famous general officers of the Confederate Army, tried to get funds for a new storehouse at Magoffinsville. Captain Longstreet was the new post commander at Fort Bliss, replacing Alexander. Brevet-Captain Pickett was a company commander.

Lieutenant Colonel Dixon Stansbury Miles returned once more for duty at Fort Fillmore, arriving on September 14. Miles brought his entire family and servants, including a Negro slave, with him. His daughter, Sallie Ann Miles, left history a magnificent description of the family journey from Baltimore, Maryland, to the dusty adobe buildings of Fort Fillmore. Through Sallie Miles's words we have a picture of what it was like for an Army family to come to New Mexico in the earliest days of the American experience there. She wrote:

> ... To resume my narrative of mother's life, Father left Baltimore for New Mexico the May or June before Alex was born and he was two months old before father could hear of his birth and was nearly three years before father saw him.
>
> In 1854, father came to Baltimore to take his family back to New Mexico. Sister was a very pretty young lady just from boarding school and considered quite accomplished. Brother

Sallie Ann Miles Marrian
1850-1926
Courtesy: Bill Kuethe Collection.

Ben was left at the Military Academy at Catonsville. Mr. Van Vockle was principal. I was a girl of over four and Alex nearly three years. Alex and I were very large fat children as you can see by the picture of us taken in our travelling suits, but I have heard mother and sister say that Mother had to carry Alex on her lap the entire journey. The negro girl, Dolly, was also of the party. She was only 9 years old, but had been trained to walk after Alex and myself after Louisa left, as a sort of nurse and I will say right here that I never pretended to dress myself, not even to put on my shoes and stockings until after the war broke out when I was eleven years old. Dolly always did it for me.

I don't think there was anything eventful happened until after we passed St. Louis as we traveled by train that far. There, Father had waiting for us, having had it built, a six seat ambulance at a cost of $500.00 It was a most complete traveling carriage. The back seat under the cushions was divided into compartments. One was a place for toilet articles, etc. and the other, having a hole clear through, you can imagine the use of. The second seat was also divided. One part was a tin-lined box for our lunch and the other contained the keg for water. The front seat was filled with boot straps and everything that could possibly be needed in the case of an accident. Around the sides were pockets of different shapes where necessaries of all kinds could be put. One was just for sister's books. There was a curtain that could be let down before the back seat, making it perfectly private. The backs of the seats were cushioned and made to let down so that when opened out in that way, there was a perfect bed formed. He also bought a pair of Kentucky mules, which were as large as horses and as fine looking, for which he paid $500.00 and then he made the whole equipage a present to Mother. I suppose it was a sort of recompense for the hardships she would have to endure in crossing the plains and in going to her frontier home. And yet, her life was not as hard as it might have been, for she carried out three servants, the coachman, the Irish woman cook and Dolly, the little colored girl.

Before leaving Baltimore, Mother had provided as well as traveling suits for herself and Sister, shirred green [?] sunbonnets, buckskin gauntlets and masks made of twill white muslin with holes buttoned for the mouth and eyes and a nose set in. They were kept on by tapes that tied in the back and soon after we started on the march in the mornings, the sunbonnets and masks were put on to save their complexions, as both had pink and white skins, and were not taken off until a halt was made for lunch and again resumed as soon as the march began. Of course, occassionally [sic] one of the young officers would ride up to the carriage to talk to Sister and the mask had to be hastily pulled off. But sister got so used to wearing it, that she finally would keep it on while the sun was shining and she was so afraid of snakes, that she would not get out of the carriage until the soldiers had well beaten down the grass.

One day as she was sitting in the carriage reading with her mask on, she saw a shadow on her book and looking up, expecting to see one of the officers, much to her surprise, there stood an Indian all dressed up with feathers, beads and paint. Her heart stood still for a moment, expecting every moment to be tomahawked, but the Indian only gazed, making unintelligible sounds and in a little while, Sister got up the courage to call for help. In a few moments he was of course surrounded by officers and soldiers. Father had enough knowledge of the language to find out what he wanted to say and as a good many of the officers also understood, there was quite a conversation, assisted as much by the signs as the tongue, passed between the Indian and Father, much to the bewilderment of both Mother and Sister. He told Father that he was a chief's son and was very rich, that he had fallen in love with the white squaw and wanted her for his wife (remember Sister had the mask on) and was willing to give 20 ponies for her. Father always loved a joke and couldn't resist carrying this on, so he told the Indian it was too cheap, that his daughter was worth more, so after a great deal of talk, he raised it to 25 ponies. Still father said, 'Too cheap.' The Indian said he had no more but would see what his Father would do for him and went away. In about an hour or so, he came back with his Father and there was another offer made for Sister, always in ponies and as Father's answer was always 'too cheap', it was raised several times until it got to be 35 ponies. By this time both Mother and Sister had gotten the idea of what was going on and, of course, were in a great state of indignation. Mother made no secret of hers, but told Father very plainly what she thought of him, carrying on such a bargain. I suppose this attracted the attention of the old chief and asked if she was Father's squaw, and when he answered yes, the old Indian asked if he would sell her. Father said, 'What will you give for her?'

The old chief said he would give his two squaws who were with him and immediately jumped off the ponies they were riding and threw their arms around Father. As this turned the joke on Father and made the officers roar with laughter, Father thought he had had enough of it and soon sent the Indians about their business. As the Indians were leaving camp, the young chief threw his arm around Sister's waist, drew her on the horse, and started to ride off with her, but he was soon overpowered and was glad to escape with his life. The incident was written up and sent to the Sun, and was published, I think, in the weekly Sun.

Our camp was a very long one, in fact, it was a mile long when on the march. They were carrying out horses to recruit the cavalry and there were a good many young officers, some just from West Point, who had been assigned to duty on the frontier and were on their way to join their regiments. Sister being only eighteen years old and just from boarding school, was quite a belle among them. There were several officer's wives along who traveled in their carriages so that when there was a halt for lunch in the middle of the day or at night, there was a pleasant time of visiting. As Sister was the only unmarried lady and Mother the oldest one, they generally congregated around our carriage and tent and Mother always had something good on hand to offer them, as had also father, for he carried his little liquor chest with him always ... . Before starting out on the trip, Mother used to bake a large bag, as large as a pillow case, full of small cakes, ginger, sugar and spice and there was a large ham boiled and a large coop of chickens taken along, some of them hens, so that we had a few fresh eggs. This coop was always filled up at every house or town we passed where we could possibly buy them. In fact, whenever we came near a house, father would send his orderly ahead to engage butter, eggs, vegetables, and in fact, anything edible that could be had to make a change in our diet. Then of course, we had a good supply of canned goods, and condensed vegetables for soups, so that altogether we did not fare badly. Mother had even a supply of candy along.

One of the officers was taking out his bride of the month—Lt. Whipple—and he had bought for her, a beautiful little pair of ponies and a handsome carriage which mother fell in love with, it made so much better show than hers and cost just the same, so she and Lt. Whipple, who was just as much in love with Mother's mules and ambulance, knowing how much more serviceable they were, began talking of exchanging them, but Father would not consent to it, at least until the journey was over. Well, to make a long story short, one evening an Indian crept on hands and knees, passed the guard, disguised as a wolf, and got into the midst of the horses that were picketed out to graze and by throwing up the wolf skin, frightened them so that in less time than it takes to tell it, there was a general stampede and in ten minutes, there were not a dozen horses left in camp out of the hundreds that had been there. And now you see how Spiritualism was of use to Father. He had become interested in it some years before and frequently received communications, being a writing medium. That evening just before dark, there was a rapping on the tent pole and Father took out the pencil and paper he always had ready and there was written out 'Have your mules securely lashed to the wagon wheels for there will be a stampede of the horses tonight.' So he went right out and made the coachman bring in his mules and horse, although the man grumbled at the idea for the pasture was fine—and had the grass cut for them. He advised the others to do the same, but he could not tell them why, for spiritualism was held in much disrepute then. They thought he was over cautious until they found their horses gone and then they were sorry enough. The very horses that Mother was about to exchange her mules for were lost and never recovered. Officers and men jumped on the few remaining animals and rode after the rushing stampeded horses and the camp was at a standstill for three days. They would come to a bunch of horses that had been stopped by the ropes they had been picketed out with—getting tangled and some of the horses had been dragged to death so that out of a bunch of twenty horses, there would not be ten that were fit to use and a great many the Indians must have gotten, for they were never heard from. One of the officers was three days and nights in the saddle, so that when he got back to camp, he just fell in a dead faint off his horse and required the doctor's care.

They got back enough animals to move the wagons, but the men who had been riding one and leading three besides, found their occupations gone. This was done by what were supposed to be friendly Indians so it showed how much dependence was to be placed in them.

Mother had had made in St. Louis, a large tin tub for bathing and every evening it was put in her tent, and one after another, we all had a bath. I was generally the first one and Alex the next. That night, Mother had taken me out of the tub and put Alex in, and after hearing my prayers, was just about to put me in the ambulance where Sister and I slept, when the stampede began. The noise and confusion were so great that Sister and the Irish cook became frantic with fright and ran to Mother, and threw their arms about her, one on one side and the other on the other side, so she couldn't move. There was I, half in and half out of the carriage and all mother could do was to shout, 'Save Alex, for he is in the tent.' The horses were rushing right for the camp and would soon have knocked down every tent and Alex would have been crushed to death, if the officers had not gotten out their pistols and by firing, frightened them and made them swerve to one side.

When we came to hostile Indians, they dogged the camp and threatened to attack us so that the utmost care had to be taken to keep together, and we never knew when we laid down at night whether we would get up in the morning alive. It was some time before this, that Sister had gotten frightened at finding a snake coiled in the little basket in which she carried her brush and comb, and had absolutely refused to sleep in the tent again, so that she and I were using the ambulance for our sleeping quarters. Father didn't like the idea of our sleeping there, for he said the Indians would come into the camp some night and run it off in the night without anyone being the wiser, so every night, just before going to bed, they would take the gay [guy] ropes of his tent (the ambulance was always put just in front of it) and pass them over the ambulance and tie them, so that if it was moved, it would jerk the tent down. He did this secretly. One night, two or three of the young officers thought they would play a joke on Sister and after all were asleep, they got up and started to drag the ambulance away. But they had not moved it more than a foot or two, when out ran Father with a pistol in each hand, expecting to see Indians. For a while there was quite an exciting time, as Father was very indignant with them.

The Indians got so bold one time that they took their stand on the banks of the river (I think the Rio Grande) and refused to let us cross. Having so many women and children along hampered the officers and soldiers very much. It was here that Mother was taken ill with dysentery caused by the water. After waiting three days and finding the Indians still determined, the officer commanding the camp determined to steal off in the night and go up the river to the next fording place, which was five or six miles off. So, quietly they slipped away in the dead of night with Mother so ill that the doctor would come to the side of the carriage every now and then and put his hand to her mouth to see if she was alive or not, and not daring to strike a match for fear of the Indians.

Well, I will briefly say that they got across the river safely and Mother was better the next morning. That was the last time the Indians showed themselves on that trip ... . One day as we were on the march, there was a dense cloud of dust and after a time, it proved to be an immense herd of buffalo and as we were right in their way, the soldiers and officers had to shoot at them and turn them in another direction or they would have trampled us down. After they are once started on their runs with an old bull at their head as leader, they turn for nothing short of fire arms.

I have not mentioned that we crossed the prairies when for miles, even days, we would not see a tree, so that we had to depend on the droppings of the buffalo for fire. Of course, it was only the dried that could be used and it burned very readily.

There was one place called the 'Jornado Valley' [Jornada del Muerto] where for one hundred miles, we were not only without wood but also not a drop of water was to be had, so that we had to make the march across in two days. Of course, it was easy to carry the water for the people, but the animals suffered dreadfully.

Well, to resume my story, I don't remember of hearing of anything further of interest on this journey. Our home was Fort Filmore [sic].[11]

Sallie Ann Miles was only four when she made her journey. The tale she told came from letters her father and mother left behind, some of which still exist. She wrote her long letter in 1901 for the benefit of "My Little Grandson Frederick" (Frederick William Kuethe), so he would know something of what she and her family had endured on that long ago journey to New Mexico Territory.

Miles and his wife Sarah Ann Briscoe Miles had eight children, four of whom died in childhood. The nineteenth century frontier military post was hardly conducive to the health and safety of children. His son Dixon, Jr., daughter Elizabeth and son Mathew were all born at military posts where Miles served. Each died before reaching two years of age. The other son who died, John, was born in Baltimore and died there at just over two years old. Three of the four surviving children, May, Sallie Ann and Alexander, spent part of their youth at Fort Fillmore.

The surviving child who did not come with his father and mother, Benjamin Bonneville Miles, died at age thirty-seven in Baltimore. We do not know why Miles named his son after Benjamin Louis Eulalie Bonneville, but it certainly was a fate-filled decision. In 1856 Colonel Benjamin Bonneville replaced Dixon Miles as commander of the 3^d Infantry Regiment at Fort Fillmore. The most probable answer is that Miles honored Bonneville's achievements as a world explorer and soldier by naming his son after him.

Assistant Surgeon George E. Cooper arrived for duty at Fort Fillmore with Miles. He may have been the surgeon Sally Ann Miles spoke of who tended her mother. Cooper replaced Charles Sutherland, who left Fort Fillmore shortly thereafter.

A group of Apache Indians came to Fort Fillmore the day after Miles returned, following a complaint by Mexicans in Doña Ana that some horses had been stolen in Las Cruces, but were now returned. Miles talked with these Indians, whom he had met earlier on the journey down through Doña Ana. Miles informed the Department:

> ... I have the honor to report when passing thro' Dona Ana on the 14th Inst. the citizens brought to me several Apaches, who they said, had just brought back a few horses that had been stolen some days before from Las Cruces and wished to know how they should be treated, or rewarded; being in a hurry I told the Alcalde to send them to this post, that I might talk with them. When I arrived at Cruzes [Las Cruces], I saw Mr. Campbell the prefect of the county and advised him to cause to be paid to these Indians some gratuity for the restitution of the horses by the owners. This I presume was done to their satisfaction, as they called upon me yesterday to the number of twenty-six and in their council never mentioned the subject.

The Captains, or Chiefs who headed the party that visited me yesterday are named Palanco and Santos. They are the Chiefs of the two bands that range west of the Sacramento Mountains to Manzana, desire to be at peace and promise to prevent any of their people from committing depredations, or if they do, to restore the property and deliver up the offenders for punishment. On my remarking to them, that it was impossible to make peace with a portion of a nation and be at war with the balance, they replied, their nation was broken up into bands. There was no head Captain or Chief, but each acted independently and as he thought proper. That there were many bad people among them and no doubt many evil disposed even in their own bands, but they were neither the sun, moon , nor stars, nor the day, night or wind to see, hear or know, every thing, or prevent the bad from stealing; what they promised they would do; but they desired to know, what were their rights and privileges. Were they to stand with folded arms and permit Mexicans to come among them and despoil them of their property with impunity? Should not the Mexicans be restrained and defined limits be pointed out for both parties to hunt, etc. etc. To these questions I had to reply, I was unprepared to answer, but would refer their talk to you, which would be given this day two months and that exacted of them, to see the other Chiefs of the Apaches ranging east of the Sacramentos on the Pecos, and south of the Guadalupe Mountains and bring them also to the council. This they agreed to, and will send runners to all they can find and bring them to this post by the 18th of Novb.

These Chiefs gave as information that besides their bands, there were seven others of Mescalero. The most hostile is headed by Santa Ana, who ranges from the Sacramento to Guadeloupe [sic]. The following named Chiefs, Barela, Francisco Hanero, El Marco Hanero to the east of the Sacramento desire peace. The band next below Marco's is Capt. Bigotes, a native of Presidio del Norte [San Elizario]. Then follows Mateo of Agua Nueva. Next Chino Guiro who is very desirous of peace and keeps his followers apart from the rest.

Palanco, thinks the peaceable party will come in, but has no expectations that Santa Anna will.

I would respectfully request of the Comdg. Genl. such instructions as may be necessary to meet the questions of these Indians and also how those disposed to peace should be treated. [12]

Most of the names of these Mescalero Apache band leaders are lost to history, but the fact that Miles names nine identified bands of Mescaleros operating between the Pecos and the Rio Grande at that time is interesting. Chief Gomez, of whom so much is made in history, is not listed, although he is believed to have come to Doña Ana seeking revenge at the time of the Cuentas Azules killing.

The town of Mesilla, although not officially transferred to United States control, acknowledged United States hegemony over the town in a letter sent to Fort Fillmore on September 25, 1854. The author was Domingo Cubero, a sub-prefect in the town. Cubero addressed Miles as 'Your Lordship,' a title of nobility not heard in the United States. This letter asking assistance against the Apaches is the first correspondence between Mesilla and Fort Fillmore, and acknowledged that the town was soon to be under United States control.[13]

In a brief note to the 9th Department, dated October 2, Lieutenant Colonel Miles told of a sad situation among the Mescalero who recently visited Fort Fillmore. Assistant Surgeon George Cooper notified Miles that he had found indications of small-pox and congestive fever in members of the bands led by Chiefs Palanca and Santos. The Apaches gathered their people together and traveled back to the Sacramentos to recover what they could of their health. Cooper added that these diseases were fatal when contracted by Indians. The Fort Fillmore troops were vaccinated against small-pox.[14]

Captain Frederick Masten arrived at Fort Fillmore on October 6 to take up his duties as the post quartermaster and commissary officer, replacing Captain John Courts McFerran, although McFerran did not leave the post. Captain Masten, an officer of the Quarter-master Corps, owed no allegiance to Colonel Miles and the 3d Infantry. He had a tragic career at Fort Fillmore and resigned in disgrace as the result of his actions there.[15]

First Lieutenant Samuel Davis Sturges arrived back at Fort Fillmore from detached service at Fort Union on September 27. He notified Miles that he was to take Company 'H,' 1st Dragoons, to his regimental headquarters at Fort Union, then under the command of Colonel Fauntleroy. Sturges had no written order authorizing such a transfer and Miles refused to release Company 'H' without one. Miles knew that Lieutenant David Hastings, with Company 'B,' 1st Dragoons, was on his way to Fort Fillmore. Miles would not release Sturges until he was officially informed of the transfer, which did not take place until October 6, 1854. At that point Miles ordered Sturges to prepare his company for immediate departure, as Hastings was then encamped at Mount Robledo north of Doña Ana and soon would arrive at Fort Fillmore.[16]

Sturges departed Fort Fillmore on October 7 with Company 'H.' The party consisted of one officer, three sergeants, three corporals, one bugler, one farrier, and sixty privates. Second Lieutenant Hastings arrived at Fort Fillmore on that same day with Company 'B,' 1st Dragoons. Company 'B' had one officer, three sergeants, four corporals, one bugler, one farrier and forty-one privates. Hastings is an interesting character. He was not a West Point graduate. In fact, he was a former enlisted man who emigrated from England and had served as a private, corporal, sergeant, and 1st sergeant of Company 'B,' 2d Infantry Regiment. Hastings enlisted in 1837 and spent eleven years in the ranks before applying for and gaining a commission in the 1st Regiment of Dragoons in 1848, at the time of the War with Mexico.[17]

Captain Henry Whiting Stanton arrived at Fort Fillmore with his family on November 14, 1854. One of Fort Fillmore's more tragic figures (see pp. 137-144), Henry Stanton was the captain of Company 'B,' 1st Dragoons, Hastings being his second in command. Stanton was thirty-one years old and had been an officer in the army since graduating from West Point in 1842. A New Yorker, Stanton was commissioned with the 1st Dragoons and remained with that regiment over his full career. He had been the 1st Dragoon regimental adjutant from August 1846 to January 1851, until promoted to captain on July 25, 1854, when he was given command of Company 'B.'[18]

Company 'K,' 3d Infantry, returned to Fort Fillmore for the third time on December 2, 1854. Brevet-Major Israel Richardson, still in command, arrived at Fort Fillmore with one 2^d lieutenant, one brevet-second lieutenant, four sergeants, two musicians, and forty-three privates. Second Lieutenant Laurens O'Bannon was a familiar face, although Brevet-2^d Lieutenant Henry Walker had not been at Fort Fillmore before. The company was transferred from Fort Thorn, which it had founded and helped construct. Brevet-Major Richardson almost immediately went on a well-deserved leave in the East.[19]

Company 'K's' arrival meant that four infantry companies and one dragoon company were at the post. There being no room for this many men, Company 'A,' 3^d Infantry, was given notice to cross the river into the Gadsden Purchase lands and to take quarters at the small village of Santo Tomás, just south of Mesilla. The overall command of this expedition was given to Major Gouveneur Morris, Miles's second-in-command. Captain Andrew Bowman went along, assisted by 2^d Lieutenant Richard Bonneau and possibly 2^d Lieutenant Laurens O'Bannon of Company 'K.' Four sergeants, two corporals, one musician, and forty-three privates were to provide the garrison. By occupying Santo Tomás, Morris was in effect also showing the flag to the larger, nearby village of Mesilla.[20]

The arrival of O'Bannon, a handsome South Carolinian, created a situation at Fort Fillmore within the Miles family. Sister, as May Miles was often referred to in the long letter written by Sallie Ann Miles, fell head over heels in love with O'Bannon, much to the dismay of her father. O'Bannon was previously married to a Doña Ana Mexican girl. Before she died in an accident they had two children. May Miles was eighteen years old, well polished, and no doubt brought west to meet an officer husband. Miles didn't want O'Bannon as a son-in-law. His choice was the equally handsome and well-born Brevet-Captain Barnard Bee who, like O'Bannon, was from South Carolina. Sallie Ann said of May Miles:

> ... Before we went to Fort Filmore [sic], Father had quite made up his mind that his Adjutant, Lt. Bee, would make her a good husband and I think from his letters, he had tried to create a little romance between them. When he found that Sister inclined toward Lt. O'Bannon, he showed very markedly his displeasure and Lt. O'Bannon says he tried to get rid of him by detailing him

to every campaign that went out to fight the Indians, and made mother keep watch so that he never had a chance to see Sister alone to propose to her. Well, there came a time when father had to go out on one of the scouting expeditions and leave the Lieutenant in the camp. His last command to Mother was, 'Don't let O'Bannon have a chance to propose to May.' Mother did keep careful guard until one day when she was going to the little Mexican town to do some shopping. After the mules were hitched to the carriage, they both were frightened and ran away and damaged the carriage so she couldn't take her ride that day. Lt. O'Bannon very politely offered to take Sister in his buggy to do the shopping. Now I think Mother was in sympathy with the lovers. Father used to say that Lt. O'Bannon had bought Mother, telling her of his Texas lands. Well, she evidently forgot all father's instructions and let Sister go and, of course, she came back engaged to be married.[21]

Santo Tomás, where O'Bannon took May Miles shopping, was another of the villages scheduled to be transferred to American control on July 4, 1855. Miles discussed that village and Mesilla in a letter to General Garland on December 2, 1854:

... Your communication of the 25th Inst. I had the honor to receive last night. Immediately orders were issued for Capt. Bowman with his Company A. 3d. Inf. to reoccupy Mesilla and Maj. G. Morris 3d Inf. to proceed there and assume command of the Troops at that station. The company will march this morning.

Maj. Morris has received instructions to protect the people in their persons and property from molestation from Mexican Officials and to assist our civil officers in the execution of their duties., etc., etc.

I am informed that at the village of Santo Tomas directly opposite from where we crossed the river there are fine large buildings, suitable for quarters for officers and soldiers. It is about three miles from Mesilla and where the bottom and mesa come together, making the road from El Passo [sic] to run through it, and truly a military position. Knowing that at Mesilla there are but jacal building of the most indifferent kind, very small, too much so for comfort. I have told Major Morris, that on inspection, if he finds St. Thomas as represented, he can take post there until you disapprove of the station. St. Thomas has from its position the great advantage of being removed from the many grogeries in Mesilla.[22]

First Lieutenant John Wynn Davidson brought a dragoon detachment to the post late in 1854. Miles called these troops a disgrace to the service. He notified the Department:

> The detachment of 'I' Company, 1st Drags arrived here destitute of clothing, the horse's appointments barely serviceable, four of the horses so poor and out of order as to be unserviceable, and with <u>one</u> camp kettle and <u>one</u> mess pan as camp equipage. Some of the soldiers of this detachment reported to Lt. Hastings, that before they left Fort Thorn they were ordered to turn over their better grade horses for those considered unfit for service.[23]

Miles may have had a reasoned prejudice against this unit, especially toward its commanding officer, Davidson. John Wynn Davidson, who gained a general's rank during the Civil War, later became known as 'Black Jack' Davidson when he commanded the colored 10th Cavalry Regiment. In 1854 his army career hung in the balance, awaiting the results of a most serious court martial. Davidson was involved in one of the worst disasters to befall the army in New Mexico during the 1850s. Official details were not available to Lieutenant Colonel Miles, but rumors of 1st Lieutenant Davidson's conduct during the incident must have reached his ears. The charges implied that in March 1854, Davidson's actions were incompetent, if not cowardly, during a battle at Cieneguilla in northern New Mexico. Twenty-one or twenty-two dragoons died as a result. Miles perhaps laid blame where he thought it belonged.[24]

Miles was sometimes hard, especially on mounted officers, but he had a heart of gold at other times, at least when it came to the soldiers of his infantry regiment. On December 29, 1854 he enlisted a nine-year-old boy into the regiment, against regulations which specified twelve years of age for drummer boys. He seems to have expected support from the Department of New Mexico in bending the rules:

... In making up my Recruiting Return, I find the enlistment of Mrs. Williamson's grandson not [expressely] forbidden by regulations. [Such] would make it doubtful if the enlistment is allowed he being but nine years of age and the recruiting regulations stating boys of twelve years may be enlisted. I have made the following endorsement on the enlistment and request you will add something to the Adjutant Genl. on the subject.

The within named boy (James Williamson) was enlisted by the particular request of Brigd Genl. Garland, Comdg. Dept. Of New Mex. under the following circumstances. The Grand Father of the boy was a meritorious soldier in the Regt. over thirty years ago. He died at Fort Jesup as Orderly Sergt. The father was raised and served as a musician in the Regt. [He] joined a Kentucky Regt. of Volunteers at the commencement of the Mexican War and was killed at Camargo, Tamaulipas. The Grandmother is now here. Old, blind, poor and helpless, dependent on a daughter married to a musician and this boy for her support. She has been a laundress of the Regt. at least thirty-five years.

I make the particular request from the above related circumstances that this last enlistment be approved. I am informed he will make a good drummer.[25]

How many women, children, and other family members lived at Fort Fillmore at any time? No records were kept of camp followers, laundresses, wives, and children, etc. This old woman, and her family, had served with the 3[d] Infantry Regiment for some thirty years, grandfather to father, and now to a nine-year-old boy. Each company was allotted four laundresses. They lived in the barracks with the soldiers, but were provided with small private rooms. This letter indicates that at least one enlisted musician was married with his wife on post, the daughter of the grand-mother, who no doubt was with the regiment as she grew up. Where they lived at Fort Fillmore with respect to the other soldiers is not determinable. Miles did not say which infantry company Williamson was enlisted in; 'C,' 'K,' and 'E' were there at the time.

Fort Fillmore ended 1854 with a total of five companies: one detached to Santo Tomás under the command of Captain Andrew Bowman who, reported to Major Gouveneur Morris; Companies

'C,' 'E,' and 'K' of the 3^d Infantry Regiment were living in quarters on the south side of the fort; Company 'B;' and the 1st Dragoon Regiment occupied quarters on the north side. Just over two hundred soldiers were at the post. An additional one hundred and nineteen recruits were required in the four companies to bring them up to strength. In addition there were five officers on the post staff, Miles, Bee, Masten, McFerran, and Assistant Surgeon Cooper. Twenty-five enlisted men of Company 'I,' 1st Dragoons were on post and scheduled to leave with Lieutenant Hastings in early January as part of the escort for Major Emory's Gadsden Purchase Boundary Commission. At the Stanton quarters, Captain Henry Stanton and his wife celebrated the Christmas holidays, probably with other officers of the post. The Captain was about to be sent into the field in early January. The Mescalero were acting up and in need of punishment.

NOTES - Chapter 6

1. Fort Fillmore Post Returns, January 1854.
2. Thomas to Garland, March 14, 1854, M1120. Roll 3.
3. Alexander to Nichols, April 10, 1854, M1120, Roll 3.
4. Alexander to Nichols, May 7, 1854, M1120, Roll 3.
5. Manypenny to Meriwether, May 9, 1854, U.S. Interior Department Microcopy No. T21: Indian Affairs Bureau records of the New Mexico Superintendency, 1849 - 1860. (Hereafter cited as Indian Bureau. Roll 2.)
6. Ezra J. Warner, *Generals in Blue: Lives of the Union Army Commanders* (Baton Rouge: Louisiana State University Press, 1964), p. 486.
7. Backus to Nichols, June 12, 1854, M1120, Roll 3.
8. Steck to Meriwether, July 8, 1854, Indian Bureau, Roll 2.
9. Steck to Meriwether, August 22, 1854, Indian Bureau, Roll 2.
10. Fort Fillmore Post Returns, August 1854.
11. Sarah Ann (Sallie) Marrian, A Letter To "My Little Grandson Frederick" From Sarah Ann ("Sallie") Marrian, Feb. 7th, 1901 (Unpublished), pp. 16-27. (Hereafter cited as Marrian, A Letter to "My Little Grandson.")
12. Miles to Nichols, September 18, 1854, M1120, Roll 3.

13. Cubero to Miles, September 22, 1854, M1120, Roll 3.

14. Miles to Nichols, October 2, 1854, M1120, Roll 3.

15. Heitman, Frederick Masten.

16. Bee to Assistant Adjutant General, Department of New Mexico, October 6, 1854, M1102, Roll 3.

17. Heitman, David Hastings.

18. Miles to Garland, November 18, 1854, M1120, Roll 3.

19. Miles to Nichols, December 3, 1854, M1120, Roll 3.

20. Ibid.

21. Marrian, A Letter To "My Little Grandson," p. 29.

22. Miles to Garland, December 2, 1854, M1120, Roll 3.

23. Miles to Nichols, December 17, 1854, M1120, Roll 3.

24. Buell or Bell to Williams, December 27, 1854, M1120, Roll 3.

25. Miles to Garland, December 29, 1854, M1120, Roll 3.

7

1855 - THE YEAR OF THE MESCALERO

The year of the Mescalero was 1855. From the first day of the year to the last, that tribe's freedom to roam and, as the military termed it, commit depredations, was greatly reduced. Before 1855, the United States Army chased the Mescalero through mountains and desert, but rarely caught them. In 1854, Fort Webster moved to the Rio Grande and was renamed Fort Thorn; Fort Bliss was established opposite the Mexican town of Paso del Norte; and Fort Conrad moved to a healthier and more suitable site at Fort Craig. There were now enough troops to secure the mail route from El Paso to Santa Fe, if steps were taken to pacify the Apache bands on the east side of the Rio Grande.

The move to confront the Mescalero began early in January 1855. Captain Richard Stoddard Ewell, 1st Dragoons, left Fort Thorn for the Mescalero country in the Sacramento Mountains to be part of a coordinated attack, in line with a new policy to get tough on Indian raiders. Captain Ewell was to link up with a mixed infantry/ dragoon force coming from Fort Fillmore. Ewell had orders to go as far as the Pecos River, where the Mescalero were reported to be raiding cattle ranches.[1]

At Fort Fillmore, Captain Henry Stanton, commanding Company 'B,' 1st Dragoons, received orders to prepare a force to join Ewell's. Stanton took four days to select and prepare his troops for the field, as well as organize supplies, horses, pack animals, and required equipment. This was to be a quick assault on the Mescalero strongholds and the troops were not taking wagons.

Correspondence from Lieutenant Colonel Miles to the 9th Department provides many details of the Stanton mission, as well as other events which transpired at Fort Fillmore that early January. The original order from the 9th Department, sent on Christmas Day, arrived at Fort Fillmore on January 1. Miles replied:

> ... Yours of Decbr. 25 Ult. I had the honor to receive on the 1st Inst. Immediately preparations were commenced to put the detachment enroute to Sineguilla [Cieneguilla] in time to join or communicate with Captain Ewell by the 15th Inst.
>
> The organization of this force is as follows. Capt. Stanton, 2d Lt. Daniels and Bvt. 2d Lieut. Walker, 2 sergts, 2 corpls, 2 buglers and 24 pvts. Of Dragoons; 3 sergts, 3 corpls and 44 pvts of Infantry; 40 mules, 8 Mexican packers, one guide and one interpreter.
>
> This command leaves this post this morning, and can by easy march reach the point of destination on the 14th Inst.
>
> In addition to instructions given me for the government of the commander of this detachment, I have ordered Capt. Stanton to attack any party of Indians he may fall in with, having sheep or cattle, as the Indians lately have been committing depredations below Fort Bliss and run off two days since Mr. White's stock at Fronteras ... .[2]

On January 16, 1855, with Stanton's force already in the field, one of those rare documented events related to the enlisted men's lives at the post occurred. Private Abraham Ferguson, Company 'B,' 1st Dragoons, was remanded, in chains, to the Fort Fillmore guardhouse. Knowledge of his problem has survived because Lieutenant Colonel Miles asked for clemency in his case. In asking for the pardon Miles wrote:

> ... I have the honor respectfully to solicit of the General Commanding of the Department, clemency in the third case enumerated in special order No. 2 (current series), that of Private Abraham Ferguson of B. Co. 1st Dragoons and request he will pardon his confinement in the guard house with a ball and chain and half of the fine of money per month, which the court has sentenced him to forfeit.

I cannot say much in extenuation of his offence, it was great, but there was an aggravation in his conflict with Corpl. Rockett that might under an excitement have caused any man in protecting himself, to have done the same he did. He is a young man, of fine soldierly appearance, great energy of character, very fair education and being on his second enlistment superior in knowledge and attainments in his duties to any soldier of his company. His conduct as a soldier must have been good, or else, at the time of his committing the outrage he did, he would not have risen to the position he held, at that time, of First Sergeant.

I feel sure if the Genl. Commanding will give his clemency in this case, it will not be misplaced, as this young man, has in my opinion grievously repented of his acts, and the trial and sentence has made such an indellible [sic] impression, as to deter him from ever engulphing [sic] himself into another crime. Besides, restoring to the service a good and efficient soldier.[3]

Former 1st Sergeant Private Abraham Ferguson, Company 'B,' 1st Dragoons, languished in the Fort Fillmore guardhouse for some act Miles did not address in detail. With Ferguson in chains and 1st Lieutenant David Hastings, Stanton's second in command, on an escort assignment for Major Emory's Gadsden Purchase boundary survey, Captain Henry Stanton went into battle against the Mescalero without two of the three other leaders of his company who might have made a difference to the mission.

Captains Stanton and Ewell linked up on January 16, 1855, and immediately set out in search of Mescalero warriors. The general policy at that time was that one Apache was like any other Apache. Any could be attacked for the crimes of another, and were. On January 19, south of Sierra Blanca in the Sacramento Mountains, the two joined commands met an enemy force, and eagerly engaged them in battle. An account of the resulting fight written by dragoon Sergeant James A. Bennett survives. Although brief, the fate of Captain Henry Stanton and two dragoon soldiers serving with him were noted. Bennett wrote:

> ... On the mountain in front of us at daybreak appeared about 100 warriors. They were dancing around a fire, "hallowing," and seemed to be daring us on. We saddled our

horses, took no breakfast, mounted in pursuit. The main body of troops moved up the stream and small parties of Dragoons kept charging out after parties of Indians. A running fight was kept up until 4 o'clock, when we encamped.

Captain Stanton with 12 men rushed up a deep ravine. The Indians in ambush fired upon him. He fell, a ball having passed through his forehead. One private soldier also was killed. The party turned to retreat. The horse of one man fell wounded. The Indians gathered around him and filled the rider's body with arrows. Those in camp heard the firing, ran to the rescue, met the Indians, had a hard fight of 20 minutes, when the red men fled. We picked up the dead and brought them into camp. 2 ponies came running into camp. They were covered with blood, showing that their Indian riders had fallen,

At night outposts were established 1/4 mile in each direction from camp. The dead bodies were buried and fires were built over the graves to obliterate all marks of the burial place. I was just far enough from camp to hear the spade and pickaxe as they struck stones. The night was as dark as "Egypt." I was lying alone upon a blanket, waiting and watching anxiously, the approach of the foe. I heard the noise of something coming slealthily through the bushes. The dry leaves rattled. My nerves were at their utmost tension, when I was pleased to discover the intruder to be a large white mountain wolf, easily frightened off. No Indians were to be seen in the morning.[4]

Sergeant Bennett did not say what kind of weapon was used to kill Captain Stanton. Given that Bennett believed it was a ball, one has to wonder whether his own dragoons might have accidently shot him down. It is not known whether the dragoons of Company 'B' used pistol and saber in this charge against the Mescalero. According to the only data available, the Mansfield Inspection Report of late 1853, many dragoon companies in New Mexico were armed with either the Colt Dragoon Pistol, Caliber .44, or the Colt Navy Revolver, Caliber .36. Colonel Mansfield did not specify caliber. Colt Navy Revolver ammunition is far more prevalent among artifact finds at Fort Fillmore, but this weapon may not have been in wide issue in January 1855.

Muskets and pistols were not common weapons possessed by the Apaches, though no doubt the better armed had them. Bows and arrows, as well as lances were far more common. Bennett noted that one of the wounded soldiers was filled with arrows by a group of milling Apaches. Had they used firearms he would have said filled with bullets.

Stanton and two other dragoons were hastily buried in the Sacramentos and the mixed force continued on the campaign trail. Three days later, January 23, Sergeant Bennett and his part of the force returned to the burial site. Bennett reported:

> ... Turned back yesterday. Saw 4 Indians in the distance but they soon disappeared. In crossing a stream we lost nearly all of our packs of provision. Those who couldn't ride became bare-footed, and to make matters worse the road was strewn with sharp fragments of rock. The Indians have been burning the grass upon our route.
>
> Came to where we buried Capt. Stanton and the two men. Found the bodies torn from the grave; their blankets stolen; bodies half-eaten by wolves; their eyes picked out by ravens and turkey-buzzards. Revolting sight. We built a large pile of pine wood; put on bodies; burned the flesh; took the bones away.[5]

According to a later report from Fort Fillmore, the bodies of Stanton and the others were brought home by Fort Fillmore Lieutenants Daniel and Walker, not by Sergeant Bennett's group, which was under Ewell. Given later comments by Bennett he may have been with the bodies on the return journey for some reason. It would seem he first returned to Fort Thorn with Ewell, in which case the entire column may have passed through Fort Thorn on the return journey to Fort Fillmore. The excavation of Captain Stanton's bones at a later date made no mention of the condition of the body, but there is confirmation of it being burned to near ashes. Sallie Miles remembered hearing stories from her father concerning the Stanton death. She reported:

> ... I remember on one of these expeditions, three soldiers and an officer, Capt. Stanton, was killed. They were buried where they fell and the troops followed the Indians. When they came back to the spot on their home trip, they found the Indians had dug up

the bodies, scalped them and left them exposed to any varmint that came along. As they had no wagons along, they had to burn the bodies and put the ashes in bags and carry them back to the fort that way. Poor Mrs. Stanton was broken hearted and they never told her that her husband's body had been burned.[6]

The exact date of the return of Captain Stanton's body to Fort Fillmore is uncertain. The only mention of his death in the Fort Fillmore records was made in a letter from Lieutenant Colonel Miles to the 9th Department on February 5, 1855. Later descriptions by Sergeant James Bennett, 1st Dragoons, do not confirm the dates given by Miles. However, since Bennett was writing from memory and Miles from the scene, this author believes the date Miles used for the arrival of Stanton's body, as well as the other two dragoons, is more accurate. Miles reported:

> ... I have the honor to report, that 2nd Lieut Daniel, 3rd Inf. Returned to this post from the scout after the Mescaleros, in command of the late and lamented Capt. Stanton's Detachment, on the 2d Inst. He brought the remains of Capt. Stanton and the two privates of B. Co. 1st Drags Thos Dwyer & Jon Henning [killed at the same time] who were intered [sic] with the highest funeral honors on the 3rd Inst.
> The horses and mules on this scout, are at present unfit for any service, owing to the scarcity of grazing, from the ground being covered with snow.
> Capt. Ewell on the death of Capt. Stanton placed Bvt. 2nd Lt. Davidson 1st Drags in command of the B. Co. 1st Drags. I have been necessitated to temporarily retain him at this post, in command of that company until an officer of that Regiment is sent to relieve him.[7]

The funerals were conducted on February 3, 1855, some fifteen days after the incident, with funeral honors "of the highest" as specified in the Army Regulations of 1847, still applicable in 1855. For Captain Stanton a full company, no doubt Company 'B,' 1st Dragoons, Stanton's own company, provided the escort for the funeral. The escort for the body would probably have been commanded by Captain William Brooke Johns, 3[d] Infantry, as senior captain, or Captain John McFerran, followed by Brevet-Captain Barnard Bee. Stanton's escort was supposed to be commanded by an officer of his rank or, if none were present, an officer of the next lower rank.

Stanton being an officer, all other officers of the post and in the vicinity would have been expected to attend. They would have worn a strip of black crepe around the left arm, if available, and also upon their sword hilt. The drums of the escorting band would have been edged with black crepe, as per the 1847 Army Regulations.

The escorting company and band were to be formed in two ranks, opposite to the adobe quarters where Stanton and his wife had lived. The corpse was carried from his quarters, borne by six resident officers of the post who held rank equal to (or above or below) Captain Stanton. Captain Johns, listed in the post returns as being present during that month, or whoever was in command, would have ordered the men to "Present Arms." As they presented arms, the band played a funeral dirge, and the coffin was carried to the right of the formation, then halted.

Captain Johns would shout "Shoulder Arms," "Company Left (or Right) Wheel, March," followed by "Column Forward, Guide Right, March." These commands were given strictly according to regulations. The column, in this case Stanton's Company 'B,' with casket following, and music playing, would have proceeded slowly up the small rise to the Fort Fillmore Cemetery, which lay beyond the hospital, south of the post.

Upon reaching the cemetery, Johns would have (after the center of Company 'B' reached the grave) commanded "Column, Halt!", "Right Into Line, Wheel, March!" Stanton's coffin would have been brought along the front of the company and then to the opposite side of the grave. Johns would have shouted "Present Arms" as the coffin started toward its resting place. As the coffin reached the grave, Captain Johns would have ordered the men to "Shoulder Arms," "Order Arms," and "Parade Rest."

It is assumed that Lieutenant Colonel Miles, present at the post for the ceremony, gave the final oration, as there was no post chaplain at Fort Fillmore. A clergyman might have been secured from the surrounding region for the duty. When Miles, and any others, finished, the coffin was lowered into the grave.

As the coffin was lowered Captain Johns was required to shout "Attention Company," "Shoulder Arms!", "Load at Will, Load!" The 1847 Regulations simply state that "three rounds of small arms will be fired by the escort."

When this duty of honor was completed, Johns would command, "By Company, Right (or Left) Wheel, March!" followed by "Column Forward, Guide Left, Quick March!" Once the Company cleared the cemetery, the band would then have begun to play again, and would have continued playing through the slow march back to the post area.

The two Privates, Dwyer and Henning, would have been buried in a separate ceremony, probably together. Their escort would have consisted of six pallbearers for each, from their own company. The escort for the pallbearers would have consisted of eight Privates, commanded by a corporal. The rest of the ceremony would have followed a like pattern as for Captain Stanton, although the officers were not required to be present. It is assumed that some of them probably were, as would have been the case for many of the enlisted men as well.

Indian Agent Dr. Michael Steck finished his first monthly report to Governor Meriwether that January. Steck had received new instructions from the Indian Bureau in Washington. The directive ordered reports be made every month thereafter and added that the agent should live in close proximity to the tribe for which he was responsible. Dr. Steck made no mention of the Mescalero tribe, only those he called the Gila Apaches. Steck was not yet the agent for the Mescalero, none having been appointed. During January, Agent Steck met with every tribal chief he could identify. Those named were Mangas Coloradas, Delgadito, Itan, Luceres, Josecito, Cuchillo Negro, Piñon, and Sergento. Steck met with the chiefs at the Fort Thorn agency and provided them and their bands with corn and beef. He said because these Apaches lived in scattered bands from the Gila River to the Rio Grande, and from the line between Mexico and the U.S. and the country occupied by the Navajos, he had not met with all of their leaders. Those that came in numbered about four hundred. Agent Steck reaffirmed his belief that the policy of feeding the Apaches, and instructing them in agriculture, was by far the best policy.[8]

A change in the command status of the 3[d] Infantry Regiment on February 3, 1855, had far-reaching significance for Fort Fillmore, the Apaches, and the people of the whole region. On that date Colonel Benjamin Louis Eulalie Bonneville was named colonel of the 3[d] Infantry Regiment following the death of Colonel Thomas Staniford. Bonneville, a noted explorer and military commander, took a different view on command. He came to New Mexico to take over the regimental reins of power from the hands of subordinates, as James Many and Thomas Staniford had not done, and place them in his own. Bonneville was then sixty-two years old but not yet ready for the rocking chair.[9]

On January 9, 1855 Company 'E,' 3[d] Infantry, up to then the longest-serving infantry company at Fort Fillmore, departed for service at Albuquerque. Except for one two-month campaign against the Mescalero in the summer of 1854, Company 'E' had been at the post since being marched there by Brevet-Major Jefferson Van Horn in September 1851. Company 'E' was commanded when leaving by 1st Lieutenant John Wilkins.[10]

The punishment expedition on which Captain Henry Stanton served when killed was only one prong of a much larger campaign against the Mescalero that winter and spring of 1855. From Fort Bliss, the future Confederate general, then a U.S. Army captain, James Longstreet, led two companies out from Fort Bliss toward the Guadalupe Mountains to provide another force bearing down on the Mescalero country from the south. Captain Richard Ewell headed the column from the west and Brevet-Major Simonson brought his force from the north. Stanton linked up with Ewell's column in the Sacramentos, as we now know. Longstreet and Simonson did not encounter any significant bodies of Mescaleros on their sojourns, but this use of troops from many forts was a harbinger of future events.

Lieutenant Colonel Miles reported on March 12, 1855, that he had received several reports of Indian depredations in the area around Fort Fillmore. Miles reported the theft of ponies, mules, cows, and oxen from a little place called Las Mulas, about eighteen miles below Fort Fillmore. The trail led toward Cook's Springs and the thieves were believed to be Gila Apaches. On the first of March, opposite Fronteras, the Mexican Commissioner, a man named Salazar, lost twenty-one horses and mules out of a total of twenty-three. That depredation occurred at ten o'clock in the morning. The people of Fronteras saw it all happen. The thieves were believed to be either Mescaleros, or New Mexicans. The last depredation occurred at Picacho Mountain where Indians ran off some mules and horses belonging to Mexicans. Pursuit was useless in all cases as the command at Fort Fillmore was not notified in a timely fashion.[11]

The months following the Senate signing of the Gadsden Purchase agreement saw increased Apache raids into Mexico by the bands on the west side of the Rio Grande. Cochise, Delgadito, Coleto Amarillo, and Mangas Coloradas all made use of the safe harbor across the American border. In the spring of 1855, a large party of Apaches planned a raid into Mexico. The bands living close to abandoned Fort Webster and the Santa Rita Copper Mines traveled west to Apache Pass in what is now Arizona. They gathered volunteers from other Apache bands and went in small war parties into Mexico. Cochise raided in Sonora while Josecito, Costales, and Itan raided Chihuahua. Upon their return, they learned the Americans, with whom they had treaties, wanted to make another, the third in the past four years.[12]

The first mention at Fort Fillmore of a new fort, named Fort Stanton after the martyred Captain Henry Stanton, occurred in a letter Lieutenant Colonel Miles wrote to the Department of New Mexico on March 28, 1855, a little over two months after Captain Stanton's death. Miles was about to leave Fort Fillmore for the Mescalero country, taking Company 'K,' 3[d] Infantry, under Lieutenants O'Bannon and Walker. Second Lieutenant Bonneau became acting assistant quartermaster. Brevet-Captain Barnard Bee accompanied Miles as his executive officer.[13]

Miles held a peace conference with the Mescalero at Dog Canyon on April 3, 1855, only five days after leaving Fort Fillmore. The Mescalero warriors were abject in pleading for peace with the Americans, a request which Miles honored. Miles then moved on with Company 'K' to a site called Camp Stanton on the Bonito River. This Camp Stanton was not located at the future site of Fort Stanton. Miles did not like the location because of its want of timber and grazing. Since the responsibility for locating Fort Stanton fell on his shoulders, he was agreeable to a site fifteen miles to the north and nearer the pine trees where wood could be obtained. He arrived at the second site on April 28, temporarily naming it Camp Garland in honor of the Department Commander, Brevet-Brigadier General John Garland. The campground was soon renamed Fort Stanton. The beginning of the end for Mescalero depredations was at hand, although it was to be another ten years before the Mescalero Apaches were finally pacified.[14]

As if he didn't have enough responsibility, in May 1855, Doctor Michael Steck was appointed the Indian Agent for the Mescalero tribe as well as for all the bands west of the Rio Grande. In effect, this meant that Steck was agent to all the Apache peoples, as well as all the tribes from the Texas border to California—a task laughably impossible for Fort Fillmore to handle as a military site, and even more impossible for one man to control.

Lieutenant Colonel Miles returned to Fort Fillmore on May 12, 1855. By May 18, the more showy aspects of command were back to normal and the mundane was once more at the forefront. Miles was concerned that units of the 3ᵈ Infantry Regiment, which he commanded but did not directly control at other posts, were baking their own bread and in this way not providing funds for the upkeep of the regimental band as per Army regulations.[15]

The regimental fund not only supported the band, it also provided temporary relief to disabled officers and soldiers, allowed for the establishment of a regimental library, and helped create the non-commissioned officers' mess. Councils of Administration at each post set aside these small amounts of money after deducting the expenses of the company bakeries. What the councils seemed to be doing, if Miles was correct, was failing to deduct the expense of a bakery, stating that since they baked their own goods, the expense of the bakery equaled the donation to the regimental fund. Why Miles did not have the power to write directly to the offending officers under his command is once again due to the independent status of each post in New Mexico Territory, as designated by the War Department in Washington. These companies, in effect, acted as independent detachments answerable only to the Department of New Mexico commander, thereby ignoring the wishes of the regimental commander.[16]

A May 18 letter from Private Henry Miller, who deserted one branch of the army to join another, provided a brief look at enlisted life at Fort Fillmore in 1855. Wilson pleaded:

> ... You will remember that I deserted from Comy 'K' 1st Arty on the 18th of May 1854 and two days afterwards I enlisted in the 1st Regiment of Dragoons at the recruiting station in New York, which fact itself will explain that it was not my intention to desert the <u>service</u>, but I could not live in Fort McHenry on account of certain persons who so annoyed me that I determined to leave the Company. I was assigned to "B" Compy 1st Drgs and came to this country, but immediately after I acquainted Captain Stanton of my Compy that I was a deserter, but unfortunately a few days after he was killed while on a scout against the Indians, so I do not know whether he ever took any steps in the matter, and my object in writing to you is for you to speak to Col. Taylor to get me transferred back to my own Compy, or use some other means to soften the rigor of this imprudent act, as I can assure you I am sincerely sorry for what I have done. You will confer a great favor if you will do this, and a still greater, if you will write to me and let me know the result, please direct to Henry Miller, Troop "B", 1st Drgs at this post.[17]

Apparently Private Miller looked at Fort Fillmore, did not like what he saw, and decided he liked it better back at dear old safe Fort McHenry. We do not know the outcome of his case but it is extremely doubtful that he was able to effect any kind of transfer. One item of interest is that Wilson used the term, Troop 'B,' 1ˢᵗ Dragoons, instead of the official title of Company 'B.' It was not until after the Civil War began, and the dragoon name disappeared from use, that all mounted companies were designated troops.

Brevet-Captain Barnard E. Bee returned to Fort Fillmore from the field on May 12 to find he had been promoted to captain. Bee was to become an infantry company commander in the newest infantry regiment in the Army, the 10ᵗʰ Infantry Regiment. The 10ᵗʰ was one of four regiments added to the strength of the United States Army in 1855. The new regiments were the 1ˢᵗ and 2ᵈ Cavalry Regiments, and the 9ᵗʰ and 10ᵗʰ Infantry Regiments. These new units were experimental in their outlook and usage. No mounted regiments with the title 'cavalry' existed in the United States Army until the 1ˢᵗ and 2ᵈ were established.

The 9ᵗʰ and 10ᵗʰ Infantry were also experimental as to the look of infantry regiments for the future. Gone were the fifer and drummer in each company—replaced by a bugler, as in the dragoon and cavalry units. The 9ᵗʰ and 10ᵗʰ also received pleated blue-colored uniform jackets, at least in the beginning. These proved very unpopular and were soon discarded..

Captain John McFerran, the Fort Fillmore Quartermaster, temporarily replaced Captain Bee as the 3ᵈ Infantry Regiment adjutant in May 1855. McFerran, an extremely competent individual, was originally sent to Fort Fillmore to bring order to the chaos over supplying Fort Webster and the multitude of small missions for which escorts had to be provided.

Captain Andrew Bowman, in command of Company 'A' of the 3ᵈ Infantry, left Fort Fillmore on May 21, 1855, for the still under construction Fort Stanton, there to relieve Company 'K,' which had accompanied Miles on the Mescalero Campaign. Bowman had four sergeants, four corporals, one musician, and thirty-one privates in Company 'A.'[18]

The 3[d] Infantry Regiment, all ten companies of which were then serving in the Department of New Mexico, was reduced to its lowest overall strength level in years by May 1855. Only 493 rank and file were then serving with the regiment out of over 780 allocated slots. Miles stated in May that the March 1855 regimental return, just being completed, had the correct total, and added that between March 31 and October 31, 1855, some 103 soldiers would be discharged, reducing regimental totals even more. The greater number of the discharges would be in June and July. He believed re-enlistments would not equal the casualties, and regimental strength might be below three hundred by October 31.[19]

One of the most important documents surviving from Fort Fillmore's active period was written on June 20, 1855. Lieutenant Colonel Miles had in storage at Fort Fillmore outdated, worn-out or useless weapons, clothing, and equipment. The letter is very enlightening concerning the paucity of artifacts later found at Fort Fillmore related to military activities. Belt buckles, cross belt plates, weapons, etc. were very rare finds, considering the number of troops who once served at the fort. Miles said:

> ... I have in magazine at this post a quantity of surplus arms (muskets of different patterns, and in all conditions, for service to being useless). Pistols, likewise, cartridge boxes, belts (Musket and Carbine) worn out and of old pattern. Mountain Howitzer pack saddles and harness worn out and out of repair - a large quantity of ammunition boxes, which I respectfully request authority to send to the Ordnance Depot.[20]

Artifact hunters and professional archeological groups have long wondered why there were so few 'important' artifacts found at Fort Fillmore, when an average of two hundred soldiers per month lived there over a period of ten years. One would expect these men to wear out cartridge boxes, belts, uniform clothing, and every variety of 'important' soldier personal equipment accessories. In fact, cartridge box plates, brass U.S. belt buckles, cross-belt plates, brass shoulder epaulettes, martingales, and even uniform buttons, are scarce, even rare, finds. Given the thousands of uniforms which must have worn out over the ten years, averaging seven or eight buttons per uniform, this author has counted less than one thousand buttons of all types in all of the major collections, a trivial number when compared to what should have been found there.

What happened to all these wonderful artifacts which hunters and professional archaeologists hoped to find? They were shipped in wagons to the great storerooms at Albuquerque or even Fort Union and disposed of by public sale. Although there has been no mention found of a public sale conducted at Fort Fillmore, that possibility also exists. No doubt much of the worn-out clothing in store was handed over to the Apaches on both sides of the Rio Grande for their use in the winter. Documents attest to this in a number of instances. The brass items, which also had lead backs to make them heavy for use as belt buckles, cross-belt plates, etc., were no doubt bought in mass quantities by investors and melted down for their brass and lead content.

Captain John Wynn Davidson, commanding Company 'B,' 1st Dragoons following Captain Stanton's death, led his horse soldiers out of Fort Fillmore on June 20, 1855. Davidson's forty-six enlisted men and approximately fifty-eight horses headed for temporary duty at the new Fort Stanton. Several of the unit's horses were broken down, over half having been rated unserviceable in the May returns. Captain Johns, then temporarily commanding the post, had two companies of infantry, 'C' and 'K,' with only seventy-two enlisted men between them. Eighty-eight recruits were needed to bring these companies up to strength. Fortunately, Indian depredations had slowed.[21]

The transfer of the Gadsden Purchase lands became official on July 4, 1855. A parade formation formed at Fort Fillmore in the morning. Led by Brevet-Brigadier General Garland and Governor Meriwether, the parade crossed the Rio Grande and took possession of the town of Mesilla. A detachment of Company 'G,' 1st Dragoons, the Governor's mounted escort, accompanied the dignitaries, as did Companies 'C' and 'K,' 3ᵈ Infantry, and Company 'B,' 1ˢᵗ Dragoons. The 3ᵈ Infantry Band provided the marching music and the ceremonial playing. A speech by the governor was translated into Spanish. A flag staff floated the 'Stars and Stripes' and three times three loud cheers were given. The band played 'Hail Columbia,' 'Yankee Doodle,' and the 'Star Spangled Banner.' The Mexicans holding office swore allegiance to the American government. Dragoon Sergeant James Bennett, who was in attendance with the Company 'G' escort, added that all Mexicans that did not wish to obey American laws were notified to leave and to take residence within the new boundaries of Mexico.²²

There is no confirmation that Lieutenant Colonel Miles had returned from detached service before the July 4 celebrations, but he may have been there. This was certainly a critical event for his command. Miles had definitely returned by July 7, and mentioned that General Garland was still at Fort Fillmore on that day.²³

On July 30 Miles made a special request for a furlough for Private Charles Mister of the 3ᵈ Infantry Regiment Band. Mister's term of service was to expire on December 20. He had been with the 3ᵈ Infantry for over twenty years. Physically in poor condition, Private Mister sought permission to enter one of the soldiers' homes in the East. Miles asked for a quick reply so Mister could travel to San Antonio with the Boundary Commission.²⁴

Captain Stanton's death was still creating waves within the army bureaucracy as of August 4, 1855. In June Captain John Wynn Davidson wrote to the Adjutant General's Department in Washington for clarification of Stanton's date of death. Davidson had replaced Stanton as commander of Company 'B,' 1ˢᵗ Dragoons. Davidson knew from experience that future promotions would be based on the exact date of that death. In effect, Davidson's promotion to captain officially came at the very moment the ball from an Apache weapon or dragoon weapon entered Stanton's forehead. The Assistant Adjutant General replied:

> ... In answer to your letter of June 1st relative to the date
> of <u>Capt. Stanton's</u> death, I have to state that Genl. Garland,

Commanding in New Mexico, reported it to have occurred January 20th, while it is noted on your muster roll as January 19, 1855. The former date was taken in carrying up the promotions consequent upon the vacancy, but the adoption of either date would in no wise change the relative rank of the officers concerned, as no other casualty took place in the Army between January 18th, when you allege that Capt. Stanton was actually killed, and the end of the same month.[25]

Regardless of their duty performance or their behavior in service, coward or noble, incompetent or brilliant, every officer was considered equal in ability and was promoted based on their position on a chart of seniority. Such a system must have made officers of merit feel very unappreciated.

The number of soldiers at Fort Fillmore was at a low point, according to a letter from Miles to Eaton on August 11, 1855. The post records show a total of only eighty-two in two companies, 'C' and 'K,' 3[d] Infantry, with no dragoons present. Ninety-two recruits were needed to fill the company strengths. Miles reported this sad state of affairs:

> ... Owing to the very few soldiers for duty at this post, I am unable to furnish but one sentry for guard, the necessary extra and daily duty men consuming more than half of this small command. There is of necessity, as at all posts, certain labor required, which obliges the old guard to work daily. This can be avoided and permit me to mount additional guard, if the Quarter Master is permitted to hire but a few Mexicans, not over five or six, who can be obtained at five or six bits per day furnishing themselves. This is decidedly cheaper to the government than the employment of soldiers and I respectfully request may be granted, until at least the recruits arrive.[26]

Miles proposed hiring local Mexicans to do the work of the missing soldiers. Had Major Backus arrived in the Territory with fresh faces, these temporary hires from among the Mexican community would be terminated, regardless of Miles's comment on the temporarily employed being cheaper.

First Lieutenant George Andrews of the 3ᵈ Regiment of Artillery camped near Fort Fillmore on August 16, 1855, as part of the escort for the Pacific Railroad Survey then being conducted through the Gadsden Purchase lands. He had fifty-one men in his red-leg infantry company—artillery personnel serving on duties unrelated to the artillery arm, most often as infantry. His animals were in poor condition and required rest and forage before returning to California. Andrews was going to Doña Ana in a day or two to find forage and to graze and rest his animals. He addressed a letter this matter in a letter from a 'Camp Near Fort Fillmore.'²⁷

Some Mescalero were back on the raiding trail in August 1855. Indian Agent Steck reported to Governor Meriwether on a murder which took place near El Paso. Steck was now responsible for the care of the Mescaleros, and for keeping a close eye on the various bands. He reported:

> ... In my letter of the 14th I promised to enquire into the Moscalero [Mescalero] difficulties said to have taken place near El Paso some seven or eight days ago. I immediately sent for Palanquito to come and see me and today he and his brother arrived at the Agency. The facts as near as I have been able to ascertain from various sources are that a small party of Indians attacked a herd of cattle, killed one of the herders and made the other captive—driving the stock—small lot some 10 or 12 head cows & oxen—the trail is said to have gone in the direction of the Guadelupe Mountains. The Chiefs who have visited me this morning deny having any knowledge of the theft & murder except what they have heard from the people —and state that as soon as they heard of it they immediately sent out two of their men to follow the trail and ascertain who the depredation was committed by and that as soon as they returned they would report to me who the thieves are.
>   Palanquito is of opinion that it was either Plumas, a Moscalero [Mescalero] Chief who might be said be avenging the stealing of a lot of horses and mules from him by people from about El Paso or a party of Jicarilla under Jose Largo who he said were encamped at the St. Augustine Spring about that time. Jose Largo's party was small numbering eight lodges and five men.

On the return of Palanquito's runners I hope to be able to report the names of the thieves. The bearer of this letter being an express direct from Fort Bliss probably carries to your excel-lency and the Commanding Genl a definite account of the whole matter.[28]

Agent Steck already had better intelligence on Mescalero (though he still didn't know how to spell the tribal name) activities than the Army had been able to obtain in the past. Using a divide and conquer technique, he used one Mescalero band, and internal tribal antagonisms, to gain knowledge of which bands committed depre-dations and under whose leadership.

As of September 7, Lieutenant Colonel Miles knew that Colonel Benjamin Louis Eulalie Bonneville, recently appointed colonel of the 3d Infantry Regiment, was about to appear at Fort Fillmore as his replacement. Bonneville requested that Miles appoint 1st Lieutenant James Noble Ward as adjutant. Miles notified the Department of New Mexico that he had done so. Ward was coming up from Texas with the party escorting Colonel Bonneville. In order to facilitate this appointment, 1st Lieutenant McFerran was transferred to Company 'K,' 3d Infantry.[29]

Brevet-Major Israel Richardson came once more to Fort Fillmore on September 21, delivering seventy recruits for Companies 'C' and 'K,' 3d Infantry, then abruptly resigned his commission as of September 24. Miles accepted the resignation without any official statements on the matter.

Dr. Michael Steck left the Apache Agency in September to visit the camps of the principal chiefs of the branch of the Apache people he called the Gila Apaches. He was well and kindly received everywhere he went. Agent Steck indicated that since the signing of the April 1853 compact between these Apaches and Governor Lane, very little trouble had been made by them. That undoubtedly accounts for why the dragoon horses at Fort Daniel Webster were safe from theft after that time. The Apaches often visited the settlements, but only for the purpose of trading skins and baskets of their manufacture for corn and other subsistence items.

The Apaches living at the headwaters of the Gila were in a most destitute condition. These people had formerly subsisted on what they could steal in the way of mules, cattle, and horses from both the Territory of New Mexico and the states of northern Mexico. Peace had not been good for them, as the government only partly supplied their wants. Agent Steck wanted to supply them with clothing, of which they were almost destitute, blankets, cooking utensils, and tobacco—winter was approaching. Apparently the natural resources of the Gila River region could not support even the small numbers of Indians who resided there. Steck indicated that game was scarce in all seasons, not just in the winter. Starving, the Apaches had resorted to eating what few mules and horses they had, reducing their level of survival even more. Steck wanted them supplied until they learned farming and sheep raising. If not, they would most certainly appear at the settlements to steal what they could. Steck firmly believed that "All experience has shown that not only here in New Mexico by the settlement of the Pueblos but in the management of the Indians of the United States, that to teach them the cultivation of the soil is the surest road to civilization."[30]

The Mescalero question was partly solved in 1855 through the use of force and threats. There was a stronger peace in place than in previous years, but no peace would hold until the United States Army and the Territorial Government gained total control over the region. By 1855, that time was close. Miles commented on the temporary situation with the Mescalero on October 11:

> ... The Mezcalero Apaches are quiet and seem disposed to be peaceful. They are very destitute and greatly in want of food. They frequently visit [here] in small parties and to induce them to continue to do so, I have liberally issued to them flour and fresh Beef. They are very anxious for the return of their treaty, that the agent may give them something to eat.
>
> I feel confident without the issue of rations to these people they must starve or steal. They should have an agent of their own. Dr. Steck, one of the best I ever knew, being identified by them with the Gila Apaches can never acquire their entire confidence or control them; and if he succeeds, would lose his

influence over the [Gila Indians] for there is considerable jealousy between these tribes.

A few days since, Baranquito [one of the Apaches who participated in the April talks] informed me, that a party of [Jicarilla] Apaches, had located themselves in the Sacramento Mountains. That they had ordered them off but they refused to go, and wanted to know what next they should do. I advised them to threaten the Jickaries [Jicarillas], if they did not go immediately, they would take their horses from them and switch them besides. He quietly replied that he believed some of their young men had taken their horses away and that their Chief was on his way here to complain ... .[31]

The talks Miles held with the Mescalero Chief Barranquita, or Barranquito, show that Indians came and went at Fort Fillmore with some regularity. Of course, there was an agency at Doña Ana and later at Apache Agency near Fort Thorn. Miles's comments about Dr. Steck fit this author's understanding of the good doctor as the type of Indian agent who put the tribes' interest first. Steck certainly appeared to be, as Miles said, "one of the best he knew." Many times he was said to have walked among the ferocious Apaches with only an interpreter as company.

There was intense jealousy between the Mescalero and Chiricahua Apaches. The same can be said of a band of Jicarilla Apaches from the north, who were unwelcome when they arrived in the Mescalero lands, although they were not attacked. This division in the Indians' forces was no doubt exploited to the benefit of the non-Indians, though Miles, as usual, gave good advice on what the Mescalero should do. He also recommended an independent Indian agent for the Mescalero and the west Rio Grande (Chiricahua) bands.

Sergeant Bennett reported Colonel Bonneville's arrival at Fort Bliss with one hundred and fifty recruits. Even a colonel had to herd recruits when required. Bonneville arrived at Fort Bliss on November 20, 1855. The sergeant was visiting Fort Bliss with Dr. Cooper and next journeyed with Major Cary H. Fry, the paymaster, to San Antonio. He did not say whether Colonel Bonneville continued onward.[32]

On December 9, 1855, in Santa Fe, Major Surgeon Eugene Hilarion Abadie, of the medical director's office, reported his findings on the state of the Fort Fillmore hospital, and others, to the assistant adjutant general of the Department of New Mexico, at that time Brevet-Major W.A. Nichols. As to the hospital at Fort Fillmore, visited August 31, 1855, Abadie said:

> ... The hospital at this post [Fort Fillmore] under the charge of Asst. Surgeon Geo. E. Cooper is remarkably well constructed for the purpose to which it is applied. It is a large quadrangular adobe house, with flat roof rooms all around it with inner court or placita. The building has in the center of its facade a hall or saguan which opens on the court, and by side doors with the rooms; it has also a corresponding one leading into the backyard which encloses the necessary outbuildings, privy, cow house and chicken house.
>
> To the left on entering is the surgery well fitted up with necessary conveniences, communicating on that side of the house with the Steward's room, dead room [?], store room, kitchen and mess room, ending in the back hall: On the right of the front hall is the entrance to the four large wards on that side of the house communicating one with the other and ending at the back hall or saguan.
>
> When the portal is erected on the three sides of the building, which it is contemplated to put up, the rooms will be completely protected from the heat, being well ventilated through the windows opening on the inner court and on the outside walls.
>
> The wards can receive 25 to 30 beds, allowing at least 1000 cubic feet of air to each. The order, neatness and police of this Hospital is excellent, the medical stores and medicine of good quality, are sufficient, although the new annual supply has not yet been received. The sick receive the best of care and attention and the books, accounts, Reports, etc. required by the Regulations are strictly kept and furnished.[33]

Dr. Abadie believed Fort Fillmore's hospital to be among the very best in New Mexico, many of which were very unsatisfactorily set up and maintained. His details concerning the building and its layout in 1855 are the only detailed information we have on the hospital and its operation.

On Christmas Day, 1855, Lieutenant Colonel Miles reported the arrival at Fort Fillmore of Company 'B,' 1st Dragoons from Fort Stanton, under the command of Captain John Wynn Davidson. Besides Captain Davidson, the company had four sergeants, four corporals, one farrier, one bugler and fifty-nine privates. Company 'B' had been absent from Fort Fillmore since June 20, leaving the post entirely without a mounted contingent.[34]

On December 31, 1855, President Franklin Pierce addressed the growing rift between north and south in his Third Annual Address. His words were most prophetic:

> ... when sectional agitators shall have succeeded in forcing on this issue, can their pretensions fail to be met by counter pretensions? Will not different States be compelled, respectively, to meet extremes with extremes? And if either extreme carry its point, what is that so far forth but dissolution of the Union? If a new State, formed from the territory of the United States, be absolutely excluded from admission therein, that fact of itself constitutes the disruption of union between it and the other States. But the process of dissolution could not stop there. Would not a sectional decision producing such result by a majority of votes, either Northern or Southern, of necessity drive out the oppressed and aggrieved minority and place in presence of each other two irreconcilably hostile confederations?[35]

President Franklin Pierce predicted the future in 1855, but few seemed to be listening.

NOTES - Chapter 7

1. John Upton Terrell, *Apache Chronicles*. (New York: World Publishing, Times Mirror, 1971), p. 206.

2. Miles to Nichols, January 5, 1855, M1120, Roll 4.

3. Miles to Nichols, January 16, 1855, M1120, Roll 4.

4. James A. Bennett, edited by Clinton E. Brooks and Frank D. Reeve, *Forts & Forays, A Dragoon in New Mexico, 1859-1856*. (Albuquerque: University of New Mexico, 1996), pp. 60, 61. (Hereafter cited as Bennett, *Forts & Forays*.)

5. Bennett, *Forts & Forays*, pp. 61, 62.

6. A Letter To "My Little Grandson Frederick," p. 29.

7. Miles to Nichols, February 5, 1855, M1120, Roll 4.

8. Steck to Manypenny, January 31, 1855, Indian Bureau, Roll 2.

9. Bennett, *Forts & Forays*, note at bottom of p. 78.

10. Fort Fillmore Post Returns, February 1855.

11. Miles to Assistant Adjutant General, Department of New Mexico, March 12, 1855, M1120, Roll 4.

12. Edwin Sweeney, *Cochise*, p. 94.

13. Miles to Nichols, March 28, 1855, M1120, Roll 4.

14. Miles to Garland, April 18, 1855, M1120, Roll 4.

15. Miles to Sturgis, May 18, 1855, M1120, Roll 4

16. *1847 General Regulations*, pp. 52, 53.

17. Miller to Sergeant Wilson, Co "K" 1st Arty, Fort McHenry, M1120, Role 4.

18. Miles to Assistant Adjutant General, May 22, 1855, M1120, Roll 4.

19. Miles to Assistant Adjutant General, May 24, 1855, M1120, Roll 4.

20. Miles to Easton, June 20, 1855, M1120, Roll 4.

21. Fort Fillmore Post Returns, June 1855.

22. Bennett, *Forts & Forays*, p. 74.

23. Miles to Easton, July 7, 1855, M1120, Roll 4.

24. Miles to Assistant Adjutant General, July 17, 1855, M1120, Roll 4.

25. W. Claude Jones to Miles, July 17, 1855, M1120, Roll 4.

26. Miles to Assistant Adjutant General, August 11, 1855, M1120, Roll 4.

27. Andrews to Eaton, July 30, 1855, M1120, Roll 4.

28. Steck to Meriwether, August 17 or 19, 1855, Indian Bureau, Roll 2.

29. Miles to Nichols, September 7, 1855, M1120, Roll 4.

30. Steck to Meriwether, September, 1855, Indian Bureau, Roll 2.

31. Miles to Nichols, October 11, 1855, M1120, Roll 4.

32. Bennett, *Forts & Forays*, p. 78.

33. Abadie to Nichols, December 9, 1855, M1120, Roll 4.

34. Johns to Nichols, December 25, 1855, M1120, Roll 4.

35. James D. Richardson, *Messages and Papers of the Presidents*, p. 2874.

8

1856 - UP FROM TEXAS

Depredations in the vicinity of Mesilla in early 1856 were attributed to Apaches living in the Mogollon Mountains. Mangas Coloradas admitted that some of his people were involved but he had been unable to stop them. A campaign initiated in January 1856, led by Captain David Chandler and using troops from Fort Craig and Fort Thorn, followed a sheep herd into the Mogollon Mountains. They surprised an Apache ranchería and recaptured two hundred and fifty sheep and twenty-one horses and mules. One Apache was killed and three or four others wounded. The leader of the camp was El Cautivo, an associate of Cochise.[1]

There were several regional problems with Indian depredations in late 1855 early 1856. Near Mesilla one man was killed and fifteen head of stock run off. At nearly the same time, in the town of Socorro, New Mexico Territory, another raid was attributed to the Mimbres Apaches. Agent Steck sent for the Apache chiefs of the Mimbres bands, but before his messengers arrived, Chief Delgadito sent an interpreter named Costales to the Apache Agency. Names were provided and Steck notified the commander at Fort Thorn, Brevet-Lieutenant Colonel Eaton, that he knew the men and that Eaton should mount no punishment forays until he could address the problem. Eaton ignored Dr. Steck's request to wait and mounted an expedition into the Mimbres country to catch the thieves. Eaton returned empty handed. This foray badly upset the Apaches. With the entire Mimbres River country in a state of alarm, Steck agreed to meet with the principal chiefs about fifty miles west of Fort Thorn. He met with Delgadito, Itan, Piñon, Lucero, Jose Nuevo, and Pajarito of the Mimbres Apaches. During these talks the murderers and thieves were identified. The Mesilla murder was done by a raiding group led by Chief Cigarito from Mexico, who may have had Mescalero connections. The actual killing was done by Cigarito's son and son-in-law, and the brother of another chief named Manguia. The stock at Mesilla was stolen by the son of Delgadito, a warrior named Jenero, and the son of Chief Negrito, the latter two being Mimbres Apaches. Except for those two, all the others crossed back over into Mexico to continue raiding there.[2]

The stock theft at Socorro was committed by a small band of Mescalero, not Mimbres, who drove the stolen animals through the Mimbres camp, possibly in order to put suspicion on the Mimbres bands. The Mescalero had been living for some months along the Rio Grande near Doña Ana and near Fort Craig. They were identified as Francisco, Flaco, and Sho-a-no, the latter termed the biggest thief and villain among the Mescalero people. He was responsible for killing three soldiers on the Jornada in 1853 and also bragged of killing fourteen white men at other times. Other robberies in Socorro and Valencia Counties were attributed by the Mimbres to Apache bands from the Mogollon Mountains. Agent Steck believed these Apaches had so fine a hiding place that the military would have to enter their country and fight them.[3]

Lieutenant Colonel Dixon Miles and Major Gouveneur Morris departed Fort Fillmore on January 8 for Santa Fe to participate in a courts-martial. While they were gone Colonel Benjamin Louis Eulalie Bonneville arrived at Fort Fillmore on January 16, 1856, to take command. Bonneville was accompanied by 2[d] Lieutenant Benjamin Franklin Davis and one hundred sixteen recruits. These men were destined to fill places in the empty ranks of the various red-leg artillery and infantry companies then in New Mexico.[4]

Bonneville was a famous figure in his day. Born in France in 1793 during the French Revolution, he emigrated to America as a youth and, through influence, probably at the behest of the Marquis de Lafayette who was a family friend, was admitted to one of the first classes to graduate from the United States Military Academy

Colonel Benjamin Louis Eulalie Bonneville.
Courtesy: National Archives.

at West Point. Bonneville became the 155th graduate on December 11, 1815, when he was commissioned a brevet-2^{d} lieutenant of the light artillery. Bonneville was promoted to 2^{d} lieutenant on January 15, 1817, and transferred to the 8th Infantry Regiment on March 10, 1819. He became a 1st lieutenant on July 9, 1820, and captain on October 4, 1825.[5]

Bonneville's fame was established from his explorations in the Far West from 1831 to 1836. Having an opportunity to enter the Rocky Mountain fur trade, he asked for a leave from the military and left Fort Osage on the Missouri River on May 1, 1832. His explorations and adventures during this expedition were included in *Adventures of Captain Bonneville*, written by Washington Irving. Bonneville was not a success as a fur trapper but he received credit for discovering Yosemite Valley and Bonneville Flats, the latter of course named for him. Many of his contemporaries believed Bonneville to be a spy for the American government, sent to gain details of Spanish California and British interests in the Oregon country. He returned to Independence, Missouri, in the summer of 1835, to learn he had been mustered out of the Army. He reinstated himself with some effort and his military career thereafter saw him involved in the Second Seminole War in Florida as a major of the 6th Infantry. During the Vera Cruz Expedition into Mexico under General Winfield Scott in 1847, Bonneville took part in the assault on Mexico City. He was rewarded with a brevet to lieutenant colonel for gallantry and meritorious conduct in two battles. He was also court-martialed on the charge of "misbehavior before the enemy," found guilty on three of ten specifications, and sentenced to be admonished by the commanding general, a form of reprimand. Upon returning to the West he served briefly at Fort Kearny, Nebraska, and Fort Vancouver, Washington. He was promoted to lieutenant colonel of the 4th Infantry Regiment in 1849. His promotion to colonel took place on February 2, 1855, on the death of Colonel Thomas Staniford.[6]

The first Indian incident in which Colonel Bonneville was involved occurred near Mesilla on January 24, 1856. He reported the incident on January 28:

... I have the honor to state for the information of the Brigadier General Comdg. the Dept. that it has been reported to me by the Probate Judge for the County of Dona Ana, living in Mesilla, that on the 24th inst. a party of Indians having stolen some cattle from near their town, were pursued by a party of Mexicans numbering [?]. The Indians were overtaken about three leagues from Mesilla going in the direction of the Mimbres. A fight took place in which three Indians were killed as proof of which the Mexicans brought in the scalps. Other than this I have heard of no depredations committed by the Indians.[7]

While Fort Fillmore troops waited in garrison for orders, mounted Mexican militia from Mesilla were active in the field. With the help of Delgadito's Apache people, three of the raiders from Cigarito's band were tracked down and killed for making the recent raid on Mesilla. Indian Agent Michael Steck was notified by Delgadito that his warriors were marking the progress of Cigarito's band through their country. When it looked as if they might be conducting a raid, Delgadito sent word to Steck at Apache Agency to warn the people in the Rio Grande communities. Dr. Steck alerted Mesilla to Cigarito's presence and, following a raid which led to the stealing of four oxen, the raiders were chased down and three were killed. The Mexican militia who did the chasing then turned around and stole some horses from the Mimbres Apaches who were followers of Cigarito and killed two of them.[8]

Colonel Bonneville did not stay long on his first visit to Fort Fillmore. By January 25, he determined to convene a board of inquiry at Taos, relative to the case against Fort Fillmore officer John Wynn Davidson and the loss of twenty-two dragoon lives at Cieneguilla. Bonneville decided it was unsuitable to hold the examination at Fort Fillmore, because there were not enough senior officers among the officers then present.[9]

Fort Fillmore Post returns report that Captain John Wynn Davidson left Fort Fillmore for Taos on February 14, 1856. He was to answer to a court of inquiry for his actions at Cieneguilla. Bonneville left Fort Fillmore about the same time, but may have traveled separately. Miles returned from Santa Fe in time to retake the command, at least temporarily. Results of the enquiry placed no blame on Davidson for the deaths of the dragoons. His principal accusers failed to appear at the hearing and the matter was dropped.

On April 4, 1856, Lieutenant Colonel Dixon Stansbury Miles prepared once again to relinquish command of Fort Fillmore. As soon as Bonneville returned from Santa Fe and Taos, Miles took command at Fort Thorn, forty miles to the north. In 1856, Fort Thorn was a more active command than Fort Fillmore, at least as far as Indian problems. Miles's last communication from this brief interval at Fort Fillmore, written just before the change of command, reported on a number of incidents which had recently transpired at or near the fort:

> ... Before I am relieved in command of this post by Colonel Bonneville, I have the honor to report the many Indian depredations committed in this vicinity, since I last had the opportunity of communicating with you—20th ultimo.
> On the 26th ulti. a party of five Indians drove off from the camp of Mr. Joseph [Capuledes], about two miles this side of Cruszes [Las Cruces] twenty mules and one horse. On the same day at Canatillo [Canutillo] this side of Frontera a party of five Indians took from a Mexican wagon six mules. On the 28th ulti. a party of four Indians about day break six miles south of this post on the El Paso road, attacked three Mexicans from Carasal [?] Mexico, killing one.
> In all these instances the trails led to the west bank of the Rio Grande. The arrows found in the dead Mexican were recognized as belonging to the Gila Apaches.
> Lt. Davis with B. Co. 1st Drags. was rapidly in pursuit of the depredators in Capuledes' and the killed Mexican cases, but having neither guides nor trailers, after vigorous pursuit of several hours lost all signs, and had to return disappointed to the post.
> The dead Mexican I had buried where he fell.
> I do not believe a Mezcalero was engaged in any of these transactions and depredations, but doubtless soon will be in open hostility, by the cowardly, [?] conduct of the brothers of the killed Mexican, who wantonly shot in Dona Ana on the 29th of March a Mezcalero squaw, killing her instantly, and shot at

another, without it is supposed injuring her. These squaws were peaceably and industriously cutting and bringing wood for sale to the citizens of the town.

I am happy to inform you, this dastardly Mexican passing Fort Thorn was recognized and Col. Eaton promptly arrested him, holding him in custody under the charge of murder, until claimed by the civil authority.[10]

One more important event took place in Miles's life before he traveled north to command Fort Thorn. The marriage of his daughter May Chase Miles to 1st Lieutenant Laurens O'Bannon on April 8, 1856, took place in the commanding officer's quarters at Fort Fillmore. O'Bannon had not been Miles's choice for a son-in-law but there is no accounting for love. First Lieutenant O'Bannon believed, perhaps tongue in cheek, that Miles put his life in danger with the Apaches so he could keep him away from the twenty-year-old May. Sallie Ann Miles provides a rare look into the private lives of the most important family on post in those days. In her 1901 letter to her grandson Frederick Kuethe she said:

> ... Our house was quite a large one and, like all the houses in that country, it was only one story. As Father describes this house in one of his letters to Mother, I can easily do so ... . It was in this house that Sister was married to Lt. L.W. O'Bannon, April 8, 1856. The dining room was cleared of all furniture, excepting a row of chairs around the walls and the walls were decorated with swords, flags and guns. The porch at the back was enclosed with canvas and also decorated with flags, etc. A table ran the full length, just loaded with good things to eat. In the center was the bride's cake which was built up in pyramid form of six cakes, each beautifully iced and decorated with little flags on sticks and the top surmounted with a larger flag. It made a very handsome show.
>
> There was one thing in the army. All trades were represented so that when Mother wanted to give a dinner, which she sometimes did, having forty guests at a time, she had only to send word to the soldiers' quarters for a confectioner and, of course, any of that trade would be glad to come to her aid on account of the extra pay and she could make just as fine a display as if she lived in the Eastern cities.

Laurens O'Bannnon.
Courtesy: Bill Kuethe Collection.

May Miles O'Bannon.
Courtesy: Bill Kuethe Collection.

Well, to get back to Sister's wedding. It must have been a very pretty scene with the officers in full dress uniform and the ladies in ball gowns. Sister was dressed in white with veil (and I will say here that if you notice, she was the only bride in our family dressed in white). Alex and I walked in front of her and acted as bridesmaid and groomsman and were her only attendants. Lt. O'Bannon had to send three hundred miles to get a minister to perform the ceremony or be married by what was called a alcoldy [alcalde] which is a justice of the peace or by a Catholic priest. The minister was a missionary, a Methodist, and when Lt. O'Bannon gave him the check, he actually cried with joy, for he had never had so large an amount of his own before. I think the check was for three hundred dollars.

There were guests from all the forts within a hundred miles as it was quite an event on the frontier. The music was the band of the fort, which was quite a good one and after the banquet, dancing was indulged in until near morning. Sister's wedding tour was just across the road to the Lieutenant's quarters.[11]

There were some very important American characters in the region at that time who might have attended. Certainly Benjamin Bonneville and James Longstreet (Fort Bliss) were in attendance. Shortly after the wedding, Lieutenant Colonel Miles and his family departed for their new duty station at Fort Thorn.

Agent Michael Steck was not at the wedding. He had gone out with the Fort Thorn contingent serving with Brevet-Lieutenant Colonel Chandler's military expedition against the Mogollon Apaches. By April 6, 1856, he had returned to Apache Agency, angry and filled with trepidation over the future for the area's Indians. Two military columns were involved in the expedition, one from Fort Thorn and the other from Fort Craig. The Fort Thorn companies traveled by way of the Copper Mines to the Gila River and up the Gila River where it left the Mogollon Mountains. They then marched two days to the northwest where they met Chandler's Fort Craig force. The merged force traveled southwest trailing a large herd of sheep into the Almagre Mountains where they surprised a small camp of Indians, firing on them, killing one Indian and wounding three or four others. They captured two hundred and fifty sheep and twenty-one horses and mules. Chandler then marched south to the Gila and the Burros Mountains, which he crossed near Santa Lucca. Chandler wanted to return a different way, but finding the Gila River impassable, returned by way of the Copper Mines to his post at Valverde. According to Agent Steck, the success of this expedition lay in the military becoming acquainted with the country and its trails rather than in the number of Indians that were chastised. The effect of a strong military force in their country must have had a salutary effect upon the Mogollon Apaches.

Toward the end of the expedition an incident occurred in which Brevet-Lieutenant Colonel Chandler's troops fired on a friendly Mimbres village and created a situation which would have severe repercussions. Agent Steck said responsibility for the incident rested with Chandler; the Mimbres Apaches had not instigated the trouble. Apparently Chandler, in an attempt to return quickly to Fort Craig, had left some troops with Brevet-Major Oliver Shepherd. Chandler took one company of infantry and a detachment of dragoons and started back for Fort Craig. Six miles down the Mimbres they encountered Delgadito's camp. Agent Steck believed Chandler was familiar with the fact that he was in the Mimbres Indian reserve. Instead of checking, Chandler ordered his men to fire upon the Indians. Delgadito had camped there to watch the command pass through and then to talk with Agent Steck. Instead, roughly sixty infantrymen fired muskets upon his peaceful people. The firing continued for twenty minutes. The Indians scattered, but one woman was killed and another wounded. Three children were wounded and another child was missing. The firing stopped when Delgadito and the Army's interpreter, a man named Costales, approached Chandler's troops and told them who they were. Chandler said he thought they were Mogollon Apaches and offered to pay for their lost goods. Agent Steck wondered if he would ever regain their lost confidence. Steck said, "... and how can he [the Apache] confide in you if when he has been promised a friendly salutation you greet him with musketry and the shreiks [sic] of the dying and wounded women and children?"[12]

Colonel Bonneville returned to Fort Fillmore and was in command once again in mid-April, reporting that Company 'B,'

1st Dragoons, being in compliance with Special Order No. 26 from the Department of New Mexico, departed Fort Fillmore for Fort Stanton on April 11. Company 'B' had one 2^d lieutenant (Benjamin Franklin Davis), four sergeants, three corporals, two buglers, one farrier, and fifty-six privates. Fort Fillmore was again without a mounted company for field service.[13]

A seemingly minor courts-martial at Fort Fillmore was in process of becoming a military law case of some consequence in April 1856. Its importance reached all the way to the President of the United States. On April 26, 1856, Irwin McDowell, writing from the Headquarters of the Army in New York City, wrote Brevet-Brigadier General John Garland concerning the Fort Fillmore case:

> ... I have the honor to acknowledge the receipt of your letter of February 5th forwarding the proceedings of a Garrison Court Martial, and drawing attention to your endorsement therein suspending the execution of a part of the sentence in the case of Musician (Private) Beyer Regt. Band 3rd Infantry. On account, in your judgement, of its illegality it will be duly forwarded for the decision of the President as required by existing orders.
>
> In your letter you refer to the case of Private Oscar F. Holmes Co C. 3rd Inf. tried by a General Court Martial for stealing a watch from a sergeant of his regiment, sent here on an appeal taken from your decision by 1st Lieut. J.N. Ward 3rd Inf. It was duly submitted to the General-in-Chief, who did not entertain the appeal because the case was definitely disposed of by your actions in the proceedings of the court; and he did not wish to re-open it.
>
> A case in point has just been tried by a General Court Martial instituted by the General-in-Chief at Newport Barracks Ky. That of Private Shanahan, convicted of stealing a jacket from recruit Kennedy, and sentenced among other things to refund to Kennedy the price of the article stolen.
>
> The proceedings and sentence of the court have been approved and confirmed.
>
> As this action is the opposite to that taken by you in a similar case, and is founded on the same rule that would cause the

General—had he now the authority—to overrule your action in the case now pending—of Musician (Private) Beyer, he instructs me to say as follows in relation to the point of military law involved.

The question is, can a soldier convicted by a Court Martial of stealing from a fellow soldier be sentenced to refund to him the value of the stolen article?

The General agrees with you in the opinion that the 32d Article of War was, and is, evidently intended to apply to depredations by soldiers on persons not in the military service. It does not, therefore, apply to the case now in question. Nor is the case specially provided for in any of the articles, and must come, if it comes at all, under the 99th.

The 99th Article provides that all crimes not capital and all disorders and neglects which officers and soldiers may be guilty of to the prejudice of good order and military discipline though not mentioned in the foregoing Articles of War are to be taken cognisance [sic] of by a general or [special] court martial according to the nature and degree of the offense.

It is clearly a crime and a disorder for one soldier to steal from another.

It is clearly not a capital crime, and it is, therefore, undoubtedly, one to be taken [care] of by a court-martial—and under the 99th as it is not mentioned in any of the preceding articles.

It may here be asked, that, as theft is a crime which can be tried by civil courts as larceny, can military courts take cognisance of it? And, if so, could a trial by a military court be pleaded by the accused in bar of another trial before the civil court and, if not, would not the accused be liable to be tried for the same offense? Which is prohibited by the Constitution.

It has been decided by the Supreme Court of the United States that, by the same act a man may commit several offences and be tried for each. That an offense in "its legal signification means the transgression of a law." As an offense is not the act committed but the law or laws transgressed by the commission of the act, and as those laws may be local or general, civil or military, it follows if a person in the military service should, in consequence of the same act be charged with an infraction of the common law and of the U.S. Mil. Law he could be tried by civil courts and a court martial.

It is highly important to the service that all questions arising between soldiers should be settled by military courts as far as the laws permit. For to have them suing each other for damages or having each other tried by the civil courts would lead to many irregularities and be hurtful to the harmony and discipline of the service. And if courts martial had not the power to try in cases like those in question it would be necessary to the well being of the Army to clothe them with it.

The punishment to be given for offenses tried under the 99th Article is left to the discretion of the court. That discretion to be exercised under the obligations of the oath taken by the members of the court, which is the sole rule by which courts are governed.

By that oath they are to administer justice according to the Articles of War—and in cases not explained by the Article—according to their conscience. The best of their ability understanding—and the custom of war in like cases.

The sentence to refund to the injured party is according to the first principles of justice among all nations, civilized or savage. And there is nothing in custom of war to prohibit it, but the contrary. The 7th Section of the act approved March 3, 1851, providing funds for the Military Asylum gives to that institution all stoppages or fines adjudged against soldiers by sentence of Courts Martial, over and above any amount that may be due for the reimbursement of government or of <u>individuals</u>.

General Orders No. 21 of 1851, to which you refer in your endorsement was intended to be simply advisory. It is defective in the first part in the enumeration of the punishment which courts may legally inflict, and the second part is, as is shown therein, an error. The General thinks it proper here to remark—as the order was issued in his name, that it was not reviewed by him before being issued, and that the last part was drawn up when he was absent from Washington where the Head Qrs. of the Army then was.

The matter could have been corrected sometime since but under the assurance that it would soon be remedied by the "new regulations." He has this day rescinded the order.[14]

This is a fine example of the machinations of military law in the 1850s. Brevet-Brigadier General Garland made a decision on the case based on some interpretation of a regulation that had never been intended to exist, or which had been overturned by

events, and was now superceded by higher authority. The bands-
man at Fort Fillmore, Musician (Private) Beyer, stole an article from
another soldier, then was let off of paying the offended soldier for
the stolen item. Apparently, General-in-Chief Winfield Scott
directed that the fine be imposed. The offending regulation, never
intended to be, was then rescinded by order.

On May 15, Indian Agent Michael Steck reported to the
commanding officer at Fort Fillmore that Mescalero Chief Shawans,
or Sho-Wa-No, had been committing depredations near the Rio
Grande along with other Mescaleros. He was in Cuchillo Negro's
camp about five to seven miles from Fort Thorn. Eighty men under
Lieutenant Williams, Major Steen, and Lieutenant Pender left the
fort after midnight on May 15 to raid Cuchillo Negro's camp. Agent
Steck guided the troops to the camp. Brevet-Lieutenant Colonel
Eaton, commanding at Fort Thorn, ordered Brevet-Major Grier,
commanding the dragoon company, to shoot all offenders among
these Mescalero, and not to bring them in as prisoners.[15]

Eaton's force went to Cuchillo Negro's camp and returned to
the post by May 31. Eaton's after-action report sent to the
Department of New Mexico explained what happened.

> ... I have the honor to write you about the 10th of this month, that
> I was in daily expectation of an opportunity to seize the Mesca-
> leros, who had taken shelter in the country of the Mimbres
> Indians.
> On the 15th Inst. that opportunity seemed to be offered
> as you will see by the enclosed letter of instructions to
> Major Grier. It was not successful. Major Grier marched at
> midnight, and, before daybreak, reached a point about one
> mile from Cuchillo Negro's camp, where his approach was
> made known by Indian sentinels posted that far from the
> camp and who passed the information from hill to hill, and
> they defeated the enterprise. By what means the Indians were
> put on their guard, it was impossible for me to determine.
> Costales, well known as one of Delgadito's party, was in the
> confidence of Dr. Steck, and my suspicions rested upon him.
> He visited the camp [Cuchillo Negro's] with Mr. Barnes who

was sent out on the morning of the 15th as a spy, and it is as likely as not that whilst passing through, he managed to convey some hints of danger.

Taking this treachery, wherever it may have originated in connection with the fact that the Mescaleros were harboring in the camps of the Mimbres Indians, or that they were at least tolerated amongst them, without a strong effort to drive them away, I thought it time to notify them all that under such a state of things they were in fact as hostile to us as the Mescaleros themselves, unless they at once put the troops in the way of securing the thieves or drove them to their own country east of the river. On the morning of the 16th Cuchillo Negro came to the post to see me with Dr. Steck, and, after he had distinctly acknowledged to me that Shawans was in his camp the day before, I told him and Dr. Steck that I would give the Mimbres Indians about the post and the agency three quarters of an hour's time to clear themselves. That if at the end of that time the post guard found any about they would be imprisoned. And that until reliable information was received that Shawans & his party had been driven across the river they must be regarded as our enemies. When I left Fort Thorn (20 Inst.) this interdict was still upon them, although Dr. Steck had been informed that Shawans had gone over the river. The Mimbres Indians offering to go and show the trail leading east of the river.

I took this course because I considered that the least favorable opportunity to seize the Mescaleros was gone, as they were now apprized of the intention & efforts of the troops to take them, and will in future be on their guard.

I have been the more particular in rendering this account to dept. Hd. Qrs, knowing that there are suspicions that Mimbres Apaches were lately the perpetrators of robberies so near Los Lunas. I do not think that suspicion well founded. About that time the entire Mimbres branch were active and engaging under Dr. Steck near old Ft. Webster in opening their farms, or were about Fort Thorn and the agent.[16]

While Brevet-Lieutenant Colonel Eaton fulminated against the perfidy of Agent Steck and the scout Costales in preventing a massacre of Delgadito's band, a mounted unit that would have so much influence on the history of late 1850s New Mexico Territory prepared to march from Texas to their new stations in New

Mexico. This unit was the Regiment of Mounted Rifles, the only regiment of its kind in the history of the United States of America. The Regiment of Mounted Rifles (R.M.R.) was created by Congress on May 19, 1846, as a garrison command for army posts along the Oregon Trail. The War with Mexico changed this original goal.[17]

The R.M.R., although mounted, was different from a dragoon regiment, not only because of its unique uniform and insignia. It was intended to ride to battle on horses, then to dismount and fight on foot as infantry. The regiment was originally equipped with the U.S. Model 1841 .44 caliber rifle, called the Mississippi Rifle after Jefferson Davis equipped Mississippi volunteer units with the weapon during the Mexican War. This rifle had rifling in the barrel as opposed to the smoothbore weapons carried by the infantry and dragoons. The Mississippi Rifle had a longer range than the standard infantry musket and was more accurate. The problem with the weapon was that it took longer to load due to the tighter fit of the bullet. During the Mexican War, the R.M.R. was also equipped with Model 1840 sabers and flintlock pistols. The War Department was said to have purchased one thousand Colt Walker Model revolvers for the regiment. By 1856, the weapons used by the R.M.R had been modified to fire the .54 Caliber Minie ball, a far more devastating round. Many examples of this round have been recovered from Fort Fillmore refuse sites.[18]

The senior officers of the regiment were selected by President Polk more for their political beliefs than for their professional merits. At the time the Rifles were ordered out of Texas in June 1856, they were commanded by Colonel William Wing Loring, a hero of the Mexican War, who had lost an arm in battle. Loring was born in North Carolina on December 4, 1818. He later went to Florida with his parents where, on June 16, 1837, he was appointed a 2[d] lieutenant in the Florida militia, then fighting a protracted war, along with United States troops, against the Seminole Indians. When war clouds started to form with Mexico, Loring parleyed his former commission into an appointment as a captain in the newly formed Regiment of Mounted Rifles. In

February 1847 he was promoted to major and, at the Battles of Contreras and Churubusco, received brevets to major and lieutenant colonel. At the final battle at Chapultepec Castle he received a brevet to colonel, losing his arm in that battle.[19]

Loring was still a brevet-colonel and lieutenant colonel when he brought the R.M.R to New Mexico. He became the youngest colonel, at age thirty-eight, on December 30, 1856.

At the time of the Mexican War, few officers appointed in the R.M.R. were West Point graduates but, by 1856, this situation had changed. Following the Mexican War, the Mounted Rifles set out on their original mission to garrison the Oregon Trail. Then Brevet-Colonel Loring led them on a two-thousand-mile journey to the Pacific Ocean, dropping his companies off at various posts from Fort Phil Kearny, Nebraska, to Fort Vancouver on the Pacific Ocean coast. By 1851, the R.M.R. was back in Texas. Gold fever took its toll among the troops. The regiment had so many desertions to the California gold-fields that it was rendered ineffective to accomplish its mission. The remaining troops were pulled back to Jefferson Barracks, Missouri. The 1st Dragoons were given their horses, and the officers of the regiment sent to recruit a new body of men. By 1851, they were garrisoning small posts in Texas.[20]

Colonel Bonneville believed the 3d Infantry Regimental Band was in fine order in July 1856. He wanted the band to tour the various posts in New Mexico where 3d Infantry Companies were stationed. Bonneville's concert route was a circle: Fort Stanton, Albuquerque, Forts Craig and Thorn, and then home to Fort Fillmore. The 3d Infantry units at far-away Fort Defiance and Cantonment Burgwin were too far out of the way. Bonneville's post was still without a mounted company in July, and would not get one until Loring brought the R.M.R. up from Texas.[21]

When Loring and the R.M.R. arrived in the New Mexico Territory in August, Company 'F' stayed at Fort Bliss. On August 10, Companies 'B' and 'H' arrived at a new camp of the regiment some twelve miles upriver from Fort Bliss. The other companies followed. The campsite was designated Camp Holmes. Loring received word from Fort Fillmore that they had no supplies to give to him, other than limited quantities of beef and corn, and that none were known to be on the way. Loring indicated he would wait at Camp Holmes until the provision problem was corrected.[22]

Michael Steck returned from a visit to the copper mining region in early August. For six days, he had tried to learn who had committed some depredations near Fort Craig. Eight mules and five muskets had been stolen from an army timber camp in the mountains. Apparently, Dr. Steck followed up on most, if not all, reports of Indians depredations which occurred in southern New Mexico, south of the Jornada del Muerto. Major Enoch Steen had reported the incident. Steen said eight men in the timber party were fired on by five or six Indians. The men ran, leaving their teams and arms. The Indians took the mules and weapons and headed in the direction of the Mimbres River. Agent Steck immediately went to the Indian camps on the Mimbres, not telling his charges why he was there, and searched for the mules and the weapons. He found no trace of them. On July 25, Mescaleros reportedly stole six head of cattle in the Organ Mountains and were pursued. When caught, they lanced the cattle and ran off. There were other depredations near El Paso during the same period. Agent Steck expected a visit from Captain John Wynn Davidson of the dragoons. Davidson, coming from Fort Stanton and headed for duty at Tucson, told Steck where the camp of the Mescalero Chief Palanquito was located. Steck wanted to visit Palanquito to transmit Governor Meriwether's views to him.[23]

The R.M.R. moved out of Camp Holmes in early September. One company, 'A,' was commanded by 1st Lieutenant William B. Lane. Lydia Lane, wife of 1st Lieutenant Lane, and by far Fort Fillmore's most famous female, arrived for a brief visit on September 8, 1856. Lydia was not impressed, reporting, "such a dreary-looking place I have seldom seen; but there were some Mexican settlements only a few miles off, which were quite accessible, and when the officers and ladies were tired of home they could go to see their Mexican neighbors. We stayed there [at Fort Fillmore] part of a day to have the ambulance repaired, and dined with Lieutenant and Mrs. John D. Wilkins." Lydia soon left for other, perhaps even drearier looking places, leaving behind friends she would meet later on her return in the cold of January 1861.[24]

The several companies of the 1st Dragoon Regiment moved out of New Mexico as the R.M.R. moved in. Colonel Fauntleroy was in command. These dragoon units under Major Steen headed for what is now the state of Arizona to provide the first garrisons in that as yet undefined territory.

Company 'G' of the Regiment of Mounted Rifles arrived at Fort Fillmore on September 5, 1856, with three officers, fifty-nine enlisted men and fifty-eight horses, eleven of which were unserviceable. Immediately after their arrival, Captain Thomas Grimke Rhett, the commanding officer, applied for leave that he might bring his family to the Department. Rhett did not say whether his family was still in Texas, although one might assume so.[25]

The second officer in rank with Company 'G' was Brevet-Captain and 1st Lieutenant Alfred Gibbs. While Rhett's career failed to attain the level it might have, Alfred Gibbs's career rose to heights of greatness. Gibbs graduated from West Point a year after Thomas Grimke Rhett, in 1846. Born in New York, Gibbs was com-missioned a 2d lieutenant of the Mounted Rifles on July 1, 1846, only a few months after Rhett. In April 1847, Alfred Gibbs received a brevet to 1st lieutenant for gallantry and meritorious conduct at the Battle of Cerro Gordo in Mexico. A double brevet, this time to captain, was awarded him on September 13, 1847, for gallant conduct at Garita de Belen in Mexico. He was promoted to 1st lieutenant on May 31, 1853. During the interval from 1848 to 1856, Brevet-Captain Gibbs was Aide de Camp to General P.F. Smith. Company 'G' was his first field assignment since the end of the Mexican War.[26]

The remaining R.M.R. companies passed near Fort Thorn and dropped off another company at that post. Dr. Steck advised Governor Meriwether that soon he would attempt to renew intercourse with the Mescalero. On September 12, he reported the results of talks held near Fort Thorn. Estrella (Star), a principal chief, had promised to bring in the Apache leaders. Brevet-Major Jefferson Van Horn, commanding at Fort Stanton, sent word that Cadete, a son of Chief Palanquito, had given proof of his desire to remain friendly. Cadete gradually took over his father's position in the tribe. Van Horne took fifteen horses from two Apaches named Sho-wa-no and Loco. These animals had been stolen from the San Miguel country. As a reward for turning these animals in for their owners to claim, Agent Steck agreed to provide Cadete's (Palanquito's) band with rations. The estimated number of Indians supplied with corn and beef during that current quarter was roughly two hundred and fifty Mescalero, three hundred from Mangas's band, and three hundred and fifty from the Mimbres band of Cuchillo Negro. Agent Steck indicated that all of these were low estimates.[27]

Dixon Miles's daughter Sallie Ann told what it was like to be near Apache Agency in those days of heightened activity. Reminiscing in 1901 she said:

> While we were at Fort Thom [Fort Thorn], Father was trying his best to subdue the Indians so that it was constant warfare and the fort was nearly always surrounded by Indians. Alex and I were forbidden to go outside of the walls of the fort and the gates leading [she must have been talking about the gates surrounding her quarters] out were kept closely locked. One day we found ours open and just took a peep outside. What did our eyes see, but the vines filled with red berries which we knew were nice to eat! Well, the temptation was too great for us to withstand. Remember we were only six and seven years old, and out of the gate we crept and on from bush to bush picking berries and eating to our heart's content, when all of a sudden, a snake sprang at us. Oh! what a screeching and squalling there was. I am sure if there had been a hundred Indians after us we couldn't have made more noise. The whole fort was aroused and rushed out of the gates, thinking the Indians had captured us. I will say right here, that we were duly punished for our disobedience and that was the only time I ever remember of my Father whipping me.[28]

Fort Thorn had no walls so the very young Sally must have been speaking of either the gate around her quarters or elsewhere.

Apache Agency was near the fort, but not directly outside. Apaches may have been near the post seeking food or whatever else they might be able to get. The close Apache presence made the post far more open to an incident than was possible at Fort Fillmore. Neither post had stockades, the threat of attack not being sufficient to warrant them.

Colonel Bonneville left Fort Fillmore on September 13 to travel to Santa Fe once again. Major Gouveneur Morris was left in command. This was a final move, although Bonneville did not take the entire regimental headquarters with him at that time. Bonneville's sojourn in New Mexico saw him take command of the Department and on then to a posting at the regimental headquarters in Albuquerque. Gone were the days of Fort Fillmore's prominence as the headquarters of the 3[d] Infantry Regiment.

The long journey of the Regiment of Mounted Rifles to their duty stations in New Mexico Territory was complete with the arrival of Brevet-Colonel W.W. Loring at the regimental headquarters established at Fort Union on October 3. Companies of the regiment were stationed at Fort Bliss, Fort Fillmore, Fort Thorn, Fort Craig, Los Lunas, Fort Stanton, Fort Defiance, Cantonment Burgwin, and Fort Union.[29]

Major Gouveneur Morris reported that the headquarters and band of the 3[d] Infantry Regiment, following on the heels of the departure of Colonel Bonneville for Santa Fe, left Fort Fillmore on October 9. The headquarters consisted of one 1st lieutenant and adjutant (John Wilkins), one 1st lieutenant and regimental quartermaster officer (Laurens O'Bannon), one sergeant major, two principal musicians, and seventeen musicians of the 3[d] Infantry Regimental Band. May Miles O'Bannon probably went along as well. On October 11, with his staff and band still on the road to Santa Fe, Colonel Benjamin Bonneville became temporary commander of the Department of New Mexico, replacing Brevet-Brigadier General Garland, who had left for the East.[30]

Second Lieutenant Charles McNally, R.M.R., left Fort Fillmore for Tucson on November 11 escorting a large wagon train loaded with flour for the military garrisons being established by the dragoons under Major Enoch Steen. McNally would not return until January 1857. The routes from Fort Fillmore to the newly established garrisons soon became well traveled. McNally took an escort of over thirty enlisted men. He also took a wagon-master along at $50 per month, ten teamsters at $25 per month, and two herders at $10 per month, hired and paid by the government.[31]

In late November 1856, Brevet-Major H.L. Kendrick, commanding Fort Defiance, reported an incident that changed many lives and involved the soldiers at Fort Fillmore in their greatest campaign. The Indian Agent for the northern New Mexico region, Henry Lynn Dodge, had disappeared and was feared kidnaped by Apaches. As these first notices went out to New Mexico military commands, Dodge was believed still alive. Kendrick stated:

> ... I regret to inform you that H.L. Dodge, Indian Agent, while hunting on the 19th Nov. some 35 miles south of Zuni was taken captive by the Apaches and carried southward entirely beyond our reach or negotiation. These Apaches are believed to be Mogollones or Gilenos probably the former. From appearances he was treated kindly. A Mexican captive who came into us says Mangus Colorado [Mangas Coloradas] or his brother will get information of Captain Dodge being captured, and if so it is presumed that he may be ransomed, which the boy thinks will be the object of the captors.
>
> The object of this note is to ask you to get the information to Dr. Steck Ind. Agent at Fort Thorn as quickly as possible by whom it is presumed Capt. Dodge's liberation can be effected.
>
> I have also to ask that this information be at once sent to the Governor.
>
> I send this by a special messenger to whom please receipt for this letter.[32]

Upon returning to Apache Agency following a visit with the Mescalero, Dr. Steck was informed of Dodge's kidnaping. Apache Chief Delgadito was at the Agency and agreed to send a man to the Almagre Mountains and southern Mogollon villages to see if the kidnaped agent was there. Steck expected them to return with information in two or three days. If Dodge's captors were not found there, Agent Steck intended sending runners to the far off villages of the Coyotero and Pinal Apaches.[33]

On December 31, the last day of 1856, Colonel Bonneville wrote to General Winfield Scott, via Lieutenant Colonel Thomas in New York City, detailing the current activities in his Department. The letter gives some idea of the area being covered—from Bent's Fort on the Arkansas to the California border. Indian Agent Dodge's whereabouts were still unknown. Bonneville wrote:

... The persons sent into the Mogollons Country, by His Excellency Governor Meriwether, to ascertain the fate of Agent Dodge, and if alive, to ransom him have not yet returned.

The Indians who committed the robbery, reported as I was finishing my last monthly dispatch, were pursued by Lieut. H. Randal, 1st Dragoons, a distance of three hundred miles, who overtook them on the eighth day. After a sharp conflict the Indians fled, leaving the stock they had stolen, some of their own, and one of their warriors dead on the field. I felt it my duty to notice this gallant officer in Orders No. 17. of this year.

Captain Bowman, 3rd Infantry, commanding at Fort Massachesetts, reports a few Indians of the Capote Band of Utahs, which came to his post, sent by their chief to ascertain the treatment they might expect. This is the first visit these people have ever made. Of course everything was done by this judicious officer to win their confidence.

It affords me pleasure to say that the good understanding established by Major Holmes with the Mezcaleros [sic], and since continued by their agent Dr. Steck is having its beneficial effects. These Indians now visit Fort Stanton with confidence and in large numbers.

The detachment sent to Bent's Fort on the Arkansas to ascertain the disposition of the Kiowas, and the condition of the Subsistence stores in deposit with the trader, are still absent.

Finding the expense of keeping a company [of the RMR] at Los Lunas large, and that an unexpected debt of several thousand dollars had been contracted, I directed the company there to take post at Albuquerque, twenty three miles distant, quite as eligible a position to afford protection as Los Lunas.

Major Steen reports that he reached Tucson on the 27th ultimo. As this point is one of deep interest to our government,

I enclose his report, which no doubt will be more satisfactory than any extracts I might make. I also append my instructions to him in reply.[34]

The year 1856 ended on a troubling note—a promise of more terrible events to come. This time, unfortunately for the Apache way of life, the United States Army finally had the assets and troops available to make retribution viable.

NOTES - Chapter 8

1. Edwin Sweeney, *Cochise*, pp. 96, 97.
2. Steck to Garland, January 7, 1856, M1120, Roll 5.
3. Ibid.
4. Fort Fillmore Post Returns, January 1856.
5. Heitman, Benjamin Louis Eulalie Bonneville
6. Thrapp, *Encyclopedia*, p. 136.
7. Bonneville to Nichols, January 28, 1856, M1120, Roll 5.
8. Steck to Davis, February 13, 1856, Indian Bureau, Roll 2.
9. Bonneville to Nichols, January 25, 1856, M1120, Roll 5.
10. Miles to Nichols, April 26, 1856, M1120. Roll 5.
11. Sarah Ann Miles Marion, who wrote the lengthy letter in which these words were penned in 1901, must have been using letters written by Dixon Miles to refresh her memory. She was only a small child in the days when her father served at Fort Fillmore in the 1850s.
12. Steck to Davis, April 6, 1856, M1120, Roll 5.
13. Bonneville to Nichols, April 16, 1856, M1120, Roll 5.
14. McDowell to Garland, April 26, 1856, M1120, Roll 5.
15. Eaton to Grier, May 15, 1856, M1120, Roll 5.
16. Eaton to Nichols, May 31, 1856, M1120, Roll 5.
17. Gregory J.W. Urwin, *The United States Cavalry - An Illustrated History* (London: Blandford Press, 1983), p. 89. (Hereafter cited as Urwin, *United States Cavalry*.)
18. Ibid.
19. Heitman, William Wing Loring
20. Urwin, *The United States Cavalry*, p. 93.
21. Bonneville to Nichols, July 15, 1856, M1120, Roll 5.
22. Loring to Nichols, August 9, 1856, M1120, Roll 5.
23. Steck to Meriwether, August 12, 1856, Indian Bureau, Roll 2.

24. Lydia Spencer Lane, *I Married a Soldier* (Albuquerque, Horn & Wallace, 1964), pp. 45, 46. (Hereafter cited as Lane, *I Married a Soldier*.)

25. Heitman, Thomas Grimke Rhett.

26. Heitman, Alfred Gibbs.

27. Steck to Meriwether, September 12, 1856, Indian Bureau, Roll 2.

28. A Letter To "My Little Grandson Frederick," pp 16-27.

29. Loring to Nichols, October 4, 1856, M1120, Roll 5.

30. Morris to Nichols, October 9, 1856, M1120, Roll 5.

31. Fort Fillmore Post Returns, November 1856.

32. Kendrick to Nichols, November 22, 1856, M1120, Roll 5.

33. Steck to Meriwether, December 7, 1856, M1120, Roll 5.

34. Bonneville to Thomas, December 31, 1856, M1120, Roll 5.

R.M.R. in the Fight - 1857
by Loren Schmidt.

1st Dragroons
1851

Mounted
Rifiles
1853

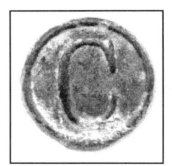

2nd Dragroons
1853

Dragoons
Unassigned

Horse Bridle Rosettes - Companies 'H,' 'C,' 'D,' and blank.
Courtesy: The Author.

9

1857 - THE BONNEVILLE EXPEDITION

As of January 3, 1857, the fate of Agent Henry Linn Dodge had still not been determined—it was over forty-five days since he went missing. Indian Agent Steck believed Dodge was dead and that Coyotero Apaches, on a revenge raid, had done the deed. There were still only the words of Indian spies as proof, but Michael Steck trusted those he sent out to gather information.

Lieutenant Colonel Dixon Miles returned briefly to Fort Fillmore in January 1857. While there he brought a number of matters to the attention of the temporary Department commander, Colonel Bonneville. Miles reported the results of a case against two Fort Fillmore enlisted men, in which there appears a mixture of both humor and tragedy in what transpired.

> ... The sentence of the Genl. Ct. Mt. of Privates Maley and Bertal of C. Co. 3rd If. spl. order No. 123 Novr 18 '51—forfeits all pay, clothing and allowances but confines the former two years and the latter one year when they are to be discharged—without further action of the Comdg. Genl. The officer commanding their company, may if he issues "the common necessary fatigue clothing" to be charged with the same; and it is absolutely necessary if kept in service that during their confinement some clothing should be given them.
>
> The case of Pvt. Maley is peculiar, and if testimony had been taken, particularly Dr. Cooper's, there would have appeared mitigating circumstances.He was charged with a violation of the 7th and 9th Art. of War and through ignorance made no defense and plead guilty. Two officers of his court

knew all the circumstances—which was, as informed by Asst. Surg. Cooper, as follows. It appears Maley more than once appealed to Lt. Whipple Comdg. his company for protection against the contumacious language of a Corpl. he [who] constantly used on all occasions the same approving term— "You damn son of a bitch." Maley on his last refusal by Lt. Whipple respectfully asked if he might lay his complaint before his Colonel [Bonneville] then in command of the post. This was granted and he presented himself to Col. Bonneville and stated his case. Who told him to go about his business nor would he listen. Maley then returned to his quarters and met the Corporal who called him again a son of a bitch for reporting him. Maley told the Corporal he had applied for redress and had been refused—he meant now to take the matter in his own hands and if he ever called him a son of a bitch again he would kill him. He went into his quarters, loaded his musket, and cap'd it. (Fortunately the cap was taken off by a soldier unobserved) and soon after this Corporal entered and the first salutation was "You damn son of a bitch." Maley sprang to his musket and snapped it at his breast.

These are all the facts—Maley before this bore the character of a good soldier, obedient, sober and attentive to his duty.

On the detail for the scout in May last he was released from confinement by Major, now Lt. Col. Morris, under his and Lt. Whipple's promise, that if he performed his duty faithfully the charges against him should be withdrawn. He served in my column and performed his duty so well that Lt. Whipple on his return did not revive the charges. But they were brought up subsequently by Bvt. Captain Gibbs of the Mounted Rifles, who temporarily fell in command of the Company and I acted on them before I knew all the circumstances. I now relate—The Corpl. I immediately brought to trial—he was found guilty and sentenced to be reprimanded by his Company Commander.

I bring this case before the Commanding Genl., that a mitigation of the sentence of Maley may be taken into consideration. If I was his Company Commander I should earnestly ask for his release.[1]

Private Maley's stand against the cruel comments of his squad corporal is a most interesting and clear example of daily life at Fort Fillmore, and the interactions of the soldiers there—proof that some conditions never really change, nor do people.

Captain Frederick H. Masten, Fort Fillmore Department Quartermaster and Commissary, was in deep trouble in early January 1857. Angry citizens wrote a letter of rebuke for Masten's conduct to the then Secretary of War Jefferson Davis on January 7. Citizens were not the only complainants. Even Masten's fellow officers turned against him, providing corroborative evidence of considerable official misconduct in his duties, charges that ended in Masten's resignation from the army less than a year later.

Another small village began to take shape in the Fort Fillmore protected region during early 1857. La Mesa was founded by several hundred farming people. An older name for the area was Victoria; one assumes the name was taken from the reigning British monarch. The name La Mesa came from a nearby lava flow called black mesa. Settlers had gradually moved into the region since 1854. Most were Hispanics, with a small mixture of Anglo European-Americans. The first post office was named Victoria, but the town was always locally known as La Mesa.[2]

The Dodge mystery was solved by late January. On January 30, at Fort Defiance, Major H.L. Kendrick was ordered to send two officers and forty men to recover Captain Dodge's body and to inter it at Fort Defiance. Apparently, Agent Dodge was killed very near the place of his capture.[3] Reaction to Dodge's murder was swift, once his fate was known. The first remarks concerning a possible expedition into the Gila River country to punish the perpetrators were included in a letter from Colonel Bonneville to Lieutenant Colonel Lorenzo Thomas in New York City on January 31, 1857. Bonneville stated there was no doubt that Captain Dodge had been killed by the Mogollon band of Apaches while he was out hunting, about a day's journey from Zuni Pueblo. Nine Pueblo Indians were killed at the same time and about twelve hundred head of sheep taken. Bonneville indicated he was preparing to take all available troops into the Mogollon country, and to remain until they accomplished their task.[4]

Regiment of Mounted Rifles Company 'G' began an active campaigning period out of Fort Fillmore in early February 1857. This was the result of the heightened tension following Dodge's death. No more sitting back and watching Indian raiders move through the region. On February 10, Captain Thomas Grimke Rhett reported the results of his first active response:

> ... In accordance with the order of the Commanding Officer of this post, dated February 5th 1857, I proceeded at daylight on the 7th with a command of twenty five men of my company to the vicinity of White's Ranch, on the road to Fort Bliss, to search for Indians, said to have fired upon two soldiers, riding express and to punish said Indians if I could overtake them.
>
> I struck a trail of three Indians, one man and two boys, about two miles the other side of White's Ranch and followed it to the mountains where it was lost on account of the rocky nature of the ground; I then returned to the river, having ridden over sixty miles that day, and next day, returned to this post.[5]

To facilitate Bonneville's planned campaign in the west, large stores were sent to Forts Thorn, Fillmore, and Bliss for the purpose of providing sustenance in the field. Fort Thorn received the most, being the military post closest to the region where the campaign was to take place. Fort Thorn received twenty thousand pounds of bacon, twelve hundred pounds of coffee, twenty-four hundred pounds of sugar, six hundred pounds of candles, twenty bushels of salt, five hundred pounds of ham, and two hundred gallons of vinegar. Fort Fillmore received three thousand pounds of bacon, one hundred and fifty pounds of ham, five hundred pounds of coffee, fifty gallons of vinegar, one hundred pounds of candles, twenty bushels of salt, and one thousand pounds of sugar. Fort Bliss received the same amount as Fort Fillmore. The supply shipments were to begin, if possible, in February.[6]

Dr. Michael Steck was concerned that innocent Apaches would be treated in the same fashion as the guilty if a large military expedition took the field. Brevet-Lieutenant Colonel Chandler's assault on Delgadito's peaceful village, which that officer may have known was inside a safe area, was a fearful precedent. The Apaches along the Mimbres, especially the bands of Cuchillo Negro, Mangas, and Delgadito, remained peaceful, trying to raise enough corn and other crops to survive with the help of Agent

Steck. They had even helped learn what happened to Agent Dodge. There were treaties between these bands and the United States. Would any of this matter when the armed troops reached their camps? Michael Steck was very worried about his charges.

Steck should have been worried. On February 17, orders were sent to Lieutenant Colonel Miles, then commanding at Fort Thorn. Miles was ordered to hire twenty-five or thirty local men as guides, interpreters, spies, packers, etc. to accompany a punishment expedition into the Gila River country. These men were to be familiar with the Florida and Burro Mountains, and the lands along the Gila River.[7]

On that same February 17 orders were sent to Major Enoch Steen, commanding the 1st Dragoon battalion near Tucson, to hire twenty to thirty men as guides, interpreters, trailers, packers, etc., for the upcoming expedition. Steen was to have whatever forces he could gather link up with the columns of Brevet-Colonel Loring and Lieutenant Colonel Miles. The Indians he hired were to be marked with a distinctive badge, so the troops would know they were friendly. That badge was a piece of red cloth, perhaps fastened in the hair. When seeing soldiers the friendlies were to call out, "Navajos! Acomas! Pinos!" to prevent mistakes.[8]

Three columns of troops converged on the Indian country—Lieutenant Colonel Miles from the south, Brevet-Colonel Loring from the north, and Major Steen from the west. Any and all Indians found by these troops were to be engaged as hostile unless they could identify themselves as working for the army. In this period of American history all Indians paid for the crimes of one.

Company 'G,' R.M.R., out hunting Apaches again on February 23, was sent to the village of Los Amoles, southwest of the fort. Brevet-Captain Alfred Gibbs led the column of mounted troops. They did not encounter Apache raiders during the foray and returned without incident.[9]

On February 24, former Fort Fillmore junior officers, Lieutenants Bonneau (at Fort Defiance) and McCook (at Santa Fe), took charge of the Navajo and Pueblo guides, trailers, and spies who would be assisting the American army during the Gila

Expedition, as the campaign was now being called. Each officer had up to one hundred men for these duties. In later days such Indian mercenaries were called scouts, but little else was different. In the war against the Apaches the army had no trouble hiring Navajo and Pueblo trackers and guides. Conversely, in 1858, when the first major conflict with the Navajos took place, there was no trouble gaining Apache assistance.[10]

The number of mules required by each post participating in the Gila Expedition was detailed in a March 7 letter. The most allocated were for Fort Union (R.M.R. staff & command, Companies 'A,' 'D,' and 'I'), a total of forty-nine pack mules; Albuquerque (Major Crittenden, Major Shepherd's command, 'C,' RMR, forty-nine pack mules; Fort Stanton, 'D,' 2d Artillery, twenty-one pack mules; Fort Bliss (Medical Officer, 'K,' RMR, 'B,' 8th Infantry and 'I,' 8th Infantry) forty-five pack mules; Fort Thorn (Colonel Miles, 3d Infantry, 'B,' RMR, 'F,' 3d Infantry) twenty-four pack mules and Fort Fillmore ('G,' RMR, 'C,'and 'K,' 3d Infantry) forty-two pack mules. This data also identifies all of the anticipated units in the southern and northern columns.[11]

The Mounted Rifles challenged the Apaches south of Fort Craig all the way to Fort Bliss in February and March. There was a fight at the Ojo del Muerto Springs on the Jornada between Company 'B' of the Mounted Rifles, stationed at Fort Craig, and the Mescalero. On March 17, a list of the casualties taken in the battle was provided. The detachment, under the command of Lieutenant Baker, R.M.R., encountered a party of Mescalero at sunrise on March 11, 1857. One man, Private Patrick Sullivan of Company 'B,' was shot in the back with an arrow and died; Sergeant Patrick Dugan was wounded in the left arm near the shoulder, also by an arrow; Corporal John Brady was hit in the right knee with a musket ball which shattered the knee; Bugler Thomas Reed was wounded in the right leg, and also on the upper part of the left clavicle near the neck; Reed's wounds were inflicted with arrows. Five horses were also wounded, three of them severely.[12]

During the first three months of 1857, nine Apache warriors, some from Mangas Coloradas's band, were killed by Mexican forces.

By the spring of 1857, Delgadito and fifty members of his group joined other Apaches living at Janos, abandoning their Mimbres River homeland. The coming American campaign drove the Apaches into Mexico in great numbers, although the incursions by troops had yet to begin.

Company 'G,' R.M.R., at Fort Fillmore, was again active in the field against raiding Apaches on March 8. This time there was a casualty of some importance. On the afternoon of the March 8, Brevet-Captain Alfred Gibbs led two corporals and fourteen men on a scout after Apache raiders near Robledo Campground, close to the future site of Fort Selden. Gibbs was severely wounded in the action that followed, a wound which could easily have caused his death. On March 11, 1857, from his place of confinement at Fort Fillmore, Alfred Gibbs documented what happened and how he came to be wounded:

> ... I have the honor to report that in obedience to instructions from your office at 2 ½ P.M. on the 8th Mar., I started from this post at 3 P.M. with two corporals and fourteen men [mounted] of Co. "G", Mounted Rifles, to proceed to Roblero [Robledo Campground], examine into the loss of certain animals by Mr. Garretson, Deputy Surveyor General of the Territory. And if circumstances should justify it, follow after and punish the robbers, and recover if possible the animals. I arrived at 7 P.M. at Roblero, distance marched 22 ½ miles. I camped there for the night, and at break of day next morning, with Messr's Garretson & Dickens as guides, started on the trail of the thieves, then twenty hours old. We followed it towards the Dona Ana Mountains for several miles, when it abruptly turned and crossed the Rio Grande about five miles above Roblero. From the crossing of the river, the trail was very difficult to follow, up and down steep hills and valleys, along the ridges of steep ravines, and over plains covered with flinty sharp stones, and scoriae. We were frequently compelled to dismount and lead our horses for miles at a time, and it required all the skill of the guides and the energy of the men in scattering to look for the trail, to enable us to follow it at a walk even. When the ground admitted we followed it at a smart trot. About eleven O'Clock, having marched about thirty five miles, we came to where the

Captain Alfred Gibbs
Courtesy: U.S. Army Military History Institute.

Indians had halted a few hours before to cook. There were seven of them; four mounted and three on foot. The immense size of the foot of one of the latter rendered this trail easily distinguishable from others, several of which, we passed. Our general course from the crossing of the river was about W. by S. towards "Cookes" Spring and "Tierra de los Mimbres". Resting an hour at this place, we pushed on more rapidly altho we feared the party had escaped us. At about half past 1 P.M. on ascending a little rise, we saw an Indian about fifty yards off coming to meet us, and at the same moment we saw the mules at the bottom of a little arroyo and six Indians looking at us and then beginning to run. The men were immediately dismounted and we commenced on them with rifles. As fast as the rifles were discharged, the men loaded and mounted, and followed at a gallop the Indians, who ran like wild turkeys. It was evident the game was up. Three were badly wounded though running still, and there was a mile before they could go to the mountains. The men were urged to be steady and to keep their revolvers to the last. As we rode on, the Chief who was badly wounded kept encouraging his men; whenever he did this they turned and charged us furiously. As I passed near him, he was making at one of our men on foot, whose horse had been shot, and I stopped and shot him a fifth shot with my revolver, he turned on me, and as my horse reared, he passed his lance into me, altho parried with my pistol. One of the men then brought him down.

Riding forward, about a quarter of a mile beyond, I came upon the rest of my party close up with the Indians, and the shot telling continually. Here becoming very faint from loss of blood, I dismounted to prevent falling off, and giving my horse to Corporal Collins, whose horse had been shot under him, directed him to keep up with the party, until he killed all the Indians, or until pursuit was hopeless, and then to rally and return to where his horse fell where he would find me. I found the Chief dead with ten balls in him, and the five men left in charge of the animals, reported that they had one horse, five mules, bows and arrows, knives, blankets etc. of the Indians. In about half an hour Corporal Collins returned with the party, and reported six Indians dead, and the other one severely wounded, had clambered on his hands and knees up the mountain abandoning his arms, and had fallen down behind a rock out of Rifle shot. They thought it useless to clamber up after him.

I have no doubt whatever but that the whole party were killed as the intense cold of the evening night, and the absence of water precluded his escape.

The seven animals captured were all those lost by Mr. Garretson. We camped where we were that night, sending in to this post forty five miles distant for assistance. At daylight next morning Asst. Surgeon Cooper with a carriage, rode into camp, and at retreat, with my whole party, with the wounded horses - three in number—and all the captured animals, arrived in safety at this post. Fortunately not a man was hurt, altho some had their clothes cut by lances and shot. This affair took place about two miles from the Eastern slope of the Sierra Mimbres, and about fifteen miles from Fort Thorn ... .[13]

On March 13, Major Gouveneur Morris, commanding Fort Fillmore, reported the wounding of Captain Alfred Gibbs to the Department of New Mexico, lauding Gibbs for his bravery. Second Lieutenant John Edson was sent to Fort Fillmore from Fort Craig to replace Gibbs in temporary command while the latter recovered in the Fort Fillmore hospital.

During late March and early April they prepared for the coming campaign. Much had to be done for such an arduous and hitherto untried adventure. For the first time, army forces throughout New Mexico Territory massed to maximize their power against a foe— in this case any Apaches found between Albuquerque and the modern Arizona border. Both mounted soldiers and infantry were to be used in a fashion which had long been discussed but never tried. As early as 1850 at Doña Ana, Major Enoch Steen had proposed such a combined arms effort.

On April 27, 2[d] Lieutenant John Henry Edson marched the main part of the garrison out of Fort Fillmore for Fort Thorn to link up with Lieutenant Colonel Dixon Stansbury Miles's Southern Column. Edson commanded up to forty-eight enlisted men of Company 'G,' Regiment of Mounted Rifles. He left behind one officer, the still-recuperating Brevet-Captain Alfred Gibbs, and twenty-three R.M.R. enlisted men.[14]

Second Lieutenant William Whipple, commanding portions of Companies 'C' and 'K,' 3[d] Infantry, left Fort Fillmore on the same mission as Edson with a combined force of one hundred and five enlisted men. Left behind were twenty-one enlisted men from those companies and no officers. The total left at Fort Fillmore on April 30, 1857, was the smallest number ever there—three officers, including Assistant Surgeon George Cooper, and forty-five enlisted men. First Lieutenant Frederick Myers, the new post quartermaster, also went with the column. Myers returned to Fort Fillmore with his train on May 3, having taken supplies to the Depot on the Gila.

The day the bulk of the troops left, Major Gouveneur Morris, who was not involved in the Gila Expedition, addressed the state of the garrison at Fort Fillmore after the troops left:

> ... I have the honor to represent to the Colonel Commanding the Department that after sending off duty men of each company on the Scout, agreeably to orders, there will not be sufficient men left to take care of the quarter master & commissary animals, and to guard this post, to say nothing of the men who will be required on extra duty to haul wood, water, and hay, and not a man left for express purposes should any be required for that duty. Under these circumstances I would respectfully suggest to the Colonel Commanding the Dept. to relieve the party detached from this post as a guard with the surveying party of the public land, and direct it return to its proper station. The surveyor is amply paid by the government for his work, and is no more entitled to a guard from the Army, than the mail, or other contractor in New Mexico.
>
> The following is a correct manuscript from the morning report of this morning, which shows the necessity of making this appeal.
>
> For duty, 2 Sergeants; 3 mus. & 5 Privates, extra and day duty, including hostlers, teamsters, butchers, bakers, Quarter Master & Com. & Sergts, cooks & attendants in hospital, on saddle and Blacksmith—20 Privates. Sick—one Sergeant and 15 Privates.[15]

Three important terms used to describe post life are defined in this letter. Regular duty often implied care of animals that belonged to the quartermaster and commissary departments, their wagons, and the storing and care of their products. Regular duty also included guard mount. Extra duty included hauling wood and hay, and making the mile trip to the river and back for water. Detached service was, as defined, any job that took the soldiers away from the post for any length of service as, in one case mentioned, serving as the infantry guard for the survey party or other such duty away from the post. Major Morris did not say whether cooks, bakers, hospital attendants, hostlers, teamsters, herders assistants, and blacksmiths were considered as regular or extra duty; one assumes possibly a little of both. Since there is no term given for what we might call a "special reaction force" dedicated to chasing Indians and other hostile factions, we must assume there was not one, nor was there much in the way of daily drill.

As the Fort Fillmore contingent arrived at Fort Thorn, they saw few peaceful Apaches at the nearby Apache Agency. Most of them had gone to Janos, Mexico, to treat with the Mexican government. Dr. Steck believed some of the Mimbres bands may have wanted to take up permanent residence in Mexico, believing the Mexican government would take better care of them than the United States government. Agent Steck stated that "The bad faith and ill treatment of our own people may also have actuated them. A few months ago two of their people were killed near this agency and about the same time many of their horses & mules were stolen by our own people." Agent Steck did not want to accompany the troops. He believed his friendly Mimbres bands would not return until the military had exited the country, and it would look bad if he was with the troops. Steck knew the Mimbres would return one day because the Government of Chihuahua had already repudiated the recent treaty between the town of Janos and the Mimbres Apaches. The Apaches could not remain in Mexico. There was only one place for them to go, back to the Mimbres and to his agency. Word came that Mexican troops were to be despatched to force the Apaches across the border into the path of Bonneville's converging forces.[16]

By May 12, Colonel Bonneville was on the trail from Santa Fe with his staff looking for a place from which he could centrally direct operations. Bonneville's goal was to find a suitable spot for a supply depot near the Gila River. By May 12 this had been done and his wagon train straggled into the new camp with their valuable supplies and sustenance. The main bodies of troops arrived later. The exact site of Bonneville's Depot on the Gila has been found on a bluff above the Gila River northwest of the present town of Silver City. Relics from there are sparse but include a number of horseshoes used by Captain Simonson's R.M.R. company who protected the Depot. Uniform buttons with the letters 'A,' 'D,' and 'R' have been found there, as well as large and small general service buttons from an overcoat. Ammunition finds are few but include both the .54 Caliber R.M.R. rifle round and Minie-ball ammunition for infantry weapons. A red-leg artillery unit serving as infantry was assigned as one of the units guarding the depot, accounting for the presence of artillery uniform buttons.[17]

Fort Bliss troops were in the field with the Southern Column. On May 15, one of the 8th Infantry companies, led by Lieutenant Thomas K. Jackson, camped southwest of the Bonneville Depot near the well-known Santa Lucia Springs (now Mangas Springs).

On May 20, 1857, Lieutenant Colonel Dixon Stansbury Miles reported on the first days of activity for the Southern Column. His command was then located on the Gila River at a point he called Camp Union. Miles explained, in detail for the benefit of Colonel Bonneville, the highlights of his journey to Camp Union and the actions taken until then. He did not clarify whether the Fort Fillmore troops joined his column before or after he left Fort Thorn on May 1. There was a four-day period between when the troops left Fort Fillmore and when Miles departed Fort Thorn. That left enough time for the Fort Fillmore troops to march to Fort Thorn, cross the Rio Grande at San Diego Crossing, and join Miles. Miles massed three hundred and ten soldiers in eight companies, five from the 3[d] and 8th Infantry regiments and three from the Regiment of Mounted Rifles. Company 'B' of the Mounted Rifles came from Fort Craig, and Company 'G' and Company 'K' (3[d] Infantry) from Fort Thorn. Second Lieutenant Edson led the Fort Fillmore contingent from Company 'G,' R.M.R. First Lieutenant

William Whipple commanded the infantrymen from Fort Fillmore, Companies 'C' and 'K.'[18]

Miles spent twenty days on the march to the Bonneville Depot and never saw an Indian while en route. Perhaps Indian Agent Steck could take a little of that blame. He alerted all of the Apaches in his area of control as to what was coming. Not being the uncaring attackers our movies would have us believe, the Apaches on the Mimbres and Gila left for cooler climes in Mexico. Their standard conduct, when threatened from either side of the border, was to cross to the other side and wait until the threat passed. No running in circles around wagons, Hollywood style, while their best warriors were picked off one by one. No head-on assault of an armed column of troops that outnumbered their small number of mature warriors. Mangas ran. Delgadito ran. They all ran, save one band, as we shall see. Only a few scattered warriors were left in the home country to light those mysterious fires which marked the route of Miles's column as it moved north. Those Apaches that dared remain heeded the warning of the fires. Miles saw nothing of them.

On May 21 Captain Claiborne, R.M.R., writing from the Depot on the Gila, reported on a mission against the Apaches which took place in conjunction with Whipple's infantry column from Fort Fillmore. Although once again the Apaches totally eluded them, Claiborne's troops found a trail estimated to have been made by five thousand sheep being driven to safety by the Apaches, one step ahead of the column. The column found the trail but they never saw the sheep or their Apache herders.[19]

Another long march with nothing to show for it save some sore feet and blisters. "As yet we have no Indians" was the opening comment in a report written by Colonel Bonneville on May 24. Bonneville's frustration was obvious. Both Colonel Loring (Northern Column) and Miles (Southern Column) had seen nothing but smoke on their journey to the Depot on the Gila, at least as far as Colonel Bonneville yet knew. He reported:

> ... As yet we have no Indians. I have waited this long before reporting—so as to give the result of our first twenty days scout.

Colonel Loring left Albuquerque on the 1st inst. with twenty days subsistence. The route given him was via Acoma [pueblo] & over the mountains & down the eastern waters of the Gila & to visit the San Mateo Mountains, laying nearly west of Fort Craig. Unluckily, Colonel Loring went west of the Mogollon Mountains & waters of the Gila—reached it for the first time on the 18th at the Depot. He was very anxious to get upon the eastern waters of the river, but his guides were either ignorant or would not.

He saw on his route nothing to evidence the presence of Indians—it is supposed they have taken their families west to the Coyoteros, & left only a few spies to watch our movements—four days before his arrival he detached Colonel Crittenden to visit the Almagre and Burro Mountains; he is just in, saw nothing.

Colonel Miles left Fort Thorn also on the 1st instant with twenty days subsistence. Took the trail of sixty-seven mules just stolen from a Mr. Mirindas; he came to the Depot on the 15th inst., having left the trail—his report is herewith. On the 17th I directed a four days reconnaissance in and about the Mogollon Mts etc., report enclosed. The trail they discovered was on the 21st taken up by Col. Loring with twenty days subsistence—determined to follow it to the end. Colonel Miles was also in chase, but took a route so as to fall on the trail by some cut off.

I suppose these sheep to be those of Montoya reported by Colonel Porter Comdg. Fort Craig, as stolen ... . The Depot is situated upon a low bluff, about 100 yards from the east bank of the Rio Gila. The country is intersected by mountains in every direction.

The Depot is under the command of Major Simonson R.M.R. [and[is conducted to my perfect satisfaction ... .[20]

On May 21 Miles again took to the field on the hunt for hostiles. He did not return to his camp near the Depot until May 30. On June 1, he gave a day-by-day accounting of what had transpired during the interval. His descriptions of the beautiful countryside are almost as true today as they were then, save for scattered human habitations that often interfere with an unspoiled view. Whatever Miles and his column saw on their journey, they did not see any Apaches. Not only that, but the few unseen Indians were still burning up the countryside wherever they proceeded. These fires warned Indians ahead of the column concerning the direction in which the column was heading. The soldiers's frustrations were building, especially when a chance meeting with a spearhead from the Northern (Colonel Loring's) Column, reported a heavy fight with Apaches only a short time before.

The sole purpose of Colonel Bonneville's Gila Expedition was to force the Apaches into battle and then to punish them all for the murder of Indian Agent Henry Linn Dodge. Until June 2, that mission had been a failure. On June 2, Colonel William Wing Loring described the details of the first Indian casualties of the campaign. Unfortunately, these came at the cost of peaceful Apache Chief Cuchillo Negro, who had always interfaced with the Americans through discussions rather than battle. The Apache leader and his people were simply at the wrong place at the wrong time. Cuchillo Negro may have believed he and his band to be true friends of the Americans. Loring's battle began on May 23. He may not have known exactly who Cuchillo Negro was, only that he was an Apache, one of the hunted. Loring explained:

> ... The canyon below was covered with timber on part of its sides. The atmosphere was smokey, so that objects could not be distinguished far away ... . The command was some distance down the hill before the Indians, who moved to be directly opposite, saw its approach. Up to this time the surprise was perfect. The camp proved to be the camp of Cuchillo Negro. Upon discovering the troops the Indians fled up the sides of the hill next to them, near 1500 feet high and very steep. A vigorous chase was at once made by those advancing upon them, followed as soon as possible by the others. In the attack I had evidence of six Indian men being killed and two badly wounded. Among those killed was the Chief Cuchillo Negro. One squaw is reported as having been accidently killed. Five squaws and four children were captured. All the camp equipment, a large quantity of packed meat, about 1000 sheep, several oxen and other animals.[21]

Cuchillo Negro was dead. Little remains of his memory and that of his people. By the 1870s, the Warm Springs Apache band to which he belonged was removed from its mountain and desert retreat near the Alamosa River in Sierra County and taken to Arizona. Two small memorials to Cuchillo Negro remain: a little village on the road to Winston, north of Truth or Consequences, called Cuchillo, and a smaller settlement north of Winston said to be named for him. Indian peoples no longer roam the land he once knew.

Lieutenant Whipple, commanding the infantry troops from Fort Fillmore, led a scout along the headwaters of the Gila River in early June. On June 8 he notified the adjutant of the Southern Column, 2ᵈ Lieutenant Henry Lazelle, as to a walking foray he and his troops made in the direction of the headwaters of the Gila River in late May and early June. Company 'C' had a major workout but saw no Apaches.

Dr. Steck was angry at Colonel Bonneville over rumors of the assault on Cuchillo Negro's village because he believed Bonneville did not care which Apaches he attacked—all were the same. He was pleased when Garland was, once again, in command of the Department, for he seemed to Dr. Steck to be more reasonable. The fear of attack and the deaths of their families forced most of the remaining Mimbres bands into Mexico. The Mimbres leaders twice sent messengers to Apache Agency to let Michael Steck know where they were, and to ask what they should do. Steck advised the Mimbres people to remain where they were until he notified them it was safe to return.[22]

The Southern Column, on June 13, headed toward the country of the Coyotero Apaches to the south, near the modern Arizona state border. On July 13 Miles documented his progress south toward what he hoped would, at last, be a major confrontation with the enemy. Colonel Bonneville accompanied the Miles column, although he did not take the field command for the coming fight. With Miles were troopers from Enoch Steen's Fort Buchanan dragoon force under the command of Richard Ewell. At last, the key elements that had always been needed to make war on the Apaches and succeed were in place—a mixed force of infantry and cavalry, along with a well-defined and operational supply system.

On June 13 Lieutenant Colonel Miles noted that his column marched only nine miles before camping at Sycamore Spring.[23] The next day the southern column marched ten miles, then camped on Dove Creek.[24]

At the Gila Depot on June 14, Lieutenant Laurens O'Bannon was in charge of the provisions. O'Bannon's list of the provisions on hand at the Depot gives a good idea of what Miles and his men might have eaten and used on the march down the Gila. On hand were four hundred pounds of ham, thirty-six thousand pounds of bacon, fifty-three thousand pounds of flour, one hundred and fourteen bushels of beans, twenty-four hundred pounds of rice, thirty-five hundred pounds of coffee, eighty-three hundred pounds of sugar, seven hundred gallons of vinegar, fourteen hundred pounds of candles, four hundred and forty pounds of soap, eighty-seven bushels of salt, ten gallons of pickles, two hundred gallons of sauerkraut, and eighteen head of beef cattle. The non-walking products were under canvas.[25]

Monday, June 15, the Southern Column marched sixteen miles. They crossed the Mogollon River running westward from the mountains, then moved on to the Rio San Francisco and crossed that before stopping for the night.[26] The next day the column remained in camp. Pack mules and horses had to be rested or they would break down and require long periods of recuperation before they could be used again.[27] On Wednesday, June 17, Miles took up the march again, trekking fourteen miles before camping at Patos, or Duck Creek.[28] Miles and his men marched nine miles in a generally westward course on June 18, arriving at Canyon Bonito. Here they connected with Colonel Loring's Northern Column. They appear not to have joined Loring's column, but rather made their first contacts with some of Loring's outlying elements.[29] On Friday, June 19, Miles marched another nine miles before camping. He made no mention this day of any of Loring's troops—the Southern Column must have passed through the Northern Column and continued on south to what may have been a pre-arranged destination.[30] Saturday, June 20, Miles marched nine more miles, the course of the march being south and southwest over rocky hills. They camped on the 'Negrita' River.[31] On Sunday, June 21, the animals had to be rested again and the troops remained in their camp. Miles believed he had arrived at the eastern frontier of the Coyotero Apache lands. Exploring troopers found extensive ruins, which Miles believed to be of Aztec origin; perhaps two hundred years or more earlier a population of thousands had lived near that camp site. Earlier he mentioned such sites as being part of a vanished civilization which the present Apache inhabitants could never duplicate.[32]

It is not clear as to where Loring's men were as Miles made his camp. He made no further mention of them after the comment of "linking up" on June 18. It is assumed they may have been waiting in camp themselves, perhaps for Miles to pass through and get to his general attack position south of Loring's column. As of June 21 the Northern Column prepared to move down the Gila River toward what is now the Arizona border. Colonel Loring gave his opinion to Bonneville on the best invasion route to take. He mentioned striking the Prieto River, where a known trail leading south could be found. The guides with the Northern Column were not as expert in this country as were the many serving with the Southern Column. Loring requested that two guides, Phillipe and Duran, be ordered to join his column, as they had better knowledge of the country than his current guides.[33]

On Tuesday, June 23, the Southern Column resumed their march. They marched fourteen miles that day, meeting other elements of Loring's main body, who were busy killing and drying broken down beef cattle for food. The two columns appeared to have camped quite close to each other that evening.[34]

The columns divided again the next day; Loring headed toward the northwest and the Prieto River, while Miles marched on a southerly route to again reach the Gila River as it wound its way toward Arizona. On June 24 the Southern Column marched only five miles and then camped in a ravine. On arriving at their campsite, guides reported that an Indian camp was discovered not far away. Miles sent out a scouting party, which he called a "light corps" of twenty men from infantry and dismounted R.M.R.

companies, along with forty mounted dragoons from Ewell's Fort Buchanan troops. All the officers were sent forward but 2ᵈ Lieutenant Edson, who maintained the rear guard with Company 'G,' Mounted Rifles from Fort Fillmore.[35]

On Thursday, June 25, an express from Ewell's dragoon force stated that his guides had captured nine Indian women; Miles called the Indian camp up ahead a barrio of the Coyotero Ranchero. Miles remained in camp and waited for further messages from Ewell which, when sent, reported that spies had discovered the Indians and for Miles to come on. Miles had to wait as it was too late in the day for him to safely climb the high mountains with his pack animals.[36]

The next day, Miles's infantry marched sixteen miles. Starting at daybreak, they marched across what he referred to as a mountain under a hot boiling sun. Captain Ewell, guided by captive Indians, moved westward toward what was believed to be the main Indian camp. The column camped at a water hole from which the surface water quickly ran out; they dug in the sand for enough water to supply needs for the night.[37]

On Saturday, June 27, the infantry marched some twenty-four miles, leaving camp about 1 p.m. At some time after four o'clock, following a tiring march over very rough country, Miles heard firing up ahead from Captain Richard Ewell's advance force contacting warriors in the Apache camp.[38] Ewell's force consisted of Lieutenants Moore, Chapman, and Davis with a detachment from the 1ˢᵗ Dragoons; Captain Claiborne and Lieutenant Dubois, with their R.M.R. detachment; Lieutenants Whipple and Steen with a battalion of the 3ᵈ Infantry Regiment; and Lieutenants Jackson, Cooke, and Lazelle with a battalion of the 8ᵗʰ Infantry Regiment. Lieutenant McCook was in charge of Mexican and Pueblo Indian spies and guides.[39]

Ewell later reported that the mountain his column approached (Mount Turnbull) was very rugged. To prevent surprise by any Apache force, the Pueblo Indians were kept to the front of the column under the command of Lieutenant McCook. The country became more level and the Pueblos soon discovered Indian signs, urging Ewell to "go on with my people." The dragoons hurried forward and soon came to an Apache Camp on the Gila River partly surrounded by thick brush. Lieutenant Moore led his horsemen through the village and across the river, taking up a position on the other side so as to cut off all Apache retreat.[40]

Lieutenants Whipple and Steen, in charge of the detachments from Companies 'C' and 'K' out of Fort Fillmore, deployed among the brush, moved forward, fighting the Indians as they advanced. The R.M.R. troops also dismounted and, fighting as infantry, moved into the brush as well. This force secured a number of prisoners. Lieutenant Steen, the son of Enoch Steen the commanding officer of Fort Buchanan, was struck by an arrow in the corner of the eye. Lieutenant Davis of the 1st Dragoons was shot in the knee in a personal encounter with an Apache. Corporal Anderson, Company 'G,' 1st Dragoons, was twice seriously wounded by an arrow and a bullet. The battle was quickly over, the surprised Apaches retiring from the field as fast as they could run.[41]

On July 13, 1857, reporting from a 'Camp Floyd,' Lieutenant Colonel Dixon Miles provided details about the battle.

> ... In making out the report on the battle with the Coyotero Apaches on the 27th of June past, I request you will refer to my journal accompanying this, to see in what manner the wings of the Southern Column were placed. The difficulty of the march in single file down a tremendous rocky precipice which extended the column to great length and which prevented the whole line from coming into action together.
>
> The Column was divided on this occasion into two wings. Altho [sic] commanding the whole I retained the command of the right, giving to Capt. Ewell, 1st Dragoons, that of the left. It was composed of "B," "G," & "K" Companies of 1st Dragoons, "C" and "F" Companies of 3rd Infantry. The guides and spies under Lt. McCook, 3rd Infy. (Being the Pueblo Indians and Capt. Blas Lucero's Mexicans) in advance. Capt. Ewell's report enclosed states in what manner the battle commenced. At that time you were riding beside me at the head of the right wing and at least a mile and a half from the battlefield, threading our way down a rocky bushy pathway,

followed by a squadron of the Mtd. Rifles under command of Capt. Claiborne and Lieut. Dubois, being in command of "B" and "K" Companies of that Regiment, and Lieut's. Jackson and Cooke commanding "B" and "I" Companies 8th Infantry. So soon as musketry was heard by us the order was given to gallop and the charge was made by all, you leading the van to the field of battle. When I arrived, which was not until after Lieut. Dubois had passed with his Company, my first object was to ascertain how the field laid, what the disposition of the troops [was] and how the enemy was placed. I soon found that Capt. Ewell under his heavy charge of dragoons had broken the Apaches. They had taken cover in the thick underwood and that it was the work of Infantry to pick them out. That the Dragoons were occupying the left bank of the Gila cutting off the retreat of the enemy to Mount Turnbull and that Capt. Claiborne and Lt. Dubois had very properly charged on the right bank and prevented them from reaching the mountains on that side. My object then was to bring into action as soon as possible the 8th Infantry and recrossed the river from where Lts. Whipple and Steen were engaged to give this order, but found to my great surprise that Lieut's. Jackson & Cooke with their Companies were already up and actively engaged in the place where they were most required. It was then a primary object to so regulate the firing that our troops should not injure each other which could easily be done, when all was so anxious to destroy an enemy in a narrow valley covered with a dense undergrowth of willow. When I crossed the river again I found Lieut. Steen had been driven out of the bushes by a volley from the Dragoons, and Lieut. Moore actively rallying his men to prevent their firing. When this was accomplished the infantry dashed into the thicket and soon captured many prisoners. Then frequent volleys showed that many a warrior was sent to his final rest.

The battle field extended for a mile on both sides of the Gila and [was] covered with a thick undergrowth. Persons within could readily see those outside but could not be seen within. This gave the enemy a great advantage and it is a miracle how so few of our officers and men, exposed as they were, escaped.

I suppose the battle commenced about ½ past 4 p.m. It lasted until near sun set, when we encamped on the field .... On the 28th June I ordered an officer with a detachment of soldiers to examine the battle field and count the dead. He found killed twenty warriors and four women. Two of these women were killed by Puebla Indians. One was killed while fighting with a bow and arrow, the other I presume was accidently shot, for at a short distance only, it is difficult to distinguish by dress the men from the women, so much are they alike.

Twenty six women and children were taken captive on the battle field. One woman was captured on the Francisco River, making 27 in all. All the camp utensils, clothing, etc. etc. were taken or destroyed. A captive woman informed me that there were forty warriors there when the battle commenced and she thought but three had escaped. On the 29th or 30th June, Col. Loring descending the Francisco captured a wounded Apache who informed him, that he was in the battle of the 27th. That there were forty warriors and but two had escaped. This corroboration of the same fact would seem to require I should report thirty seven or eight killed, but only twenty could be found ... .

The wounded are as follows: 2nd Lt. Davis, 1st Dragoons, in the knee. 2nd Lt. Steen in the corner of the right eye. Both of these wounds were made by arrows. Corpl. Henderson of "G" Co. 1st Dragoons, was wounded twice by bullet and arrow. Pvt. Donnelly of the same Co. was wounded, also Pvt. [?] of Co. "D" 1st Dragoons.

Sergt. Heron of Co. "K", 3d Infy. was wounded through the arm, also Pvts. Johnson & McNamara of "C" Comp. 3rd Infy. were wounded by arrows ... .[42]

Monday, June 29, the Southern Column broke camp, marched eighteen miles, moving east at first and then west again upon hearing of cornfields on a river thirty miles further west. Colonel Bonneville was with the Southern Column at that time.[43]

The next day the Southern Column marched sixteen miles down the Gila before turning northwest onto a trail that led over a high, rocky, barren plain to the Francisco River, which lay to the southwest of Mount Turnbull. Mexican and Pueblo Indian guides called this river Tularosa. Near this camp were extensive cornfields. Indians appeared bearing white flags and asking for peace. During these talks one Indian leader said "that our coming was an act of God's, in revenge for their many outrages and sins." This

Indian also said his nation held many captive Mexicans, which they wished to exchange for their women and children taken during the Gila battle. Bonneville told them to bring their chiefs and head men and he would talk of an exchange. He also told the Apaches he would destroy all their corn crops unless they acted quickly and came in.[44]

Friday, July 3, the Southern Column once again broke camp and marched twelve miles in the general direction of the Gila Depot, to which they intended returning. Scouting troops found the body of a missing Mexican packer who had been killed by the Apaches. Miles remembered him as being from Mesilla with a wife and two children. The column arrived at the Depot on the Gila River on July 12, not having encountered any other hostile force of Apaches.[45]

With Miles's troops back in camp on July 14, Colonel Bonneville acted on orders from Brevet-Brigadier General Garland to relieve Colonel Loring of the R.M.R. from duties with the Gila Expedition.[47] That same day Dixon Miles reported that five horses belonging to the 1st Dragoons had died during the recent campaign against the Coyotero Apaches; one horse had died from disease during the march, one was shot by accident, and three died from exhaustion. Three horses from Company 'B,' R.M.R., one horse from Company 'G,' R.M.R. and five horses from Company 'K,' R.M.R., also died during the campaign. Miles continued: "... these horses, except those named by Captain Ewell, were shot for giving out—10 of them on one night by Captain Claiborne." From these cryptic comments we learn how broken-down horses or mules were treated in that time. They were not freed when they could not go on, but were shot to prevent their use as work animals or food by any Apaches who happened to be in the area.[47]

In a letter to Colonel Bonneville, Miles stated that soldiers of Company 'C,' 3d Infantry, and Companies 'B' and 'I,' 8th Infantry, with few exceptions, were barefoot by the end of the campaign. Their shoes had fallen off their feet and there were no replacements at the Depot. The men had to walk back to their respective posts barefoot unless they adapted replacements. Some men resorted to the expedient of making cowhide sandals and moccasins, although many marched barefoot. The men of the Mounted Rifles were believed in a similar condition. The mules of the southern column were in such bad shape that many did not recover. The sores on their backs and sides sometimes reached to the bones. Miles believed this was the result of uncaring packers or defective pack saddles.[48]

After thirty-two days of campaigning in the field, the Northern Column, under Colonel Loring, arrived back at the Depot on the Gila on July 16 to learn they were ordered north immediately to Fort Defiance, where there was a growing problem with the Navajo. Loring wrote that he required fifteen or twenty days before taking the long journey because of the broken down condition of his horses—the result of their walking some seven hundred and fifty miles during the campaign. Procedures for dismantling the depot and marching the troops back to their far-flung bases began in earnest. The departure of all troops continued into the month of August.[49]

While Fort Fillmore troops engaged hostiles in Arizona, back at Fort Fillmore good news arrived for Major Gouveneur Morris, commanding the post. On June 30, 1857, orders from the War Department to Santa Fe notified the Department of New Mexico that Morris had been promoted Lieutenant Colonel in the 1st Infantry Regiment, upon the death of an officer named Bainbridge.[50]

On July 27 or 28, a strange caravan of wagons, up from Texas, passed through Fort Fillmore on the road to Albuquerque and then to Santa Fe. Their destination was California. Two years earlier on March 3, 1855, at the urging of Secretary of War Jefferson Davis, Congress appropriated $30,000 to import camels to the United States for testing in the southwest areas. Seventy-seven animals were eventually imported. Their base of training was Camp Verde, Texas. The mission that led these strange critters and their handlers into and past Fort Fillmore that July was designed to determine how sturdy camels would be in hauling goods across a dry southwest countryside. On June 19 Edward Fitzgerald Beale, a onetime friend of the famous Kit Carson, set out from Camp Verde with twenty-six of the best camels. These, he led up the San Antonio-El Paso Road that ran through Fort Davis and then on to Fort Bliss. No Fort Fillmore officer took note of their passing, even though their route allowed for a brief stop there before continuing on to the villages of Las Cruces and Doña Ana.[51]

The camels eventually completed the journey to California, but their utility and value received only lukewarm support in high places. It was General David Twiggs, Commander of the Department of Texas since the summer of 1851, whose adamant denials regarding the usefulness of camels helped end the experiment. Due to inaction in high places, the experiment simply fizzled out. Many of the animals were released to the wild where they were killed by Indians, hunters, etc. For years, strange animals were seen in the wild by travelers.[52]

The news spread quickly through Indian country that Bonneville was leaving the Gila River region. Cochise and his followers, having departed on Bonneville's approach, showed up at Janos in August. His warriors were a destabilizing influence on the Mexican Janos peace program. Edwin Sweeney, in *Cochise*, told of stories of poison rations being issued in an attempt to rid Mexico of the Chiricahua problem. These rumors caused Cochise and the other Apache leaders to take their bands back to the Chiricahua Mountains, the Gila, and the Mimbres.[53]

Major Gouveneur Morris departed Fort Fillmore for Texas and his new duties as commanding officer of the 1st Infantry Regiment on August 10, 1857. Orders sent Lieutenant Colonel Miles to Fort Fillmore once again, as Morris's replacement.[54]

Company 'C,' 3d Infantry, and Company 'G,' Mounted Rifles, escorted the Indian captives to Fort Fillmore. Miles temporarily detoured to Fort Thorn and then quickly left for Fort Fillmore. These changes proved to be a bad omen for the thirty-six Indian captives taken during the Bonneville Campaign, principally along the Arizona-New Mexico border. Had they gone to Fort Thorn directly, they would immediately have been with their fellow Apaches at Apache Agency. Now, the captives were destined for the adobe guardhouse at Fort Fillmore.[55]

Company 'C,' 3[d] Infantry, under the command of Lieutenant William Whipple, and Company 'G,' R.M.R., led by 2[d] Lieutenant John Henry Edson, returned to Fort Fillmore with their prisoners on August 16, 1857. They had been in the field since April 17. Both Whipple and Edson surrendered their commands upon reporting and were directed to other duties at other posts before the end of the month. No doubt fellow company mates gave the men of Companies 'C' and 'G' a hearty welcome back. The men of Company 'C' reported to 2[d] Lieutenant Henry 'K' Freedley, then commanding both Company 'C' and Company 'K,' Captain Sykes having gone on leave the day before. Company 'G' men were once more under the command of Captain Thomas Grimke Rhett, who, surprisingly, was not sent to the field with his men, even though he had returned from leave some time earlier.[56]

The captive Coyoteros were in poor condition when they arrived at the fort. They had marched in chains from the lower Gila River in Arizona to the Depot, and then from there on the long route to the post. Assistant Surgeon George Cooper was shocked by their ragged appearance and the potential for disease among them. His memorandum on August 18 described the captives, who were only women and children. He addressed his concerns to 1st Lieutenant Alfred Gibbs, still recovering from his lance wound and serving as adjutant. Gibbs forwarded the Doctor's letter to the Department of New Mexico.

> ... In consequence of the sickness existing amongst the Indian prisoners, women and children, who have today arrived at the post, caused in a great necessity by the close confinement in which they have been kept, I respectfully recommend that the irons now on them be taken off and that they be allowed to move about, outside of their quarters as much as possible consistent with their safe keeping.

They are entirely devoid of suitable covering, having not sufficient to hide their nakedness. I therefore [ask] that a blanket be furnished to each of the poorer Indians.

The rags upon them, all most disgustingly dirty and covered with vermin, tend to keep them in a great measure [unable to contend] with their change of manner in living, the [agues] and fevers of a typhoid character, as well as the purulent opthalmus from which they are now suffering.

Could it be done, I would recommend that each be furnished with a sufficiency of domestic to make clothing, in order that the rags now upon them may be burnt up. I would also recommend that they be compelled to wash themselves daily until the vermin, now covering them, be destroyed, and they become clean, as medicine will have but little effect upon them as long as they remain so disgustingly dirty.[57]

No doubt the soldiers arrived at the post in a like condition, barefoot, their field clothing ragged and in need of being discarded or replaced. The Depot on the Gila had been woefully inadequate in the number and types of available replacement equipment and clothing. During some campaigns the soldiers dressed in whatever civilian clothing was available, or in a mixture of civilian and military clothing. As noted from past correspondence, military replacement clothing was not only tightly controlled, it was parsimoniously handed out. The relatively small number of military buttons found at Fort Fillmore, below one thousand identified, points to a simple truth. The uniforms were exchanged, not thrown into any dump. In fact, the most common buttons found at Fort Fillmore are civilian, not military. Everything was rare in a society dependent on ox and mule train transport.

The mention of domestic cloth for use by the Indians indicates the military may have used shirts and other garments made of that same cloth when they could not attain suitable military uniforms. Wearing a uniform in the field on a long campaign, given their difficulty of acquisition, was perhaps asking for problems. Chances are better than even that Company 'C,' 3[d] Infantry and Company 'G,' Mounted Rifles, went to the field wearing a mixture of rugged clothing similar to that worn by Custer's troopers when they rode out to the Little Big Horn in 1876—broad-brimmed, locally made hats as protection from the sun and flannel shirts of a variety of patterns and colors. It is even possible they went into the field dressed in their very best Mexican War period short jackets and military pants. Many may have worn the ubiquitous Model 1839 Field Cap, again a Mexican War holdover, although no buttons from this cap were found at the Bonneville Depot. Few had boots, except the officers, and their low pattern shoes did not last.

No sooner had the troops returned than many of their prisoners broke out of confinement and escaped. One cannot be sure but what the escape of the Indian women and children was contrived out of sympathy by some of the very men who brought them back. Whatever the case, on the night of August 21, 1857, only six days after the return, and with their chains finally removed, twenty-two of the thirty-six broke out, or simply walked away, from their confinement. Captain Thomas Grimke Rhett commanded the post and he had to take the responsibility for the escape. In an August 24 report Rhett stated:

> ... I have the honor to request that you will inform the Commanding general, that on the night of the 21st August the guard over the Indian prisoners allowed twenty-two of them to escape. I was informed of the fact at ten minutes before 5 O'Clock in the morning, and before six, two parties were sent out, and somewhat later a third (two of them being mounted). The trail of some of them was found some two or three miles from the post, and followed on a gallop to the Organ Mountains, where it was lost, they having scattered and hid among the rocks. The second mounted party, also took a trail, and followed to the same range, and there lost it, the mountain at that point being scarcely ten miles from the post. There was a severe storm, the whole night, and under cover of it, they must have escaped some hours earlier, than was reported. Upon the arrival of the prisoners at this post, and on recommendation of the Assistant Surgeon, their chains were stricken off, because the whole of them were suffering from fever and diarrhea. They were assigned to a room where the windows were barred, and locks and chains put on the doors, and in the next room with a door between, was placed, an Acting Non-Commissioned

Officer, and three men as a guard, with orders to lock them up during the night. And that the other portion of the guard should attend them when necessary for them to go out during the day, the sentinel remaining at his post. It seems that on the night in question that the sentinel allowed some twenty six, or more, women and children to go out to the rear together, without informing the Acting Corporal, or the rest of the guard. And afterwards reported to the Corporal that he believed all the prisoners were gone. Two boys and an old woman were retaken within some fifty yards. The rest have not been recovered, but are supposed to have gone up the range of mountains towards the San Nicholas Springs, where a large band of the Fort Stanton Apaches were encamped. The want of sufficient numbers of horses and men prevented my sending a party to that point. Two of the Indian women have died since reaching the post and the remainder are all sick.[58]

At least as important as the escape is the fact that from August 16 to August 24 two of the Coyotero women died. Many of the others, including the escapees, were very ill. This sad incident involving the Apache women and children captives was the low point in the history of Fort Fillmore's relations with the Apaches. The situation among the Indian prisoners, as of September 5, was deteriorating, and included further deaths. This time it was Lieutenant Colonel Miles who provided details on their condition.

> ... I have the honor to report the death of an Indian captive child on the 3rd Inst. Day before yesterday a herder reported he found in the hills east of this post, the dead body of an Indian woman, doubtless one of those that escaped from here last month.
>
> There is now in confinement here, three women, all helplessly sick, two very old. The other a young woman, the daughter of the Chief of the Coyoteros. One boy 12 years old and eight little children all sick but the boy he having just recovered. A more pitiable sight could not be seen than these captives and humanity requires, that their sufferings and condition be alleviated, beyond the power or authority vested in me.
>
> I would recommend that these captives (children) be distributed or given to anyone who would take them, the women and boys turned over to the Indian Department.[59]

On September 20, Indian Agent Dr. Michael Steck received a letter from Superintendent James Collins, stating the remaining Coyotero Apache prisoners were to be placed in Dr. Steck's care. Steck had recently returned from a six-day visit to the Mescaleros at Fort Stanton. By September 28, Miles had his solution to the problem of the Apache women and children captives remaining at Fort Fillmore, but not before another death took place. He sent nine captives to Fort Thorn, but did not say how he had disposed of the eight or nine who died, nor whether the young daughter of the Coyotero chief was among either group. The last Apache to die at Fort Fillmore was a child, who died on September 20.[60]

Chino Penio, a high chief of the Coyotero Apaches who promised to return to Apache Agency to sue for peace and regain Coyotero prisoners taken by Colonel Bonneville's troopers, arrived on September 29. He brought several chiefs and sub-chiefs with him. Dr. Steck warned the Coyoteros that they must live in peace and it was the policy of the U.S. Government not to injure them but to do them good. The remaining prisoners arrived from Fort Fillmore in time to be turned over to the chiefs. Of the forty-two prisoners brought to Fort Thorn in July, only nine remained to be delivered to their friends. Some escaped and as many as fifteen died from diseases contracted in confinement. The surviving nine had fevers and diarrhea when turned over. Dr. Steck thought it best that these latter leave for the Coyotero country at once.[61]

Orders generated on October 5 at Santa Fe transferred Company 'G,' R.M.R., from Fort Fillmore to Fort Union. The peaceful and slow days of post activity returned now that campaigning was at an end. Lieutenant Colonel Miles, accompanied by his son-in-law 1st Lieutenant Laurens O'Bannon, left Fort Fillmore in October for the headquarters of the 3d Infantry at Santa Fe. Miles eventually returned but O'Bannon, the regimental quartermaster and commissary, did not. After years of service in and around Fort Fillmore since 1850, Lieutenant O'Bannon said goodbye to the area for the last time. Captain Thomas Rhett, Brevet-Captain Alfred Gibbs, and the rest of Company 'G,' R.M.R., left Fort Fillmore for Fort Union as per the orders generated on October 5.

Gibbs and Rhett later returned to Fort Fillmore, but under completely different circumstances. Rhett eventually became Department Paymaster, while Gibbs did not return until July 1861, when he arrived in time to participate in the ignoble surrender of Isaac Lynde's troops at San Augustine Springs. Because the order denuded the fort of its mounted command, and Captain Sykes of Company 'K' was still on leave, command of Fort Fillmore fell upon the shoulders of lowly 2^d Lieutenant Henry Freedley, who now commanded 'C' and 'K,' 3^d Infantry, and the post. Captain Frederick Myers and Assistant Surgeon George Cooper were present, but they were not line or command officers, Myers served as quartermaster and Cooper was in charge of the hospital. One hundred and nineteen enlisted men were present for duty. How did Freedley feel about his new assignment? This must have been a signal honor to a twenty-five-year-old man.[62]

Indian Agent Steck, then at Apache Agency, confirmed in a November 21, 1857, letter that he received word from Mangas Coloradas in Janos that the latter wanted to return to the Santa Rita area and was suing for peace. Mangas told of the terrible sickness among the Apaches in Janos and that he believed they were being poisoned. Steck believed the poison may have been administered through whiskey or even through their rations. Mangas reported the number of sick among his people at about sixty.[63]

On December 8, President James Buchanan addressed the question of a Territorial status for Arizona in his First Annual Message:

> ... I recommend to Congress the establishment of a Territorial government over Arizona, incorporating with it such portions of New Mexico as they may deem expedient . [It is no wonder the Mesilla secessionists could form a government without it being put down by force.] We are bound to protect the lives and property of our citizens inhabiting Arizona, and these are now without any efficient protection. Their number is already considerable, and is rapidly increasing, notwithstanding the disadvantages under which they labor. Besides, the proposed Territory is believed to be rich in mineral and agricultural resources, especially in silver and copper. The mails of the

United States to California are now carried over it throughout its whole extent, and this route is known to be the nearest and believed to be the best in the Pacific. [64]

Buchanan was speaking of the miners at Pinos Altos and the Santa Rita Copper Mines, as well as communities farther west. At this time the intent was to place New Mexico lands west of the Rio Grande in the new Arizona Territory. The present-day boundaries were a result of conditions which arose during the American Civil War.

Second Lieutenant John McLean Hildt arrived at Fort Fillmore for duty on December 14, 1857. Hildt was assigned to Company 'C' but also served briefly as post adjutant. An 1856 graduate of West Point, Pennsylvanian Hildt was only twenty-one when he arrived at the post. He was commissioned a brevet-2[d] lieutenant in the 6th Infantry on July 1, 1856, and as quickly transferred to the 1st Infantry in Texas on October 31. Somehow, perhaps without ever reporting to his Texas assignment, Hildt was transferred to the 3[d] Infantry on February 13, 1857.[65]

First Lieutenant John Alley reported for duty for a second time at Fort Fillmore near the end of the year and took command of Company 'C.' An 1850 West Point graduate, Alley was supposed to be assigned to Fort Fillmore when the post was established in September 1851. Just before his arrival he effected a trade with another officer that sent him to Company 'B,' 3[d] Infantry, then going to Fort Conrad from Doña Ana. Alley, born in Maine in 1827, was thirty years old and a 1st lieutenant as of December 31, 1856. His was a strange career. He was involved in the surrender of the 3[d] Infantry Regiment in Texas in early 1861. He was a Confederate prisoner of war for over two years, being promoted to the rank of captain on May 14, 1861, while a prisoner of war. What happened to Alley after his capture was one of the stranger stories of the war. The Union Army forgot that he was a prisoner and, while other 3[d] Infantry officers were quickly paroled, Alley remained a prisoner in San Antonio until 1862. When he was finally remem-bered and a parole attained, Captain Alley made no attempt to reach the States. Instead, he went to Denver where he was assigned to handle recruits. Then he simply walked away and disappeared—perhaps as the result of his treatment by the Regular Army when in Texas.[66]

NOTES - Chapter 9

1. Miles to Nichols, January 4, 1857, M1120, Roll 6.
2. T.M. Pierce, *New Mexico Place Names: A Geographical Dictionary* (Albuquerque: University of New Mexico, 1965), p. 83.
3. Nichols to Kendrick, January 30, 1857, M1012, Roll 2.
4. Bonneville to Thomas, January 31, 1857, M1120, Roll 6.
5. Rhett to Whipple, February 10, 1857, M1120, Roll 6.
6. Grayson to Schroeder, February 10, 1857, M1120, Roll 6.
7. Nichols to Miles, February 17, 1857, M1012, Roll 2.
8. Nichols to Steen, February 17, 1857, M1012 Roll 2.
9. Gibbs to Whipple, February 23, 1857, M1120, Roll 6.
10. Nichols to Kendrick, February 24, 1857, M1012, Roll 6.
11. Nichols to all commands, March 7, 1857, M1012, Roll 6.
12. Lieutenant L. Baker report, March 11, 1857, M1120, Roll 6.
13. Gibbs to Whipple, March 11, 1857, M1120, Roll 6.
14. Fort Fillmore Post Returns, April 1857.
15. Morris to Nichols, April 27, 1857, M1120, Roll 6.
16. Steck to Acting Governor Davis, May 6, 1857, Indian Bureau, Roll 3.
17. Bonneville to Nichols, May 12, 1857, M1120, Roll 6.
18. Miles to Bonneville, May 20, 1857, M1120, Roll 6.
19. Claiborne to Lazelle, May 21, 1857, M1120, Roll 6.
20. Bonneville to Nichols, May 24, 1857, M1120, Roll 6.
21. Loring to Bonneville, June 3, 1857, M1120, Roll 6.
22. Steck to Collins, June 8, 1857, Indian Bureau, Roll 3.
23. Miles to Bonneville, July 13, 1857, M1120, Roll 6.
24. Ibid.
25. O'Bannon Report, June 14, 1857, M1120, Roll 6.
26. Miles to Bonneville, July 13, 1857, M1120, Roll 6.
27. Ibid.
28. Ibid.
29. Ibid.

30. Ibid.

31. Ibid.

32. Ibid.

33. Loring to Bonneville, June 21, 1857, M1120, Roll 6.

34. Miles to Bonneville, July 13, 1857, M1120, Roll 6.

35. Ibid.

36. Ibid.

37. Ibid.

38. Ibid.

39. Ewell to Miles, July 13, 1857, M1120, Roll 6.

40. Ibid.

41. Ibid.

42. Miles to Nichols, July 13, 1857, M1120, Roll 6.

43. Ibid.

44. Ibid.

45. Miles to Nichols, July 13, 1857, M1120, Roll 6.

46. Bonneville to Nichols, July 12, 1857, M1120, Roll 6.

47. Miles to Nichols, July 14, 1857, M1120, Roll 6.

48. Miles to Bonneville, July 14, 1857, M1120, Roll 6.

49. Loring to Nichols, July 16, 1857, M1120, Roll 6.

50. Floyd to Morris, June 30, 1857, M1120, Roll 6.

51. Odie B. Faulk, *The U.S. Camel Corps - An Army Experiment*. (New York: Oxford University Press, 1976), p. 106.

52. Ibid.

53. Edwin Sweeney, *Cochise*, p. 106, 107.

54. Fort Fillmore Post Return, August 1857.

55. Ibid.

56. Ibid.

57. Cooper to Gibbs, August 18, 1857, M1120, Roll 6.

58. Whipple to Nichols, August 19, 1857, M1120, Roll 6.

59. Miles to Nichols, September 5, 1857, M1120, Roll 6.

60. Miles to Nichols, September 28, 1857, M1120, Roll 6.

61. Steck to Collins, October 2, 1857, Indian Bureau, Roll 3.

62. Freedley to Nichols, November 4, 1857, M1120, Roll 6.

63 Edwin Sweeney, *Cochise*, pp. 108, 109.

64. James D. Richardson, *Messages and Papers of the Presidents*, p. 2987.

65. Heitman, John McLean Hildt.

66. Heitman, John Alley.

Fort Fillmore - Regiment of Mounted Rifles button.

Fort Fillmore - Late 1850s General Service Enlisted button.

Fort Fillmore - Model 1839 Forage Cap button.

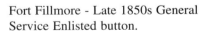

Photos Courtesy: Gernomino Springs Museum

10

1858 - THE NAVAJO CAMPAIGN

Changes were made in the armaments situation as 1858 opened. New and more effective weapons were soon in the hands of troops. On January 9, 1858, the ordnance office in Washington described the type and numbers of weapons, ammunition, slings, cap pouches, belts, and plates, etc., being sent to New Mexico for the year 1858. The most destructive weapon in American history up to that time, the range-lethal .58 caliber elongated Minie-ball-firing rifle/musket, was about to be sent to the Territory in large numbers. Although available since 1855, it was just beginning to make an appearance in New Mexico. So much more effective were these weapons than the former .69 caliber smoothbore muskets, that the new arm had a similar impact on the American Civil War as did the machine gun in WWI, and the tank in WWII.

These new weapons would not to be in the hands of the New Mexico troops for the upcoming conflict with the Navajo tribe. A few of the rifle-muskets were in the Territory by late in the year, but the majority of the conflict was fought with the old smooth-bore .69 caliber muskets.

Eleven hundred .58 caliber rifle-muskets were prepared for shipping. As the year opened, the ten infantry companies comprising the 3^d Infantry Regiment required almost nine hundred of these. The rest were probably placed in storage. The Regiment of Mounted Rifles could have used this weapon, but the abundance of .54 caliber Minie balls found at Fort Fillmore and at the Bonneville Depot site testify to the presence of the Model 1844 rifle. In addition, .52 caliber Sharps carbine rounds are known from ammunition finds at Fort Fillmore, as well as the Depot on the Gila. Hence, one assumes that dragoon and Mounted Rifle needs were not part of this arms and equipment package.

This data also implies that when the 3^d Infantry transferred to Texas in 1860, they went fully equipped with these lethal .58 caliber weapons, only to surrender some of them to Confederate Texans without a fight in 1861.

On January 18 the new Territorial governor, Abraham Rencher, transmitted a Resolution of the Territorial Legislature to Colonel Bonneville and the officers of the Department of New Mexico who had participated in the recent Gila Expedition, thanking them for their actions.

Therefore be it Resolved

1st That the thanks of the Legislature of New Mexico be hereby tendered to Colonel B.L.E. Bonneville 3rd U.S. Infantry, the Commander of the late Gila Expedition against the several Tribes of Mimbres, Gila and Coyotero Apache Indians, and through him to the brave officers and soldiers he had the honor to command, for their zeal, intelligence, and fortitude, in accomplishing the successful results of the expedition in the midst of so many privations and dangers.

2nd That the Governor of the Territory be requested to transmit a copy of the foregoing to the Hon. Secretary of War, the General Commanding in Chief the Army, and to the Commanding Officer of the Department of New Mexico, and to Colonel B.L.E. Bonneville 3d. U.S. Infantry.[1]

Apaches were rumored to be back in the Mesilla Valley, or at least the thieves among them were, early in the year. On January 23, several mules were stolen from Don Pedro DeGuerre near Doña Ana. The thieves were supposed to be Indians but Dr. Steck believed the animals may have been taken by Mexicans. Having no mounted troops to respond to depredations, the infantry were sent forth to chase Apache, Mexican, or American thieves and murderers no matter how ineffective they were without mounted support. On February 8, 1st Lieutenant John Alley wrote his second in command of Company 'C,' 2ᵈ Lieutenant John McLean Hildt, a formal letter. That letter makes one of the few known references to the small Indian settlement of Tortugas not far from Fort Fillmore. This letter also mentions a group of Mexican men from Mesilla who called themselves the 'Mesilla Guard.' This informal militia organization's growing reputation was about to make its name a watchword for violence in Doña Ana County. Alley reported an attack on an Apache camp near the village of Doña Ana by the Mesilla Guard:

> ... I respectfully report that in obedience to the instructions of the Comdg. Officer, I this day proceeded to Dona Ana and Mesilla, making diligent inquiries from all available sources with the view of informing myself as to the correctness of certain reports which called forth the order under which I acted, having reference to alleged outrages committed by Mexicans upon the Mescalero Apaches, living in terms of amity with the residents of the former place. At the little settlement of <u>Tortugas</u> about 4 miles from this post, and nearly opposite Mesilla I was informed that the Indians had passed on Saturday night with animals stolen from that vicinity. In Las Cruces I could gather no other information respecting the subject other than that inducing me to believe that the perpetration of the alleged outrage were actuated by wantoness. The people of Donna Ana [sic] with whom I had occasion to make enquires concerning the matter asserted that certain people from Mesilla came into the town in a [cruel] and wanton manner, and without warning commenced an indiscriminate attack upon the Indians, killing and wounding them, even after they had taken refuge in the houses of certain citizens. It was related to me that the Mexicans had pursued the trail of the Indians to a camp about 3 miles from Don Ana [sic], where some of the tribe were living, and after killing three Indians came into the town in a condition of semi intoxication, following women and children, who were fleeing there for protection. It seems to be a subject of complaint from the people of Dona Ana, that the peace of the town should be thus violated. Some of the Indians had endeavored to conceal themselves in the house of a Mexican, who with his son and wife, with arms, successfully forbade the entrance of the party; the Chief of which upon being so reported, summoned the protector of the

Indians to appear with them at a certain hour in Mesilla which summons they did not obey. I saw 2 women, one a very old one, both badly wounded, and was told that the bodies of 3 women, most horribly mutilated by the Mexicans, were buried today.

From the best sources of information I could obtain, I gather that this Mexican band is held in high esteem by the people of Mesilla, a party seems to be constantly held in readiness, to punish Indians, retake stolen property from them, and when not employed on active service of this nature, enjoying certain civil privileges in that town, they are known as the Mesilla "Guard."

I believe as the result of my inquiries that 8 or 9 Indians, principally women were killed, 2 women wounded, and one child taken captive and carried to Mesilla. I would also add that it seems the Mescaleros are a portion of the tribe, at least, are permitted by the Indians Agent, to come into and linger about Don Ana [sic].[2]

Vigilantes or militia, the Mesilla Guard must have been condoned by at least the Mexican people of Mesilla, and perhaps Territorial authorities as well, as a contemporary rapid reaction force. This all-Mexican unit responded to Indian thefts mainly through the killing of Indian women, children, and the aged—the vulnerable Apaches were easy to kill. What seems troubling is the complacent attitude of 1st Lieutenant Alley to the slaughter. He appears annoyed that it happened, but made no attempt to hunt down and deal with the murderers, nor to recover the child taken to Mesilla.

On February 9 Miles addressed an angry letter to the civilian Prefect of Doña Ana County, whose offices were in Mesilla, concerning the Doña Ana massacre. Miles said:

... I have understood that some of the people of your town on Sunday last killed one Mescalero Apache and eight women and children of that Tribe and also took a child captive which is now in Mesilla. This act whether right or wrong you must be sensible will excite the whole Apache Nation to revenge and a bloody retribution, to avoid it if possible. I shall endeavor for the sake of the innocent who will be the sufferers, to make every exertion to pacify the Indians by asking them to let [us] settle the matter.

But it is incumbent for you to take an active part and have the captive child returned to its parents or relatives in the first place, and such other course as your sense of duty prompts.

I see signal fires in every direction doubtless to collect the Indians: it would be well for you to warn the inhabitants of the impending storm that apparently will break soon over them, and guard with watchful care, their flocks and themselves. At any alarm of danger, I will come to your assistance with whatever troops I can spare from this fort. You know I have but two <u>foot companies</u> and shall not be able to make pursuit. I can defend but cannot pursue with any probability of success in overtaking.[3]

Miles' letter must have stirred panic in Mesilla, especially his warning that the Apaches usually took revenge for such acts. There was bias as well. Miles clearly pointed out that Mexicans and Americans were considered part of the United States. Apaches were not. He did not send for the aggrieved Apaches from Doña Ana and tell them he would send his infantry to protect them from Mesilla Guard attacks. Nothing came of these complaints. The Mesilla Guard's day was yet to come.

On March 3 Miles was informed the Indians had erected a rack of skulls and bones on the outskirts of Mesilla, a warning to the townspeople of what was going to happen to them for what they had done to the Doña Ana Apaches. A party of Mesilla citizens had gone out a few days before chasing Indians suspected of stealing cattle. They found the cattle and killed some Indians. On the return journey to Mesilla, seven of the party went missing and did not return to the town. It was supposed the citizens had been killed. Fear was rife among the Mesilla citizenry that the rumored skull rack was their bones.[4]

Miles notified the Department of New Mexico of the growing trouble. He told of receiving a communication requesting federal troops to defend Mesilla if necessary. Miles also mentioned the Mesilla Guard and its growing use against the Apaches:

... I have the honor to enclose the following communication from the Alcalde of Mesilla and Mr. Bull of the same place on yesterday. I replied that "I could not on the vague report of

"Skulls & bones" being erected in their neighborhood order troops to that town. Before my communication left a third express arrived, stating the seven absent men had been found. That two Indians had been killed and many horses & mules had been captured by the Indians.

The people of Mesilla have raised and maintain a volunteer company of Mexicans. This company carries on war against all Indians wherever met, and it seems by extending its sphere of action have penetrated as far as the Mimbres and attacked the Indians peaceably living there, despoiling them in their recent foray, of horses, etc. on the pretense of having had cattle stolen. Should this independent action of the inhabitants of Mesilla continue, the Indians will to a certainty unite and carry out their threat, as reported, by erection of "skull & bones", by wiping this town out.[5]

Miles had more sympathy with the Apache cause than with the vigilante-type Mesilla Guard who raided Indian camps as far away as the Mimbres River. Perhaps because of Miles's failure to react to their need for assistance, a rumor began in Mesilla and spread to Doña Ana and Las Cruces that Fort Fillmore was about to be closed. The townsmen of Mesilla responded to the rumor of a Fort Fillmore closure on March 24, 1858, by petitioning Brevet-Brigadier General John Garland. The petition was signed by hundreds of Mesilla residents. In truth, there seemed no purpose to the post now that Forts Bliss, Stanton, Thorn, and Craig protected the more critical Indian haunts.[6]

First Lieutenant John Alley returned to Fort Fillmore from Fort Buchanan in April. Paymaster-Major Brice was expected soon to pay the troops. Alley brought word of a problem with coordinating mail from Fort Fillmore to Fort Buchanan along the San Antonio-San Diego Mail Line, the only postal system available until the Butterfield Overland Mail Route came into operation later in the year. Lieutenant Colonel Miles notified the Department adjutant, Major Nichols, that the San Antonio-San Diego mail stage arrived at Fort Fillmore on the fourth or fifth of each month, and passed on immediately to points west. The problem was that the Santa Fe mail usually failed to arrive before the seventh of the month and, therefore, had to be held at Fort Fillmore until the next month. Miles was not concerned about civilian mail being late. He was concerned that dispatches to Fort Buchanan from the Department were being delayed for almost a month each time. Miles asked that the Postmaster at Santa Fe compel the carriers of the San Antonio-San Diego mail to delay at Fort Fillmore until the Santa Fe mail arrived.[7]

Just when the Apache-Mexican problems seemed to be settling down following the early February attack on the Apache camp at Doña Ana, the Mesilla Guard struck again, this time at Apache Agency near Fort Thorn. On April 17, thirty-six members of the Guard attacked what were obviously peaceful Apaches under the care and supervision of Agent Steck. The attack resulted in the death of seven Apaches, three men, three women, and one boy. This time, however, there was an immediate response from the nearby Fort Thorn military garrison. The commanding officer at Fort Thorn, 1st Lieutenant William H. Wood, reported the massacre of the Apaches to the Department of New Mexico, providing all pertinent details, including the fact that troops from the fort captured all thirty-six of the Mexican raiders soon after.

> ... I have the honor to report for the information of the Genl. Comdg. the Dept., that this morning about daybreak, a party of armed Mexicans, from Mesilla, charged into the Indian camp at the Indian Agency near this place, and butchered indiscriminately men, women, and children.
>
> Immediately on ascertaining what was going on , I ordered the garrison under arms while the Rifles were saddling up, went out with the Infantry and succeeded in capturing the whole party about ½ mile from the Post, as they were retreating with a number of little children whom they had made captive. In a few minutes, Lieut. Howland, with as many of his men, as he had been able, in the great hurry, to mount, came up; all the prisoners, thirty six in number including their leader, one Juan Ortega, were marched into garrison, disarmed and placed under a strong guard, where they still remain.
>
> After disposing of the prisoners, a party was sent out to collect the dead bodies. They soon returned bringing in seven, three men, three women, and one boy, all of whom were [buried]

in rear of our burying ground. Three of the women, two men, and one boy have been placed in hospital.

Upon the first alarm the Indians flew in every direction, seeking shelter and protection. Mr. Tully at the Indian Agency, Mr. Beck living on the Island, and another American living at the ranch, each were fortunate enough to save a number of lives. As some of the Indians were [thrown] into the river bottom, where they had fled to hide among the trees, it is feared that a number were killed, whose bones have not yet been found. Parties are still out in search.

This affair is but a repetition of the horrible massacre recently perpetrated at Dona Ana. To show the temerity with which they acted I have only to state that one of the women was [shot] and killed within 500 yards of the Fort, to which place she was evidently running for protection.

These Indians, for the last four or five months, have been at peace and on friendly terms with all in this vicinity, have been daily in and about this garrison, quiet and well behaved, and sincerely believe have given no cause for this cowardly outrage. It is moreover extremely unfortunate that this affair has recurred at the present time, as their Agent, Dr. Steck, to whom they quite ready [obey], is temporarily absent on business connected with his agency. [8]

The arms and weapons taken from the Mesilla Guard were listed on April 17, the day of the massacre. Wood provided some details—thirty-six horses, bridles, and saddles, thirty-five rifles, fourteen Colt Revolvers, and six common pistols.[9]

Only six days after the massacre at Apache Agency, on April 23, a United States Judge in Santa Fe, Kirby Benedick, wrote the commanding officer at Fort Thorn concerning the progress of the case against the thirty-six Mexicans. A Lieutenant Craig acted for the United States Army and placed charges before Benedick related to the fate of the Mesilla men. The Mesillans were taken to Socorro, in the County of Socorro, for examination. The sheriff of Socorro County was to travel to Fort Thorn to take possession of the men. Because of the number of accused involved, he required a 'posse' to help with the escort. He was cleared to request that the 'posse' be made up of soldiers with an officer commanding. Judge Benedick intended to travel to Socorro from Albuquerque to meet the posse when they arrived and to dispose of the case according to the law.[10]

Lieutenant Colonel Dixon Miles, responding to the situation at Fort Thorn, left Fort Fillmore on April 27, accompanied by 2[d] Lieutenant Henry Freedley, his adjutant, and approximately forty-six members of Company 'K,' 3[d] Infantry. Miles wanted to reinforce the small Fort Thorn garrison in the event the capture of the Mexican militiamen raised issues among the local populace.

On April 28 1st Lieutenant William H. Wood personally led the escort which left Fort Thorn acting as a posse for the sheriff of Socorro County. Lieutenant Colonel Miles arrived at Fort Thorn the following day and immediately took command of the fort. He made his presence known to both the local Mexican populace and the Apaches at Apache Agency in case trouble should arise. Wood arrived safely at Socorro, no problems being encountered en route.[11]

Lieutenant Colonel Miles outlined conditions at Fort Thorn as he found them on May 2, 1858. He also described the makeup of the Mesilla Guard.

> ... I have the honor to report that all disquietude at this post is settled into tranquility. The Indians are perfectly satisfied at the course adopted by the Command. General of the Dept. and have left (except the wounded) for their location where they intend planting corn. The wounded are improving and will soon be well.
>
> The Agent Dr. Steck leaves tomorrow morning for the Gila to meet the Mogollons and plant corn for them at the mouth of the St. Lucia. All the Indians I have seen promise most faithfully to remain quiet and await the decision of the U.S. District Court for redress for the grievous injury done them by the people of Mesilla.
>
> So far as I have heard, the Mesillan people are satisfied that the prisoners have been removed to Socorro and I do not think you will ever hear again of the independent action of their volunteer company.
>
> So far as I can learn, this company is composed of one hundred land holders, but when the company is called into service, any of the landholders disinclined to march, are obliged to furnish a substitute, always of course one of his peons, and since among the company that came here and perpetrated the

recent outrage; were mostly peons, (as I hear) not over five land holders among them. The balance [being] peons, runaway's from Corolitas [sic] and deserters from the Mexican Army. I have stated this to Lt. Wood in my instructions to him. To get the character of each and their nationality, and transmit the same to the Comdg. Genl. of the Dept. by express.[12]

Miles found the situation at Fort Thorn to be stable, with no apparent threats, and returned on May 11 to Fort Fillmore. He made no mention of the Fort Thorn Massacre after he returned, simply notifying the Department that he was once more in command. Since no record of court proceedings related to the Guard's appearance at Socorro has been found, it has to be assumed that all thirty-six men got off on some pretext or another, probably as the result of their being part of the New Mexico Territorial militia system.[13]

Dr. Steck visited both the Mimbres and Mescalero lands in May and found the Mimbres, Mescalero, and part of the Mogollon Apaches planting corn. On May 20 he told Superintendent Collins that he believed everything would turn out fine if the 'outlaws' from Mesilla did not attack them. Since the raid on Apache Agency, Dr. Steck had tried to quiet the fears of the Indians that the Mexicans would return. Steck knew violent threats were still being made by the people of Mesilla. Supposedly, the Apaches had resumed stealing animals from Mesilla and its outskirts. Since receiving these reports, Agent Steck had looked for any and all stolen animals, but had found none. He believed the Mesilla people were lying about the thefts, or at least who the thieves were, so as to shift the blame for the massacre away from themselves. In fact, the situation which brought about the massacres had not changed. By the end of May, Fort Fillmore remained without a mounted contingent, and Lieutenant Colonel Miles refused to tramp his infantry back and forth across the desert chasing Apaches in vain. The need for the Mesilla Guard must have seemed greater than ever to the residents of Mesilla.[14]

The Utah campaign, which eventually fizzled into nothingness, severely impacted the ability of the United States Army in New Mexico to protect the Mexican and American populations and of controlling or stopping Indian depredations. One result was the Mesilla Guard and the massacres at Doña Ana and Apache Agency. With Fort Fillmore denuded of its mounted company, other changes were in the works. The U.S. Army in New Mexico was quite small at the best of times, consisting of ten companies of the 3ᵈ Infantry, the entire Regiment of Mounted Rifles, a few red-leg artillery companies acting as infantry, and the dragoon units in what is now Arizona. During the summer of 1858, Colonel Loring took one-third of the mounted force of the Territory and one-fifth of the infantry to Utah. Such a shock to military strength was immediately felt. Some points were left without protection. At Fort Fillmore the two remaining infantry companies were soon impacted. Considered for deactivation, Fort Fillmore continued its daily duties that summer. Strictly a two-company ('C' & 'K') infantry post, its importance to the overall strategic outlook in New Mexico was soon reduced even further by events happening far to the north.

The Butterfield Overland Mail Stage Company arrived that summer of 1858. On June 28 Abel Rathbun Corbin laid out the route of the intended Butterfield Stage Line, which was to begin operations September 16, 1858. Fort Fillmore may have survived 1858 as a military post strictly because it was listed as a stop on the Butterfield line. Corbin told the Secretary of War:

> ... Referring to your kind expression in regard to furnishing thorough protection to the Overland Mail from St. Louis & Memphis to San Francisco, I have the honor to say to you, in behalf of Messrs. John Butterfield & Co., that they will commence regular semi-weekly mail service over the whole line on the 16th of September next.
>
> The route begins at St. Louis and Memphis and converges at Fort Smith on the Arkansas River. From Fort Smith the route passes to Preston on the Red River, to Fort Belknap, to Camp Cooper, thence along Marcy's Trail of 1849 to the Big Springs of the Colorado of Texas; thence along the trail or route of Lieut. Michler to Mustang Springs, to the springs in the White Sands hills, and to the Rio Pecos; thence to the crossing of the Pecos three miles below the junction of Delaware Creek, up the Delaware Creek, and through the Guadeloupe [sic] Pass, along

the usually travelled road to Fort Bliss near El Paso. Thence up the Rio Grande to a point not far from Fort Fillmore, and thence through the Messilla [sic] Valley, and Tucson near Fort Buchanon, to Fort Yuma. From Fort Yuma, through San Bernardino Valley, and by Fort Tejon, and through the Tulare Valley, on to San Francisco.

The distance from St. Louis to San Francisco by the above described route exceeds (very little) 2600 miles, and is to be traversed in 25 days from end to end; the mail is to be carried by four horse coaches, twice a week, each way; each coach must be suitable for the conveyance of passengers.

Such is the route for which Messrs. Butterfield & Co. have instructed me to apply to you to obtain military protection, of both life & property, against all hostile attack. Indians, Mexicans, Mormons & lawless robbers frequent certain parts on this extended route, and protection against their predatory attacks is indispensible [sic] to the success of our enterprise. Such protection is therefore applied for.[15]

Fort Fillmore's garrison was further reduced on June 30. Company 'C' departed for Fort Craig, under the command of 2[d] Lieutenant John McLean Hildt, where they were to take up temporary duty. The strange thing about this transfer is that although the soldiers were physically gone from Fort Fillmore, the company records and accounting process were left under the control of Lieutenant Colonel Miles. A few infantrymen of Company 'C' remained at Fort Fillmore, probably to watch the barracks and company public property as well as to keep up the records for the monthly return. Company 'C's' status as the longest-serving infantry company at the post remained, at least officially, unbroken.[16]

A greater slaughter of the Apaches than that committed by the Mesilla Guard at Apache Agency took place in July at the small Mexican town of Fronteras. A number of Chiricahua peace overtures had been made at Fronteras in June. On July 14, 1858, Fronteras officials agreed to hold peace talks with the significant Chiricahua leaders. There are some discrepancies regarding what actually transpired but there is no doubt that, while in a drunken stupor caused by liberal amounts of alcohol, Apache representatives at Fronteras for the peace meetings were attacked and slaughtered. The Mexicans blamed the slaughter on an Indian who killed a soldier. The Apaches told a different story. Whatever the cause, twenty-six Apache men and ten women were killed. Chief Colchon was among the dead. The Mexicans were said to have captured twenty lances, seven horses, three mules and two burros. The Chiricahuas later admitted to twenty-five casualties in their ranks.[17]

Abel Corbin, agent of the Butterfield Overland Mail, requested, through the commander of the Department of New Mexico, that military protection be provided the mail stages within the jurisdiction of the Department. The Department adjutant notified the Adjutant General's Office in Washington, that "the demands upon the Army at the present time, place it out of the power of the Department to furnish the assistance desired." With the Utah Campaign still holding critical Department resources in the form of Loring's troops and troubles with Apaches and Navajos always on the horizon, the truth of the Department's inability to support a heavy level of escorts appears hard to challenge. Dismounted infantry, the only force available along the Butterfield route at the time, would have been of little use to a fast-traveling mail coach.[18]

One of the more interesting letters to come out of Fort Fillmore in the 1850s was one Lieutenant Colonel Miles created in the last days of his service there. The letter, dated July 22, 1858, dealt with an operating den of iniquity somewhere close to Fort Fillmore. Insights into these combination stage stations, bars, and probable whorehouses are difficult to find, as the military kept mention of them very close to the vest. The stage station referred to was not the new Butterfield Overland Mail, which had yet to see service, but was probably the coach mail line to Santa Fe, then active over the Jornada del Muerto. No matter, history can withstand the impact of a thousand such letters which describe daily life at the post in a way fiction cannot. It was addressed to Major Nichols at a time when Lieutenant Colonel Miles was not pleased by his lot; he had been at Fort Fillmore for most of seven years.

> ... To correct the misrepresentation that doubtless will [be] made, of an occurrence that happened on the 8th and 11th Inst.

in the vicinity of this post. I have the honor to present the following report.

Severe indisposition from which I have not recovered, has prevented me making this report at an earlier date.

On the 8th Inst. Pvt. P. Cunningham of K Co. 3d Inf., on leave of absence, got drunk at the mail station kept by a discharged soldier named Albert Kuhn in this vicinity. A row commenced between him and Snyder over a game of cards. Kuhn separated them and assumed the quarrel and after various banters etc., engaged Cunningham in a fist fight. On the latters approaching him he shot him in the abdomen and as Cunningham turned and was leaving fired three more shots into him. These wounds caused his death in a few hours afterwards.

On the 9th I directed Lt. Freedley to proceed to Mesilla with witnesses and take out a writ for the apprehension of Kuhn for murder. He went there and while the writ was being made out, Kuhn delivered himself up to the Alcalde of the adjoining town who happened to ride into Mesilla at that moment. Miller refused to deliver Kuhn on the writ but held him to appear before him at Mesilla (contrary to law) on the next morning at 8 0'clock.

On the 10th Lt. Freedley was unable to go to Mesilla but the witnesses were sent. These were tampered with in every way by the mail stage men, and at the last made drunk. The trial came off and as anticipated , Kuhn was held to bail in $100. To appear at the next term of Socorro Court to answer the offended dignity of Dona Ana County for riot. Kuhns on this [10th] Saturday afternoon returned to the store in a mail stage, surrounded by his friends as in triumph, uttering denunciations against the soldiers with threats etc., etc. Many of the soldiers heard this and vowed vengeance.

Anticipating a disturbance on the 11th [Sunday] strict orders were given to the guard to patrole [sic] the road to Kuhn's store every half hour and apprehend and confine every soldier found in that direction. Not withstanding the order and vigilance of the guard , about 2 o'clock P.M. a portion of the men of K Company, unperceived, slipped out of their quarters and proceeded to Kuhn's store, with the intention of lynching him for the murder of their companion. They had left but a short time before it was discovered and were promptly followed by another and the 1st Sergeant—who arrived after two shots had been fired at Kuhn's closing his door. One of these shots slightly wounded a citizen (herder for the mail party) when the sergeant with great daring threw himself into the open window and ordered the infuriated soldiers to cease firing, as there were women and children in the house. This act saved Kuhn. The Sergeant informed him, he must leave immediately with him, or he could not guarantee his life. That he could take him to the guard house, when, by that time the officers at the fort would become aware of the difficulty and save him. About the time of the arrival of the Sergeant at Kuhn's I was informed that the soldiers were assaulting the house. I instantly gave Lt. Freedley orders to take with him any & all soldiers he could readily find and suppress the riot. He arrived at Kuhns as the sergeant was marching from the house and the men fell into ranks and marched as orderly and as obediently to his orders as if on parade. Lt. Freedley brought Kuhn down and delivered him up to me. After keeping him in my parlor for an hour or so, a horse was procured; Lt. Freedley and myself escorted him out of the garrison; and he left unmolested —promising me to leave the store and never return to it. He expressed many thanks to Lt. Freedley & the Sergeant for saving his life, etc., etc.

But he no sooner considered himself safe than he commenced threatening the Sergt's life—as well as the soldiers. On his leaving the store the excitement [?]. No soldier has been there since and I suppose never would go there again, if the whisky was not kept there to entice them. The wounded citizen was brought to our hospital, where he was promptly and skillfully treated by Dr. Cooper. He is recovering rapidly. The men of K Company have subscribed I am told $100. for him and he is perfectly satisfied.

I should not omit to state that Kuhns is only a clerk of the mail company, employed by Dr. Nangle the agent.

This is the whole transaction as it occurred. Had the soldiers got possession of Kuhns they would doubtless have hanged him. Hardly able to hold a pen, must be my excuse for this feeble and unimportant report.[19]

What Miles calls a "feeble and unimportant report" is one of the most interesting personal and historical documents to survive from Fort Fillmore's history. Where was the stage line store? Although diligently searched for on the lands surrounding Fort

Fillmore, no sign has yet arisen of any building. The letter confirms there was a whisky-buying point and probable brothel on the road to the village of La Mesa. Was the La Mesa road the same as the Mesilla or Santo Tomás road? The quickness with which the 1st Sergeant and 2ᵈ Lieutenant Freedley were able to reach the bar indicates the place was closer to the fort than La Mesa. The bar must have been of some size as the sergeant indicated during the fracas there were women and children in the house as well as possible bar customers. The owner and local stage line manager, a Dr. Nangle, was not involved in the incident.

Lieutenant Colonel Dixon Stansbury Miles left Fort Fillmore forever on August 1, 1858. He had been the post commander between September 1851 and July 1858, save for brief periods on leave or on other assignments in the Territory. Miles was fifty-four years old and headed north to take command of the most remembered mission of his army career—the campaign against the Navajo Tribe. That, like the 1857 campaign into the Gila Country, was underway in a similar fashion before Dixon Miles arrived to take command. By August 19 guides and spies were hired from among the Mexicans and non-Navajo Indians.[20]

Help was on the way to New Mexico for Miles' use in the coming campaign. Major Electus Backus, slowly plodding westward on September 1, encamped near Fort Atkinson, Kansas Territory. Backus brought three hundred and twenty desperately needed recruits for use in the campaign.

Miles arrived at his new post of Fort Defiance, located in what is now northern Arizona, on September 2. Stationed there were eight officers and three hundred and ten soldiers ready to take the field, as well as Blas Lucero's spy company. Miles intended to travel to Canyon de Chelly first, the very heart of the Navajo lands, and then go to wherever the Indians could be found. He was also to link up with Major Backus. Backus, with troops from Fort Union as well as his recruits, was to sweep toward Canyon de Chelly from the north and east. Miles also expected to be reinforced by Captain Lindsay's R.M.R. company from Fort Union and George Washington Howland's company from Fort Thorn, as well as to receive support from 8th Infantry units coming up from Fort Bliss.[21]

On September 4 Miles issued Special Order No. 3. This order outlined the nature and intent of the campaign, as well as spelling out the particulars for the column Miles would be leading. All posts in the south—Fort Fillmore, Fort Bliss, Fort Thorn, and Fort Craig—were barely operational at that time. Had the Apaches struck the denuded area with force, the outcome would have been grim and probably unopposed. Fortunately, the Apaches were never able to coordinate a combined operation of any size.[22]

At Fort Defiance on September 8, former Fort Fillmore officer 2[d] Lieutenant Henry Harrison Walker reminded the other officers at the post as to the reason for the Navajo Campaign, and also brought them up to date on what was expected to happen soon. Walker noted: "Sufficient time has been given the Navajo tribe of Indians, to seek, secure, and deliver up, the murderer of Mj. Brooks' negro to atone for the insult to our flag, and the many outrages committed upon our citizens. They have failed to do so. Our duty remains to chastize them into obedience to our laws. After tomorrow morning [September 9] war is proclaimed against them."[23] In 1855 and 1857 the army had massed forces to punish the Apaches as a people for the acts of a few. In 1858 the massing of forces was to be directed at the Navajos for the killing of the slave property belonging to a Major Brooks, then serving at Fort Defiance. In either case the actual murderers were never caught, although many innocent lives were severely impacted and a great deal of funds expended.

While Walker urged the troops to heightened effort during the coming fray, the Navajo leader Sarcillo Largo informed Miles that the murderer was being hunted by the Navajo head men and chiefs. The killer was seen at Bear Spring, near Laguna, and other places. Then on the morning of September 8, 1858, Sarcillo Largo came to Miles and said that the murderer had been caught, was mortally wounded, and had died the previous evening. Largo requested a wagon to bring the body to Fort Defiance. Miles told Major

Brooks to send for the body. This was done and the corpse was brought to the fort where those who knew the murderer came to view the body. All who attended the viewing said the man was an imposter and the body was not that of the murderer. Miles, furious at the Indian leader's attempt to foist an imposter upon him, refused to talk to Largo and the others. The attending surgeon believed the body to be that of a Mexican Navajo captive who had sometimes visited the fort. He appeared to have been shot on the morning of the 8th, not the night before. After this incident there was no stopping the cries for war.[24]

Dixon Miles marched the next day with Companies 'A,' 'I,' and 'F' of the Regiment of Mounted Rifles, Companies 'B' and 'C' of the 3[d] Infantry (save for the six men still at Fort Fillmore), in addition to Mexican militia Captain Blas Lucero and his guides and spies.[25] On the 10th Lucero's men brought in a well-dressed, fully-armed, and well-mounted Indian warrior who had been spying on the column. He said a great number of Navajos were waiting to fight the soldiers at Canyon de Chelly. The warrior also informed Miles that the dead imposter had been the slave of a Navajo chief, who had him murdered to provide the false identification. Miles then did something truly unusual, at least based on his past actions. After the Navajo warrior told what he knew, Miles had him shot as a spy, being reluctant to free him to fight again.[26]

On September 11, the column entered Canyon de Chelly over a precipitous rocky path. The path was almost a mile long, very narrow and overhung with large rocks. Miles said: "... when I reached bottom the men on the top looked like pigmies [sic] and the mules like rats." Upon closing up the column in the canyon, Miles was notified by 1st Lieutenant Averill, commanding the rear guard, that he had been fired on by Indians and had killed one. Miles gave thanks for the advice of his Zuni guides, as the Navajos apparently had been surprised by their entry into the canyon from this particular pass. While moving down the huge Canyon de Chelly, Miles saw Navajos everywhere on the heights. The troops captured some squaws and children while chasing a warrior.

Failing to find the other side of the canyon before nightfall, Miles camped that night in a wide spot in the canyon. The column could see great numbers of Navajos all around them but not close enough to fire on. Brevet-Major Elliot of Company 'A,' R.M.R., reported he had a fight with ten Indians, killed one for certain, perhaps more, and had wounded several. Almost immediately after the troops camped, the Indians closed in and began firing, especially from the north. Miles asked that an old Indian captive be brought to him. Miles asked the man if he knew the chief leading the men to the north. The man replied that it was his son. Miles told him to call out to the Navajos and tell them, that if they fired into the camp during the night he, Miles, would hang the old man next morning. The Navajo's warning was heeded by his people and the camp slept peacefully the rest of that night.[27]

The next day the Infantry quickly cleared both sides of the canyon, making secure the march of the mounted troops and pack mules up the center. During the day they had a few minor skirmishes and, later in the afternoon, a Navajo chief under a white flag came forth to talk to Miles. Miles demanded once more that the murderer be brought in, otherwise the war would go on.[28]

On the 13th, after a hard march, Miles reached a group of small lakes, some twelve miles from where he had encamped the previous night. Here he found 1st Lieutenant Lane of Company 'A,' R.M.R. in charge of six thousand head of recently captured sheep. Lane reported that after a long chase after the Indians, during which one of Captain Blas Lucero's guides killed a Navajo, he had come back to the lakes. It is not clear what Miles meant by lakes; perhaps he meant small bodies of water. He added there was no grass there for his animals. They marched on in the direction of some cornfields and camped near there for the night.[29]

The morning of the next day Miles decided to release the captive women and children. He may have remembered what happened at Fort Fillmore to the Coyotero captives. He stated: "I could not kill them and they were too great an encumbrance to retain." About three o'clock that morning, the command suffered its first casualty when Navajos attacked the piquettes around the camp, mortally wounding Private Marius Sweeney of Company 'A,' Mounted Rifles and wounding Sergeant James Watson. Private George Dunn of Company 'I,' R.M.R. and Private William Mank of Company 'C,' 3d Infantry, were slightly wounded. All the wounds were inflicted with arrows. Progress the rest of that day was slow as Private Sweeney had to be carried on a litter. During the march Miles ordered 1st Lieutenant Averill to attack and capture what was thought to be a herd of sheep. After marching further, Miles realized what he had thought were sheep were simply white rocks. He then ordered 1st Lieutenant Lane and a bugler named Fisher to ride toward Averill's command and, when close, Fisher was to blow the Recall. After doing this, Lane ordered Fisher to cross over the trail and await the arrival of the column. Fisher failed to do as he was told, and instead pushed ahead. Some time shortly thereafter, Bugler Fisher was the first of the column to be killed in action during the Navajo campaign. Miles found his stripped body, naked except for his gloves and shoes, pierced by two arrows. He ordered Fisher's body buried where he was found.[30]

Shortly after leaving Fisher's burial place, Miles found the column facing a narrow wooded pass in the canyon. He ordered 1st Lieutenant Whipple's infantry to ascend to the left and 2d Lieutenant Hildt and his infantry to the right. Whipple soon encountered a large number of concealed Indians, waiting to attack, who fled on his approach. By three o'clock that afternoon they had reached the cornfields in what Miles called the Puebla Clorada, a beautiful valley with good water, wood, and grass. There he camped. That night, after the usual attack on the piquettes by the Navajos, quiet again fell over the camp. Miles added that about 8:00 p.m. the wounded Private Sweeney died, the second army casualty.[31.]

Miles marched his soldiers back to Fort Defiance on September 15; his rear guard under 1st Lieutenant Averill fought occasionally with the Navajos as the column progressed. Miles recorded that during the march through Canyon de Chelly, six Navajos had been killed and undoubtedly many others had been wounded. The column captured four or five horses, six women and children, an old man, and between five and six thousand sheep.

Two of his soldiers were killed and three wounded.[32]

On September 16, 1858, with the army in the field against the Navajos, the first stage coach to travel over the new Butterfield Stage Line route to California left St. Louis, Missouri. The coach traveled through Missouri, Arkansas, Oklahoma, and across Texas to present-day El Paso. The first stop in Doña Ana County was at Cottonwood Station, near what is now Canutillo, then on to Fort Fillmore and places west. The stage arrived at San Francisco on October 10, 1858, ending a journey of twenty-three days and 23.5 hours. There is no mention in the post records of the stage's arrival at Fort Fillmore or the accommodations to be found there. No mention has been found of any special modifications to buildings at Fort Fillmore, although there must have been a great flurry of activity all along the new line. Stage stations were built, horses gathered, and the workers who manned the line arrived from the East taking their places on the route at stations generally twenty miles apart.

Roscoe Conkling's book, *The Butterfield Overland Mail*, reported that the Butterfield station at Fort Fillmore was an adobe building with an attached corral located near the sutler's store on the west side of the barracks quadrangle.[33] The mail road traversed the fort reservation in a general southeast-northwest direction and passed west of the fort buildings and north of the fort garden, following the acequia (supplied with water from the Rio Grande) which bounded the reservation about half a mile southwest. From the station on the west side of the post, the mail road continued in a northwest direction past the fort for about four and a half miles. There the road forked—the Santa Fe road diverged from the California Road, or as was sometimes called, the Butterfield Road. The Santa Fe Road continued northwest through Las Cruces and then northward to Doña Ana and over the Jornada del Muerto; the California or Butterfield Road curved westward and crossed the Rio Grande a mile and a half slightly southeast of Mesilla. The branch road leading to Mesilla from Fort Fillmore was part of Colonel Leach's road-building program and was completed early in 1858.

Prior to that time, travelers on the California Road between Fort Fillmore and Mesilla took a circuitous route, crossing to the west side at a point about a mile and a half southwest of the fort, then turning northwest and passing through the Bosque Seco Ranch before continuing on up the bottom lands to Mesilla.[34]

From 1850 to 1865, due to frequent shifting of the river channel, the ferry on the road used to transport the stage across the river to Mesilla was moved from one location to another. In 1858, the ferry on which the Overland Mail coaches were transported across the Rio Grande was located a quarter of a mile southeast of the present Santa Fe Railroad station at Mesilla Park. The Rio Grande in those days was wild and uncontrolled; it was noted for being a river which could overflow its banks one day and be completely dry soon after. How the stage crossed the river in the muddy periods is not known. No doubt they used Yankee ingenuity, most of the people employed on the Butterfield Line being from New York State.[35]

Upon his return to Fort Defiance Miles immediately prepared for further action. He asked that all men from companies in the field who had, for any reason, been left behind be sent to their companies. All soldiers issued 'Long Range Rifles' were to be sent to him. Miles undoubtedly referred to the new Model 1855 .58 caliber Rifle-Muskets that used the oblong Minie-type round. These weapons, slowly arriving at Fort Union from the East, were not distributed in large numbers. The majority of troops in the field used the smoothbore percussion musket that fired the .69 caliber round. Differences in range and accuracy between the two weapons were like night and day—approximately one hundred effective yards with the .69 caliber musket and six hundred effective yards with the .58 caliber rifle. With the new weapon Miles's men could have reached some of the Navajos above them in the Canyon de Chelly.[36]

The huge sheep herd captured from the Navajos could not be preserved. Roughly five hundred to a thousand were kept for the use of the troops and the rest, some five thousand animals, were destroyed. Miles said his decision to destroy the enormous herd of captured Navajo sheep was because he could not send enough troops to guard the sheep and still keep up a "vigorous campaign" against the Navajos.[37]

Fort Fillmore's longest resident infantry company, 'C,' under the command of 2[d] Lieutenant John McLean Hildt, was ordered out of Fort Defiance on September 25 to escort the contractor's supply train as far as Gallos Spring, and then to return to Fort Defiance. Captain Lucero supplied four guides and spies to accompany Hildt. On the day Company 'C' left on escort duty, Lieutenant Colonel Miles requested an additional twenty thousand to forty thousand .69 caliber buck and ball cartridges. Miles also asked for fifty thousand cartridges for the Mounted Rifles' Mississippi Rifles and twenty thousand Navy Colt pistol cartridges.[38]

At Fort Fillmore on October 2, thirty-seven soldiers from Company 'H,' 3[d] Infantry, marched into the post under the command of Brevet-Major and Captain William Hamilton Gordon. Gordon's post was normally at Fort Thorn but, because of the impact of the Utah and Navajo Expeditions upon the assets in the Department of New Mexico, he was ordered to take command of both Fort Fillmore and Fort Thorn.

Brevet-Major Gordon was not a West Point officer. He was commissioned a 2[d] lieutenant in the 3[d] Infantry Regiment on July 31, 1838, during the Seminole War. He was promoted to 1st lieutenant on June 21, 1841, and to captain on September 21, 1846.[39]

Miles, on the campaign trail again as of September 29, reported on that action on October 3. He was accompanied by Captain Elliot with Company 'A,' R.M.R, 1st Lieutenant Averill with Company 'H,' R.M.R., and Captain Lindsay with Company 'I,' R.M.R. First Lieutenant Whipple with Company 'B,' 3[d] Infantry and 1st Lieutenant Willard with Company 'K,' 8th Infantry and their troops were also part of the command. Militia Captain Blas Lucero and twenty-two guides and spies accompanied the column as did Captain McLane with additional personnel. This force traveled northeast of Fort Defiance about twelve miles before descending east six miles and entering the plain of an extensive basin. Elliot and Averill were the first to engage the hostiles; Averill's command captured nine horses and one thousand sheep. Elliot reported later killing two Indians and wounding four. On the morning of September 30, Miles moved his camp a mile and a half north to a large lake which he named Lake Lucero in honor of his Mexican scout, Blas Lucero. In all, the brief campaign led to the killing of ten Indians, the wounding of many others, and the capture of Chief Kay-a-tana's camp equipage. Eighty horses and sixty-five hundred sheep were captured before the men returned to Fort Defiance on October 3. Two privates lost their lives. One sergeant was wounded.[40]

On October 6, 2[d] Lieutenant Henry Freedley led sixty-six men of Company 'K,' 3[d] Infantry, out of Fort Fillmore to Albuquerque where they were to be temporarily stationed. That left at the post only Assistant Surgeon George Cooper, four men each from Companies 'C' and 'K' of the original garrison, and whatever portion of Company 'H,' 3[d] Infantry, could be spared to guard the post public property.[41]

The Fort Defiance post horse herd was savagely attacked about 7:00 a.m. on October 17 as it passed out of the Canyon Bonito. This included Company 'G,' R.M.R.'s horses, under the protection of fifteen Mounted Rifles and ten infantrymen. Estimates were that three hundred mounted Navajos, lying in wait, attacked the herd. The herd commander, Sergeant Bernard W. Clark of Company 'I,' Mounted Rifles, defended as best he could. He saved the horses and most of the sheep and cattle, but lost about sixty-two mules. He was sustained in the fight by the men under his command and by Zuni Indians who had been encamped near the place of conflict. As soon as possible, troops were sent from from Fort Defiance, but they could not find the hostiles.

While Company 'C' from Fort Fillmore operated from Fort Defiance, Company 'K,' under Henry Freedley, was in the field near Jemez Pueblo with the northern column. This force included

Company 'I,' or 'F,' 8th Infantry and Company 'K,' 3[d] Infantry.

On October 23, Miles reported on the progress of a five-day scout westward into the Navajo country. They had passed through Puebla Colorada before turning southwest for an examination of the valleys in that region. He took with him Companies 'F,' 'I,' and 'H,' R.M.R., a total of 127 rank and file, and Companies 'C,' 3[d] Infantry, and 'K,' 8th Infantry, 116 rank and file, as well as 20 Mexican guides and spies. Also with Miles's column were one hundred and sixty volunteers from the Zuni people, the latter out for whatever Navajo loot they could find. Miles sought to attack the camp of Navajo Chief Manuelito on October 20. The Zunis, traveling as the lead element, captured some one hundred horses, but established such a visible camp (their smoke could be seen for thirty miles) that the Navajos were warned of their coming. On the 21st Miles split his Mounted Rifles force, sending each company, escorted by Zunis, in a different direction. Lindsay went south, Lane north, and Captain McLane west. None of the columns found a fight. On October 22 Miles started early, intending to march northward toward Canyon de Chelly once more. The Zuni refused to guide Miles as they had decided to go home. The further north Miles marched the colder the weather became. A snow-storm threatened. Fearing that with no guide, and no sun as a marker of direction, he might get lost in the snowstorm and lose the column, he decided to return to Fort Defiance. The column turned around and traveled through a blizzard as Miles hastened the men and animals forward, fearing they might all perish if they did not soon reach the fort. Miles believed the Zunis to be unreliable auxiliaries. The horses they captured were useless for any government service. He left them as well as the cows and calves in the Zuni camp, as remuneration for their inadequate services.[42]

By October 25 Miles believed it was time to treat with the Navajos, but before doing so he wanted to combine forces with Major Backus and sweep through the territory in which the murderer's band was often known to reside. Miles left Fort Defiance to link up with Major Backus's column on October 29. Before departure he had word from the Navajo chiefs that "their hearts were sore and they beg for peace." The murderer was now reported to be with a band of the Utahs, whose tongue he spoke. Miles reported that earlier two rich Navajo women rode up within hailing distance of the Fort Defiance pickets, but their hearts had failed them and they had not come in.[43]

Fortunately for the army the Apache bands remained at peace during the Navajo conflict. On October 30 Agent Michael Steck sent a list of needs for Apache Agency to Superintendent Collins. Among the items mentioned were eight hundred yards of scarlet cloth, ten thousand yards of domestic cloth, one hundred fifty dozen hickory shirts, three hundred and fifty pair of scarlet Makinaw blankets, thirty-five hundred yards of blue print, fifty Barcelona handkerchiefs, seventy-five military frock coats with red trim, two-hundred dozen assorted spools of cotton, twelve hundred copper kettles, one-hundred dozen butcher knives, sixty-three squaw axes, twenty half-axes, fifty gross needles, five hundred pounds of brass wire, thirty dozen two-quart tin pans, twenty dozen four-quart tin pans, seventy-five dozen tin cups, thirty-five dozen scissors, one set of carpenter's tools, one set of blacksmith's tools, three heavy plows, fifteen dozen spades, sixty dozen hoes, and one hundred pounds of tobacco. These supplies were to meet the needs of the Apache, Mescalero, Mimbres, Mogollon, and Coyotero bands.[44]

Brevet-Major Gordon returned to Fort Fillmore by October 19. He was at the fort on October 31 when the monthly report was completed. The relatively vast, for its period, fort complex had only forty-five soldiers present, not enough to fill one barrack. It is assumed that four men from Companies 'C' and 'K occupied their old barracks on the south side of the fort. Gordon's Company 'H' troops probably took up residence in the barracks of their choice. Certainly a few may have occupied the mounted troops barracks on the north side near the sutler's store.[45]

The Miles and Backus columns joined forces in camp at Zuni Chez, near Zuni Chez Mountain, by November 3. The troops found that all the Indians in the region appeared to have fled west with their herds. Miles ordered Major Backus to take his command through Canyon Blanco about fifteen miles north of Zuni Chez, where Chief Kay-a-tana usually resided, then west. Miles intended to march through Washington Pass to Cienega Negra and then north, coursing the base of Zuni Chez Mountain until the two commands met again. The combined force would then move westward through Canyon de Chelly to its mouth, then southwest. Miles asked that his writing be excused, as "... the thermometer must be several degrees below zero. My ink freezes before I can use it and my fingers are so cold that I can hardly hold my pen."[46]

Meanwhile, Brevet-Major Gordon reported thefts of public property in and around Fort Fillmore and Fort Thorn. The situation was at disaster level since some of the thieves were soldiers. Gordon, unable to be at both places at once, saw thefts occur at one when he was at the other, and vice-versa. He reported the thefts in a letter to the Department while temporarily at Fort Thorn on November 4:

> ... I have the honor to inform you for the information of the commander of the Dept. That on the night of the 2nd Instant, my acting Command Sergt. at this post deserted after being detected in stealing Coms. & Qr. Mr. Stores; also that at Fort Fillmore Lieut. Freedley's company store room has been broken open and all the clothing it contained stolen.
>
> These robberies have been committed during my absence from one or the other of the posts. Under present arrangements I consider the public property in a very unsafe position, and would respectfully request that some officer be sent to assist or relieve me of the duties of one of these posts.
>
> Since the desertion of Norman I have no person to assist me who understands making out the necessary papers to be supplied to the different Departments.
>
> Most of the clothing stolen at Fort Fillmore has been recovered. I can learn nothing about, nor can I tell, to what extent the property has been lost. I think however it cannot be very great from the appearance of the store rooms.[47]

When you can't trust your senior sergeants, who can you trust? No doubt Sergeant Norman made a few dollars on the side and hoped no one would miss a little of what he took.

On November 15, 1858, Miles wrote of his final expedition

against the Navajos. The scout began on October 30 and ended on November 15. This scout, except for some rough traveling conditions, was uneventful until November 6, when they came across a small Indian camp in which the signs of a hurried departure were evident. The Indians had killed their dogs and left their fires burning. On November 7, the combined column, which included Major Backus's troops, came upon a Navajo horseman with a white flag. The Navajos asked for a peace conference. The murderer still had not been caught, but three members of his family were now involved in the search. Miles' reception was cold. He wanted the Navajos to suffer a little more before peace came.[48]

The column's course was toward the southwest next day, November 8. Traveling over rough and rocky ground some of the army mules gave out and were shot to prevent them falling to the enemy. One private was struck in the back by a ball when a small Navajo party opened fire on Captain Lindsay's company. The next day saw significant fighting, at least by the front and rear guards of the column. One Indian was killed and many were believed wounded. The column still moved southwest. During the day of November 9, Miles received more signs that the Navajos wanted peace. One of these was an erected small cross with a large white leaf tied on it. Many footprints were found around this cross. Miles believed these footprints were from the feet of many women and children, indicating a disruption in the Navajo life.[49]

On the 10th, anticipating the arrival of Major Backus's command, Miles retained his force in camp. During the day, 1st Lieutenant Lane met with a party of Navajos who once again pleaded for peace. The Indians told Miles that Major Backus was not far away, near the Rio de Chelly—the first news Miles had of Backus's whereabouts —and that the soldiers were strong and the Navajos were weak. Miles arranged to meet with Navajo Chief Barboncita in seven days. Terribio, another Navajo leader then a prisoner at Fort Defiance, would meet Barboncita at La Jolla and ask him to bring in other chiefs, all to talk with the Indian agent for the Navajos. For the first time, the demand for giving up the murderer was dropped as a condition for peace. On November 11, Miles started back in the direction of Fort

Defiance, his animals in too poor a condition for further field service.[50]

As with the column led by Lieutenant Colonel Miles, that of Major Backus was unable to bring the main body of the Navajos to a direct fight. The Indians, who knew the country well, simply kept ahead of the column and out of its way. In one incident which took place on November 15 or 16, some of Valdez's spies held talks with several Navajo warriors. While these Navajos talked, others crept close to the group. The hidden Navajos fired at Captain Valdez and his men, killing Valdez's horse and wounding him in the forehead. The next morning several Navajos approached the column under a white flag, protesting they were the ones asking for peace the day before and not the ones who had fired on Captain Valdez. These Indians told Major Backus that peace was being made and Lieutenant Colonel Miles had returned to Canyon Bonito. On November 18, Major Backus and his command reached Fort Defiance. He reported four Navajos dead, four or more wounded, thirty-five horses captured, and an additional ten horses shot. Two hundred and seventy-eight goats and twenty-two sheep were captured.[51]

Miles agreed to a request by Indian Agent Yost to meet with the Navajo chiefs and discuss peace. The murderer who had caused the Navajo War was still a fugitive. Miles drafted an armistice agreement which the Navajos signed, unconditionally. The day after the signing Miles recommended that the commander of the Department accept the armistice and that a garrison of one company of Mounted Rifles and three companies of infantry be stationed at Fort Defiance on a permanent basis. While Fort Defiance was touted as very important to the army's future, Fort Fillmore's future was in doubt; Fort Thorn was ordered closed. The latter order was issued by the Adjutant General's Office in Washington on November 27, 1858, although the post was not closed until March 1859.[52]

In a letter to Brevet-Major Brooks, 1st Lieutenant William Whipple proposed a settlement of the question over Brooks's slave, whose death had caused the war with the Navajos. Whipple offered a compromise:

> ... The Lieut. Col. Comdg. Directs me to acknowledge the
> receipt of your communication of this date, and to say—not
> commenting on your inference and deductions in regard to the
> cause of the war, and the means of carrying it on—that he did
> promise you that a demand should be made on the Indians for the
> payment of your negro boy, and he is still under the belief that
> it would be just; but since then this matter has passed into other
> hands than his, and your payment for this loss will have to be
> made under the head of a claim on the government for Indian
> spoliation, as other individuals for Indian depredations.
>
> The Lieut. Col. comdg. would suggest that there is one
> resource for this payment which he will recommend to the Col.
> commanding the Department (as he refuses to deliver captured
> sheep as payment) & that is to deliver to you the goats from
> twelve hundred to fifteen hundred now with the captive sheep at
> Fort Craig, which the Depot Commissary refuses to receipt for,
> and which demand a ready sale on the Rio Grande. But that you
> may not be disappointed, it is surmised that this fund if the goats
> are sold, will be appropriated "pro rate" to reimburse other
> claimants for lost property other than yours, since the war
> commenced. [53]

The price of an African slave was significant in the 1850s and
constituted a serious financial loss to Brevet-Major Brooks.
Although basically invisible to the historian, the presence of Negro
slaves in New Mexico, especially as servants for the officer corps,
may have been a common sight. Servants were mentioned by
William Whipple and Lydia Lane as being hard to find and hold in
the Territory. The Lanes had African slaves as servants at one
point, although Lydia Lane does not declare the presence directly.
Lieutenant Colonel Miles, a Marylander, brought a female slave
named Dolly to New Mexico in 1854 to serve his wife and family.
There were many southern officers serving at Fort Fillmore during
the 1850s and early 1860s. Many of these no doubt were rich enough
to own slaves. How many did, and how many blacks were at Fort
Fillmore in a serving capacity, will probably never be known.

President Buchanan's Second Annual Message, on December

6, addressed the continuing concerns with Kansas and Utah, and told of the Mormon capture and burning of a seventy-five-wagon train loaded with U.S. Army provisions. No doubt this incident reached the ears of the officers at Fort Fillmore, as did the fact that the Mormons were finally brought to a state of agreement with United States law after the army's arrival there. President Buchanan threatened Mexican independence in his Second Annual Address:

> ... there is another view of our relations with Mexico, arising from the unhappy condition of affairs along our southwestern frontier, which demands immediate action. In that remote region, where there are but few white inhabitants, large bands of hostile and predatory Indians roam promiscuously over the Mexican States of Chihuahua and Sonora and our adjoining territories. The local governments of these States are perfectly helpless and are kept in a state of constant alarm by the Indians. They have not the power, if they possessed the will, even to restrain lawless Mexicans from passing the border and committing depredations on our remote settlers. A state of anarchy and violence prevails throughout that distant frontier. The laws are a dead letter and life and property wholly insecure. For this reason the settlement of Arizona is arrested, whilst it is of great importance that a chain of inhabitants should extend all along its southern border sufficient for their own protection and that of the United States mail passing to and from California. Well-founded apprehensions are now entertained that the Indians and wandering Mexicans, equally lawless, may break up the important stage and postal communications recently established [the Butterfield Overland Mail] between our Atlantic and Pacific possessions. This passes very near to the Mexican boundary throughout the whole length of Arizona. I can imagine no possible remedy for these evils and no mode of restoring law and order on that remote and unsettled frontier but for the Government of the United States to assume a temporary protectorate over the northern portions of Chihuahua and Sonora and to establish military posts within in the same; and this I earnestly recommend to Congress. This protection may be withdrawn as soon as local governments shall be established in these Mexican States capable of performing their duties to the United States,

restraining the lawless, and preserving peace along the border.[54]

President Buchanan's protectorate over the Mexican States of Chihuahua and Sonora was never implemented. The fact that he mentioned a colonial policy tool, the protectorate, like that applied by Great Britain and France in those days, certainly indicates how close America came to carrying out such a policy. In fact, few at that time would have challenged the United State's right to do so —formerly independent tribal areas all over the world were falling under the sway of colonial administrations.

Apache Chief Cochise supposedly had his first contacts with American officials in late 1858. In December 1858 he met with Indian Agent Dr. Steck at Apache Pass in what is now eastern Arizona. Here they discussed the safety of the Butterfield Overland Mail through Apache Pass and the stage station there.[55]

Christmas of 1858 found Fort Fillmore still under the command of Assistant Surgeon George Cooper. Brevet-Major Gordon, who signed the end of month returns, had been at Fort Fillmore from December 6 to December 22, before he returned to Fort Thorn. The number of men at the post varied from seven to forty-four, dependent on whether Gordon was there. The year ended with Fort Thorn about to be abandoned and Fort Fillmore about to take on new life.[56]

NOTES - Chapter 10

1. Rencher to Garland, January 18, 1858, M1120, Rolls 7/8.
2. Alley to Hildt, February 8, 1858, M1120, Rolls 7/8.
3. Miles to Doña Ana County Prefect, February 9, 1858, M1120, Rolls 7/8.
4. Bull to Miles, March 3, 1858, M1120, Rolls 7/8.
5. Miles to Nichols, March 4, 1858, M1120, Rolls 7/8.
6. Citizens of Mesilla to Garland, March 24, 1858, M1120, Rolls 7/8.
7. Miles to Nichols, April 7, 1858, M1120, Rolls 7/8.

8. Wood to Nichols, April 17, 1858, M1120, Rolls 7/8.

9. Ibid.

10. Benedict to Wood, April 23, 1858, M1120, Rolls 7/8.

11. Miles to Nichols, April 29, 1858, M1120, Rolls 7/8.

12. Miles to Nichols, May 2, 1858, M1120, Rolls 7/8.

13. Miles to Nichols, May 12, 1858, M1120, Rolls 7/8.

14. Steck to Collins, May 20, 1858, M1120, Rolls 7/8.

15. Corbin to Floyd, June 28, 1858, M1120, Rolls 7/8.

16. Miles to Nichols, June 30, 1858, M1120, Rolls 7/8.

17. Edwin Sweeney, *Cochise*, pp. 112, 113.

18. Williams to Adjutant General's Office, July 22, 1858, M1120, Rolls 7/8.

19. Miles to Nichols, July 22, 1858, M1120, Rolls 7/8.

20. Fort Fillmore Post Returns, August 1858.

21. Miles to Nichols, September 3, 1858, M1120, Rolls 7/8.

22. Miles, Special Order #3, September 4, 1858, M1120, Rolls 7/8.

23. Walker to Fort Defiance Officers, September 8, 1858, M1120, Rolls 7/8.

24. Miles to Nichols, September 8, 1858, M1120, Rolls 7/8.

25. Miles to Nichols, September 16, 1858, M1120, Rolls 7/8.

26. Ibid.

27. Ibid.

28. Ibid.

29. Ibid.

30. Ibid.

31. Ibid.

32. Ibid.

33. Roscoe P. & Margaret B. Conkling, *The Butterfield Overland Mail 1857-1869,* Volume II. (Glendale CA: The Arthur H. Clark Company, 1947), p. 98.

34. Ibid., pp. 101-102.

35. The United States Census taken in 1860 indicated a predominance of persons from New York at the stage stations in Doña Ana County. Whether this was an expedient given that the company was from New York, or whether it was felt better to have some kind of kinship based on locality, is not known. It is assumed some of the persons working for the company may have been locals as time passed.

36. Miles to Assistant Adjutant General, September 17, 1858, M1120, Rolls 7/8.

37. Miles to Assistant Adjutant General, Santa Fe, September 18, 1858, M1120, Rolls 7/8.

38. Miles to Assistant Adjutant General, September 25, 1858, M1120, Rolls 7/8.

39. Heitman, William Gordon.

40. Miles to Assistant Adjutant General, September 25, 1858, M1120, Rolls7/8.

41. Fort Fillmore Post Returns, October 1858.

42. Miles to Wilkins, October 23, 1858, M1120, Rolls 7/8.

43. Miles to Wilkins, October 30, 1858, M1120, Rolls 7/8.

44. Steck to Collins, October 30, 1858, Indian Bureau, Roll 3.

45. Fort Fillmore Post Returns, October 1858.

46. Miles to Wilkins, November 3, 1858, M1120, Rolls 7/8.

47. Gordon to Wilkins, November 5, 1858, M1120, Rolls 7/8.

48. Miles to Nichols, November 15, 1858, M1120, Rolls 7/8.

49. Ibid.

50. Ibid.

51. Backus to Lane, November 19, 1858, M1120, Rolls 7/8.

52. Cooper to Bonneville, November 27, 1858, M1120, Roll 7/8.

53. Whipple to Brooks, December 1, 1858, M1120, Roll 7/8.

54. James D. Richardson, *Messages and Papers of the Presidents*, pp. 3045, 3046.

55. Edwin Sweeney, *Cochise*, p. 119.

56. Fort Fillmore Post Returns, December 1858.

11

1859 · LAZY DAYS IN THE SUN

D r. Michael Steck, in the Chiricahua Mountains on January 1, 1859, had recently returned from meeting with Chiricahua and Coyotero leaders at Apache Pass. At the request of the Superintendent of Indian Affairs he traveled to the Pass, some eighty-five miles from Fort Buchanan and far from his Apache Agency, to give presents to the 'Coyotero' Apache bands, as he termed them. Some of these Apaches may have been Chiricahua under Cochise, although that name was not used by Dr. Steck in his correspondence. The Indian Agent seemed astounded and a little concerned by the fact that he was surrounded by some six hundred Indians at that meeting, "large and small." The bands he visited lived along the route of the Butterfield Overland Mail and had been peaceable during the recent operations of that company. Steck referred to the Chiricahua Mountains as the "Chilihuihui Mountains." While there, Agent Steck met with forty Apache warriors who were headed for Sonora on a marauding expedition. He convinced them to turn around and go home. Michael Steck was without a doubt one of the bravest men to live in the West, yet he is generally forgotten by history. He went into Apache lands with only a few hired guides—Steck not only survived, but stopped many depredations.[1]

Steck met more Apaches in January near the Mogollon and Pinal Mountains. At that time he expected to be escorted by Captain Richard Ewell and dragoons from Fort Buchanan. The Agent intended to be back at Apache Agency by January 25. Fort

Thorn was in process of being abandoned, but no mention was made of any impact on Apache Agency, nor on Dr. Steck's work. In this period, the Agent had responsibility for all of the Apaches in southern New Mexico and what is now Arizona. Word came to him that an Indian Agency was to be established near Fort Buchanan, although an agent had not yet been assigned. He suggested that a better sharing of duties would be for the new agent to take the Mescaleros on the east side of the Rio Grande, and allow him to manage the west bank bands. His suggestion was not adopted.[2]

Navajo Chiefs were still appearing at Fort Defiance in the early days of January to sign the peace treaty. Major Electus Backus, in command at the fort, stated that it might still be good to send four or five mounted companies through the Navajo country in May or June to reinforce the meaning of the treaty.[3]

The situation was looking up at Fort Fillmore with the Navajo Campaign temporarily over. On January 13, 1st Lieutenant George Washington Howland rode into the post with seventy-one men of Company 'C,' Regiment of Mounted Rifles, the men recently involved in the Navajo Campaign and now released for new duties at Fort Fillmore.[4] Howland was thirty-four years old, a native of Rhode Island and an 1848 graduate of West Point. He was appointed a brevet-2[d] lieutenant of the Regiment of Mounted Rifles on July 1, 1848, and a 2[d] lieutenant on June 30, 1851. This was a remarkable length of time spent in what was actually no assignment at all. A brevet-2[d] lieutenant slot was normally used until a permanent position opened up. If the information on Howland is correct he served almost three years in a non-officer position until he received that appointment.

First Lieutenant Howland left two lasting memories of his service at Fort Fillmore, one architectural and one literary. A corral he built in the Burro Mountains while on detached service late in 1859 still stands, a remarkable testament to his engineering skill. While in the field, he received a poetic message from higher command. During the construction of his corral Howland was ordered to return to Fort Fillmore, "when the grass fails and the cold weather sets in." This famous order has been repeated in several historical works on that period. In fact, Howland returned early, subsequent orders caused him to abandon his engineering project almost at the moment of its completion.[5]

George Howland was promoted to captain on May 14, 1861, and participated in the Battle of Valverde against the Confederate Army from Texas on February 21, 1862. He received a brevet to major for heroism during that battle where he faced his former second in command at Fort Fillmore, 2[d] Lieutenant Henry C. McNeill, in direct combat. At Valverde, Howland still commanded Company 'C,' but by then the name had changed from Regiment of Mounted Riflemen to the 3[d] Cavalry Regiment. Henry McNeill was then a lieutenant colonel in the 5th Texas Cavalry. In January 1859, Henry McNeill was still at Fort Thorn when George Howland led the rest of their company to Fort Fillmore.[6]

Fort Fillmore lost its long-time infantry companies, 'C' and 'K,' 3[d] Infantry, to the Navajo Campaign, but a few soldiers from those companies remained in the barracks on post. That situation was soon to be remedied. Orders arrived indicating a final displacement of Company 'C' and 'K' public property. Two officers, 2[d] Lieutenant Henry Freedley of Company 'C' and 2[d] Lieutenant John McLean Hildt of Company 'K,' soon arrived to take charge of the remaining property.[7]

As of January 21, Brevet-Major Gordon was still not sure of the status of either infantry company, or of Lieutenant Colonel Miles, who was listed as part of the Fort Fillmore garrison. Of course, such changes raised havoc with the orderly transition of the military day. Gordon pleaded for orders on how he was to handle any transfers. Gordon soon learned Miles would not be returning. As of January 19 Miles became Colonel of the 2[d] Infantry Regiment, with a posting to Fort Leavenworth, Kansas Territory. The old man, then fifty-five, left New Mexico for good. After seven years his promotion had finally came through.[8]

Early in January the Apaches under Cochise stole horses in the vicinity of the Sonoita and Santa Cruz Rivers in Arizona. Dr. Steck went with Captain Richard S. Ewell and some dragoons to Apache Pass to meet with Cochise and get the stock back. Cochise returned the animals and agreed not to raid American ranches in Arizona. Steck did not try to get an agreement with Cochise to cease raiding in Sonora. The American army was not yet strong enough to prevent those raids.[9]

On February 2, writing to Superintendent Collins, Dr. Steck mentioned for the first time the subject of the removal of all of the Mimbres River and Mogollon Mountains Apaches to a reservation on the Gila River, far to the south of their present homelands. Such a move would have included the bands of Mangas Coloradas, Delgadito, and the Warms Springs Apaches formerly belonging to the decimated band of Cuchillo Negro. Some of the Indians appeared willing to go, others were hesitant. Dr. Steck advised waiting a year or so after any reserve was established before attempting to remove them. There was duplicity in Agent Steck's next words, however. He stated, "let a beginning be made with the Mimbres and Mogollon and before two years with a little management half the band can be got there without their knowing that it is the design to compel them to remove." Steck was worried that if all Apaches in these bands were crowded upon the reserve at one time it would take "an immense amount of provisions to supply them." That Steck's recommendations were not carried out can only be attributed to a heightening of tensions due to the coming American Civil War. The war provided the Apaches with a temporary respite and may have saved the northern states of Mexico—Chihuahua, and Sonora—from annexation.[10]

Brevet-Major Gordon was ordered to furnish an officer and fifty men from Company 'H,' 3[d] Infantry and Company 'C,' R.M.R. to serve with another Boundary Commission, then residing at Fort Bliss. Only one other officer, 1st Lieutenant George Washington Howland, was then at Fort Fillmore. Howland served as quartermaster and commissary officer of the post, in addition to his company duties. Second Lieutenant McNeill, Howland's junior officer in Company 'C,' was at Fort Thorn, a post which Brevet-Major Gordon still commanded. Second Lieutenant McNeill was preparing the public property for that post's abandonment in March. Gordon recommended that McNeill be the officer to serve with the Boundary Commission detail and he would send 1st Lieutenant Howland to Fort Thorn to look after the property there. Gordon indicated he made arrangements with a Major Donaldson to hire transportation for removing the stores from Fort Thorn to Fort Fillmore, and that this move would be accomplished as quickly as possible.[11]

While the officers and men at Fort Fillmore worked hard to bring the public property then at Fort Thorn to Fort Fillmore, an incident took place on or about January 28 at Dog Canyon, involving troops from Company 'D,' Regiment of Mounted Rifles, under the command of 1st Lieutenant Henry Lazelle, 8th Infantry. Lazelle, who later commanded Fort Fillmore, was severely wounded in that battle. An accounting of the incident was made at Fort Bliss on February 11, 1859, upon the return of Lazelle's column.

> ... I have the honor to report that 2nd Lieut. Lazelle, 8th Infantry left with post on the 21st ultimo in command of thirty men of Co. 'D' R.M.R. with ten days rations and orders to pursue the Indians who drove off a herd of mules from the vicinity of St. Elizario until he overtook them, and then to destroy the marauders. The command returned this morning, and Lieut. Lazelle informs me that after following the trail seven days he found himself first at night in Dog Canyon with fifty or sixty warriors in his front, armed, painted and prepared to resist his further progress, finding himself with his men mounted in a narrow defile while the Indians occupied a position that was perfectly impracticable for horses & within an easy range of their arrows. He withdrew his men from the canyon and encamped near its mouth [at] dark. About midnight after leaving a guard with his horses he with twenty six men returned to the point where he had left the Indians, hoping to surprise them in camp, but on his arrival he found they were no longer there.
>
> At the dawn of day he continued his march up the canyon. When he had progressed about a mile he found the Indians had been notified of his night march and were ready in a strong position to receive him. He immediately attacked them and a very hard fight ensued, which lasted two and a half hours, when Lieut. Lazelle, finding himself unable with his small force to drive them from their position in the rocks above him, and many

of his men being disabled by wounds, resolved to withdraw from the canyon. This he effected in good order, carrying the wounded men who could not walk. The Indians pursued him to the mouth but could not be induced to leave the mountains and fight in the plains. About one third of them were armed with guns, the remainder with bows & arrows. The result of the fight was nine Indians killed (counted). Our loss of life was three men killed, and seven wounded. Among the latter I grieve to say is the gallant commander of the brave party who received a very dangerous wound, being shot through the lung with a rifle ball. Several of the [men] are severely though not dangerously wounded.

The American troops are so accustomed to perfect success that anything approaching a repulsion is looked on with suspicion. I claim this to be an exceptional case, that the men behaved admirably well, and that the young officer in charge acted with good judgement, perfect coolness, and a degree of chivalrous enterprise worthy of all commendation. As soon as Lieut. Lazelle's wound will permit him to write I will forward his detailed report.[12]

The writer pointed up the ease with which the United States army had dealt with Apache raiders in the past, when they could track them down. Now, the army had suffered a reverse in battle for the first time in the short history of American stewardship in southern New Mexico. Such a reversal might stain, even ruin, an officer's reputation, if not properly documented. Henry Lazelle became a hero, his wound mitigating the minor defeat by the Mescaleros, especially in an army that prided itself on any incident involving armed conflict with such an elusive enemy. A wound taken in battle was a source of great pride, and perhaps even envy, among the other officers—if it was not too serious.

Brevet-Major Gordon received news of the fight at Dog Canyon from civilian messengers while the defeated soldiers treated their wounded at San Nicholas Springs, a known site just north of San Augustine Springs in the Organ Mountains and on the old Apache trail to Sierra Blanca. Their request for aid was immediately filled in the form of troops, wagons, and medical support. The Fort Fillmore rescue party met Lazelle's column at San Augustine

Springs. Lazelle survived his wounds and was carried safely back to Fort Bliss where he quickly recovered. Three soldiers from his command were killed and seven wounded.

The Department of New Mexico, then headed by Colonel Bonneville, was incensed over the fight between Lazelle's command and the Mescaleros. Bonneville directed Brevet-Major Gordon to assess the need for a major campaign in the Mescalero country. On February 20 Gordon responded. He stated that the nature of the terrain, which he had not seen, would make a small force of less than one hundred to one hundred-fifty men ineffective. The canyons and mountains of the region would literally swallow up such a force. As an alternative, Gordon recommended that one column of troops from each nearby post (probably Fort Stanton, Fort Craig, Fort Fillmore, and Fort Bliss) converge on the Mescalero stronghold, each pushing inward toward the center, forcing the Mescalero backward onto the bayonets of a column approaching from a different direction. Gordon believed overcoming the Mescalero, "be where they ain't" type of vanishing strategy, would leave the Indians little option except to either leave their country or make peace on army terms.[13]

Fort Thorn was in effect abandoned by mid-February of 1859, but Brevet-Major Gordon reported there was still finalization work to do. The post cannons (two twelve-pounder mountain howitzers) were yet to be relocated, as were the post corn supply, window blinds, panels, doors, lumber, etc.[14]

Some Mescalero Apaches, terrified of possible army reprisals over the Lazelle incident, came to the still-operational Apache Agency for assistance. Dr. Michael Steck addressed the problem in a February 27 letter to Superintendent Collins:

> ... I have the honor to report that careful enquiry has been made into the fight between Lieut. Lazelle & the Mescalero Indians at Dog Canyon on the 22nd Inst. Benancio [Venancio] & Mateo with fifteen men & boys with their families came to this agency and report[ed] the fight and say that they were not engaged in it and further report that Manuelito and Jose de la Paz were in command of the party and they alone with their people should be

held responsible. They state[d] that they, Mateo and Venancio, were encamped on the Tularosa at the time of the fight and as soon as they heard of it they came directly here and wish to remain west of the river among the Mimbres bands. I have cross questioned them carefully and also some of the Mimbres Indians with whom they are encamped and am inclined to the belief that they were not present. It was reported that Venancio was recognized but Jose de la Pas dresses very much like him, wears a hat & speaks good Spanish and might easily be mistaken for him. They contend that they are innocent & knew nothing of the robbery until after the fight. I told them they were blamed for the robbery & the killing of the soldiers and that they would be held responsible, to which they replied "we had nothing to do with it and you can do as you please with us."[15]

Fortunately for the Mescalero, Henry Lazelle was not dead, only badly wounded. Had he died, the ghosts of Stanton, Dodge, and the negro slave Jim would have no doubt added a fourth to their number, and a new campaign against the Mescalero begun. Steck recommended evaluation rather than suppression, removal rather than retention. At this time he believed the Mescalero and the Mimbres bands would one day have to be sent to reservations to save further trouble and raiding, and perhaps even to save the bands themselves.

Second Lieutenant Henry McNeill arrived at Fort Fillmore from the now-abandoned Fort Thorn on March 23, 1859. He joined his men with the rest of Company 'C,' R.M.R., raising the total number of soldiers available for duty in that company to sixty-seven men. McNeill was the number two officer in the company commanded by 1st Lieutenant George Washington Howland. McNeill left behind an unprotected, but still operational, Apache Agency.[16]

Just when it seemed as if Fort Fillmore, like Fort Thorn, was to be abandoned as no longer meaningful to the control of the Apaches, new life was breathed into the old fort. On April 13, 1859, 2d Lieutenant Richard S.C. Lord, recently at Fort Buchanan, brought Company 'D,' 1st Dragoon Regiment, to the post. Company 'D' was almost fully staffed with enlisted men, having seventy-three soldiers on the duty roster. This brought about a rare event in the history of the United States Army. Company 'D,' 1st Dragoons, joined Company 'C,' Regiment of Mounted Rifles and Company 'H,' 3d Infantry in comradely friendship at the old post. This may have been the only time, in the history of either organization, that a 1st Dragoon company and a Regiment of Mounted Rifles company were stationed together. R.M.R. green, dragoon orange, and infantry blue formed an appealing color panoply when men of the three regiments gathered on the Fort Fillmore parade ground.[17]

A soldier who arrived from Fort Buchanan with 1st Lieutenant Lord was murdered near Fort Fillmore soon after. The suspected murderer was apprehended. On April 25, 1859, Brevet-Major Gordon reported on the particulars of the case to the Department of New Mexico:

> ... I have the honor to report circumstances connected with the murder of a soldier belonging to Lt. Lord's Company, in the vicinity of this post, showing the course I have pursued.
>
> Five or six days since a report reached me that one of the men of this command had been found dead at the Ranch near here. Supposed to have been murdered. I immediately set to work, and after some investigation, found strong suspicions to rest upon a citizen by the name of McDermot. I then sent to Mesilla for the sheriff, who was prompt in attending upon my call. There was a coroner's inquest held over the body and from the evidence aduced [sic] before it, I was advised to send the prisoner over to Mesilla, for further investigation before the magisterial court, which was accordingly done. And upon the latter investigation McDermot was indicted for murder, and sent back to the post for me to imprison in consequence of the insecurity of the County jail. This request was made in writing by the sheriff and I have complied with it. McDermot is now under charge of the guard at the post, to await the meeting of the next term of County Court to be convened at Socorro some time in May next.[18]

The jail at Mesilla was apparently not escape proof, so the prisoner was held under guard at the more secure Fort Fillmore stockade. What is more amazing than the insecurity of the local jails is that Brevet-Major Gordon did not mention who was killed or provide any details of the incident. The man was taken to the Fort Fillmore cemetery and buried, hopefully with military honors, but was not provided a tombstone or marker for his grave.

May 1859 was one of the laziest months in Fort Fillmore's history, as it was for all of the Department of New Mexico. Correspondence between commands was at an absolute low and there seems to have been no event at Fort Fillmore worth reporting. How ironic that just when Fort Fillmore was at its greatest potential for responding (two mounted companies and only one infantry company), there was nothing for the horsemen to do. An active response against the Mescalero for the attack on Henry Lazelle's force had been shelved, due mostly to the quick response of the Mescalero leaders in seeking peace. The Navajos were quiet in the north and Apaches west of the Rio Grande were at peace with the Americans. The Mesilla Guard was no longer active in the field following the previous year's forays and arrests. Perhaps Colonel Benjamin Bonneville expressed the mood of this month of peace best when he said, "The Indians in the Department appear to be quiet, and I am happy to state that persons passing through the Navajo country report them as much more kindly and peaceably disposed than ever before." The same was true in the lands of the Apaches. Nothing to report.

Fort Fillmore came back to active life on June 12. Twenty men from Company 'C,' R.M.R., under the command of 2^d Lieutenant Henry McNeill, left the post for the Santa Rita Copper Mines. McNeill was to protect the miners until ordered to other duties.[19]

Indian Agent Michael Steck returned in June from assisting the Apaches near the mines and along the Gila River in planting crops. He met with Colonel Bonneville at Mesilla while Bonneville was on an inspection tour of forts and the general region, but not including Fort Fillmore. Bonneville wanted to send troops west to be stationed near the Apache farms in the location of the Burro Mountains. A new fort could be anticipated. The Apaches also farmed several locations along the Mimbres River near abandoned Fort Daniel Webster, as well as near the Alamosa River. There is no information that Colonel Bonneville visited Fort Fillmore for accommodations. Mesilla was growing and better quarters could be rented there.[20]

As of June 15, with 2[d] Lieutenant McNeill on his way to the mines, Agent Steck believed he must travel there as well to protect Indian interests and the peace of the region. The farming experiment was going well, at least for the Mimbres and Mogollon bands. So well, in fact, that Mangas Coloradas, the Mimbres Chief, told Agent Steck that if he would help him build a house he would live in it just as the white men and Mexicans did. Steck wanted to take four loads of corn and some beef cattle with him to the Burro Mountains camp. He seemed favorably disposed toward the stationing of troops there, adding that with a military post in the region, there should be few troubles with the area Apaches.[21]

Apaches crossing the border into the United States from Mexico had recently stolen some animals near Cook's Springs. This same band also raided the copper mines. Two of them were killed following the killing of one Mexican. Colonel Bonneville ordered twenty-five men and one officer be temporarily stationed at the mines. The Mescalero were initially blamed for a raid near Fort Craig, but the perpetrators were later found to be Mexicans. One of these thieves was captured and an animal retaken. In a turnabout, Indians near the Santa Rita Copper Mines reported two horses stolen from them in one incident and eight in another. The thieves were chased down, the stock recaptured, and the perpetrators turned over to the Alcalde at the mines.[22]

Colonel Bonneville, who mistrusted Dr. Steck as being too humanitarian, traveled to the Gila River country to assess the situation for himself. Bonneville had preconceived notions that the Apaches were simply addicted to theft and outlawry and the only means of controlling them was by force of arms. On his journey of inspection through Apachería, Bonneville met the Mimbreno Chief Mangas Coloradas. He was surprised to learn that the Mimbres bands had actually not caused a lot of trouble for the miners since Fort Webster closed in 1853. Steck advised him that such a situation could not hope to continue unless the Apaches were provided with more provisions as an insurance against raiding.[23]

*   *   *

More new and revolutionary weapons gradually made their way to the soldiers in the Department. On June 18, 1859, the Chief of Ordnance notified the adjutant of the R.M.R., Dabney Maury, at Fort Union, to expect sixty Maynard carbines and twelve thousand metallic cartridges for the weapons to be sent from the St. Louis Arsenal to the care of William Shoemaker, the Military Storekeeper at the Fort Union Depot. The Maynard carbine was destined for testing and possible future use by the Regiment of Mounted Riflemen. In addition, unspecified numbers of the new Burnside carbine would also be coming to the Department of New Mexico for testing. A Burnside carbine shell casing was found at Fort Fillmore in the 1970s.[24]

Brevet-Major Gordon left Fort Fillmore on June 27 headed for the Santa Rita Copper Mines in response to Bonneville's concerns. Second Lieutenant Henry McNeill and twenty men were already on guard there. Gordon's approximately fifty-three infantrymen were accompanied by 1st Lieutenant George Howland and forty-three rank and file of Company 'C,' Regiment of Mounted Rifles, along with a small detachment from Company 'D,' 1st Dragoons. There were over one hundred troops with the column, a force that probably terrified the Apaches when they saw it coming into their lands. Howland and his men established the camp and began construction of the necessary outlying structures.[25]

Brevet-Major Gordon returned to Fort Fillmore on July 28, having left Howland out on the grasslands. On August 16 an interesting letter was sent to the Department adjutant confirming the building of a stone corral on a site near the southern part of the Burro Mountains. Howland built it strong and permanent, as would befit the needs of the rising fort he intended would follow soon thereafter. He noted:

> ... I have indirectly heard today that the balance of my Company property which, [was] on route for this place, had reached as far as Cook's Springs, was ordered back by express on account of an order directing Company "C" to be [placed] on detached service.

I would most respectfully state that I have nearly completed stone stables for my horses. My men are quite comfortable, and if I am to remain here it will be necessary to have the balance of the Company property. I have provisions to last to January not with the exception of fresh meat, and have made every arrangement for the winter.

If I am not to remain here I most respectfully request I may be informed of the fact, and I will stop building.

And I would further state for the information of the Colonel comdg. the Dept. that the place selected is about 9 miles from Cow Spring and on the most direct route for the California mail. There is an abundance of grass, wood & water. A fine spring about 15 feet in diameter has been dug out and walled with fine stone. The surplus water runs to about 300 yards to a basin which is large enough to water all the animals. The soil is such here that in time I could find enough vegetables for the command. Wood is plenty, the best of pine limbs is only 12 miles from camp and lumber can be obtained to almost any amount. I am immediately in the midst of Indians. There are many of them at my camp daily [who] are pleased that I am here. They are glad that the government takes such an interest in their welfare. When they go below they ask my permission. They are very peaceful. I have learned all their camping grounds, and I think that it is for the interest of the service that this place should not be abandoned. Much more I might say favorable to this solution but I do not, knowing that it is not long since the Colonel Comdg. was on the ground and knows most all the advantages.[26]

Second Lieutenant Henry C. McNeill and his detachment returned to Fort Fillmore on August 20, 1859, their duties at the Santa Rita Copper Mines completed. McNeill left Fort Fillmore with a small escort for the Burro Mountains camp on September 2, 1859, to join the rest of his company still on duty there.

Fort Fillmore had not been inspected by an army-level Inspector General since the Mansfield inspection in 1853. On September 9 Lieutenant Colonel Joseph Eggleston Johnston, 1st United States Cavalry Regiment, arrived to inspect the post. Johnston filed a report on conditions at Fort Fillmore on September 12. Unlike usual references to the companies at the post, Johnston chose to use formal terminology in his descriptions. Brevet-Major

Gordon was in charge; 2^d Lieutenant Lord and Assistant Surgeon Cooper were the only officers present for duty with Company 'D,' 1st Dragoons, and the remnants of Company 'C,' R.M.R. Johnston referred to the companies as being commanded by Brevet-Major Fitzgerald ('D') and Brevet-Lieutenant Colonel Roberts ('C'); neither officer had appeared at Fort Fillmore to be with their company. The army at that time did refer to each company as belonging to its most senior officer, no matter whether he was present or not. Johnston was simply following tradition. He reported:

> ... I reached this place from Fort Craig on the 9th Inst. & have been engaged, since that day, in the inspection of the post. Bvt. Major Gordon's Company (H) 3rd Inf—Bvt. Major Fitz-gerald's (D) 1st Dragoons & Bvt. Lt. Col. Roberts' (C) R.M.R. compose the usual garrison. The Company last named is now temporarily detached. There are present a Capt., 2nd Lieut. Asst. Surgeon, hospital steward & 163 enlisted men. 31 of the latter are on extra & daily duty, 27 sick, & 7 confined.
>
> The arms, accoutrements & clothing of the infantry company are in good order—like those of the 3rd Infy. already reported upon. The men, however, who were seen both in close order & as skirmishers, are not well instructed. The firing was equal to that at Los Lunas. All the companies of this regiment have exhibited a want of skill which justifies me in regarding the differences observed as accidental. Major Gordon thinks unfavorably of Maynard's primer—his company had made some progress in the bayonet exercise; & is the only one I have seen which has commenced it. Several of the men have not activity enough to be efficient as skirmishers.
>
> The dragoon company is not well armed. All the men have sabres & Colt's navy revolvers—a majority, the pistol carbine —some Sharps & a few rifles of the Cal. .54 of an inch. The clothing and the accoutrements of the men are very good, but the saddles are much worn. The appearance of the backs of the horses proves that the shape of the saddles are bad—& Lieut. Lord reports that all the officers of his regiment whom he knows, condemn them. The 75 men have 45 horses. About 45 of these men have joined the company this year. There are 15 old soldiers—& 25 joined 2 years ago. The discipline of the company is better than the proficiency of the men in field

exercises. The main deficiency is in horsemanship. 10 of the horses were in the Mexican War. 32 have served 8 years, 14 years, & 22 years. The use of the revolver on horse back has not been taught as yet. The shooting with carbines, on foot, was equal to that of the infantry. The young officer now in command of the company, Lt. Lord, shows commendable zeal in its instruction.

Three of the men in confinement are undergoing sentences of General Courts Martial. Charges against the other four, who have been in confinement near two months, have been sent to department head quarters. It is here said to have been always difficult to bring prisoners to trial in this department. Most of the military offences committed by the garrison are consequences of the neighborhood of low drinking houses.

The quarters (for 4 companies), hospital, store houses, guard room & prison, are the best I have seen, altho' ragged in external appearance. The barracks rooms, however, are not quite large enough for full companies. The magazine & bake house, altho' apparently substantially built, are not well roofed.

The "books, papers & files" of the post, companies, Qr. Mr., Comy & surgeon, are complete. The store rooms good and secure, & the clothing & other property of both companies, kept with due care. The mess furniture, & messing arrangements generally, are very good. As each company has a large fund— that of Comy H being $1499.25, & that of Compy D $969.73. The post bake house is capacious enough to produce (44) rations of bread daily.

Major Gordon has $994 of regimental recruiting funds in his hands.

The hospital might serve as a model. The surgery, store room, wards & kitchen, are well organized & extremely neat— There have been 85 cases since the 1st of August. On being asked if the "supply table" contains all the medicines necessary here, & in sufficient quantities, Dr. Cooper gave me the enclosed memorandum. As he has served several years in this region, knowing its diseases, & is very capable of learning their treatment, I think it may be useful to his department.

The quarter master's stores are in excellent condition. He has 12 wagons, 1 serviceable ambulance, & 101 mules, 23 of which are to be sent to Albuquerque. Forage is good & comparatively cheap. The amount of money on hand is $3288.05.

The subsistence stores are in good order. The supply, received last fall, is sufficient for a year. The balance of money on hand is $790.42. Lieut. Lord, the officer acting as Qr. Mr. & Comy., seems to be very attentive to his duties.

There are four mountain howitzers at the post, with about 100 rounds of ammunition. The only available ammunition for small arms, in the magazine, is for Colt's navy revolver, of which there are 19000 cartridges. There is a quantity of old musket cartridges which might supply material for ammunition for target practice, if ball moulds were provided. Each company has in its possession a small quantity of ammunition for the arms with which it is equipped.

A chaplain has entered upon his duties in the few weeks. There are 8 pupils, soldiers children, in the post school.

The four senior sergeants are detailed as acting officers of the day—The others as non-commissioned officers of the guard.[27]

Lieutenant Colonel Joseph Eggleston Johnston was born in Virginia in 1807 and was fifty-two years old when he inspected Fort Fillmore. A West Point graduate, Class of 1829, he was a classmate of Robert E. Lee, whose career followed Johnston's closely. On June 18, 1860, he was appointed quartermaster general of the United States Army, with the rank of brigadier general. Johnston gave up that position and his army career on April 22, 1861, when he accepted a position as brigadier general in the Army of the Confederacy. Performing well at 1st Bull Run in 1861, Johnston was raised to the rank of full general and placed in command of the Army of Northern Virginia, later Lee's command. He was ranked fourth in seniority for Confederate generals, behind Samuel Cooper, Albert Sidney Johnston, and Robert E. Lee. While leading the Army of Northern Virginia at Seven Pines in 1862 he was severely wounded. It was then Lee replaced him in command. Johnston was later named commander of the Department of the West. He was involved at Vicksburg and was Hood's replacement in command of the Army of the Tennessee, an army which suffered defeat after defeat, mostly due to the fact that they were invariably outnumbered and outgunned. According to sources, Johnston was one of the senior Confederate officers who refused a parole following the war, in effect never surrendering.[28]

Lieutenant Colonel Johnston, as had Mansfield before him, raised as many questions concerning Fort Fillmore as he answered during the 1859 inspection. Obviously, the enlisted men were no longer wearing the Mexican War era uniforms as they had been in 1853. Had they been doing so Johnston would have remarked on it, as did Mansfield. They were possibly still wearing Model 1839 Forage Caps, although the previous year had seen the introduction of the French-influenced kepi as standard wear. The kepi may have been worn by the newest recruits, many of whom were resident in the dragoon company.

The mention of weapons provides other changes from 1853. The .69 Caliber Musket was replaced in the infantry company ('H') by the more powerful and long-range .58 Caliber Rifle-Musket, firing the elongated Minie ball. Johnston did not specifically note this change, but he remarked that there were still many of the "old musket cartridges" available which could be used as practice if melted down and re-cast as Minie balls. In the 1970s an entire box (over eight hundred complete rounds) of the old .69 caliber cartridges was excavated at Fort Fillmore. These were the buck-and-ball type cartridge having one .69 caliber ball and three small buckshot balls. The fact that these were found entire may indicate Johnston's recommendation was not adopted, or they may have come to the post later with the 7th Infantry.

The .36 caliber Colt Navy Pistol ammunition commonly found at Fort Fillmore, indicates the weapon of choice for mounted units in the late 1850s. Interestingly, the dragoon soldiers were not yet fully trained in using that weapon from the saddle. The Colt was a cavalry weapon initially and Lieutenant Colonel Johnston was a cavalry-man from the 1st Cavalry Regiment. He would have quickly noted inefficiency in the use of that weapon. Johnston's mention of the presence of what might have been the Model 1855 .58 Caliber Pistol-Carbine is interesting. Surely, he was referring to the then-modern weapon rather than some ancient Mexican War period piece. If so, dragoon soldiers in Lord's company were using the Colt Revolver and the

Pistol-Carbine, a weapon combination normally associated in most modern references with the two existing cavalry regiments.

The mention of Brevet-Major Gordon's dislike of the Maynard primer, then in use on at least some of the .58 Caliber Rifle-Muskets, is interesting. Lieutenant Colonel Miles also never liked the system. The Maynard, which operated much like a child's cap pistol, often misfired. Its use was eventually discontinued. No sign of that primer, or of any excavated materials related to it, has been identified among Fort Fillmore artifacts. A few of the weapons may have been brought to the fort for testing.

William H. Gordon left Fort Fillmore for Fort Marcy in Santa Fe on September 26, 1859. The infantrymen of Company 'H' went with him. Fort Fillmore was reduced to one officer, an assistant surgeon, seventy-two enlisted men of Company 'D,' 1st Dragoons, and nineteen enlisted men from Company 'C,' R.M.R., left behind to protect public property.[29]

First Lieutenant George Washington Howland and an escort of six men returned from Burro Mountain Camp on October 17. Second Lieutenant McNeill and the rest of Company 'C,', R.M.R. were still on detached service there. The situation at Fort Fillmore was changing rapidly, making Howland's return an absolute necessity. First Lieutenant Richard Lord and Company 'D,' 1st Dragoons', departure in late October would leave no officer in charge who knew the post. Assistant Surgeon George Cooper prepared to leave as well. Preparations were made to receive troops from an 8th Infantry Company coming up from Fort Bliss. They had to be properly welcomed and settled. Howland was the only officer available who could perform that task.[30]

Captain William Elliot stayed briefly at Fort Fillmore and reported on a field expedition that the Mounted Rifles of his Company 'A' were about to conduct. Apparently, 2d Lieutenant Richard Lord and Company 'D' were to be involved in Elliot's campaign, although Captain Elliot did not mention Lord in his brief letter to the Department on October 22 detailing the coming expedition. He mentioned Company 'C,' R.M.R., rather than the dragoons as being part of the expedition. Company 'C' was still at Burro Mountain. Elliot reported:

... I have the honor to inform the Department Commander, that the details from Fort Bliss Texas, and Fort Fillmore N.M. have been organized as required by S.O. 121 Sept. 26th. 1859. And that the command will leave tomorrow for the depot on the San Pedro. Col. Reeve has been notified of this. Fifty rounds per man, of rifle and carbine cartridges, and 24 of pistol is being taken. Also a pair of horse shoes, and a pair of mule shoes, with nails for same, and extra nails. Twelve head of beef cattle will also be taken. A <u>notice</u> from Capt. Wainright, of Ordnance Stores having been <u>ordered</u>, has been received at this post. The horses of Co. 'C' Rifles, having recently joined from "the field", and the greater portion of those of Co. 'A' Rifles having been received from Fort Leavenworth are thin, and require corn, which I have arranged to be taken, 8 lbs. to the animal for 15 days. Without this the horse would not be in condition for the campaign, or reaching the depot. The Dept. Commander has in this, a report of the equipment etc. of my command, which I consider <u>all</u> that can be taken for the march.[31]

Whatever Elliot intended to say, 2[d] Lieutenant Richard Lord led Company 'D,' 1st Dragoons, numbering seventy-two soldiers, left Fort Fillmore on October 23, 1859. Lord's troops, destined for a long campaign in the field against the Apaches, did not return to Fort Fillmore until January 1860. We cannot be sure Assistant Surgeon George Cooper left with Lord, although he may have. Cooper was replaced by Assistant Surgeon James Cooper McKee. Until McKee arrived the Fort Fillmore hospital was without a doctor. Hospital Steward Fitzwilliams had to suffice.[32]

On October 26 Fort Fillmore received an infantry contingent to replace the company that left in September with Brevet-Major Gordon. For the first time in its history Fort Fillmore spent a month without an infantry company at the post. This was highly unusual for a major nineteenth-century United States Army post. The infantry's primary job was to guard public property and the post itself. The arrival of Company 'E,' 8th United States Infantry Regiment, from Fort Bliss, restored the ancient equilibrium of post life. Company 'E,' at about half regulation size, had two of its three officers present—1st Lieutenant Milton Cogswell, commanding, and 2[d] Lieutenant Royal Thaxter Frank. The headquarters of the 8th Infantry was in Texas, although not at Fort Bliss, which still nominally belonged to the Department of New Mexico. Moving Company 'E' to Fort Fillmore was almost like making an orphan of the unit, as was so often the case with dragoon companies in New Mexico.[33]

On November 6, 1859, Indian Agent Steck traveled to Apache Pass in the Chiricahua Mountains with rations suitable for feeding about four hundred people. While he was there Cochise returned a few stolen animals and again promised to watch over the route of the Butterfield Overland Mail, which was peacefully going about its business. However, Apache stock raids north of the border were on the increase and the army threatened to mount a campaign against the Chiricahua in Western New Mexico (now Arizona) if the raids did not cease.[34]

Dr. Steck held a huge ceremonial smoke with some two thousand five hundred Coyotero, Mogollon, Pinal, and Mimbreno Apaches near what became the town of Safford, Arizona. About this same time, in November 1859, a small band of Gila Apaches attacked a rancho near Santo Tomás, across the river from Fort Fillmore, killing two or three people and making off with stock. The Mescalero were accused but they were innocent. The editor of the new local newspaper, the *Mesilla Miner*, prompted: "How long, oh! how long are we to endure these outrages. Will Congress never give us protection?" The raid probably took place as described in the newspaper even though the military command at Fort Fillmore took no written notice of it in its correspondence with the Department.[35]

Michael Steck returned to Apache Agency following a month-long trip and, on November 25, informed Superintendent Collins of what he found. He distributed presents to members of the Gila and Mogollon bands at the Burro Mountains on October 29. Eight hundred Indians, nearly the entire tribe, met Agent Steck, who had been among them without an escort. From the Burro Mountains he proceeded west to the San Simon River. Here he met with the 'Chilicagua' Apaches and distributed presents to some four hundred. He never mentioned the presence of the great Chief Cochise by name. The Butterfield Overland Mail coaches on the "great road to California," as Dr. Steck called the passage, traveled, without incident, directly through the Chiricahua country while he was there.[37]

Dr. Steck recommended in this letter that the 'Chilicagua' be settled with Mangas Coloradas and his people at Santa Lucia on one large reservation. The Coyoteros, Pinals, and Tontos would, if Dr. Steck got his way, be "compelled to confine themselves to the country north of the Gila until the wants of our people render it necessary that they should be confined to smaller reservations." By fixing them north of the Gila, with no permission to roam south, the land between the Gila and the Mexican border could be opened to settlement.[38]

Even more powerful test weapons appeared in New Mexico Territory as the year 1859 ended. A November 20, 1859, letter from the Ordnance Office in Washington to Colonel Loring, commanding the R.M.R., stated that the Colt's Revolving Rifle was being considered as a weapon destined for use by Loring's Riflemen. Two hundred ninety-eight Colt Rifles and two hundred fifty ball cartridges per rifle were being shipped from the St. Louis Arsenal as soon as practicable. The two hundred ninety-eight Colt Rifles were to be supplied to ten companies. Probably only a few of the R.M.R. companies were issued these weapons. Perhaps this was intended as a test of the usability of the weapon in the field.[36]

President James Buchanan presented his 3[d] Annual Message on December 6, 1859. He addressed the recent bloody incident at Harpers Ferry in which John Brown led a force of armed men in an attempt to free the slaves. Buchanan pleaded "... let me implore my countrymen, North and South, to cultivate the ancient feelings of mutual forbearance and good will toward each other and strive to allay the demon spirit of sectional hatred and strife now alive in the land." He spoke of the slave ship *Wanderer* and its cargo of three to four hundred, saying that the laws against new slaves coming into the country by any means had to be enforced. He also spoke of the vested rights of slave owners to take their property into any of the new territories, including New Mexico, without fear. President Buchanan spoke of the continuing problems with Mexico, Cuba, and with the British in Washington near the Canadian border. He repeated his request of the previous year, which had not been acted on, to establish United States Army posts in Chihuahua and Sonora. He also called for the establishment of a territorial government over Arizona. Had President Buchanan had his way the town of Paso del Norte, now Juárez, would have been transferred to American soil as Mesilla had been in 1855.[39]

At Fort Fillmore on the last day of 1859, there were three companies—Company 'E,' 8th Infantry, remnants of Company 'D,' 1st Dragoons, and remnants of Company 'C,' R.M.R.. There were three officers and ninety-five enlisted men, with 1st Lieutenant George Howland in command. First Lieutenant Milton Cogswell and 2[d] Lieutenant Royal Thaxter Frank were in charge of Company 'E,' but undoubtedly helped watch over the remnants of the other two. There was no doctor, as Assistant Surgeon James Cooper McKee had not reported for duty. The Reverend H.S. Bishop tended to the religious needs of the men. Four twelve-pounder mountain howitzers sat rusting on the parade ground, seeing only ceremonial use. The custom of having one howitzer with each infantry company had ended at some point and there is no mention of any of these guns traveling with a detached unit. Their next official use in the field was not until July 1861.[40]

NOTES - Chapter 11

1. Steck to Collins, January 1, 1859, Indian Bureau, Roll 4.
2. Ibid.
3. Backus to Wilkins, January 14, 1859, M1120, Rolls 9/10.
4. Gordon to Wilkins, January 14, 1859, M1120, Rolls 9/10.

5. Heitman, George Washington Howland.

6. Ibid.

7. Fort Fillmore Post Returns, January 1859.

8. Gordon to Wilkins, January 21, 1859, M1120, Rolls 9/10.

9. Edwin Sweeney, *Cochise*, pp. 124, 125.

10. Steck to Collins, February 2, 1859, Indian Bureau, Roll 4

11. Gordon to Wilkins, February 3, 1859, M1120, Rolls 9/10.

12. Unknown to Wilkins, February 11, 1859, M1120, Rolls 9/10. The name of the author cannot be deduced from the report, though it must have been one of the officers serving at Fort Bliss.

13. Gordon to Wilkins, February 20, 1859, M1120, Rolls 9/10.

14. Holmes to Gordon, February 21, 1859, M1120, Rolls 9/10.

15. Steck to Collins, February 27, 1859, Indian Bureau, Roll 4.

16. Fort Fillmore Post Returns, March 1859.

17. Fort Fillmore Post Returns, April, 1859.

18. Gordon to Wilkins, April 25, 1859, M1120, Rolls 9/10.

19. Fort Fillmore Post Returns, June 1859.

20. Steck to Collins, June 15, 1859, Indian Bureau, Roll 4.

21. Ibid.

22. Ibid.

23. John Upton Terrell, *Apache Chronicles*, p. 215.

24. Craig to Maury, June 18, 1859, M1120, Rolls 9/10.

25. Fort Fillmore Post Returns, August 1859.

26. Howland to Acting Assistant Adjutant General, Santa Fe, M1120, Rolls 9/10.

27. Johnston to Assistant Adjutant General, September 12, 1859, M1120, Rolls 9/10.

28. Ezra J. Warner, *Generals in Gray*, pp. 161, 162.

29. Fort Fillmore Post Returns, September 1859.

30. Fort Fillmore Post Returns, October 1859.

31. Elliot to Wilkins, October 22, 1859, M1120, Rolls 9/10.

32. Fort Fillmore Post Returns, October 1859.

33. Fort Fillmore Post Returns, November 1859.

34. Edwin Sweeney, *Cochise*, pp. 132, 133.

35. John Upton Terrell, *Apache Chronicles*, p. 217.

36. Craig to Loring, November 20, 1859, M1120, Rolls 9/10.

37. Steck to Collins, November 25, 1859, Indian Bureau, Roll 4.

38. Ibid.

39. James D. Richardson, *Messages and Papers of the Presidents*, pp. 3083-3107.

40. Fort Fillmore Post Returns, December 1859.

Dragoon soldiers leaving a comrade on the Jornada del Muerto.
Courtesy: Loren Schmidt, artist.

Horse breast decorative martingales from Fort Fillmore.
Co. 'E,' 2^d Dragoons - 1852; Co. 'F,' R.M.R. - 1861;
Co. 'G,' R.M.R. - 1856-57; Co. 'D,' 2^d Dragoons - 1852-53.
Courtesy: Author

12

1860 - WAR CLOUDS IN THE EAST

On January 14, 1860, relations between the Apaches and the Butterfield Stage Line began to deteriorate. Stage line employees heard rumors that Indians living near the Apache Pass stage station were threatening to attack the stations or the coaches. Less than a week later, on January 18, 1860, Apache raiders seized forty head of stock between San Simon and Apache Pass, but did not kill anybody. Other Apaches, like the Pinal, told them that Cochise's group and the Coyoteros were raiding in the area of the Gadsden Purchase and in Sonora and Chihuahua.[1]

Apaches were not the only raiders operating early in 1860. On January 21, the Consulate of the United States in Paso del Norte (modern Juárez) reported the presence of a band of four or five hundred Mexican bandits operating in the state of Chihuahua, plundering towns and ranches. The Consulate feared the bandits would take Paso del Norte, leading to a situation wherein the lives of American citizens would be at risk. The Consul, David R. Diffendorffer, expected to call upon the commanding officer at Fort Bliss to come and help the Mexican military forces defend Paso del Norte if it was attacked. There was a precedent for such action. At Matamoras, a threat from a bandit named Cortinas to attack that town led the authorities of Brownsville, Texas, to send a force across the border to help in the defense. Had such an attack occurred, there is no doubt Fort Fillmore's mounted troops would have been sent south.[2]

On January 22, 2^d Lieutenant Richard Lord, Company 'D,' 1st Dragoons, and 2^d Lieutenant Henry McNeill, Company 'C,' R.M.R., brought their respective detachments back to Fort Fillmore following campaigning in the West. The Burro Mountain Camp and Howland's corral were now officially abandoned. No new fort was to be built near the Gila River at that time. Brevet-Major and Captain E.H. Fitzgerald, whose company Richard Lord commanded, died in Los Angeles, California of consumption. Fitzgerald had not been with his company when it was at Fort Buchanan or Fort Fillmore.[3]

Assistant Surgeon James Cooper McKee arrived at Fort Fillmore on January 22. During the three-month absence of a medical officer, the Fort Fillmore soldiers were not necessarily without medical care. A medical technician, one assumes we would call him a nurse today, by the name of Fitzwilliams was available. Sergeant Fitzwilliams wore a distinguishing uniform and only performed service at the hospital. He was not available for other duties.[4]

On February 1, 1860, the 10th Legislative Assembly for New Mexico Territory attempted to do something about the impossible situation arising from the size of Doña Ana County. That entity stretched from Texas to the California border. The Territorial Legislature proposed to Congress that a new County of Arizona be created out of Doña Ana County at a point one mile east of the Apache Canyon mail station on the Butterfield line. The end point of Arizona County was to be the current California border. The town of Tubac was designated the county seat. No effective government was established by the time the Civil War began, but certain citizens in the Mesilla Valley and the mining regions to the west took the proposal be a fact and set up an Arizona government. The would-be Arizonans wanted all lands up to the Rio Grande River, including the town of Mesilla, to be part of a new Territory rather than just a county. On July 8, 1861, the county seat of the still mythical Territory of Arizona was changed to Tucson.

Fort Fillmore, according to the Mesilla filibusterers—among the most ardent supporters of the proposed Territory of Arizona— would remain part of New Mexico Territory and Doña Ana County. On February 4, 1860, 1st Lieutenant George Washington Howland made no mention of any political decisions related to Mesilla across the river but did report to the Department on the condition of the cavalry horses at Fort Fillmore:

> ... I have the honor to acknowledge the receipt of your letter dated Jany. 29th 1860, in relation to horses, and would state in reply for the information of the Dept. Commander, that I have carefully examined the horses at this post and find in Company "D" 1st Drags nine (9) that in my opinion are unfit for Cavalry service and six (6) in Company "C" Regt. Mounted Rifles, and think they could be used in a light battery. They are mostly sore backed.[5]

The term 'Drags,' used in reference to the dragoon-mounted company, has been noted before in other correspondence. Was this a nickname all the soldiers used for that mounted arm or was Howland simply abbreviating and forgot his period? The Regiment of Mounted Rifles is referred to in several abbreviated ways. In this letter Howland almost used the entire name, abbreviating the word "Regt." and omitting the word "of." Others used "R.M.R.," "Mounted Rifles," or simply "Rifles." R.M.R. was always the favored acronym, a term used today by the few who still remember that elite U.S. Army mounted regiment of the pre-Civil War days.

Howland's recommendation that the broken down horses be used with light artillery is interesting. The lack of use of the many pieces of light artillery available in the Department of New Mexico, especially in the late 1850s and early 1860s, is incomprehensible. The guns simply rusted away wherever they happened to be. When a fort was abandoned, the cannon were hauled to another place to sit, as happened to the two Fort Thorn twelve-pounders when that post was abandoned. Not since Brevet-Major Israel Richardson towed a mountain howitzer to Fort Daniel

Webster in late 1851 had a Fort Fillmore artillery piece been used in action.

On February 22 United States Marshal George Frazer reported to Howland that disturbances occurring in Mesilla had led to three deaths and the wounding of one other person. Frazer did not say what had sparked the killings, only that he feared more disturbances might occur and Fort Fillmore troops might be needed to bring stability to the town.[6]

Howland quickly acknowledged the marshal's note, but wanted more confirmation before sending troops. The Lieutenant requested that Frazer send a petition to the fort signed by the prominent citizens of the town, asking that troops be sent.[7] A petition appeared almost immediately, signed by most of the early Mesilla persons of influence—Samuel Bean, Samuel Cozzens, Steven Ochoa, B. Hamilton, A. Layman, Rafael Ruelas, Jesus Cordoba, Benito Varela, Antonio Lopez, George Lucas, G. Oury, Jesus Lucero, D.W. Hubbard, Octaviano Ruelas, and others.[8]

Upon receiving the petition, Howland ordered 1st Lieutenant Milton Cogswell of the 8th Infantry to take a detachment of eighty troops to Mesilla to quell any disturbances between the citizens.[9] Mesilla had become so dangerous that Marshal Frazer formally requested permission to quarter his family temporarily at Fort Fillmore, rather than at Las Cruces.[10]

On February 24 Cogswell provided details about what had happened to cause the three deaths:

> ... In compliance with Order No. 53, I left Fort Fillmore on the 22nd. inst. with Lt. Frank & 80 men & encamped the same evening near the Town of Mesilla.
>
> I found that considerable excitement prevailed, but the mere presence of the troops gave confidence to all good citizens, and order was fully restored.
>
> It appears that the difficulty originated in some steps taken by the Prefect Barilla, (since resigned) and was greatly complicated by the killing of one woman (Mexican) and three men (Mexican) on the evening and night before my arrival.
>
> The woman was accidently shot in an affray; one man was killed in a street brawl; the other two were killed by American

patrols—All were killed by Americans—The Mexican population were perfectly willing that the law should take its course, but before any action was taken the rioters had escaped. A considerable excitement still prevails among the Mexican population, and I think it will be some time before it subsides; yet, there is a sufficient number of good citizens in Mesilla, if they should act in concert, to preserve law & order.

I returned with my command to the Post, this day, and I am under the impression that a force is not required in Mesilla to protect good citizens.[11]

When Cogswell used the term 'American,' and when it is used elsewhere in this book, he meant the community of Anglo-European-American people who came to the region following the War with Mexico. Several deaths among the 'Mexican' population had been caused by 'Americans.' Anglo vigilantes roaming the streets brings back memories of the Mesilla Guard roaming Apache camps. The cultures, which got along most of the time, were creating hardships that would be remembered in the coming bad times. No doubt Marshal Frazer was involved in the killings, or else he would not have asked to send his family to the fort. With Cogswell's troopers in town the storm quickly abated.

Apache Agency was still functioning in March 1860, although Fort Thorn was now abandoned. The badly overworked and over-extended Agent Steck received word on March 5 that an agent named Archuleta was to be sent to Fort Stanton to take charge of the Mescalero. Throughout the latter 1850s Michael Steck had requested a new agent to take on part of his load. Steck reported that because of the price of corn near Fort Stanton he would be supplying less corn meal to the Mescalero than he had intended. There was a plus side to this. The Mescalero benefited because they could not ferment as much of their intoxicating 'liquor' as a result. Four or five beeves per month were necessary to feed the Mescalero, and he recommended they wait to give beef cattle until the planting season, then issue them about twenty so the Apaches would carry forth with the farming effort. If they were too content and well fed, the Mescalero seemed to slack off in their farm work. The farming was done that season on the Rio Peñasco, about thirty-five miles south of Fort Stanton. The bands of Negrito and Jose Pino had farmed there the previous year and the location was far from any settlements. The situation with the Mescalero was tense, ever since the fight with Lieutenant Lazelle.[12]

North, east, and west, trouble with the Indians was brewing. Cochise, with some one hundred warriors, returned to Sonora and to raiding. His raiding band ambushed and killed four travelers and soon after killed another eleven Mexicans, all soldiers, followed by an additional seven victims. He had not yet struck against Americans, or the Butterfield Overland Mail.[13]

The Prefect of Doña Ana County, L.S. Owings, then in Mesilla, wrote 1st Lieutenant Howland at Fort Fillmore requesting a company of U.S. troops to chase a band of Indians, leader unknown, headed for the Mimbres. The raiders had committed outrages near Mesilla on the night of March 7, 1860. Forty men from a reconstituted Mesilla Guard were already in pursuit. On March 9, 1st Lieutenant Howland ordered 2d Lieutenant Henry McNeill and thirty soldiers from Company 'C,' R.M.R. to chase the raiders. No Apaches were found during the hunt and the troops returned to the fort.[14]

Howland reported that Daniel Griffin, a former Company 'C,' R.M.R., soldier, discharged about a month before, was killed by Indians on March 8. Griffin, working for a Mesilla mercantile house, was traveling about nine miles south of Fort Fillmore when the Indians struck. Griffin was wounded in the fight and died of those wounds about one-half hour after the fight.[15]

Company 'C,' R.M.R., commanded by 1st Lieutenant Howland and assisted by 2d Lieutenant McNeill, left Fort Fillmore for duty at Fort Craig on March 17, 1860. First Lieutenant Milton Cogswell, commanding Company 'E,' 8th Infantry, took command of the fort. Troops remaining at Fort Fillmore included Company 'E,' 8th Infantry and Company 'D,' 1st Dragoons, comprising a total of one hundred twelve soldiers.[16]

The first recorded trouble along the Butterfield Overland Mail route occurred on April 7, 1860. Warriors reported to be from

Cochise's band stole some stock at the Dragoon Springs Stage Station. When Samuel Cozzens of Mesilla interviewed Cochise on the matter, the latter denied any responsibility for the act.[17]

In April 1860 the settlements and towns of southern New Mexico elected delegates to a citizens' convention in Tucson to set up a provisional government for southern New Mexico and what is now Arizona. James A. Lucas of Mesilla served as president of the convention. Granville Oury from Doña Ana County served as secretary. A provisional constitution was adopted and Mesillans predominated in appointive offices. Dr. Lewis S. Owings of Mesilla was elected provisional governor. Ignacio Orrantia, a prosperous trader and politician from Chamberino, was appointed lieutenant governor. Dr.Owings filled out the Arizona Provisional Government cabinet by appointing James Lucas as secretary of state. Samuel Bean, who was Doña Ana County sheriff at the time, was appointed marshal for the as yet hypothetical Territory of Arizona. Another Provisional Territory district judge was S.H. Cozzens, attorney for the Butterfield Overland Mail Company.[18]

The 3[d] Infantry Regiment, still under Bonneville's command at Albuquerque, was ordered out of the Department and back to Texas following eleven years of duty in New Mexico. First Lieutenant John Darragh Wilkins, himself 3[d] Infantry and acting assistant adjutant general for the Department of New Mexico, notified a Captain 'H.B.' at Fort Union that his company and Company 'H,' 3[d] Infantry, would take the route of the Pecos River into Texas.[19]

On April 28 Major C.C. Sibley was directed to take Companies 'F' and 'H,' 3[d] Infantry, from Fort Union into Texas as soon as possible, picking up 1st Lieutenant Joseph Whistler, and Company 'I' en route. Company 'I' was on the march from Fort Craig and not yet at Fort Fillmore when this order was issued.[20]

The 7th Infantry Regiment, most of its soldiers still stationed at Camp Floyd, Utah, that April, was the regiment intended to replace the 3[d] Infantry in New Mexico Territory. On April 29 Colonel Fauntleroy, rising to the command in New Mexico with Bonneville leaving, mentioned the impending arrival of the 7th in a letter to the Army Assistant Adjutant General. Most of the 7th Infantry companies were to garrison posts in Arizona and new sites in western New Mexico.[21]

Company 'I,' 3d Infantry Regiment, under the command of 1st Lieutenant Joseph Nelson Garland Whistler, arrived at Fort Fillmore on April 30, 1860, just in time for Whistler to take command of the post on the day when the monthly data was recorded. Company 'I' had two officers and fifty-one enlisted men. The second officer was 2d Lieutenant Richard Gregory Lay. On the day Whistler arrived, 1st Lieutenant Milton Cogswell, Company 'E,' 8th Infantry, left Fort Fillmore for an assignment in the East at Fort Columbus, New York. Second Lieutenant Royal Thaxter Frank took command of Company 'E.' The mounted company at Fort Fillmore, Company 'D,' 1st Dragoons, remained under the command of 2d Lieutenant Richard S.C. Lord.[22]

On May 1, 1st Lieutenant Henry Lazelle, then stationed at Fort Bliss, was ordered to proceed as quickly as possible to Fort Fillmore to take over the public property at that post, as the 3d Infantry company then serving there was soon to leave for Texas as per orders.[23] Preparation to leave orders were sent to other 3d Infantry companies at the same time. Captain George Sykes, a former Fort Fillmore alumnus now commanding Company 'K' at Los Lunas, was ordered to abandon that post, with no replacement company expected, and to move toward Texas.[24]

The 3d Infantry companies at Fort Defiance, including Company 'C,' were ordered on May 6 to prepare to leave that post. Troops from Utah were due to arrive soon. The name of the regiment coming from Utah was not provided but would have included companies from the 5th Infantry Regiment.

On May 13 a letter was sent from Mesilla to 1st Lieutenant Whistler at Fort Fillmore under the heading of La Mesilla, Arizona, and signed by the Provisional Governor of the Territory of Arizona. This was the officially unrecognized 'Governor' Owings of Arizona, and he said:

... I have the honor to transmit to you a letter just received by express from the Rio Mimbres—from my acquaintance with the writer thereof I am well convinced of the [truth] of its contents. I have therefore most respectfully to request that if in your power to do so, you will dispatch a company of say 30 United States troops to the Mimbres for the better protection of those families residing there. Should you be unable to do this soon, I would most respectfully ask that you furnish me from the United States Government Stores at Fort Fillmore, rations for 30 men for a term of thirty days, and I will immediately dispatch that number of mounted volunteers to the relief of the settlers. I regard the settlements upon the Mimbres as of vast importance to the future well being of the Territory, and desire to do everything in my power to protect them. A reply by bearer will greatly oblige.[25]

First Lieutenant Whistler no longer had a mounted force to send; undoubtedly he would not have sent it if he did. Instead, he notified the Department of New Mexico of 'Provisional Governor' Owings's request for assistance, underlining the prestigious title.

... Enclosed herewith I have the honor to forward communications received from the <u>Provisional Governor</u> of Arizona. In answer to these communications I informed him that owing to the present Dept. Orders, it was impossible to furnish any troops from this Post, and as to the second request for provisions, I did not feel authorized to furnish them to Volunteers without special instructions from Dept. Hd. Quarters.[26]

At some point, exact date unknown but certainly before the arrival of 2ᵈ Lieutenant Henry Lazelle at Fort Fillmore, Company 'E,' 8ᵗʰ Infantry, commanded by 2ᵈ Lieutenant Royal Thaxter Frank, departed the post, probably headed back to Fort Bliss. The destination of Company 'E' was supposed to be 'Fort Butler,' a proposed new fort on the Pecos or Red Rivers. A Fort Butler Military Reservation was established, but an actual Fort Butler was never constructed or manned. The American Civil War got in the way.[27]

The *Mesilla Miner* reported on June 9 an Indian raid on the farming community of Santo Tomás, just across the river from Fort Fillmore. The raid lead to the death of José M. Montoya and members of his family. One peon and one nine year old were left alive, while the rest were killed and the ranch house burned to the ground. The newspaper appealed to the government to save the people of the Mesilla Valley. The event was not even reported to higher headquarters by 1st Lieutenant Joseph Whistler commanding Fort Fillmore. It must have been clear to the farmers and ranchers that fifty infantrymen could not assist in staving off a hit and run raid anywhere in the area. Given the conditions in the town and at the fort, it would appear to have been better to move the troops into Mesilla where they could at least react. Government concern for Fort Fillmore's valuable public property rendered such a decision unsupportable. The Santo Tomás raid was not the only recent Indian incursion in the area. Unidentified Indians stole six mules from the Fort Fillmore Mining Company in the Organ Mountains and some oxen from a party traveling near Cook's Springs to the west. One man was wounded in the latter affray.[28]

The 1860 Census, for the first time, provided a detailed analysis of one company actively serving at Fort Fillmore. That census caught Joseph N.G. Whistler's Company 'I,' 3d Infantry Regiment, in a snapshot of time. A ten-man fragment of the 8th Infantry company led by Henry Lazelle was also included. The Census gave more than just the muster role names of soldiers; it provided the name and function of every person at the post.

Assistant Surgeon J. Cooper McKee, aged thirty, was listed first. His name was followed by that of 1st Lieutenant Joseph Whistler (thirty-seven), 2d Lieutenant Richard Lay (twenty-six) and 2d Lieutenant Henry Lazelle (twenty-six). These officers were single or their wives and families were not present at the post. Richard Lay had a civilian guest visiting at the time, W. Worth (age twenty) from New York. One civilian clerk and former soldier, James Griggs, performed office duties.

Women were at the post serving in a number of capacities. George Hayward, the Post Sutler, was assisted by his wife Ellen, who also was mother to two little girls, Florence (three) and Maria (two). Mary Landreth (thirty), an Irish immigrant, served in an unknown capacity. Four laundresses were allowed at the post. Maria McKane, Mexican (twenty-five), wife of John McKane a laborer on the post and a former soldier from Ireland, was probably one laundress. Bridget Lander (thirty), wife of clerk William Lander (twenty-seven), may have been a second laundress. The Landers were also Irish immigrants. Onez Snyder, Mexican (thirty-one), may have been a third laundress. She was the wife of C. Snyder (thirty), a German immigrant listed as a laborer. None of these ladies had children at the time. Another woman at the post was Dolores Mendez (thirty-seven), who may have been married to Christian Duper (thirty-three), a merchant working for the Post Sutler. Married or not, Dolores had three children, Enacia, a female (fifteen), Joseph, a male (four), and Emelsa, a female (two). There was one other married soldier. William McBride (thirty-eight), from Ireland, was married to Mary McBride (twenty-seven). They had three children, William, James, and Patrick. It is interesting to note that one of Mary's children was classified as a Kentuckian, while the other two were said to be New Mexicans, having been conceived in the Territory.

Jacob Kiluntz [sic] (thirty-three), from the State of Baden in what eventually became Germany, was a working blacksmith. His salary of fifty dollars a month was a tidy sum in those days when soldiers received ten. A second blacksmith, P. Hughes, (thirty-three), from Texas, may have served the needs of the company other than the one Jacob served. There was a carpenter from New York as well, but his name is unreadable.

Probably of most interest are the nationalities of the soldiers listed. Were they Americans, or were they foreign immigrants as general tradition would have it? Twenty-eight of the forty-nine soldiers were listed as Irish immigrants, while fourteen were from Germany. There was no Germany at that date, so the men are listed as being from the German States of Baden, Bavaria, Wurttemberg,

Prussia, etc. One man was from Canada. Only six were American citizens, most of them from the Northeast rather than from the South where it seems only officers were recruited. Such numbers explain why the enlisted men were not open to future Confederate blandishments to jump sides and join their cause. Most of these young men probably didn't know there was a cause. They served the Government of the United States to earn citizenship.

There were very few teenagers, unlike our modern force, but many men in their early twenties. The average age was about twenty-two to twenty-three, with the oldest being Irish immigrant William McBride, age thirty-eight. He may have been the 1st sergeant of Company 'E.' Several of the soldiers were over thirty.

The Department was changing its base units even as the census was being taken. Colonel Fauntleroy considered detaining six companies of the arriving 7th Infantry Regiment, destined for what Fauntleroy was himself now calling 'Arizona,' and companies of the 5th Infantry Regiment, for use against the Navajos near Fort Defiance. Brevet-Lieutenant Colonel Canby, 10th Infantry, was designated to command an expedition into the Navajo lands. Fauntleroy did not intend a major campaign against the Navajos in 1860. He wanted to inflict as much damage as he could during the fall with a few troops and then strike them even harder with a larger force during the spring of 1861. On August 7, Colonel Fauntleroy reported sending Brevet-Lieutenant Colonel Pitcairn Morrison with the 7th Infantry HQ and two companies to southern Arizona and Major Isaac Lynde, with an additional two companies of the 7th, to the Santa Rita Copper Mines and Mimbres River region.[29]

The 7th Infantry gradually moved into Arizona and New Mexico Territory that summer of 1860. No 7th Infantry troops were yet ordered to Fort Fillmore. By late August the total troop strength at the post had dropped to thirty-eight, barely enough to mount a guard and protect the public property and animals. In order to accomplish the post mission, also present were a civilian carpenter, at $50 per month, a blacksmith ($50), a post herder for the quartermaster animals ($25), and two herders for the

Subsistence Department stock ($25 each). The single deserter that month, from Company 'I', 3ᵈ Infantry, probably walked away without pursuit.[3C]

Fort Fillmore was virtually abandoned by early September. Second Lieutenant Henry Lazelle, 8ᵗʰ Infantry, reported the departure of Company 'I,' 3ᵈ Infantry, for duty in Texas. Fort Fillmore's association with the 3ᵈ Infantry Regiment was ended. Since the first days of the fort in September 1851, when the regimental headquarters was established there, to those final September days in 1860, there had been only brief periods when no 3ᵈ Infantry troops paraded and worked there. An old era had ended and a new one opened. In mid-September 1860 that new world appeared to be the post's final abandonment. As 2ᵈ Lieutenant Henry Lazelle penned his words to Assistant Adjutant Dabney Maury, there were only ten soldiers from his Company 'I' present for duty. Outsiders, including Mescalero raiders, could have taken Fort Fillmore's remaining public property, including four mountain howitzers, for the price of walking across the barren and almost empty parade ground.

Out on the plains of western New Mexico, south of old Fort Webster, a new army post was being established that September. It was to be called Fort Floyd in honor of reigning Secretary of War John Floyd. Fort Floyd bore John Floyd's name but a short time after the election of Abraham Lincoln later in the year. Floyd was a Southerner, and subsequently resigned to take up duties with the secessionist cause.

Second Lieutenant Lazelle reported to the Department of New Mexico that he could no longer supply escorts for the Santa Fe-El Paso mail. There were only eleven mules present as public animals. The herders required two and that left but nine for the hauling of water from the Rio Grande and wood from the surrounding area. There had been twenty-nine mules, but nineteen went with Major Sibley's 3ᵈ Infantry column to Texas and ten were killed in a freak accident when the post corral wall fell on them.[31]

Fort Fillmore's corral barn where the mules were kept had a high wall. Built into this adobe wall was a chain that extended the

Major Isaac Lynde
Courtesy: Museum of New Mexico.

length of the structure. The chain was there to prevent Indians from sneaking up and cutting a hole through the adobe to steal the animals. Obviously the walls of the structure were weak. Time and rain had weakened the walls until they simply fell in, killing the mules stabled in the collapsed section.

As of September 15 there were but nine soldiers remaining. One of these soldiers, Private H.W. Weld of Company 'D,' 1st Dragoons, was being discharged. Weld, an invalid, was left at the fort when his company was sent to Fort Buchanan. He was to be sent East where he had received permission to enter a 'Soldier's Home.' Men of the Regular Army, who served honorably, were entitled to live at these establishments, one of which was in Washington D.C. There was no mention of how Weld was to be transported or exactly where he was going. He may have been under the care of Fitzwilliams, who was still at the hospital, while awaiting transport.[32]

The man whose name has become synonymous with Fort Fillmore and with cowardly defeat was in the Department of New Mexico by September 16, 1860. Major Isaac Lynde of the 7th Infantry Regiment had orders to establish a battalion-size post somewhere in the region of Pinos Altos and the Santa Rita Copper Mines. Lynde was an experienced officer with thirty-four years service, all of it honorable up to that time. He once commanded Fort Laramie, Wyoming Territory, one of the most critical posts on the far-flung American frontier, and did his duty honorably. An 1827 graduate of West Point, the Vermonter Lynde was fifty-seven years old in September 1860.[33]

The total number of Indians in the region where Lynde was about to establish his new fort was not as high as Easterners of the day believed. During October 1860 and into November, Indian Agent Michael Steck sought an agreement with the Mescalero and the Mimbres region bands to establish a reservation for both tribes at Santa Lucia Springs in Mangas Coloradas's country northwest of present-day Silver City. Steck counted the total Indians in Lynde's battalion area of control as three hundred warriors and sixteen hundred women, children, and elderly, hardly a threat to Lynde or to the large numbers of non-Indians entering the mining region. The Mescalero who were outside Lynde's control numbered one hundred twenty men and six hundred women and children. These numbers seem incredibly small, considering the number of Hollywood movies portraying great numbers of Apaches swarming around a wagon train, disdainful of casualties. The numbers Steck provided scarcely allowed the taking of casualties at such levels. Of course, the more numerous Apaches living near Apache Pass were not counted in Steck's survey, yet were the nearest to open hostility. Lieutenant Colonel Pitcairn Morrison, Lynde's regimental commander in the 7th Infantry Regiment, then stationed at Fort Buchanan in what is now Arizona, recommended that the Apache peoples be either fed or exterminated.[34]

Just east of Isaac Lynde's new fort, a relative population boom was underway among the non-Indian peoples. Eight years after Doña Ana County was established, Federal census takers across the vast eight-hundred-mile width concluded that the county had 6,239 residents. The center of population was in Mesilla with approximately 3,100 residents. Las Cruces, which had grown steadily since its founding eleven years previously, accounted for 823 people. Stevenson's mines in the Organ Mountains had 149 people, while the gold mines at Pinos Altos near Silver City had about 300 prospectors. In comparison, the pre-El Paso area settlement had 428 people.[35]

Fort Fillmore's public property was saved from further theft on October 11, 1860, as 2[d] Lieutenant Royal Thaxter Frank returned from duty in the north at Hatch's Ranch, bringing with him the rest of Company 'E,' 8th Infantry. When combined, there were now two officers and over fifty-two men of that company ready for duty. Not for long, however.[36.]

By November 6, 1860, there was serious doubt as to the future of a Union of United States. On that date Abraham Lincoln was elected President, an act sure to bring civil conflict. The people at Fort Fillmore, Mesilla, Las Cruces, Doña Ana, La Mesa, and

Santo Tomás probably received the results of the election from Texas first. The first reports coming out of El Paso were that John Breckenridge, the Democratic Party candidate for whom Fort Breckenridge in the future Arizona was named, was totally victorious over Abraham Lincoln. Out of 1,052 votes recorded in El Paso County, only eleven were cast for Lincoln.

With Abraham Lincoln elected, however, and possibilities of secession looming, problems with the Indians in the Department of New Mexico increased daily as the year 1860 ended. A November 13-dated military circular brought the news that Captain George McLane had been killed in a battle with Indians. Captain McLane was one of the original appointees to the Regiment of Mounted Rifles at the time of the Mexican War. He was twice breveted for gallantry in battle and lost his life while leading a charge with his company against the Navajos. As a mark of respect, the officers of the Regiment of Mounted Rifles wore black crepe on their left arms and on the hilt of their sabers for thirty days. As with Captain Stanton in 1855, there was a clamor to name one of the new posts in his honor.[37]

With few soldiers manning the ramparts at Fort Fillmore, 2[d] Lieutenant Royal Frank had one of his privates lose his sanity. On November 19, Frank notified the Department that a soldier by the name of Kelly, serving with Company 'I,' 8th Infantry, was judged insane while confined in the post hospital. He was diagnosed with the disease of 'melancholia,' and could not have any other patients in the same room.[38]

On November 28, Brevet-Captain Dabney Maury, at Santa Fe, notified 2[d] Lieutenant Frank that the insane Private Kelly, then confined in the Fort Fillmore Hospital, was to be sent to Fort Union with the proper papers, to enable the army to send him East to the insane asylum of the District of Columbia.[39]

Abraham Lincoln may have won the office of President of the United States, but Judge Ned McGowan was elected over Indian Agent Michael Steck in the election of November 9 as the delegate from the 'Arizona Territory' to the United States Congress.

McGowan beat Steck handily but refused to acknowledge Lincoln's election. According to the *Mesilla Times* of November 22, McGowan was not willing to represent Arizona under a Republican administration. The *Times* said that if the South should separate, McGowan would attend the Southern Convention and pledge Arizona to the Confederacy. The *Mesilla Times* went on to say that of the total of one thousand American or 'white' population in Arizona, nine-tenths were for a disruption of the Union of States.[39]

The secessionists in Mesilla reached a peak in their anti-Union rhetoric on November 29, 1860, when the *Mesilla Times* printed an editorial which was nothing short of treasonous, given there was no Confederacy yet, Texas had not seceded, and Abraham Lincoln was not yet inaugurated. The Mesilla Americans were among the most vocally ardent secessionists in the country, with as little reason for being so. New Mexico Territory not a state in the Union, and slavery and states' rights were not problems. The editor, Mr. Robert Kelley, used words of sedition so strong that 2[d] Lieutenant Royal Frank at Fort Fillmore could have arrested him for treason had he had available the abrogation of habeus corpus, which the Department commander only promulgated after Isaac Lynde surrendered his command at San Augustine Springs in July 1861. Kelley editorialized:

> Arise! Let the Tocsin sound! Hang out your banner on the outer wall! Let a living bulwark of fiery valor guard your rights and your bodies! Go not beyond them. Let your boundary eastward be the brink of fate where the hell of northern fanaticism yawns beneath! Where the upas [sic] of abolition, as it poisons liberty, erases her charter and blackens the holiest memories of the past! Men of the South, look up! There is a star beaming in your glorious Southern sky, with a fixed light. It is the star of destiny. Smiling on hope as she points to a regenerated race, a renovated government, and the highest and noblest form of freedom. Remember that eternal vigilance is the price of liberty. Every son of the South is now a sentinel on the watchtower. Stand to your posts, and never surrender while there is a sod beneath your feet, or a thread on your banner! Awake![41]

At Fort Fillmore, where the candlelight of union still burned brightly, 2[d] Lieutenant Frank must have read the article. If he did, he did not report news of it to Santa Fe.

On December 3 President Buchanan, about to give his fourth and final annual message, was on his way out as president and Abraham Lincoln was about to be sworn in, an event for which Buchanan had morbid feelings. He asked that the South be allowed to answer to God in their own way for the issue of slavery and that they be allowed to go about their business in their own way. Then, in a reference to Lincoln without mentioning his name, President Buchanan said, "... and this brings me to observe that the election of any one of our fellow-citizens to the office of President does not of itself afford just cause for dissolving the Union." In order to justify a resort to revolutionary resistance, Buchanan warned, the federal Government must be guilty of a "... deliberate, palpable, and dangerous exercise of powers not granted by the Constitution. The late Presidential election, however, has been held in strict conformity with its express provisions. How, then, can the result justify a revolution to destroy this very Constitution?"[42]

The following day Lieutenant Colonel Pitcairn Morrison, commanding the 7th Infantry Regiment in Arizona and New Mexico, requested a leave of absence for the sake of the health of his wife and of himself. Morrison's departure meant that, eventually, the number four officer in the chain of command of the 7th Infantry, Major Isaac Lynde, would take Morrison's place and assume his responsibilities.[43]

As 1860 ended and turmoil was abroad throughout the rest of the nation, Fort Fillmore was still at peace. The small garrison, Company 'E,' 8th Infantry, had one officer and forty-six enlisted men, sufficient to protect the four cannon and other public property the post retained. Wind blew through a number of abandoned officers' quarters and barracks. Frank was unmarried, or at least did not have his wife with him at this time, so the row of six houses Lieutenant Colonel Dixon Miles had constructed were mostly empty. Only one of the four enlisted barracks were occupied, provided the men did not spread out to give themselves more room. One can only wonder how they celebrated this last year of full occupancy. The next December 31 would see a totally different tenant living among the adobe quarters and would include a terrible and tragic story about how they got there.[44]

NOTES - Chapter 12

1. Edwin Sweeney, *Cochise*, p. 134.
2. Diffendorffer to Walker, Commanding Fort Bliss, January 21, 1860, M1120, Rolls 11/12.
3. Fort Fillmore Post Returns, January 1860.
4. Ibid.
5. Howland to Wilkins, February 4, 1860, M1120, Rolls 11/12.
6. Frazer to Howland, February 22, 1860, M1120, Rolls 11/12.
7. Howland to Frazer, February 22, 1860, M1120, Rolls 11/12.
8. Mesilla Petition, February 22, 1860, M1120, Rolls 11/12.
9. Howland's Order Number 53, February 22, 1860, M1120, Rolls 11/12.
10. Frazer to Howland, February 22, 1860, M1120, Rolls 11/12.
11. Cogswell to Howland, February 24, 1860, M1120, Rolls 11/12.
12. Steck to Collins, March 1, 1860, Indian Bureau, Roll 4.
13. Edwin Sweeney, *Cochise*, p. 135.
14. Owings to Howland, March 8, 1856, M1120, Rolls 11/12.
15. Howland to Wilkins, March 9, 1860, M1120, Rolls 11/12.
16. Fort Fillmore Post Returns, p. 135.
17. Edwin Sweeney, *Cochise*, p.135.
18. Paxton P. Price, *Pioneers of the Mesilla Valley,* (Las Cruces: Yucca Tree Press, 1995), pp. 16, 17.
19. Wilkins to Captain H.B., April 15, 1860, M1012, Roll 2.
20. Wilkins to Sibley, April 28, 1860, M1012, Roll 2.
21. Fauntleroy to Thomas, April 29, 1860, M1012, Roll 2.
22. Fort Fillmore Post Returns, April 1860.
23. Wilkins to Pitcher, May 1, 1860, M1012, Roll 2.
24. Wilkins to Sykes, May 3, 1860, M1012, Roll 2.
25. Owings to Whistler, May 13, 1860, M1120, Rolls 11/12.
26. Whistler to Assistant Adjutant General, May 14, 1860, M1120,, Rolls 11/12.
27. Fort Fillmore Post Returns, May 1860.
28. *The Mesilla Miner*, June 9, 1860, Volume 1, Number1.
29. Fauntleroy to Thomas, August 7, 1860, M1012, Roll 2.

30. Fort Fillmore Post Returns, August 1860.

31. Lazelle to Maury, September 15, 1860, M1120, Rolls 11/12.

32. Lazelle to Sloan, September 15, 1860, M1120, Rolls 11/12.

33. Heitman, Isaac Lynde.

34. Edwin Sweeney, *Cochise*, p. 140.

35. Paxton P. Price, *Pioneers of the Mesilla Valley*, p. 53.

36. Fort Fillmore Post Returns, October 1860.

37. Jackson circular, November 13, 1860, M1120, Rolls 11/12.

38. Frank to Maury, November 19, 1860, M1120, Rolls 11/12.

39. Maury to Frank, November 28, 1860, M1120, Rolls 11/12.

40. *The San Francisco Herald*, Volume 11, #158, December 4, 1860, reporting on an article in the *Mesilla Times*, November 22, 1860.

41. As reported in the *Southern News*, Los Angeles, Volume 2, #42, December 7, 1860, from *Mesilla Times,* November 29, 1860.

42. James D. Richardson, *Messages and Papers of the Presidents,* p. 3159.

43. Morrison to Assistant Adjutant General, December 4, 1860, M1120, Rolls 11/12.

44. Fort Fillmore Post Returns, December 1860.

Texas Confederate militia buckle found at Fort Fillmore.
Courtesy: Private Collection.

Texas Star roundel for 2[d] buckle found by the author
in 1972 on Dragoon Hill at Fort Fillmore.
Courtesy: Geronimo Springs Museum

13

1861 - SAN AUGUSTINE SPRINGS

Second Lieutenant Royal Thaxter Frank and the forty-two men of Company 'E,' 8th Infantry received orders to vacate Fort Fillmore. They were to join their regimental comrades in transferring to Texas, not as a force designed to prevent Texas from seceding from the Union but only as part of a normal regimental move which came at a very strange moment in history. Frank must have wondered into what kind of a situation he was marching. All around him hostile forces were demanding an end to old agreements and relationships.

Company 'E' was headed toward a potential buzz saw, although whether they were fully aware of the implications is not clear. The state of Texas was about to secede from the Union. On February 1, a resolution of secession passed an emergency meeting of the Texas Legislature by a vote of 168 to 8. On February 23, the people affirmed this decision. Company 'E,' as noted above, was transfered to Texas as part of a normal transfer, not the result of secessionist talk. This incredible move in a time of crisis was a cruel twist of fate that severely affected the rank and file soldiers of Company 'E,' no doubt for the rest of their lives. By February 18, General David Twiggs had surrendered all public property in Texas to the state. By the end of February, all 8th Infantry troops, including Company 'E,' were on the road to San Antonio walking into a trap.

By April 23, all companies of the regiment had surrendered to Texas state forces, without firing a shot. Most of the soldiers in Company 'E,' less the officers, were held prisoner in Texas for the duration of the American Civil War, some being sent to former army posts in Texas to serve the Confederacy as unpaid soldiers fighting Indian depredations. Had the 8th stayed in New Mexico, they would have been safe and the later Confederate invasion of New Mexico might never have taken place.

As 2[d] Lieutenant Frank prepared to leave Fort Fillmore in January, the post's most famous female resident was in the process of moving there. She was Lydia Lane and her husband was 1st Lieutenant William Lane, Company 'A,' Regiment of Mounted Rifles. Lydia Lane became famous because of her book, *I Married a Soldier*. This account of her life at various military posts in the Southwest from the 1850s to the 1880s included comments on her life at Fort Fillmore.

The Lanes and Company 'A' departed Fort Craig in early February, arriving at Fort Fillmore on February 9. Lydia Lane noted she was glad to be going to the post because of the presence of a couple of small settlements nearby, unlike being buried at Fort Craig with little opportunity to acquire the goods she needed.

As the Lanes were in transit, a terrible incident occurred at the Butterfield Stage Station at Apache Pass on the future Arizona border. This incident ended a mostly peaceful ten-year period of relations between Apaches and the American government. The conflict between Indians and white men that began at Apache Pass did not end until the final slaughter at Wounded Knee in 1890. The incident started simply. Pima Indians kidnapped an eleven-year-old white boy named Felix, the adopted son of a squatter named John Ward. An army lieutenant fresh from West Point, George Nicholas Bascom, was sent to rescue the boy. Bascom took fifty-four soldiers from Fort Buchanan to the stage station at Apache Pass to meet with Cochise, who was an Apache, not a Pima. Cochise appeared under a white flag. During negotiations Bascom blamed Cochise and his people for the abduction as well as the theft of a number of cattle. He demanded Cochise bring the boy and the cattle to Fort Buchanan. When Cochise appeared both offended and indignant Bascom had the peace talks tent surrounded by soldiers. Cochise drew a knife, slit the tent side open and escaped. Firing erupted, a bullet striking Cochise in the arm, wounding him. Six Apaches were taken prisoner. Fighting continued until nightfall with several soldiers wounded, although none were killed. Shortly after this incident the Overland Mail stage was attacked; one horse was killed, the driver wounded, and another passenger shot.[1]

On the morning of February 3, 1861, a lone Apache under a white flag approached Bascom's position. Cochise wanted to parley and Bascom agreed. Two selected groups met in a nearby canyon for talks. While they talked two Butterfield employees, James F. Wallace and Charles W. Culver, plus another man, took matters into their own hands and went out among their Apache friends to make a separate peace. Instead, angry words were exchanged and the talks degenerated into open warfare. Wallace and several others were captured. Later, Cochise asked that his family members among the captives be freed in exchange for Wallace and sixteen government mules. Bascom refused, repeating that Cochise's family would only be released if the boy were released. In response to these demands Cochise murdered the stage line employees, which in turn led the soldiers to hang some of their Apache captives.[2]

The incident continued for several days before the Apaches and the troops disengaged. Now, with the imminent breakup of the American Union, relations between the army and the Apaches would have no chance to be repaired through negotiation. War was at hand, Americans versus Americans and Americans versus the Apaches and, eventually, every other Indian group still living in the old way.

On February 10 in Santa Fe, orders were sent to Major Isaac Lynde to punish any Apaches in the vicinity of Fort Floyd, now renamed Fort McLane following the defection of Secretary of War Floyd to the South. Major Lynde did not know of Bascom's problems as yet; the two messages informing him of the battle and charging him to do his duty against the Indians may have arrived at about the same time.

While Indian troubles mounted to the west, the Lanes made their appearance at Fort Fillmore. Lydia Lane, obviously depressed at what she saw at the fort, remembered those first impressions and commented on them several years later. Unconcerned with Indian problems, her eyes and thoughts were on the appearance of the home she was going to make there in the desert. She noted:

> ... Most dreary and uninviting did Fort Fillmore look to us as we approached it. It was a cold, gray day, with a high wind which blew the loose sand and dust in clouds all around us. The stiff line of shabby adobe quarters on three sides of a perfectly bare parade-ground suggested neither beauty nor comfort, and for once I felt discouraged when we went into the forlorn house we were to occupy.
>
> It was filthy, too, and the room we chose for a bedroom must have been used as a kitchen. The great open fireplace had at least a foot of dirt in it, which had to be dug out with a spade before a fire could be lighted. It took time to make the quarters comfortable; but by hard scrubbing and sweeping they at last looked clean and habitable. The woodwork was rough and unpainted; the modern method of oiling pine was not known in army quarters then.
>
> I was the only lady at the post except for the wife of the post sutler. Lieutenant Lane and Lieutenant Wheeler, and possibly one other officer, attended to all duties of the garrison. Lieutenant Lane was in command.[3]

Lydia's husband, 1st Lieutenant William Lane, as senior officer, took command of Fort Fillmore at once. Company 'A' of the R.M.R. was not his company, belonging as it did to the absent Captain Washington Lafayette Elliot, then on leave. A Kentuckian by birth and not a West Point graduate, 1st Lieutenant Lane was a former U.S. Army enlisted man who, through ability, obtained a commission. Lane's second in command, 2d Lieutenant Joseph Wheeler, was to have a different career as one of America's leading cavalry generals of the nineteenth century—the result of his service to the Confederate cause during the Civil War and for the United States in the War with Spain in 1898. Wheeler's stay at Fort Fillmore was very short as the trumpet call of destiny blew loudly for him out of the East.[4]

War with the Apaches was truly joined following the Bascom incident. On February 15 William Buckley of the Butterfield Overland Mail Company wrote Lieutenant Lane. Buckley was in Mesilla, awaiting more bad news from his stations further west in the Apache country. Stage traffic west would end if assistance could not be provided by the military. Actually, the Butterfield Overland Mail Company was about to go out of business for the duration of the American Civil War anyway, Indians or no Indians. Buckley warned:

> ... The Indians [Cochise's band] in the vicinity of Apache Pass on the Overland Mail route between Mesilla & Tucson have committed serious depredations within the past two weeks. They attacked the station at Apache Pass, fired about fifteen shots [and] wounded the driver severely. They attacked a train of five wagons near the Apache Pass & killed eight men and burnt them to the wagons. They stole from the Apache Pass forty two mules belonging to Government and seventeen belonging to the Overland Mail Co. They also stole three hundred head of sheep six mules and three oxen from the San Crimoni [?] Station. As there are many bad passes in the Mountains between Stein's Peak and Dragoon Springs, I do not consider it safe for the stage to travel without an escort. The stations also are in danger of being attacked by Indians. If you can possibly send troops to escort our mails through the bad passes I would like very much to have you do so, as I am fearful the Indians will attack the stage if we do not have an escort.[5]

Lane enclosed his response to Mr. Buckley's request for military assistance in the mail to Santa Fe, stating that he had too few troops at Fort Fillmore to give support. His reply is interesting, if unhelpful to Buckley's situation.

> ... I have your note of February 16th, giving a detailed account of the Indian depredations on the Overland Mail line between this and Fort Buchanan, and asking for an escort for the mails through the bad passes, etc. etc.—I am unable to comply with

your request for the following reasons—There being only one Compy. at this post, and the scene of the Indian depredations is so distant comparatively, it would be impossible to give the escort asked for.—If I was to divide my command and send a part of it to the passes spoken of, it would leave the settlements on the river, in the vicinity of the post almost unprotected, and I might by these means, defeat the object of the Dpt. Commander in sending my Company to this post,—But I will enclose to the Dpt. Hd. Quarters, your letter, in order that any steps deemed necessary in the matter may be taken.[6]

As was usual for the Department of New Mexico, independent action could not be taken at the forts without an of order of approval from headquarters. It did not matter if Americans were being killed along the Butterfield route; without a direct order to do so, Lane would not have moved an inch to save them. Arizona was simply too far away. Such was the antebellum army, at least as it existed in New Mexico. At Fort McLane, Major Isaac Lynde was given carte blanche on responding to any Indian provocation. Had Lane been given such an order he might have responded differently, even sending troops out that far to engage hostiles.

Brevet-Lieutenant Colonel George Bibb Crittenden, then at Fort Union and soon to resign his commission to join the Confederacy, was ordered as of March 1, 1861, to lead an expedition against the Mescalero Apache bands east of the Rio Grande. Crittenden was told to establish his base of operations at Fort Stanton. He was to be provided with additional troops from Forts Stanton and Fillmore. A supply depot was to be set up in the mountains south of Fort Stanton before the troops moved.[7]

First Lieutenant Lane was told to consider himself and his post under the command of Brevet-Lieutenant Colonel Crittenden. Lane was to report by letter to Crittenden at Fort Stanton, informing him of all available resources ready for field service, such as rank and file, pack saddles, horses, mules, wagons, subsistence, and ordnance stores. Lane was also to provide Crittenden with information related to known haunts of the Apaches in the region of Fort Fillmore. The campaign against the Mescalero was to be a horse soldier campaign, while the campaign against Cochise, in revenge of Bascom, was to be fought by foot soldiers only.[8]

Second Lieutenant Joseph Wheeler's request for leave in early March was denied due to the Apache troubles. On receiving news of the denial, Wheeler immediately resigned his commission and notified Santa Fe of that fact. He left Fort Fillmore soon thereafter without waiting for the customary acceptance of his resignation. Wheeler wanted to be in the South before war officially came, regardless of whether he left his troops in the time of their emergency.

The cause for Joe Wheeler's leaving Fort Fillmore, or at least the excuse, was sworn in as President of the United States on February 4, 1861. Most people forget that it was not Abraham Lincoln in office that triggered the rapid secession of the Southern States, but his election.

The divider of the nation, Abraham Lincoln, was born in Hardin County, Kentucky on February 12, 1809. His parents were Thomas and Nancy Hanks Lincoln. The family moved to Indiana on the Ohio border in 1816 and Lincoln grew up there. At six-feet four-inches, he was unusually tall for that period. Lincoln served as a private in one of the fights with Indians in the area. After mustering out he served as postmaster of New Salem, Illinois for three years and was elected to the Illinois State Legislature in 1834. In 1837 he moved to Springfield, Illinois, and in 1842 married Mary Todd Lincoln, daughter of Robert S. Todd, of Kentucky. Lincoln was elected to Congress in 1846, serving only a single term. In 1858 he was chosen by the newly constituted Republican Party to run for the United States Senate. His opponent was Steven A. Douglas, and the resulting campaign became famous for the debates between the two men. Douglas won the contest if not the debates. In May 1860, Abraham Lincoln was nominated for President on the third ballot by the Republican Party. On November 6, 1860, he was elected President. The electoral vote was Lincoln 180, John Breckinridge (the Southern favorite) 72, John Bell 39, and Steven A. Douglas 12. The process toward secession and civil war began, in fact, on November 7, the very next day.[9]

The coming dissolution of the nation was more obvious to national-level business interests than to the military in southern New Mexico. Financial hardship and the coming of the American Civil War put an end to the Butterfield Overland Mail Company. The last Butterfield stage from the West traveling through Apache Pass without being attacked reached Fort Fillmore safely in mid-March.

A group of Southern sympathizers met in Mesilla on March 14 to adopt a resolution declaring, in part, that "the people of New Mexico would not recognize the present black administration [in Washington]," and they "would resist any officers appointed to the Territory by said administration with whatever means in our power." Whether 1st Lieutenant Lane at Fort Fillmore was aware of what was happening in Mesilla is not known. One has to assume he was, although he was also in no position to do anything about mere words as no actions against the government had yet taken place. Besides, he would never act unless he had orders from Department of New Mexico to do so, and the Department was in the hands of future Confederate leaders during this period.[10]

Colonel William Wing Loring replaced Thomas Turner Fauntleroy as New Mexico Department Commander on March 22. Virginian Fauntleroy returned immediately to the East where, on May 17, 1861, he resigned his commission and accepted a commission as brigadier general in the Virginia Volunteers. Colonel Loring, also a Southerner, from North Carolina, certainly sympathized with the South but, since North Carolina had not yet seceded, he was under no obligation to tender his resignation.

First Lieutenant Lane and Company 'A' departed Fort Fillmore on March 30 for Dog Canyon to join Crittenden for a hoped-for fight with the Mescalero. He left behind his wife, Lydia Spencer Lane, and a small detachment of fifteen men (Lydia reported only ten). In effect, Lydia Lane was in command of the post for about five days, from March 30 to April 4, when Company 'K,' 7th Infantry Regiment, arrived from Albuquerque. Years later Lydia wrote of her experience:

... A sergeant and ten men, all that could be spared from the little command, were left behind to guard the post and our small family, and they were picked men. Those in the guardhouse were taken on the scout. I was left in command of Fort Fillmore. All public funds were turned over to me, and the sergeant reported to me every day. He slept in our house at night, heavily armed, which gave us a sense of security.

There was a flag-staff on the parade ground, but no flag. Husband sent to Fort Bliss for one before he left for Dog Canyon. I knew I would feel safer to see it floating above us, and it was run up at reveille every morning through the summer before the post was abandoned. When was the flag ever more needed than in those anxious days before the war was declared, to cheer the weak-hearted and bid defiance to its enemies.

The public money in my hands gave me considerable uneasiness, and I hid it away in what I considered a secure place; then it seemed to me that would be the first spot searched, and I found a safer one. I was determined no one should have that money while I was alive to defend it. Just how I would act circumstances must decide; if I lost my life in protecting it, I would have done my whole duty.[11]

Lydia Lane later added her thoughts that the state of affairs at Fort Fillmore and the surrounding country had been misrepresented at Santa Fe. She noted the folly shown in sending all the troops away from the post, when right in their midst was a real danger. She did not say what that danger was. Lydia noted she relinquished the command of Fort Fillmore only when Company 'K,' 7th Infantry arrived. According to post records the length of her 'command' at Fort Fillmore could have been as many as four days —of course her tenure was never officially noted in Army records.

First Lieutenant Augustus Plummer's Company 'K' was the first 7th Infantry Regiment unit to arrive at Fort Fillmore. William Lane and Company 'A' were back in garrison by April 7, their part in the Mescalero campaign being rather uneventful. The Mescalero quickly pleaded for peace when troops were first encountered and, given the degraded condition of the military at that time, their pleadings must have been accepted with relish.[12]

On April 7, Company 'D,' 7th Infantry, commanded by 1st Lieutenant Edward J. Brooks, arrived at Fort Fillmore, the second of the companies to arrive safely and without incident. On the day Brooks arrived, 1st Lieutenant Lane reported to Captain D.H. Maury in Santa Fe that the troops under his command had not been paid since August 1860, almost eight months previously. Lane pleaded that the morale of his troops was affected as a result. With civil conflict a possibility, failure to pay the troops could lead to wholesale desertions in the command.[13]

On April 14, 1861, South Carolina State militia fired on Fort Sumter in Charleston Harbor. The initial cannonading lasted thirty-three hours. No casualties were taken on either side although the provocation was enough to allow the beginning of fighting in earnest. The first major engagement between the Northern and Southern armies did not take place until July at Bull Run, Virginia. In the interval between Fort Sumter and Bull Run both sides engaged in a war of words, including those living in southern New Mexico and west Texas.

Second Lieutenant Edward Brooks left Fort Fillmore for Fort McLane on May 10 to become adjutant of the 7th Infantry Regiment under Major Isaac Lynde. He returned to Fort Fillmore with Major Lynde in July.[14]

On May 13 Colonel William Wing Loring officially resigned as Colonel of the Regiment of Mounted Rifles but did not give up command of the Department of New Mexico until he was replaced by Brevet-Lieutenant Colonel Edward Canby on June 11. Brevet-Captain Dabney Maury, another future Confederate general officer like Loring, also resigned his position as Department of New Mexico adjutant in May, although the exact date is not certain. His initial resignation was not accepted and, like Colonel Loring, he remained in the Department until late June when he was dismissed from the army for failure to pledge loyalty to the Union. By early 1862, Maury was colonel on the staff of General Earl Van Dorn, who was in charge of the Confederate troops in Texas while Maury was assistant adjutant in the Department of New Mexico.

The incoming Department commander, Brevet-Lieutenant Colonel and Major of Infantry Edward Richard Sprigg Canby, was jumped two ranks to the grade of colonel of the 19th Infantry Regiment as of May 14, 1861. An unprecedented promotion, Canby's rise meant the coming civil conflict was beginning to affect the careers of many Regular Army officers. By 1862 he would be a general officer.[15]

On May 14 Captain Cadmus Wilcox, commanding officer of Company 'K,' 7th Infantry, arrived at Fort Fillmore. Wilcox was, like Maury, another interesting character with strong secessionist leanings. Wilcox bided his time, waiting for North Carolina to secede. By October 1861 he was a brigade commander in Longstreet's Division, Confederate States Army.[16]

Another key character in the story of Fort Fillmore's final days arrived at the fort on May 29. Captain Robert R. Garland, a Virginian, was probably aware that his state had seceded before he reached Fort Fillmore. He remained a Federal officer only briefly and his stay at Fort Fillmore, like Wilcox's, was short. His conduct while there was very suspicious, especially since, for a period, he commanded the post.

Companies 'D,' 'I,' and 'K,' 7th Infantry, and Company 'A,' R.M.R., were at Fort Fillmore on May 31, 1861, when the monthly returns were filled out. Brevet-Major Gabriel Paul, arriving with Company 'I' late in the month, was in command. There were some disciplinary problems within the ranks. An unusual total of four enlisted men deserted from Lane's Mounted Rifles company during May. More left in the days to come, but not the flood some might have expected.

Many future Confederate officers passed through Fort Fillmore in May-June after resigning their commissions. Lydia Lane remarked on their passing. Her confusion as to who was there was probably due to the fact she wrote her book many years later. She said, "Many of our oldest and truest army friends resigned and went South, several of them passing through Fort Fillmore on their way out of New Mexico. Among them were General Longstreet [then a major-paymaster], who came into post driving his own ambulance en route to Texas; Cadmus Wilcox, Colonel W.W. Loring, Lawrence Baker, Major Sibley [Henry

Hopkins Sibley, the future invader of New Mexico], and others [Marmaduke and Garland] whose names I have forgotten. Colonel George B. Crittenden, one of our best friends also went down to Texas and I never saw him again."[17]

Cochise returned to the warpath in Arizona in early June. His band stole forty-four mules at the San Pedro Butterfield Station, then swung south along the Santa Cruz River. Estimates place eighty to one hundred warriors in the band. At Canoa Inn the Apaches ran off four hundred cattle and killed four men with no mounted troops in the region to oppose them. The road from Mesilla to Tucson was often cut off by Apache raiders during this period. On June 3, 1861, a wagon train was ambushed at Cook's Peak with two Mexicans killed and two mules stolen.[18]

While Apache depredations raged to the west, 1st Lieutenant Lane reported the possibility of a total breakdown of morale and discipline at Fort Fillmore, the result of the failure of the Federal Government to pay the troops there. He pointed to eighteen or twenty desertions in his command, only eleven of whom were listed in the Post Returns of the period as leaving because of failing to receive pay. Lane said:

> ... I have the honor again to call the attention of the Dept. Commander to the great length of time it has been since my Company has been paid. I have lost by desertion since about the middle of Feby. last eighteen or twenty men & I believe it has been almost solely on account of the impression that they were not to be paid. The men that have deserted were all recruits but it has been with the greatest difficulty that I have satisfied some of the "old men" of the Company that they were certain to receive their pay. I have [given them] our [word]. Again to be assured that there was no doubt about their getting all that was due by the government, but it has become such an old story, that I am not sure but they think I am a party to the wrong that is being done them. The majority of the Company was paid in August 1860 but a great many have not been paid since April of last year.
>
> I would also call the attention of the Department Commander to the fact that it is almost impossible for an officer to

dispose of his pay accounts to pay his debts, & it is not at all [?] to hunt the country over, to find a man to <u>discount</u> a pay account. In consideration of these facts, I would most earnestly request that money, if not a paymaster, be sent to this post to pay the troops.[19]

Another factor resulting in low post morale was the unknown potential for sympathy for secession within the ranks of the Fort Fillmore troops. Mesilla and the El Paso region were hotbeds of Southern sympathy. An ardent Unionist, W.W. Mills, then residing in Mesilla, stated : "I assure you that I find matters here in a most deplorable condition. A disunion flag is now flying from the house in which I write, and this country is now as much in the possession of the enemy as Charleston [South Carolina] is."[20]

When news of North Carolina and Virginia's secession arrived in the Territory, Colonel William Wing Loring immediately tendered his resignation. On June 11, soon-to-be private citizen Loring left Santa Fe for southern New Mexico and the Texas escape route. Loring arrived at Fort Fillmore where he is known to have stayed for several days before going on to Fort Bliss, possibly under the care of Captain Robert Garland and local Rebel sympathizers. Loring retained command of southern New Mexico until he was able to safely cross the new border to the Confederate State of Texas. Only then did Canby gain command in the southern part of the Territory.

On that same day, Brevet-Lieutenant Colonel Edward Canby took command over the northern portion of the Department of New Mexico. Fortunately for the Union forces, Canby immediately began to change Loring's spider-like hold on Department affairs. Canby at once contacted the Assistant Adjutant General in Washington, detailing the state of affairs in the Department he now commanded in all but name, reporting:

... I have the honor to report that <u>Colonel Loring</u>, Regiment of Mounted Riflemen, in anticipation of the acceptance of his resignation, left this place today after placing me in the general charge of the affairs of the Department and in the immediate command of the Northern district. He has not formally relinquished the Command and will await at Fort Fillmore the action of the President upon the tender of his resignation.

I have no reason to apprehend any immediate political trouble in this Department, and in the future this will be contingent upon the action of Missouri with which the people of this Territory are more intimately connected in their com-mercial relations and associations than with Texas or the States of Mexico. The disaffection in Arizona is, in my judgement, confined to a small portion of the population of that Territory and the disaffected are believed to be without the means of effecting anything against the Government as they have earnestly and expectantly applied for the assistance of the troops in settling their local difficulties.

A demonstration against Arizona by the people of Texas may be apprehended, although there is nothing known here of any movement, in that direction. I will take measures to increase materially the force at Fort Fillmore by withdrawing and transferring a portion of the troops from the interior part, and if possible an additional mounted force from the upper country.

The long deferred payment of the troops aided by the mischievous efforts of some individuals in that country have created some dissatisfaction among the troops at some of the posts, but this will be removed by the payment at an early period of a portion of the arrearage now due. The funds in the hands of the paymasters will not be sufficient to pay the whole amount, but will leave for the troops in Arizona about four months arrearage. It is hoped that a sufficiency of funds to meet these may soon be received.[21]

One-two-three—all was immediate action once Canby took command. Missions were performed and jobs done which had been put off for months by the foot-dragging of the secessionist officers in Santa Fe. Troops were ordered paid; an additional mounted force was targeted for the southern New Mexico region; additional troops were to be sent to Fort Fillmore. Canby used the word mischievous when he might have used the word treasonous when referring to the problem of non-payment of troops. No doubt there were many hands involved in that disgraceful action.

The fact that Colonel Loring gave Brevet-Lieutenant Colonel Canby only command of the Northern District of the Department, while he kept command of the Southern District, including Fort Fillmore, is another curiosity of this letter. No doubt Loring kept the command to avoid being arrested for any disloyal acts until he safely left New Mexico Territory. Loring may have wanted Fort Fillmore for use as a transit point for future resigning Confederate officers. His control there ensured their safe passage.

Special Order Number 134 of the Headquarters of the Army arrived at Santa Fe on June 14, 1861. This order directed all Federal troops to leave New Mexico as soon as possible and return to the East. A New Mexico militia was to be raised to protect the territory as best it could. On June 16 a letter went out to Brevet-Major Gabriel Rene Paul, 7th Infantry, commanding Fort Fillmore, notifying him of the instructions that Major Isaac Lynde had received to move the 7th Infantry regimental headquarters to Fort Fillmore from Fort McLane. The 7th was then to depart from the New Mexico Territory after gathering its companies at Fort Fillmore.[22]

On June 22, 1861, unknown persons stole the entire Fort Fillmore horse herd. Major Paul immediately reported the theft to Canby. Paul blamed Texans from Fort Bliss for the act and also indicated the theft may have been planned as early as June 12 at Hart's Mill in El Paso. He did not place any blame on Colonel William Wing Loring, who is thought to have been at Fort Fillmore up to the day after the horses were stolen. Whatever the case, Company 'A,' the only mounted company then available in southern New Mexico, was on foot after June 22.

Major Isaac Lynde, still commanding at Fort McLane as of June 30, was notified of the theft of the Company 'A' horses. If he received this letter before arriving at Fort Fillmore in July, he was aware that he was heading toward a situation in which all loyalties, especially among the officer corps and the surrounding citizenry, were in question. Once Loring left, Canby appointed Lynde the commanding officer for the Southern District of New Mexico.

Captain Anderson, the new adjutant at Department of New Mexico, warned of the possibility of future acts from hostile forces in now-seceded Texas, saying:

... Major Paul's communication of the 22d instant, reporting the loss of 41 horses, of Company A, Mounted Rifles, and other communications from Fort Bliss in relation to the same subject, have been received, and I am instructed to say there is sufficient evidence here to show conclusively that this robbery was not the unauthorized act of a band of robbers, but was planned at Hart's Mill as early as the 10th or 12 of this month, and is only one of a series that will be undertaken if prompt measures are not taken to defeat them. The horses were stolen for the purpose of mounting one of the companies of Texas troops now on their way to Fort Bliss. The reward offered by Magoffin and the disclaimers of the Texas authorities are mere blinds, to throw you off your guard and keep the troops inactive until Fort Bliss is re-enforced. When this object is secured there will be demonstrations against your post, the trains that supply it, or against Fort Stanton.

The movements of the Texans at Fort Bliss have been watched, and although the precise object and the details of their contemplated movements cannot be ascertained, it is positively known that movements against New Mexico are on foot; that officers who recently left the country by that route have aided and counseled in the plans, and it is alleged that others still in the service are implicated in these transactions. There is no doubt that these movements will be undertaken the moment that the instigators feel assured of a probability of success. The leading secessionists in Mesilla are apprized of these plans, and to the extent of their ability will assist in carrying them out.

The State of Texas is avowedly at war with the Government of the United States. The character of the enemy you have to deal with has been fully exhibited in the last few months, and they now expect to be able in a few days to carry the war into New Mexico. It is hoped that before this time you have a sufficient force under your control to make them feel that the war is not to be entirely upon one side.

The surplus horses at Fort Craig will be sent down as soon as possible to Fort Fillmore for the purpose of remounting a part of Company A, but it will be very difficult to procure a sufficient number in the department to remount the whole company. As many as can be procured will be sent [none were!].

Orders have been sent direct to-day for the abandonment of Fort Buchanan; the garrison to report to you at Fort Fillmore as soon as possible.

The lieutenant-colonel commanding directs me to repeat his assurance that you will be supported in any measures that you may undertake by all the means that he can control, and that there is no intention of withdrawing any portion of the regular force under your command until the affairs within the limits of your command are placed upon a satisfactory footing. He desires that you will keep him fully advised of matters that transpire in your neighborhood, and that you will keep the commanding officer at Fort Stanton advised of any matters that may affect this post.[23]

First Lieutenant Charles Hely McNally left Fort Craig on June 30 for duty in the south at Fort Fillmore. McNally's Mounted Rifles Company 'F' was not his normal unit. McNally was no stranger to Fort Fillmore, having served there in September and October 1856 after the Rifle Regiment arrived in the territory from Texas. McNally then served under Captain Thomas Grimke Rhett who, as a Regular Army paymaster in the Spring of 1861, had taken the Fort Fillmore payroll and handed it over to Texas authorities before heading back East to take a major's commission in the Confederate Army.[24]

On paper, the Fort Fillmore strength consisted of five officers and two hundred and three enlisted men on post at the end of June. These numbers grew as Major Isaac Lynde brought in the companies previously serving at Fort McLane. But numbers do not make an army. Many definable qualities lead to a proud and victorious force, foremost among them good and *familiar* leadership. The force gathering at Fort Fillmore had few redeemable qualities. The 7th Infantry Regiment at the end of June was demoralized, unsure of its commanders, and filled with suspicion—one man against the next, especially among the officer corps. That situation was about to degrade even further.

On July 2 Major Lynde abandoned Fort McLane and, with all troops and the public and private property of four companies, began the long journey to Fort Fillmore. Lynde led the way with the regimental band and his adjutant, Edward Brooks. Lynde was accompanied by Company 'E' under the command of Captain

The author at Fort Daniel Webster with the Apache's
Dziltanatal (Mountain Holds Its Head Up Proudly)
in the background.
Courtesy: Author

David Porter Hancock, a Pennsylvanian, and hence an officer loyal to Lynde and to the Union.[25]

First Lieutenant George Ryan commanded Company 'A,' Captain Mathew Rider Stevenson, Company 'B,' and Captain Joseph Haydn Potter, Company, 'G,' 7th Infantry. These were the last of the companies to follow Lynde from Fort McLane. Next to Major Isaac Lynde, Potter was the most senior officer present. A future general officer during the American Civil War, Joseph Potter had seventeen years of army service. Two other officers either traveled with Major Isaac Lynde or preceded him to Fort Fillmore. They were 1st Lieutenant Charles Bryant Stivers, the regimental quarter-master and commissary officer, and Assistant Surgeon Charles Henry Alden. Alden was sent by Department of New Mexico to help Assistant Surgeon James Cooper McKee with the large force then concentrating at Fort Fillmore.[26]

Isaac Lynde's march from Cook's Peak to Fort Fillmore must have been observed closely by the Apaches. Believing they had driven the Americans out of their lands, Cochise and Mangas Coloradas made a temporary headquarters at Cook's Peak, a mountain called by the Apaches *Dziltanatal*, 'Mountain Holds Its Head Up Proudly.' Here they hoped to cut off the former Fort McLane-protected Pinos Altos region from the town of Mesilla. What pride the Apaches must have felt, watching the long train of bluecoats at last leaving their lands. One can only wonder whether they truly believed they were the cause of the exodus.[27]

Major Isaac Lynde's four Companies, 'A,' 'B,' 'G,' and 'E' arrived at Fort Fillmore from Fort McLane on or just after Independence Day. The commander at Fort Fillmore at the end of June was Captain Robert Garland; Brevet-Major Paul had departed to serve with Canby in Santa Fe. Just before Major Lynde's arrival, Garland deserted to the Confederates. We cannot be sure of the exact date since the Fort Fillmore Post Return for July was not completed.

Major Lynde wrote to Colonel Canby shortly after his arrival on July 7:

> ... I have the honor to report that I arrived at this position on the 4th instant with the regimental staff, band, and Company E,

Seventh Infantry, and found that no demonstration from Texas had been made on this post. The remaining companies of the Fort McLane command, viz., B and I, Seventh Infantry, will be here to-day. I shall then have very little fear of the result of any attack that will be likely made from Texas. From the best information that I can obtain, there are four companies of Texas troops at Fort Bliss, with two 18-pounders and four or more small guns. It is stated that they are fortifying for their own defense. It is probable that there are two companies now at Fort Stanton. With the force that I shall have at this post in a few days I do not think that the enemy will attempt to attack us, but if they do, I think we shall give them a warm reception.[28]

Another of Isaac Lynde's responsibilities, seeing to the abandonment of Forts Buchanan and Breckinridge and the transfer of their troops to Fort Fillmore, was partially accomplished by July 10, 1861. Fort Breckinridge, once named for John Breckinridge, Vice-President under President Buchanan and also a future Confederate general, was burned to the ground. Fort Buchanan, south of Fort Breckinridge, was still preparing for the withdrawal of its troops and public property as Lynde arrived at Fort Fillmore.

On July 17, at Albuquerque, Captain Alfred Gibbs received an order directing him to take a herd of one hundred cattle to Fort Millard Fillmore. Thereafter he was to report to Major Lynde and serve under his command. Gibbs left Albuquerque for Fort Craig the next day on what was to be a very fateful journey. Ten days later Gibbs was be a prisoner of the Texas Confederates, an event which at the moment of his leaving he could not have conceived as possible. The Fort Fillmore forces were considered too strong for any Confederate force to overcome.[29]

Major Lynde notified the Department of New Mexico on July 21 of the presence of Texan scouting parties out of Fort Bliss penetrating into southern New Mexico below the fort. Lynde advised:

Since my last weekly report no material changes has occurred in affairs at this Post, or in this valley. Scouting parties from Fort Bliss penetrated this country as far as the Cotton-woods (22 miles below this place) and on one occasion detached a column of Infantry from this side and a column of Rifles for the other side of the river, to capture or drive back a party said to be at the Mesa, a town ten miles below this Post. The command returned without finding any suspicious bodies of men. On the 18th Inst. I detached two Companies of Infantry under command of Captain J. H. Potter 7 Inf. and occupied the town of San Tomas, on the opposite side of the river and distant about 2 ½ miles. From its location, the town commands the road from El Paso to Mesilla. A [line] of Lagunas between the town, and hills prevents the passage of artillery or wagons, and only horsemen could pass over the lava ridge in rear of the town. A detail of one Non Com officer and ten mounted men is sent to Captain Potter daily, for such service as may be necessary.

Information has reached me that ammunition is being sent from Fort Bliss to Mesilla. I have accordingly ordered all wagons from that direction to be stopped and searched.

The effective force at present under my command is 450. Exclusive of sick (38). There are 98 men on detached service, nearly all of whom will [return] within a week.

Nothing has been heard of the troops from Forts Buchanon & Breckinridge, since the acceptance of the order requiring the abandonment of those Posts.

Enclosed I transmit Oaths of Allegiance of Lieuts. Lane Rifles and Stivers 7 Infy.[30]

Armies were not yet engaged in battle in the East, but smoke was in the air and the President of the United States Abraham Lincoln required oaths of allegiance from all officers. In his July 21 letter, Major Lynde referred to 1st Lieutenant Lane and 2d Lieutenant Stivers taking their oaths. What Major Isaac Lynde had no way of knowing was that on that very day the American Civil War truly began, blood being shed by both sides at the 1st Battle of Bull Run in Virginia. When he abandoned Fort Fillmore a few days later, Lynde knew Texas had seceded but there was, as yet, no armed conflict or declaration of war between North and South.

Fort Buchanan was evacuated and burned on July 23, 1861. Mining, ranching, and all parts of the economy in what was then the western part of New Mexico came to a standstill. The Apaches, who believed they had caused all the turmoil in the ranks of their enemies, for at least a short time once more held sway over the lands of their fathers.

On July 24, while Fort Buchanan was still smoking and its 7th Infantry troops starting out on the long dusty road east, Colonel John R. Baylor, commanding the 2d Texas Mounted Rifles, marched 258 Texas troops north out of Fort Bliss along the east bank of the Rio Grande, destination Fort Fillmore or Mesilla. This was naked aggression, there being no declaration of any conflict between the seceded state of Texas and the United States, at least as far as Baylor or Lynde could have known. Of course, many Texans believed they were at war, regardless of the absence of a formal declaration.

By a stroke of fortune, deserters from Baylor's force alerted the garrison at Fort Fillmore of Baylor's surprise attack in time to prevent it. Lynde reported:

> ... I have the honor to report that on the night of the 24th instant a deserter from the Texas troops was brought in by our Picket, and he informed me that a large body of mounted men between 3 & 400 under Command of Lt. Col. Baylor, Texas Troops, were moving up the river, and that he left them at Willow Bar about 12 miles below the Post. Presuming their object to be an attack on the Post, I immediately ordered the two Companies of the 7th Infantry from San Tomas and kept the garrison under arms until after daylight, when mounted parties were sent out to reconnoiter.[31]

Having detected the Texan presence on the eastern side of the river, numbering by estimate some three hundred to four hundred troops (258 by Baylor's count), Lynde did exactly as he should have done given that estimate. He pulled Potter's two companies from temporary defensive positions at Santo Tomás on the other side of the river and brought them back to defend the fort.

His attack thwarted by the now alerted Federal garrison, Colonel Baylor took the next best path. He later reported:

... On the morning of the 25th I determined to occupy Mesilla, and prevent, if possible, the enemy from getting a position there, as it was one that would be easily held, and would enable them to hold the country. I reached Mesilla in the afternoon of the 25th, and was soon informed that the enemy was marching to attack us. I posted my men in position and awaited the arrival of the enemy.[32]

Baylor knew he would receive a friendly welcome in Mesilla, given the open support provided secessionist views by that town's newspaper and most of its American citizenry. His move across the river was unopposed. Once Major Lynde became aware of the presence of the Texas forces in Mesilla on July 25, he planned a march to the town. No surviving document exists giving us his original plan. Most likely, Major Lynde wanted to clear the road west so the troops from Forts Breckinridge and Buchanan could pass through Mesilla to Fort Fillmore as per his July 15 order.

There are as many versions of what happened during the Battle of Mesilla as there were observers of the battle, a study beyond the scope of this book. Facts are confused, including the number of artillery pieces used, the shots fired by artillery, whether there was a cavalry charge or a slow walk, how many were killed and wounded, etc. We only know for sure that Baylor's Texans crossed the Rio Grande on July 25, 1861. At some point after the Texans were safely in the town, an undetermined number of troops under the command of Major Isaac Lynde crossed the river and advanced upon Mesilla. Upon arriving, the Federal representative(s) demanded the Texans surrender the town, were refused, deployed their forces, and opened the battle with artillery—the numbers and results of which are confused in all accounts. The Rebels responded, killing and wounding some of the Federal soldiers, one of whom was 1st Lieutenant McNally. This maneuvering and firing took time, and darkness fell. The Federal force then returned to Fort Fillmore.

Neither side wanted further fighting that night. The withdrawing 7th Infantry troops safely re-crossed the river and entered Fort Fillmore. We know little of the next day, July 26, perhaps the most important day of all. This was the day the decision was made to abandon Fort Fillmore. The only known fact is that Major Lynde decided to abandon Fort Fillmore during the night of July 26-27.

Why did Lynde decide to pull out? He clearly indicated why in a letter written later that day. First, Fort Fillmore was indefensible, especially if artillery was brought to bear, or there was an attack from the east out of the sand dunes. Because of the high sand dunes, mesquite, and tall grass, the enemy could not be seen until they were on the post. In fact, the only two defensible directions were to the west and south, although an artillery attack would be difficult to repel from either of those directions. Lynde knew Baylor had artillery forty miles to the south at Fort Bliss, if he didn't yet have it in Mesilla. If he dug in permanently, Lynde knew he would one day face that artillery with his women and children in the midst of the fight. With the families at the post vulnerable to a four-sided attack and artillery bombardment, and having an order to abandon Fort Fillmore at his discretion in his pocket, Major Lynde decided he could not mount an effective defense.[33]

Isaac Lynde believed he was outnumbered, and soon to be outgunned in artillery as well. His initial estimates were four hundred Texas troops in Mesilla when they attacked that town. If he was outnumbered slightly by the basic Texas force, how much greater was that force than his when the secessionist militia in Mesilla was added and additional forces brought up from Fort Bliss, as were rumored? During the day of July 26, 1861, Major Isaac Lynde decided to abandon Fort Fillmore and attempt to save his soldiers, their families, and servants, as well as the public and private property of the 7th Infantry Regiment. Some of the public property, such as Dr. McKee's hospital bottles, had to be destroyed; other items, including hospital beds, and possibly a crate of .69 caliber cartridges, were left behind. Much of the private property and household furnishings belonging to the soldiers was also left behind. Lynde explained, "Other officers, with myself, became convinced that we must eventually be compelled to surrender if we remained in the fort, and that our only hope of saving the command from capture was in reaching some other military post."[34]

Two routes to safety were open to Lynde. The first was the most obvious, and the closest—across the Jornada del Muerto to Fort Craig. About that route Lynde had this to say: "I have sent an express to Captain Gibbs directing him to return to Fort Craig with his command as he can not join this Post now. They have possession of the road above." Lynde seemed to believe (perhaps he was fed false information) that the road above Doña Ana was in Confederate hands.[35]

Major Lynde commented on the decision he finally made in an August 7 letter to the Department of New Mexico:

> ... at 1 O'clock a.m. on the 27th of July I took up the line of march for Fort Stanton, which was believed to be the most practicable point to reach, and was reported to be threatened by the enemy. I had no personal knowledge of the road, but it was reported to me that the first day's march would be 20 miles to San Augustine Springs, where there would be abundance of water for all the command.[36]

No one in the Federal or Texas commands said anything about the night march, save for this briefest of comments by Major Lynde. The chain of events is picked up at dawn, July 27, 1861, somewhere on the Fort Stanton road, as Lieutenant Colonel Baylor later called it. Lynde reported with the greatest brevity: "Until daylight the command advanced without difficulty, but when the sun arose the day became intensely hot, and soon after the men and teams began to show signs of fatigue, and I found that the distance was greater than had been represented."[37]

With the coming of the sun, and the promise of the hottest of hot days, the infantry, especially in the rear—those who were exposed to the speed-up/slow-down motion of a column on the move—truly suffered. Lynde remarked on the head of the column approaching the final steep rise some six miles from San Augustine Springs: "About 6 miles before reaching the Springs commences a short ascent to a pass in the Organ Mountains, and here the men and teams suffered severely with the intense heat and want of water, many men falling and unable to proceed."[38]

We don't know where the column was when the forces of Colonel John Baylor first saw them. Baylor's words on the sighting are confusing because of his phrasing. Unfortunately, we have no others. Baylor said:

> ... On the morning of the 27th, a little after daylight, my spies reported a column of dust seen in the direction of the Organ Mountains, distant 15 miles, on the Fort Stanton road. I could from the top of a house with a glass see the movements of the enemy. I immediately ordered the command to saddle and mount, for the purpose of intercepting them at San Augustine Pass.[39]

When Baylor's forces arrived on the scene, the sun-shattered remnants of the Federal rear-guard infantry companies must have been a sight to behold. The soldiers of the most important fighting element in the Federal column were lying prostrate by the side of the road, or off seeking the shade wherever they might find it. Certainly Baylor expected a fighting rear guard, that being standard military procedure for a column of troops on the move. Lynde is known to have assigned two companies to that duty. Because Lynde never received a hearing, knowledge of the officer(s) assigned to those companies has not come down to us. Colonel John Baylor made no mention of encountering a disciplined formation which in any way opposed his advance. The infantry rear guard and the officer who commanded it were singularly responsible for protecting the forward elements of the column. If that rear guard collapsed before Baylor's arrival, as it certainly appears to have done due to the heat, the entire column was lost, no matter what Major Lynde chose to do later. As far as Major Lynde knew, at least up until the very last moments of this travesty, his rear guard was obeying orders to fight and delay, as they were required by U.S. Army regulations to do. What a shock it must have been to find they had not done their duty!

An unexpected event occurred as the troops filed through the pass toward the springs. Captain Gibbs, driving the herd of cattle destined for Fort Fillmore, appeared with his small force. During the interval in which Captain Gibbs arrived on the scene, reported to Lynde in some fashion, and then came back down the mountain, Baylor seems to have gone to a secondary spring for water. Captain Gibbs's force, according to his somewhat confusing account, moved toward the rear of the column. Gibbs reported sighting the Confederates:

> ... On arriving at the mouth of the canyon I assumed command of the cavalry force, consisting of Companies F, B, and I, and a part of G, Mounted Rifles—70 men strong. The Texans, under Colonel Baylor and Major Waller, and about 320 strong (all cavalry), with some dismounted men, and what seemed to be a couple of pieces of artillery, at this time debouched from behind the point of the hill below me to the left, and captured the beef cattle and my two wagons. I deployed 50 men as skirmishers, with 20 men as a reserve; but finding that I was entirely outflanked, I formed column of sections and prepared to charge with drawn pistols.[40]

Not much of a rear-guard fight was conducted by Gibbs and his mounted soldiers either, as had been true of the infantry rear guard Major Lynde thought would save his column. Captain Gibbs may have ordered pistols drawn but he never fired a single shot in answer. Here's what Baylor reported:

> ... The road for 5 miles was lined with the fainting, famished soldiers, who threw down their arms as we passed and begged for water. At the Springs the enemy had drawn up in line of battle some 200 or 300 strong. I ordered Major Waller to charge with Captain Hardeman's company until he reached the end of the line of straggling soldiers, then to form and cut them off from the main body. I followed, disarming the enemy, and as fast as our jaded horses would go.[41]

Here is what Lynde said:

> ... Soon after it was reported to me that a part of the teams had given out and could not be brought up, and that large numbers of the infantry had become totally overpowered with the intense heat. At this time an express from Captain Gibbs reported that eight companies of mounted men, supported by artillery and a large force of infantry, were approaching our rear guard. I had

the "Call to arms" sounded, and found that I could not bring more than 100 men of the infantry battalion on parade. Captain Gibbs, with a mounted force, now rode into camp, and stated to me that eight companies of mounted Texans (supported by a regiment of infantry, more or less) were approaching; that they had driven in or captured our rear guard and the men that had given out in the rear. Three of the four mountain howitzers that we had with us were with the wagons in the rear and captured. They were guarded by one company of infantry acting as artillery. Captain Gibbs also reported that his company, men and horses, had been without water for twenty-four hours.[42]

What happened next is well known. Isaac Lynde surrendered without fighting. The truth of why awaits a more detailed accounting beyond the scope of this book.* Whatever the truth, history has treated him on a par with Benedict Arnold; the vilification continues to this day as the old fables surrounding the surrender are repeated again and again.

On August 16, 1861, Captain Joseph Haydn Potter, who then commanded the 7th Infantry Regiment in place of Major Isaac Lynde, totaled the numbers of 7th Infantry Regiment soldiers taken prisoner at San Augustine Springs on July 27, 1861. Released on parole were one major, two assistant surgeons, two captains, five 1st lieutenants, one 2d lieutenant: total commissioned, eleven. One sergeant-major, one quartermaster-sergeant, one principle musician, twenty-three sergeants, twenty-two corporals, seven musicians, 344 privates: total enlisted, 399. Aggregate, four hundred and ten. In confinement as prisoners of war: one sergeant, fifteen privates: total, sixteen. Deserted to the enemy: one hospital steward, one sergeant, twenty-four privates: total, twenty-six. All included, there were 452 soldiers of the 7th Infantry who began the march.[43]

Adding 7th Infantry and R.M.R. numbers, a total force of 543 soldiers was in Lynde's command. The regiment also had forty men

---

* See, *Incident at San Augustine Pass: A Hearing for Major Isaac Lynde*, by Richard Wadsworth, Las Cruces, NM: Yucca Tree Press, 2002, for an in-depth analysis of Major Lynde's actions.

on detached service who were not there at the surrender. Three other companies of the regiment, on the march from Forts Buchanan and Breckinridge in Arizona, escaped the Texans. They served the Union cause at the Battle of Valverde in February 1862.[44]

The tragedy at San Augustine was over. When the troops returned to Las Cruces they were in a Confederate world, no matter what the local Hispanics thought. Former Hospital Steward Charles E. Fitzwilliams was the only man to return to Fort Fillmore. He chose the Confederate side and returned to the post to begin treating Confederate soldiers as he once had boys in blue. One sergeant and twenty-four soldiers took up the Rebel cause. All the officers remained loyal to the Union. Of the 7th Infantry officers, only Lieutenant Francis Crilly left an account of the battle, and that written decades after the fact. The rest demurred.

Major Lynde was unceremoniously dropped from the roles of the United States Army by Abraham Lincoln without any trial or hearing. Following the Civil War, Lynde was restored temporarily to active duty by President Andrew Johnson, who simply revoked the order of dismissal. He served for one day as major of the 18th U.S. Infantry before being retired permanently on a pension.[45]

NOTES - Chapter 13

1. John Upton Terrell, *Apache Chronicles*, pp. 219, 220.
2. Edwin Sweeney, *Cochise*, pp. 155-158.
3. Lydia Spencer Lane, *I Married a Soldier*, pp. 97, 98.
4. Fort Fillmore Post Returns, February 1861.
5. Buckley to Lane, February 15, 1861, M1120, Rolls 13/14.
6. Lane to Buckley, February 17, 1861, M1120, Rolls 13/14.
7. Maury to Crittenden, March 1, 1861, M1012, Roll 2.
8. Maury to Lane, March 1, 1861, M1012, Roll 2.
9. James D. Richardson, *Messages and Papers of the Presidents*, pp. 3204, 3205.
10. La Posta, Volume II, #6, November-December 1970, p. 4.
11. Lydia Spencer Lane, *I Married a Soldier*, p. 101.
12. Fort Fillmore Post Returns, April 1861.

13. Lane to Maury, April 7, 1861, M1120, Rolls 13/14.

14. Fort Fillmore Post Returns, April 1861.

15. Heitman, Edward Richard Canby.

16. Heitman, Cadmus Wilcox.

17. Lydia Spencer Lane, *I Married a Soldier*, pp. 102, 103.

18. Edwin Sweeney, *Cochise*, p. 170.

19. Lane to Assistant Adjutant General, June 7, 1861, M1120, Rolls 13/14.

20. La Posta, Volume II, #6, November-December 1970, p. 4.

21. Canby to Assistant Adjutant General, New York City, June 11, 1861, M1012, Roll 2.

22. Paul to Assistant Adjutant General, Santa Fe, June 16, 1861, M1120, Rolls 13/14.

23. Anderson to Lynde, June 30, 1861, M1012, Roll 2.

24. Fort Craig Post Returns, June 30, 1861.

25. Heitman, David Hancock.

26. Heitman, George Ryan, Mathew Rider Stevenson, Joseph Haydn Potter, Charles Bryant Stivers, and Charles Henry Alden.

27. Edwin Sweeney, *Cochise*, pp. 180, 181.

28. Lynde to Canby, July 7, 1861; various editors, *Confederate Victories in the Southwest - Prelude to Defeat* (Albuquerque: Horn & Wallace Publishers, 1961), pp. 58,59. Hereafter known as *Texas Data*.

29. Anderson to Gibbs, July 17, 1861, M1012, Roll 2.

30. Lynde to Acting Assistant Adjutant General, July 21, 1861, M1120, Rolls 13/14.

31. Lynde to Assistant Adjutant General, July 26, 1861, M1120, Rolls 13/14.

32. Baylor to Washington, September 26, 1861, Texas Data, pp. 34-37.

33. Lynde to Assistant Adjutant General, July 26, 1861, M1120, Rolls 13/14.

34. Lynde to Assistant Adjutant General, August 7, 1861, M1120, Rolls 13/14.

35. Ibid.

36. Lynde to Assistant Adjutant General, August 7, 1861, M1120, Rolls 13/14.

37. Lynde to Assistant Adjutant General, August 7, 1861, M1120, Rolls 13/14.

38. Ibid.

39. Baylor to Washington, September 21, 1861, Texas Data, pp. 34-37.

40. Gibbs to Assistant Adjutant General, August 6, 1861, M1120, Rolls 13/14.

41. Baylor to Washington, September 21, 1861, Texas Data, pp. 34-37.

42. Lynde to Assistant Adjutant General, August 7, 1861, M1120, Rolls 13/14.

43. Potter to Assistant Adjutant General, August 16, 1861, Texas Data, p. 32.

44. Ibid.

45. Heitman, Isaac Lynde.

In the 1970s a broken stirrup was found at
Fort Fillmore and inspired this sketch.
Courtesy: Loren Schmidt, artist.

Insignia found at Fort Fillmore
Bugle, infantry regimental insignia-1861; R.M.R. regimental numbers
for 1st, 2d Dragoons and 3d Infantry; Dragoon cartridge box plate, the
infantry style was larger; Pom pom or felt hat eagle.
Courtesy: Geronimo Springs Museum.

14

THE LAST DAYS OF
FORT MILLARD FILLMORE

Following the surrender of Major Isaac Lynde and the 7th Infantry Regiment at San Augustine Springs, Colonel John Baylor established the Confederate Territory of Arizona, capitol at Mesilla. Baylor's creation lasted through a true invasion of New Mexico Territory by General Henry Hopkins Sibley in early 1862. The invasion culminated in the Battle of Valverde on February 21, the capture of Albuquerque and Santa Fe thereafter, and the final Battle of Glorieta Pass in the period of March 26-28, 1862. After losing at Glorieta, the Confederate Army slowly retreated from New Mexico Territory. The approach of the California Column under General James Carleton forced the Rebel troops out of southern New Mexico entirely and pushed them well back into Texas. After that, the normal peacetime routine of the New Mexico garrisons was followed, save that the forts were under the control of troops from California, assisted by the New Mexico Volunteer Militia. The Regular Army, following participation at Valverde and Glorieta, left the Territory, not to return in significant numbers until 1866.

After July 27, 1861, Fort Fillmore passed temporarily into the hands of the Confederacy; specifically, troops from Baylor's command occupied the site after a night of looting by the local Mexican, and no doubt American, populace. Fort Fillmore was for a while part of the Confederate Territory of Arizona. The Fort Fillmore garrison now flew the Stars and Bars or the Lone Star Flag of Texas, rather than the Stars and Stripes.

Confederate Fort Fillmore evoked sparse comment in the local community, though one valuable source does exist. The Confederate history of the fort can be broken into two parts, the occupation by Lieutenant Colonel John Baylor's troops and the occupation by the troops from Henry Hopkins Sibley's force. Most of the data on the first period of Confederate occupation comes from the journal of Morgan Wolfe Merrick, a Texas soldier in Baylor's command. His journal, *From Desert To Bayou,* was published by the University of Texas at El Paso. Private Merrick's journal begins with the extinguishing of the fire started at the fort when Major Lynde and his troops departed. Merrick saw a scene of attempted mass destruction:

> ... After extinguishing the fire the fed's had started, we began looking around the post. They had left the place in a topsyturvey state, the Q.M.D. [quartermaster] was a confusion of boxes, barrels, paper, etc. At the hospital they had thrown the bedding in a pile & emptied and broken bottles of medicine over them, had pulled or turned over the shelving in the dispinsary [sic] into the middle of the floor, making a fine mess.[1]

For the next few days the Texans cleaned and made the barracks presentable for their use. Private Merrick was attached to Teel's artillery company, but they had not yet brought their cannon from Fort Bliss. Whether the four Federal mountain howitzers captured at San Augustine Pass were brought to the fort was never stated. Unfortunately, by August 7th Merrick was at Doña Ana, establishing a dispensary there and was thus unable to give further information on what transpired at the fort.[2]

The only other information Merrick offered about Confederate Fort Fillmore was that while in Las Cruces, another "Mex town population abot [sic] the same as Mesilla," he came across former Fort Fillmore Hospital Steward Fitzwilliams (he called him Fitzsimmons), who defected to the Confederate cause after the surrender at San Augustine Springs.[3]

Apparently Colonel Baylor kept troops at both Fort Fillmore and Mesilla and was at the height of his glory during the period following the surrender. On August 2, 1861, Baylor issued his famous Proclamation to the people of the Territory of Arizona, in effect establishing a military dictatorship. The first paragraph stated:

> ... The social and political condition of Arizona being little short of general anarchy, and the people being literally destitute of law, order, and protection, the said territory, from the date hereof, is hereby declared temporarily organized as a military government until such time as Congress may otherwise provide.[4]

John Baylor had what he wanted: control. The troops at Mesilla and at Fort Fillmore provided that control. Unfortunately, no Confederate official ever stated what they did with the hundreds of military rifle/muskets, bayonets, pistols, wagons, and ammunition Baylor's forces captured. We cannot even be sure what happened to the cannon, several of which were captured at Fort Bliss and four more at San Augustine Springs.

By August 8 Colonel Canby was fully aware of events and concerned enough to issue a decree suspending the writ of habeous corpus in the Territory of New Mexico for the duration of the rebellion. This proclamation would have given Lynde the power to shut down the seditious *Mesilla Times* and arrest all secessionists before Baylor invaded again. Colonel Canby noted:

> ... The writ of habeas corpus has been suspended in order to enable every commander to guard against the treasonable designs of persons disloyal to the Government of the United States, particularly agents and spies, persons engaged in furnishing information to, or in other treasonable correspondence with, the enemy, or in inciting insurrection or rebellion.
>
> Care will be taken to guard against any abuse of this power by unauthorized arrests or by annoyances to peaceable and well-disposed citizens, and, except in the case of overt acts, arrests will only be made by the superior commander of any district, post, or body of troops in the service of the United States, and only upon probable cause of suspicion of being dangerous to the public safety.

When arrests are made, the person arrested will immediately be examined, and if there be no ground for suspicion,
will be released; if otherwise, held in confinement until his case
is disposed of by the proper authorities. If there be evidence of
treason or misprision of treason, he will be turned over to the
civil courts for trial.

In the execution of these duties the troops will at all times
unite with and assist the civil authorities in maintaining order
throughout the country.[5]

The 7th Infantry troops leaving Forts Buchanan and Breckinridge, at least two companies, eluded Baylor's trap. On August 14
Colonel Baylor reported from his headquarters at Fort Bliss that
on August 7 the column of Union troops received an express from
Fort Craig notifying them of the surrender of Fort Fillmore. The
commander of the column ordered the wagons and supplies
burned, and set off for Fort Craig with the remaining troops.[6]

On August 25 Lieutenant Colonel Baylor reported a brief
skirmish with Federal troops near Fort Craig. Baylor's troops
captured a Captain Hubbell of the New Mexico Volunteers and
nine of his men. He learned there were now three hundred and fifty
Regular Army troops at that fort and one hundred and eighty New
Mexico volunteers. Baylor also believed there were as yet no
artillery batteries at Fort Craig, and said he could take the place
were his horses not so jaded. Baylor recommended to San
Antonio that strong Confederate forces be based in Arizona to
contain both the Federal and Apache threats.[7]

The Chiricahuas were in the vicinity of Cook's Springs, west
of Mesilla in late September, lying in wait for a wagon train
expected to pass through the area. Because of the presence of the
Confederate Arizona Guards under Captain Thomas Mastin, the train
made it to the safety of Pinos Altos. On September 27 the Apaches
attacked the mining camp. Captain Mastin was killed in this attack;
casualties were said to be heavy on both sides. The Apaches may
have lost as many as twenty or thirty, whereas the Americans lost
five. Both Mangas and Cochise were believed involved.[7]

After the fall of Fort Fillmore, Apaches could see the breakup of the white man's nation all the way from the Pecos River to the California line. They tried, as Mangas did at Pinos Altos, to take advantage of this turmoil to rid the land of the whites, or at least to cause them great grief. Fort Stanton was abandoned by Union troops, freeing the Mescalero at Sierra Blanca to begin raiding again. In the Davis Mountains, Apaches under Chief Nicolas attacked the Confederate garrison at Fort Davis, Texas, killing two guards while stealing a number of cattle from the fort beef herd. The Indians temporarily found themselves back in control not only of their lands, but their lives. The Mescalero even manned the old ambush site near the Point of Rocks on the Jornada, cutting off Confederate Fort Fillmore from Federal Fort Craig.[9]

In late October John Baylor requested support from General Henry Hopkins Sibley. Baylor felt the pressures of a hostile surrounding environment, as Lynde had before him. Most Americans in the region around Mesilla and Fort Fillmore still held Southern sympathies, but such was not true of the Mexican population who had no love lost for Texans, nor for the Apaches, whose raiding Baylor seemed unable to stop. Identification of the Confederacy with Texas in the minds of most of the Hispanic population doomed any efforts to sway them to the Confederate cause.

Robert P. Kelley, editor of the *Mesilla Times*, used his editorial license one time too many as the year came to an end. In the pages of his paper, Kelley accused Baylor of cowardice. Baylor demanded an apology when the two met on a Mesilla street on December 12, 1861. When Kelley refused to accede to Baylor's demand, the latter knocked Kelley down with a gun and then proceeded to shoot him. Baylor left him for dead, but the wounded Kelley hung on for two weeks before expiring. Baylor was not charged with the murder.

On the day Baylor shot Kelley, General Henry Hopkins Sibley, one-time commander at Fort Union and a visitor to Fort Fillmore in the days just before Major Isaac Lynde's arrival, returned with a Confederate army to make his temporary headquarters at Fort Bliss. The rebels were on the move at last and in the direction of

Fort Craig where Canby had concentrated most of his forces. As the partially combined forces of Sibley's and Baylor's commands moved north into the Jornada, events happening in far away Richmond, Virginia, were supposed to justify Baylor's conquests in southern New Mexico. Confederate-occupied Fort Fillmore, as well as the rest of Confederate-occupied Arizona, became officially a part of the Confederate States of America on February 14, 1862, when President Jefferson Davis gave territorial status to Arizona.

The Battle of Valverde, the first major battle between the two forces in New Mexico, took place on February 21, 1862, resulting in what was probably a draw but is usually considered a Confederate victory because the Union forces withdrew. There are many fine descriptions of the battle and at least one excellent book. In general, the Confederate approach was well known, rather than unexpected, as was Baylor's invasion of New Mexico in a time when war had not yet been declared. The Union forces were ready to defend Fort Craig or any other point nearby. General Sibley chose to bypass the fort and not make a frontal assault, hence the battle took place some miles north, near Valverde Mesa, an easily recognized landmark.

The battle involved a few former Fort Fillmore officers. Captain Richard S.C. Lord, who commanded Company 'D,' 1st Dragoons at Fort Fillmore from April 1859 to early in 1860, was still in command of Company 'D,' now re-named as part of the 1st Cavalry Regiment. Lord's company was in reserve along with the 2^d New Mexico Militia Regiment under Colonel Pino; initially both units were across the Rio Grande from where the battle took place. Pino's group disgraced itself that day while Lord's contribution to the battle was minimal, his reputation being sullied as a result.

Captain Lord's battalion (two companies) supported Alexander McRae's battery of Artillery. McRae was the widely recognized Federal hero of the Battle of Valverde, defending to the death his cannon from capture during a Confederate charge. At about 2:45 p.m. on February 1, Lord was positioning his reserve cavalry force on the east side of the river, well back of

McRae's battery, when the battery came under attack. The Confederate attack overwhelmed the battery before reserves could be brought forward. Lord, when notified of the situation, got his men in position as quickly as possible and ordered a charge. He did not get there in time. New Mexico Militia troops defending the McRae battery broke and ran. The battery was overwhelmed and McRae was killed.

Another casualty of the fighting for control of McRae's Battery was 2[d] Lieutenant Lyman Mischler, who served at Valverde as an artillery officer under Captain McRae's command. Formerly of Company I, 7th Infantry, he served at Fort Fillmore only during June 1861 and was sent on detached service before Major Lynde arrived. Mischler was not involved in the surrender at San Augustine Springs; hence, young Mischler was one of the few former 7th Infantry officers not on parole and available for service at Fort Craig. Lyman Mischler was born in 1839 and, as an 1860 graduate of the United States Military Academy, he was barely twenty-three when he fought the Rebels. He died during the second Confederate charge on the battery, shot in the chest while preparing his piece for firing.

Parts or all of Companies 'C,' 'F,' and 'H' of the 7th Infantry were engaged in the battle. These companies, not with Lynde at Fort Fillmore, fought under Captain Peter Plympton. Plympton's former company, 'B,' was surrendered by Lynde at San Augustine Springs. Company 'F,' under Plympton at Valverde, took an astounding seventy-one percent casualties, killed and wounded, trying to defend McRae's battery during the battle.

Without a doubt the most interesting fact about the Battle of Valverde as it pertains to former Fort Fillmore personnel is the possible meeting of Captain George Washington Howland, Company 'C,' 3[d] Cavalry (formerly Regiment of Mounted Riflemen), with newly promoted Colonel Henry C. McNeill, 5th Texas Cavalry, on that battlefield. McNeill was Howland's second in command of Company 'C,' R.M.R., at Fort Fillmore, from March to May 1859. They served together at Burro Mountain Camp. Howland and McNeill may have known of each other's presence at Valverde—

their units being in the same area of the battlefield. Both survived the battle. Howland remained with the Regular Army throughout the war in the East, returning to New Mexico and Fort Craig after the war. McNeill also survived the war.

Captain Powhaten Jones was at Valverde with the 7th Texas Cavalry. The 7th Texas was commanded by Colonel Steele, who, was also commanding Confederate Fort Fillmore. Jones reported to Steele concerning his unit's service at Valverde. He was with the 1st Battalion of the 7th Texas, guarding the Sibley expedition wagon train south of the battlefield. After the battle began, the men of the 7th Texas and a detachment from the 5th Texas, McNeill's regiment, received orders to move toward the sound of battle. Three companies remained with the train and four com-panies joined the fray—three from the 7th and one from the 5th. Jones described the loss of Colonel Sutton, his commander during the battle, and also described the conflict which involved their charging the Federal batteries, possibly including that of Captain McRae.[10]

Following the Confederate capture of McRae's artillery battery the battle ended. The Union troops withdrew to Fort Craig; the Confederates moved upriver toward Albuquerque and Santa Fe.

On March 1, 1862, Colonel William Steele reported on what he had heard concerning the Valverde battle. His letter is headed 'Camp Near Fort Fillmore,' a mysterious notation indicating that either Fort Fillmore proper was no longer occupied by Steele's regiment or the rundown fort could not accommodate all of the Confederate troops. Colonel Steele reported:

> ... I have received a verbal express from General Sibley, the numerous parties of Mexicans in the employ of the enemy rendering it dangerous to write. Our forces turned the enemy's position by crossing the river to the east side, which drew him out of his entrenchments, and an engagement ensued just above Fort Craig, which commenced about 9 o'clock on the morning of February 21, and lasted, with little intermission until near sunset, when the enemy was driven in confusion from the field. We captured seven pieces of artillery and a considerable number

of small-arms were picked up. Much of the Mexican portion of the enemy fled to the hills. The regulars and Pike's Peak Volunteers returned to the fort. Our forces were encamped on the field when my informants left. Our loss is stated at 38 killed [36 in some sources] and 106 wounded [150 in other sources]. Major Lockridge is recollected as one of the killed. General Sibley had been sick some days previous to the action, and the command devolved upon Col. Thomas Green, who was in command most of the day.

This account agrees with the information I had a few days previous as to the contemplated movement. I received this intelligence the day after the stage left for San Antonio and have delayed writing, hoping to get some more particulars, but as yet have none.[11]

Sibley's army moved slowly on up the Rio Grande, unharried by Canby or any forces from Fort Craig. Their destinations were Albuquerque and Santa Fe; the latter was captured on March 4, 1862. The next goal was Fort Union—General Sibley's former command post before he took up the Confederate cause—which held supplies and equipment the Confederates desperately needed.

The battles that determined the fate of New Mexico Territory were fought southeast of occupied Santa Fe on March 26-28. There the Santa Fe Trail crosses La Glorieta Pass. Major John Chivington of the Colorado Volunteers was ordered to attack Confederate Major Charles Pyron's force at Pidgeon's Ranch near the pass. The two forces numbered four hundred and eighteen soldiers—Chivington with two hundred, and Pyron with three hundred. Chivington gained the upper hand during a brief fight and the Confederates retreated to Johnson's Ranch. The two forces met the next day with reinforcements on both sides. Although the Confederates believed they won the battle, the Union forces, in effect, won the war. By one of those odd events in history, Major Chivington, who was later castigated for the slaughter of Black Kettle's Cheyenne band at Sand Creek, went to Johnson's Ranch, found the Confederate supply column and burned the wagons, killed five hundred to six hundred mules and horses, and captured seventeen prisoners. It was immaterial which side won the Second

Battle of Pidgeon's Ranch, or Glorieta Pass as it is so often called. When the Confederates lost their supply train, their war in New Mexico was over.[12]

Sibley slowly retreated down the Rio Grande towards Fort Fillmore and Texas. The Confederates always waged war on a shoestring. When something interfered with their meager supplies, the best of bravery and courage meant nothing.

General Edwin Vose Sumner, the former 9th Military Department commander in New Mexico during the early 1850s, was in charge of the Department of the Pacific, which included California. In August 1861 he heard about the fall of Fort Fillmore, the fort Sumner had helped establish in September 1851. Sumner ordered then Colonel James Carleton to move his headquarters from San Francisco to southern California to intercept any Confederate threat that came toward the state. By February, a strong force was established which was to retake 'Confederate Arizona' and those parts of southern New Mexico Territory then under the threat of Sibley's invasion. If severe weather had not intervened, Carleton's troops might have pushed into Baylor's area of control before Sibley could complete his retreat.[13]

By May 2 the advance units of the California Column, as General Carleton's military force was called, were at Fort Yuma on the southern California border. Carleton had the 1st California Infantry, 5th California Infantry, the 1st California Cavalry, part of the 2[d] California Cavalry, and Company 'A,' 3[d] United States Artillery. The force strength was two thousand men and two hundred wagons in a long caravan. As they marched toward New Mexico, Carleton did something Major Isaac Lynde might have copied. He broke the column into smaller units which arrived at water holes in intervals and the available water was not exhausted, which could have happend if two groups of soldiers arrived at once.[14]

On May 18, 1862, a one-hundred-man Confederate force led by Captain Sherod Hunter abandoned Tucson when they received word of the approach of the California Column. The next day, May 19, Cochise ambushed the Confederates and killed four men, capturing thirty mules and twenty-five horses. The first elements of the California Column, under the command of Colonel Joseph Rodman West, occupied Tucson by May 20. On May 21 Carleton ordered the reoccupation of Forts Buchanan and Breckin-ridge. He declared martial law on June 8 in what he began calling the Territory of Arizona. He also declared himself the military governor of that Territory. Carleton stated in the proclamation:

> The Congress and the United States has set apart a portion of New Mexico and organized it into a Territory complete in itself. This is known as the Territory of Arizona. It comprises within its limits all the country eastward from the Colorado River which is now occupied by the forces of the United States known as the column of California; as the flag of the United States shall be carried by this column further eastward, these limits will extend in that direction until they reach the farthest geographical boundary of the Territory.[15]

In reality, there was no Territory of Arizona as General Carleton proclaimed. Congress did not pass the act creating the Territory of Arizona until February 4, 1863, some six months later. The General anticipated what he had been told was coming.

The lead elements of the California Column, Companies 'B' and 'C,' 1st California Cavalry, reached the abandoned stage station at Apache Pass by June 25. They met Cochise, who assured them he was friendly to them. By July 4, old Fort Thorn on the Rio Grande was reoccupied. One officer who came with the California Column to Fort Thorn and later traveled on to Fort Fillmore, was John Cremony. Cremony visited Fort Fillmore in the early 1850s with the Bartlett Commission. He had been a Boston newspaperman. Cremony, both an Indian fighter and a friend of the Apaches, compiled a dictionary of the Apache language. Cremony's book, *My Life Among the Apaches,* details numerous accounts of his love-hate relationship with the Apaches. In 1862 he was a lieutenant serving with the California Column.[16]

Sibley's Confederate Army abandoned Mesilla on July 21, leaving one hundred sick and injured men there in the hospital, as

California Column advance troops reached San Diego Crossing, some forty miles north of Mesilla. By July 23 Lieutenant Colonel Eyre, 1st California Cavalry, was in Las Cruces where he found stored government property left there by the Confederates. These items may have come from Fort Fillmore. Eyre noted in a letter to another officer named Van Vliet:

> ... I have the honor to report the arrival at this place last night of an express from Fort Thorn with a package directed to General James H. Carleton, Tucson. I received no instructions whatever in regard to the package—but presume it is the desire of the District Commander, that I should forward the same to its destination. I am endeavoring to find three men with good horses, to whom I can entrust the package, and send them by Fronteras through Mexico, to Santa Cruz, and down that river to Tucson. That is the only route a small party can, with any degree of safety in assurance of getting through, at this time take. I discovered today a large lot of Government property concealed in an adobe building in this town. An inventory of which is being made out, and which when complete I will forward for the information of the District Commander consisting in part of shovels, spades, axes, kettles, etc. which were taken possession of by Lieut. Baldwin a.a.q.m. for my command. The articles have been used. They will be safely stored until orders for their disposal have been received by me. I also caused a lot of lumber and other property belonging to noted secessionists in Messilla [sic] to be seized, the owners thereof having gone to Texas. An inventory of which I will forward to the District Commander without delay. I also had seized the records and papers of this District as well as those of this County, that they might not fall into the hands of individuals to be used to their advantage and to the prejudice of this Community. I learned today of a number of hospital bed steads belonging to Government, which Colonel Steele C.S.A. caused to be sold, and which are stored in, as I am informed, in a town a few miles below here. I will send a party tomorrow in search of them.[17]

It is obvious what happened to the Fort Fillmore hospital beds, and perhaps the post shovels, spades, axes, and kettles as well. The

Confederates sold them to the local citizenry for cash. When Colonel Eyre mentioned that the hospital beds were in a town a few miles below, he probably meant Mesilla. He may not have known that Fort Fillmore, the source of the beds and tools, was nearby.

Carleton began his personal advance beyond Tucson on July 23. His lead forces were already at Fort Thorn on the Rio Grande, but had not yet reoccupied Fort Fillmore. From Fort Craig on July 25, Colonel Howe of the 3^d Cavalry reported that Texas Confederates, who had been under medical care at Doña Ana, Las Cruces, Mesilla, and Fort Fillmore, were sent by 'Steele' to Franklin, where a number of them died. About twenty-five or thirty of the men were still at Franklin, under the care of a C.S.A. surgeon. Colonel Howe ordered all of these soldier taken as prisoners of war. In addition, a number of Texas deserters were still in the Las Cruces and Mesilla area. These were ordered to take the oath of allegiance to the United States. Secessionist talk was still heard in Mesilla, especially from certain unnamed citizens, property owners who were among the Texans at the Valverde and Glorieta Pass battles. These men took the oath of allegiance, but still acted like secessionists. Howe reported that beef cattle were scarce in the Mesilla Valley as they had been driven to Mexico to keep them out of the hands of the Texas Confederates. In El Paso, Hart's Mill (Hart was a Confederate sympathizer) was placed under guard by the California Cavalry to protect it from being destroyed by secessionist sympathizers living across the border.[18]

General James Carleton arrived at Fort Thorn on August 7, some fifteen days after he left Tucson. On August 10 Carleton headed south from Fort Thorn in the direction of Mesilla, his principal goal. The occupation of the abandoned Fort Fillmore was secondary, although he converged his forces on that location as the best place to camp in some safety. While in Las Cruces, General Carleton issued an order to "Commanders of Towns living along the Rio Grande between the Jornada del Muerto and Fort Bliss Texas." The people were told the rebellion was over and they must clean up their streets and dwellings, establish sanitary regulations, and police their towns. One newspaper man accompanying Carleton estimated the populations as follows: Doña Ana, five hundred; Las Cruces, seven hundred; and Mesilla, one thousand.[19]

The number of forces General Carleton had at Fort Fillmore and in the nearby region was discussed in a letter to General Canby on August 15, 1862, just over a year after Lynde's surrender. Fort Fillmore was then listed as being in the District of Arizona, Carleton having established all lands as being Arizona on which his flag was planted. The General informed:

> ... The enclose[d] General Orders numbers 14 and 15 from these Head Quarters, will give you an idea of the force stationed in Mesilla. In Las Cruces there are four Companies of the U.S. 5th Infantry; at Fort Fillmore there are Shinn's Light Battery U.S. 3rd artillery, Companies "A" and 'E', 1st Infantry, Cal. Vols. Company "B" 5th Infantry, Cal. Vols. and Companies "B" and "D", 1st Cavalry, Cal. Vols., and Company "B", 2nd Cavalry, Cal. Vols.
>
> I placed all the Cavalry and nearly all of the Quarter Master wagons-and-teams at Fort Fillmore on account of the good grazing in that vicinity and the abundance of mesquite beans now to be found in that neighborhood, which for the present precludes the necessity of purchasing much forage.
>
> As there are sufficient at La Mesilla for the four Companies of the 5th Infantry, I shall establish them in that town unless otherwise directed by yourself—at least for the present. The emulation which will naturally spring up between them and the volunteers as to who shall best perform their duties, will, in my opinion to be of great service to both. Besides, there is a fine building there where the supplies —Qr. Mr. and Subsistence— can be kept free of expense, and the town of Mesilla is said to be a cooler and healthier locality than Las Cruces. Colonel Howe wrote to me, desiring that I would send these four Companies to Fort Craig. But this I do not feel authorized to do unless you order it. Mr. Woods—the Beef contractor—wrote me a note in relation to furnishing beef for my command. It is herewith enclosed together with my reply.[20]

For the first time since that fateful July 1861, a return was filed from a United States Army command at Fort Fillmore. As of

August 31, 1862, there were 390 soldiers at the post, including sixteen officers. The cavalry and artillery units grazed 305 horses in the region. Four artillery field guns, type unknown, sat on the parade ground. This was the last great flurry of activity for the old post. Many buildings were in poor condition and no one believed the post should be reoccupied permanently.[21]

This large California unit stayed only briefly. The Regular Army Artillery Company 'A,' 3[d] Artillery, and Companies 'A' and 'B,' 1st Cavalry, California Volunteers, chased Confederates down the road to San Antonio. Company 'B,' 2[d] Cavalry, California Volunteers, and. Company 'B,' 5th California Infantry, pulled duty at Fort Craig. By the end of September only one infantry company, Company 'A,' 5th California Infantry, remained. It was the last military unit to serve at Fort Fillmore.

Perhaps the most interesting event in the final days of active history at Fort Fillmore came when 1st Lieutenant Pennock, 1st Cavalry, United States Regular Army, passed through the post with ninety-two ragged Confederate prisoners of war on September 12, 1862. Pennock was taking his charges to Camp Johnson, Texas, where a POW camp was being established near El Paso. Given that the Rebels were paroled they were probably released when they got to the camp. All Confederates were gone after this from New Mexico, driven deep into Texas past Forts Bliss, Quitman, and Davis. Carleton followed Colonel Steele, Fort Fillmore's last Confederate commander. Steele's retreat led to the destruction of ammunition and wagons at Fort Bliss. Carleton's troops trailed Steele's rear guard all the way to Fort Davis, where they found one dead Confederate soldier in the hospital and battled Mescalero Apache Indians. At El Paso, General Carleton recovered twelve wagon loads of hospital and quartermaster stores which had once been United States equipment. Perhaps some of this came from Fort Fillmore. Twenty-six Confederate soldiers were captured at Franklin, Texas. These were paroled and sent on their way to San Antonio.[22]

Fort Fillmore saw its last days of military activity that September 1862, when final orders for abandonment were given.

The last commanding officer was Captain Joseph Smith, Company 'A,' 5th California Infantry Regiment. He was assisted in his duties by 1st Lieutenant Thomas B. Chapman and Physician W.A. Kittridge. Smith commanded only thirty-eight enlisted men. Another officer and thirty-nine enlisted men were on detached service.[23] One of the officers who arrived with Company 'A,' 3[d] Artillery, was Captain George Fillmore, a relative of President Fillmore for whom the fort was originally named. Fillmore departed the post on September 6.[24]

General Carleton and Colonel Eyre briefly set foot on Fort Fillmore soil on September 11, arriving and leaving the same day. Carleton had been at Franklin, Texas, chasing the retreating Rebels down the San Antonio road and learning the El Paso secessionists had disappeared into Mexico.

General Carleton left Fort Fillmore for Santa Fe soon thereafter, where he outlined a plan for the elimination of the Indian threat in New Mexico. His plan was terrible in conception, almost as harsh as Baylor's. Carleton proposed to end the Indian problem by moving all Indians from their native lands onto reservations where they could be permanently cared for. The plan was similar to the one Doctor Steck proposed in the late 1850s. The Indians would be taught. They would be fed. Although not a new idea, Carleton's plan was the first time the reservation massing concept was to be put into practice. The events Carleton set into motion were acts of finality. The great movement to pacify, once and for all, the Apache Indians, began in the last month that Fort Fillmore was in active military service.

Also during that last September of Fort Fillmore's use, Kit Carson, the famous frontier scout, led five companies of mounted New Mexico Volunteers to reoccupy Fort Stanton in the Mescalero Country, Isaac Lynde's elusive goal in July 1861. Carson was to rendezvous with two columns of California troops, one led by a Captain William McCleave, coming from Mesilla, and another led by Captain Thomas L. Roberts, coming from El Paso. Their orders were to slay all Mescalero Apache men they saw and bring all Apache women and children into captivity. The Mescalero fled into the Guadalupe Mountains. Two leaders, Manuelito and José Largo, names known to former Fort Fillmore commanders, came to plead for peace. Tragically, they were killed, along with ten of their followers.[25]

War Crimes trials of a kind were held in Mesilla that September as well. Three former secessionists, George I. Firer, William B. Clark, and Eli Radford were bound over for trial by a military commission. The chief witness against the men was Corporal Patrick O'Grady, who swore they had made secessionist comments in August while in his presence. A known Union supporter, William Dexter, accused Clark of asking the Confederate Texans to hang him after their arrival in Mesilla. Clark was also said to have fought on the Texan side at the Battle of Valverde. The *Mesilla Times* closed down and one of the town's influential Mexican citizens, Rafael Armijo, lost a house and other property by means of confiscation.[26]

Captain Joseph Smith filled out the final Fort Fillmore Post Return, the 120th under Federal command, on September 30, 1862, and a few days later led his men out of the post. Smith left behind three California men buried in the Fort Fillmore Cemetery— Private George Martin, Company 'C,' 5th California Infantry, Corporal Robert Welch, Company 'A,' 5th California Infantry, and Private Thomas J. Varner, Company 'F,' 5th California Infantry.

Fort Millard Fillmore's active life came to an end with Company 'A's' departure. The old fortress deteriorated rapidly, from weather first and foremost, followed by military contractors, squatters, farmers, relic and souvenir hunters, not to mention two professional archaeological excavations. All saw to the final destruction of what was once the first American fortress in southern New Mexico, as well as the first to be built in the heart of Apachería.

NOTES - Chapter 14

1. Morgan Wolf Merrick, *From Desert to Bayou*. (El Paso: Texas Western Press of the University of El Paso, copy undated). There were no page numbers in the copy the author utilized for this work. Since this was the version used, all other references to this work will cite the name Merrick only.

2. Ibid.

3. Ibid.

4. Baylor Proclamation, *Confederate Victories in the Southwest*, p. 37.

5. Anderson to all commands, August 8, 1861, *Texas Data*, p. 62.

6. Baylor to Van Dorn, August 14, 1861, *Texas Data*, p. 39.

7. Baylor to Van Dorn, August 25, 1861, *Texas Data*, p. 41.

8. Edwin Sweeney, *Cochise*, pp. 186, 187.

9. John Upton Terrell, *Apache Chronicles*, pp. 222, 223.

10. Jordan to Sibley, February 27, 1862, *Texas Data*, p. 168.

11. Steele to Cooper, Adjutant General, March 1, 1862, *Texas Data*, p. 167.

12. *Historical Times*, p. 422.

13. *Historical Times*, p. 106.

14. Ibid.

15. *La Posta*, Volume II, #6, November-December 1970, p. 7.

16. Ezra Bowen, *The Soldiers*, pp. 119, 120.

17. Eyre to Van Vliet, July 23, 1862, M1120, Rolls 15/16.

18. Howe to Chapin, August 5, 1862, M1120, Rolls 15/16.

19. *La Posta*, Volume II, #6, November-December 1970, p. 8.

20. Carleton to Canby, August 15, 1862, M1102, Rolls 15/16.

21. Fort Fillmore Post Return, August 1862.

22. Carleton to Canby, September 9, 1862, M1120, Rolls 15/16.

23. Fort Fillmore Post Return, August 1862.

24. Ibid.

25. Odie B. Faulk, *Crimson Desert: Indian Wars of the American Southwest*. (New York: Oxford University Press, 1974), pp. 161, 162.

26. West to Cutler, September 28, 1862, M1102, Rolls 15/16.

15

COMING UP TO DATE/
FORT FILLMORE TODAY

The military abandoned Fort Fillmore early in October 1862. In 1866, when the Regular Army returned to garrison New Mexico Territory, they brought a different soldier and a different kind of campaigning. After 1866 New Mexico forts were usually garrisoned by one or more companies of Anglo, European-American troops, who often shared the post with an African-American company, then called United States Colored Troops. The latter were led by white officers and strictly segregated from their European-American counterparts. There were new forts as well, strangely named and unfamiliar to veterans who had served at Fort Fillmore only ten years before. In southern New Mexico were Fort Selden, situated to the north of Doña Ana, Fort Cummings, near Cook's Springs, with Fort Bayard to the west near the site of old Fort Webster. Fort Craig, Fort Stanton, and Fort Bliss were reoccupied, remodeled and updated. Fort Bliss moved several times before finding a permanent home in the growing El Paso area. Fort Fillmore, however, was not rebuilt—the site was left to deteriorate in the hot sun of summer and the cold winds of winter.

The first severe blow to old Fort Fillmore did not come from Mexican marauders, Confederate burning, or an uncaring abandonment by Carleton and Canby. The fort was brought to instantan-eous ruin in 1863 through the actions of the U.S. Army itself. The story of the pillage of Fort Fillmore was told as part of a court case tried in the U.S. Court of Claims, General Jurisdiction Case #9521, August 30, 1878. Testimony concerning the old fort was given by Jonathan Evans, a former soldier in Company 'C,' 1st Infantry, California Volunteers. Evans testified:

> ... I first saw Fort Fillmore in the month of August 1862. At that time I was a soldier in Co. C 1st Infantry California Volunteers... . In the winter of 1862 and 1863 the company to which I belonged, then stationed at Mesilla, N. Mex., was ordered by General West to proceed to Fort Fillmore and to take out all doors, door frames, windows and window frames and fixtures, joists, mantle pieces and flooring, in fact all lumber and wood work in and about the post. In obedience to the order the company did proceed to the fort and took out of it and carried away to Mesilla N. Mex. about 300 doors and door frames, about 450 windows and window frames and fixtures, about 75 mantle pieces, about 2100 joist, about 500 water spouts, and about 2500 yards of chain taken from the walls of the Quarter Master's Corral ... . There was from 150 to 186 mule wagon loads of material taken from Fort Fillmore and hauled to Mesilla ... . We counted the rooms at Fort Fillmore. I did not keep any memorandum of the number of rooms. I cannot say positively how many rooms but think 140 ... . There was a great number of the windows with broken glass.[1]

Additional testimony by Emil Duchesne, a former Fort Fillmore soldier, and Benjamin Dowell, a merchant, gave similar accounts as to numbers of items taken from the fort, or available for taking. Duchesne said there were about one hundred and fifty windows, whereas Evans listed three hundred windows and frames —approximately the same number if there were one hundred and fifty windows and a frame for each window.[2]

What is important to note is that the most devasting blow to Fort Fillmore's historical survival was dealt by the Californians in 1863. What remained thereafter was a great mass of adobe which took its normal allotment of time to settle back into the ground. Some of the materials salvaged by the Californians were hauled to the Gila River where they were used in building Fort Joseph Rodman West early in 1863. This author visited the Fort West site looking for Fort Fillmore window glass and was not disappointed. In a hole on the north side of the old fort, much glass was found on top of the ground, some possibly from Fort Fillmore windows hauled to the Gila in wagons. Fort West was used only one year and the windows are said to have next been used in the construction of a nearby farmhouse.

The final military reference to the old fort was the result of a flurry of activity in 1866 and 1868 relative to the Fort Fillmore Cemetery and the men and women who were still buried there. The cemetery was constructed away from the main fort area to the south of the hospital, a convenient choice as bodies could be taken straight from the hospital to the walled adobe enclosure. In 1868 William R. McCormick, Forage Master at Fort Selden, described the cemetery for the only time in its early history. McCormick said:

> ... The Cemetery is 225 feet long and 90 wide. The wall enclosing it is in a very bad condition and to put it in repair will take 12000 adobes. Parties living in the vicinity will make the adobes and put them in the wall for twenty dollars per thousand ... . There are from seventy to ninety graves, and but one head board—and all that can be read on that is—Capt. H.W. Stanton, January 20 1855. A number of graves are buried in sand drifts, and I can find no one who can identify any of these graves.[3]

Perhaps ninety graves, and but one marker for the only officer buried there. McCormick's effort began in 1866 when the Adjutant General's Office in Santa Fe directed the Assistant Quarter Master's Office at Fort Selden to determine the number of military burials in the region of that fort. The Assistant Quarter Master, Captain W.L. Rynerson, did his duty in the matter but there was a hitch. The National Cemetery Act, passed by Congress in 1862, contained a provision for a marker with each soldier's name on it. This meant Rynerson was to find the graves of all 'eligible' soldiers in his region. He did so. Unfortunately for Fort Fillmore's already forgotten soldiers' graves, most of the graves in the Fort Fillmore Cemetery fell outside the dates of the National Cemetery Act. Only three Fort Fillmore burials were considered to have taken place during the Civil War, all Californians, and were hence 'eligible.' According to the National Cemetery Act, Rynerson was to report these three and did, although he had no clue as to the location of the graves. The other soldiers, including Captain Stanton, were not included in the total. They received no marker from their uncaring government. As it turned out, the other three didn't either. Note that the graves of the three 7th Infantry soldiers who fought in the Battle of Mesilla were not counted as Civil War burials.

According to Rynerson, his team found six graves at Fort Selden which qualified, ten at Mesilla, three at Fort Fillmore, and twenty at Las Cruces, all Californians. There was also an abandoned cemetery at Fort Thorn but, like most of the burials at Fort Fillmore, the soldiers at Fort Thorn did not come under the National Cemetery Act.

Fort Selden had a National Cemetery. The three California soldiers could have been moved there. The problem was how did one find the three eligible graves among many when none were marked save Captain Stanton's? In the face of this dilemma, nothing was done. An unknown person wrote a notation on Rynerson's report concerning the old cemeteries and the soldiers buried there:

> ... Inasmuch as no sufficient cause is shown for the removal of bodies from Mesilla, Fort Fillmore, & Las Cruces, and that they appear to rest very well where they now are, & their removal to Fort Selden is not approved. They should be put in good condition and enclosed at their present place of interment, and all the graves of U.S. soldiers at those places properly cared for, enclosed, and headboards erected where necessary, as should also, the graves at Fort Thorne [sic].[4]

Of course, nothing was done, at least at Fort Fillmore, and probably at any of the named places. A report was asked for and given. The matter was closed.

Fort Fillmore on September 23, 2001,
the 150th anniversary of its founding.
Courtesy: Author.

On May 19-20, 1868, a delegation made the final military visit when William R. McCormick visited. On his return to Fort Selden he estimated that the rapidly deteriorating Fort Fillmore Cemetery could be put into decent condition at a cost of $240 for 12,000 adobe bricks, made locally, and a gate costing $25, total, $265.[5]

No answer was made about money for upkeep. A reply on June 16, 1868, from the Deputy Quarter Master's Office at the Division of the Missouri Headquarters in St. Louis, stated that he concurred with Colonel Ludington's (Santa Fe, Department of New Mexico) recommendation that the body of Captain Henry Stanton be removed and brought to Fort Selden. This action was taken. No further report on any maintenance of the old cemetery exists and it has disappeared back into the desert. The soldiers, and others who might be buried at the site, are still there.[6]

During the next one hundred years, the land on which Fort Fillmore sat passed through the hands of many individuals. Through the years many persons visited the site; one group in a buggy even stopped to photograph it in 1903, the only known picture of the fort while there were still enough of the buildings standing to show the layout. That photograph shows a mass of decaying ruins in the forty-first year after abandonment, and forty years after the doors and windows had been stripped. Surprisingly, there was still some height to the adobe, although little detail can be made out in the old photograph.

On June 28, 1931, noted author Roscoe Conkling, who wrote about the Butterfield Overland Mail and other subjects, visited Fort Fillmore with Thomas Snyder, one of the last surviving soldiers who had served there. Snyder was one of Sibley's Confederates who supposedly served under Colonel Steele at Fort Fillmore while Sibley's forces drove north in 1862. Conkling related their visit as follows:

> ... It was the author's privilege to visit the ruins of Fort Fillmore, on Sunday June 28, 1931, in company with Captain Thomas S. Snyder of Dallas, Texas. Captain Snyder enlisted in the

Confederate Army and was with the command of Colonel William Steele, when his company occupied Fort Fillmore in the fall of 1861, shortly after the disgraceful surrender of the post by General Lynde [Major Lynde of the 7th Infantry], on September 26, 1861. The captain was in his ninety-second year at the time of this visit, and in spite of his advanced years, he was remarkably active and his mind unusually alert, as he recalled the happenings of sixty-nine years ago with rare vividness. He was able to accurately identify the location of the mail station, the parade grounds, and a number of the officer's quarters and barracks buildings, and after a diligent search among the mesquite covered sand dunes, he located the burial place of his tentmate and three other soldiers whose names he recalled were, John Poole, Timothy and Benjamin Sellers. All were victims of an epidemic of typhoid fever which scourged the camp at the time. He further recalled helping a sergeant named McMordie mark the graves by cutting with their jackknives, the names of the four unfortunate men on the plain wooden markers. Captain Snyder is believed to have been the last man living who had been stationed at Fort Fillmore, or among those who could recall the fort in its original state.[7]

During the 1940s, when the land on which Fort Fillmore sat was owned by Sixto Duarte, three sisters, Rose Apodaca, Nermina Paz, and Carolina Carbojal, played in the ruins. Their father was a Tigua Indian from the Tortugas Pueblo just up the road toward Las Cruces who worked for Duarte. The girls claimed Duarte was a former gunman in Pancho Villa's army and that he came north after the revolution with enough money to buy the land on which the fort stood.

Rose Apodaca was born in Brazito, Nermina Paz, and Carolina Carabajal were born near Fort Fillmore. The sisters told of many people searching the Fort Fillmore grounds and how angry Duarte became with all the unwanted visitors. Nermina spoke of her father finding a gun at the fort which Duarte took, saying he would return it later but he never did.

The ladies are still much drawn to the land and had a family reunion there—some seventy family members, who all consider themselves Tigua Indians from the small Tortugas Pueblo (the

Turtles) south of Las Cruces and just north of Fort Fillmore. Tortugas Pueblo was there when Fort Fillmore was active and may have been the first community in southern New Mexico. There are few historical references to Tortugas. Only a few army letters reference the site from 1851 to 1862.

The girls had one very fond memory of the ruins. A relative told them gold was buried in that old ruin. If they looked over there at night from where they lived and saw a light, they were to tell him where. That would be the spirits saying where the gold lay. The mischievous little girls decided to play a trick. They spoke of seeing ghostly lights and pointed to where they had seen them. The men, their father included, dug for some time at the spot and produced nothing. The girls thought it funny that adults fell for their trick. Of course they never told what they had done, and many years later this was still a memory they held with great delight.

In 1966, Dr. John Wilson conducted the first professional excavation of the fort, concentrating his efforts on two buildings on the south side of the complex—an infantry barracks and an officers' quarters. The effort was funded by the National Park Service with a $2,000 grant. The Hanes Corporation in Winston-Salem, North Carolina, provided an additional $1,000. The owner of the land on which Fort Fillmore lay, Mr. John Salopek, provided field headquarters for the party. The Museum of New Mexico provided the archaeologist, field vehicles, tools, and other equipment.[8]

Excavation began on May 16, 1966, and work was completed by July 12, 1966, when the final recording was completed. Dr. Wilson made use of convict labor from La Tuna Prison as well as other volunteers during the course of the excavation.[9]

One structure, the officers' quarters once believed occupied by Dr. McKee, a latrine, and half of an infantry barracks were completely excavated in the time allowed. During the officers' quarters excavation Dr. Wilson found signs of an early stick and mud structure called a 'jacal,' which existed up to 1852. This was followed by a mud adobe structure which was in place by 1853. There were signs an additional four rooms had been added to the northeast end of the building sometime, possibly in 1858 or 1859. The officers' quarters building contained ten rooms, eight of which Wilson believed were living rooms, one a kitchen, the other a storeroom.[10]

Very few artifacts were found in the rooms. Dr. Wilson noted, "Nails, rusted scraps of iron, broken pieces of bottles and window panes, and occasional bones made up the meager inventory." Some restorable cups, horseshoes, and a cannon ball were among other items recovered.[11] The china items were among the best finds. Military artifacts were very sparse indeed. Fort Fillmore's soldiers were never the best-dressed military our nation has fielded. They were frontier soldiers and their uniforms were frontier uniforms —meaning they wore whatever was at hand. Dr. Wilson believed the adobe infantry barracks were erected at the same time as the officers' quarters, but the Dixon Miles letter of October 9, 1851, states that the commanding officers' adobe quarters were constructed before any other adobe structure and was completed before the men got out of their tents into the jacal-type structures.[12]

The most interesting find during the barracks excavation was that sometime in the late 1850s (so Dr. Wilson believed) a red brick tile floor was put into six of the barracks rooms. Such a change seems more likely for the middle 1850s, when there were more troops at the fort. The tiles were mostly in place when Dr. Wilson made his excavation and the floor underneath was a packed adobe surface.[13] Six fireplaces were uncovered in the excavated part of the barracks.[14]

As to artifacts, the barracks were more military-productive, as one might expect. Dr. Wilson noted: "In addition to plate and bottle glass, fragmentary iron objects and military items such as buttons, bullets, percussion caps, and rare hat ornaments or company letters were recovered."[15] A thorough study of thousands of Fort Fillmore artifacts has led this author to believe Dr. Wilson found (in the barracks) military accouterments left behind when the 7th Infantry Regiment abandoned the fort. The 3d or 8th Infantry companies would not have left buttons, cap ornaments, and bullets on the floor. They had to keep the place policed as a matter of army policy. It is firmly believed that no 3[d] or 8th Infantryman at Fort Fillmore wore a company letter on his hat. The only unit so magnificently accoutered was Isaac Lynde's 7th Infantry, which had been in the East and was at least partially configured with the latest fashion. The 3[d] had not been off the frontier since the Mexican War and their equipment was often ragged and far out of date. The longest-serving company in Fort Fillmore history was Company 'C,' 3[d] Infantry. No letter 'C' has been found there, which was worn on a hat, even though most reference books say the uniform of the day required one. What was correct for the recruiting service and the artillery units manning the Eastern coastline did not apply to the frontier in the 1850s. Niceties of military dress were not always observed. Until the Bonneville Campaign of 1857 the 3[d] Infantry still wore Mexican War uniforms, at least in the field. The quantity of letter buttons found attests to that fact. These buttons were supposed to be replaced in 1854 at the latest, but clothing stocks had to be used up first. Hence, letter buttons ('I,' 'A,' and 'R') were common finds at the Bonneville Depot site constructed in 1857 during the Gila River Campaign. No company letters were found after extensive searching of the Bonneville camp site in the summer of 2000. Given previous Fort Fillmore and Fort Webster finds, none were expected.

When the 7th Infantry marched into Fort Fillmore, no Company 'C' came with them. The only hat letters ever found at Fort Fillmore conform exactly to the seven companies of the 7th Infantry who arrived at Fort Fillmore after April 1861. They probably wore the plumed felt hat or the earlier issued shako, with an eagle plate and company letter on the front. At least parts of each were found by Dr. Wilson in Barracks B.

It is not known how many of the barracks quarters were used by the Confederates; perhaps none. The California troops may not have lived in the ramshackle living quarters either. Both may have relied on tents, which would account for the undisturbed 7th Infantry finds Dr. Wilson made on the barracks floor. Colonel Steele's letter headed 'Camp near Fort Fillmore,' is an indication he may have chosen not to stay inside the fort buildings, perhaps because they were burned during the abandonment or wrecked during the brief period of looting.

There have been claims that both Confederate States of America (CSA) and Confederate States (CS) belt buckles have been found at Fort Fillmore relating to the Baylor and Sibley invasions. Such claims are doubtful. There are two examples of Texas belt buckles (see page 302) or parts of Texas belt buckles known to exist. Neither was found in a complete condition. Found separately were a belt buckle frame and catch. In the same area was a roundel with the Texas star raised on the face. The roundel fits perfectly into the frame found nearby and is a known type of Texas militia buckle from the Republic, Mexican War, and Civil War periods. In the early 1970s the author found a second star roundel of the same size and design, believed to be from a second Texas belt buckle. This is now in the collection of the Geronimo Springs Museum in Truth or Consequences, New Mexico. A third possible Texas item was found during the New Mexico State University excavation at Fort Fillmore in 1986-87. This is a small, five-pointed star made from the rowel of a spur. No known Confederate or Texas militia buttons have been reported.

Intense 'citizen' artifact hunting in Fort Fillmore history took place after the Wilson Excavation up through the 1970s, generally with the permission of the then current landowner. In 1974, the best of the metal detectors (an artifact hunter using a metal detector only) at Fort Fillmore declared the site cleaned of any worthwhile military artifacts. He was right up to a point. There were few 'important' artifacts found at Fort Fillmore. The requirement to turn in all belts, buckles, harnesses, saddles, rifles, pistols, etc. to the ordnance and quartermaster offices for public sale disposal meant they were simply not thrown away. As a result, a belt buckle or horse harness martingale were rare and important finds.

Uniform buttons of all kinds were the most common ties to the individual soldiers and officers. Even these were often turned in to be disposed of at auction in the 1850s. The author has seen and recorded less than a thousand military buttons from Fort Fillmore. Considering the large garrison of troops over twelve years, this

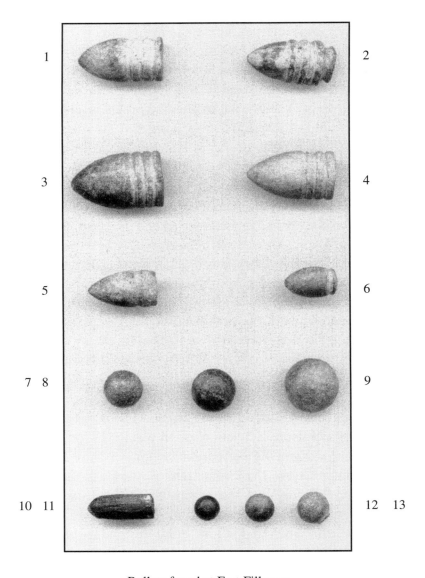

Bullets found at Fort Fillmore
1. .54 caliber Mississippi Rifle. 2. .52 caliber Sharps Carbine.
3. .69 caliber.   4. .58 caliber 1855 Rifle/Musket.
5. .44 caliber Colt Dragoon Revolver. 6. .36 caliber Colt Navy Revolver.
7. .44 caliber ball. 8. .52 caliber ball.
9. .69 caliber standard infantry musket and dragoon musketoon round.
10. Unknown.
11, 12, 13 - types of buckshot used with .69 caliber paper cartridge.
Courtesy: Author.

yield is small indeed. The material from two professional excavations and many of the most important private collections is included
in this count. With six to ten buttons, or more, per uniform, even
fifteen hundred buttons would be only two hundred uniforms, less
than twenty a year. These small numbers mean either the trash areas
were never found, or an efficient quarter-master department collected
even the rags the soldiers discarded for resale in the civilian and
commercial markets of Albuquerque and Santa Fe. Much of the brass
and lead were also melted down and used to make other items.

In 1986 and 1987 students from New Mexico State University,
under the leadership of Dr. Edward Staski, performed the second
professional excavation at Fort Fillmore. The work was conducted
over two seasons. The year 1986 saw student excavation teams in
the field from January until August. Fieldwork began again in May
1987 and continued until early July. The work proceeded while the
surrounding area was plowed and planted with pecan trees. The
area covered was almost the same as the 1966 excavation, except
there was no attempt to reveal any buildings. Areas where flooring
or walls were found received special treatment and some extensive
excavation. The work was usually done in small grids, many
roughly two meters by two meters, with depth excavations conducted down to where artifact materials were no longer found.

The best artifact finds in 1986 and 1987 were in the types of
ammunition uncovered, of which there were several spectacular
finds not previously known from Fort Fillmore. Dr. Staski, the
instructor and chief archeologist during the classes, documented
these finds in an article written for *Historical Archaeology*.[16]

After the excavations were completed in the summer of 1987
Fort Fillmore was forgotten again, for the most part. No doubt
others went to the fort with relics in mind. They were in for a hard
time. The best remaining relic areas were under pecan trees. After
1987, until 1999 most people believed the old fort no longer existed.

When this author first began to study old Fort Fillmore in the
summer of 1998, he made no attempt to visit the Fort Fillmore site.
The word was the fort was completely gone, vanished under a forest

of pecan trees. Research continued for over a year before any attempt was made to reach the fort. At a meeting of the Doña Ana County Historical Society in Las Cruces in early November 1999, one of the speakers, New Mexico State Representative Paul Taylor, mentioned the importance of Fort Fillmore to the history of the area, and that the fort should not be forgotten. Paul Taylor also believed the fort area had been plowed under. After that meeting, the author approached Mr. Taylor and asked his help in contacting Mr. Salopek, the current owner. Paul Taylor agreed and, on November 8, 1999, the author met with Mary and Paul Taylor in their Mesilla residence. Mary Taylor is a well known area historian and spoke of her many past visits to Fort Fillmore. During the interview, Paul Taylor called John Salopek and arranged a visit. This author fully expected to find nothing but trees. Since we could not enter the Salopek property through a gate, and not knowing where exactly to enter, the decision was made to go by way of the neighboring property, owned by Ms. Charlotte Priestley. Her name was often mentioned in connection with the lost Fort Fillmore Cemetery.

We approached the Priestley land after passing row after row of majestic pecan trees, thousands of them. What happened next is best explained from the author's notes. According to those notes:

The land and the gate we entered belonged to Charlotte Priestly, a lady I knew was the owner of the land on which the Fort Fillmore Cemetery lay. Mr. Taylor indicated he knew her well, and pointed to her house off to the left as we traveled down a dirt road on her property, paralleling the Salopek property. On the right, a forest of pecan trees. On the left the desert landscape I always associated with Fort Fillmore. At least Dr. Wilson was correct so far, in that the land on which the cemetery supposedly existed was as if it had been laid out without the hand of man involved. We traveled a short distance and then ran out of passable dirt road. From there, we went on foot. We crossed the Salopek fence, a small barbed wire fence easy to cross, and, since we had permission, we traveled down a well-maintained dirt road along the edge of the line of trees. After moving downward quite some distance toward where I thought Fort Fillmore might be, we turned right, and walked into the forest.

Paul Taylor indicated a clearing lay in the distance, about one hundred yards or so away. There we found quite a wide expanse, which I easily recognized as being the jumbled landscape of melted adobe which formed what remained of Fort Fillmore. The fort was not gone! There it was, more than 25 years since I had last seen it, and still intact to a great extent. True, the hospital was gone, as was any sign of dragoon hill, the dragoon barracks, or the post sutler's area. They were under the trees. Some of the officers' quarters area and at least one of the infantry barracks were intact. We began at the corner where an infantry barracks or final officers' building might be expected and started finding signs immediately. Between taking pictures and picking up related artifacts such as small pieces of china, a pocket knife, a ladies shell button and a bottle bottom, I was kept busy while walking the site from south to north, and then west. Someone had been there digging, and recently. There were many broken fragments of the red tile flooring lying here and there, plus fresh sign that a digger had made a hole and then covered it up with fresh dirt, without putting recovered floor pieces back. Such holes were to be found around the site in several places. I asked Mr. Taylor to advise the owner of the fact that someone might be working the site. I don't like them digging into the buildings. Diggers didn't do that in the past, and besides, there are few relics to be found there. Any relics would be outside the building area and in the tree lines. We stayed until my camera refused to operate [about twenty minutes], and then began to walk back. (Author's notes)

What was thought completely gone was not. Mr. John Salopek had saved what he thought was important, the area where the two archaeological excavations were performed. In truth, fully half of the fort was still there. The second great pleasure of the day was being introduced to Charlotte Priestley, a former president of the Doña Ana County Historical Society and a person very interested in supporting the Fort Fillmore work after the intent was explained to her. Fort Fillmore and its cemetery, if the latter could be found, were both available for study.

Many trips were made thereafter, primarily to the cemetery area, looking for where ninety-plus people might still be resting. Three possible sites were identified, but the exact location could only be guessed at. On Thursday, February 3, 2000, the answer as to the cemetery location was finally determined. On that day this author left Truth or Consequences, New Mexico, for Mesilla, to meet with several individuals concerning the fate, or preservation, of the Fort Fillmore Cemetery, now on land owned by Charlotte Priestley. We were to meet at the El Patio Restaurant in Mesilla for lunch then go out to the Priestley land. Those present at the El Patio lunch were: Charlotte Priestley, Judge Jim Martin, Dr. Glenna Dean (Historic Preservation), Dave Kirkpatrick of Human Systems Research (a private archaeological firm), Ron Burkett (White Sands Missile Range Museum), Robert Torrez (State of New Mexico Historian), Bob Hart (Farm & Ranch Museum), Darien and Don Couchman (historians, and Don the author of a book on southern New Mexico history which features a Fort Fillmore section), Karl Laumbach (Human Systems Research), Toni Laumbach (New Mexico Farm & Ranch Heritage Museum), the author, and Deborah Dennis (Human Systems Research).

Following lunch, a list, partially created by Dr. Wilson after the 1966 Excavation, was passed around. This list contained the names of some of the soldiers believed buried at the Fort Fillmore Cemetery.

Dr. Glenna Dean, representing the Historic Preservation group in Santa Fe, brought a map of the Fort Fillmore region which was developed during the 1966 Excavation. This map had two references to the location of the cemetery with respect to the fort proper. Dr. Dean used these references to locate the best possible candidate spot where the cemetery might be found. This location was one of three previously mentioned, a location close to what was once a site for a mobile home. Very quickly, the archaeologists found what they believed was part of the old adobe wall which once surrounded the cemetery. This wall had degraded until it was almost even with the ground. During a later testing of the depth of the wall it was found to be less than one-half foot in height. We cannot be sure how tall the wall was during the period when Fort Fillmore was active. Also at a later time, Dr. Meade Kemrer of New Mexico State University located the eastern part of the wall with a magnetometer. This discovery led to the finding of the Fort Fillmore Cemetery gate, which was known from an old Confederate drawing to be near the eastern end. The gate was about six feet wide, which meant that most burials were hand-carried from the fort. This would have met army regulations of the period. The exact position of the gate was easily determined and is now clearly marked. The cemetery is surrounded by wire cable and outlined with telephone pole sections.

There was certainly an odd feeling about the place. It was hard to believe that under our feet somewhere, the bodies of up to one hundred people might still be resting, people who lived and worked at Fort Fillmore during its most active history. There were infantry-men of the 3[d] Infantry Regiment buried there, the regiment of Dixon Stansbury Miles and Benjamin Louis Eulalie Bonneville, and dragoon and Mounted Rifles soldiers, at least two of whom were killed by Apaches with Captain Stanton. There were 8th Infantrymen, as well as men who came over from Fort McLane with Isaac Lynde and died in the Battle of Mesilla. There were at least three Texans from Sibley's army and three boys from the California Column. There may even have been, and probably were, women and children buried there as well. Apache Indians—women and children from Bonneville's 1857 Expedition—could be resting there if the U.S. Army allowed such burials at the cemetery. At that moment the author felt closer to Fort Fillmore history than at any other time.

On October 15, 2000, a small group of people, the author included, visited the Fort Fillmore Cemetery to conduct an excavation. Dr. Karl Laumbach, acting for the State of New Mexico and monitoring the excavation as sponsoring archaeologist, had obtained the required permission. Based on observations made earlier by the author, a 2 x 2-meter square was roped off on the south side of the Fort Fillmore Cemetery. Charlotte Priestley had wanted to know if there were still bodies buried on her land, or whether the army had removed them. In fact, it was only conjecture that there were still bodies at the cemetery. To protect the site and preserve it for the future, an answer had to be obtained. The author and

Fort Fillmore Cemetery - August 10, 2001.
This view is looking toward Fort Fillmore.
The first graves were found behind the cactus in the foreground.
Courtesy: Author.

representatives from the Friends of Fort Selden group, including John Smith, Leroy Grizzel, Steven Grizzel, Russell Schneider, and Jerry Saige, provided the digging crew. The author had probed this spot a week earlier as part of an effort to map the cemetery outlines and was convinced that at least two burials were detectable.

Artifacts at Fort Fillmore were rarely found deeper than three feet and it was suspected that burials in the cemetery might be shallow as well. Army regulations specified a ceremony and a coffin when possible, but did not specify depth. The first body was found at less than four feet. The author uncovered a partial jawbone as the first artifact, although coffin-wood pieces, nails, and a musket cap were found at a slightly higher level. This body was still partially inside a badly decayed pine coffin, very crudely constructed of unfinished wood. There was a problem; the burial had been disturbed at some time in the past, for the bones were gathered into a group, the skull on top, and surrounded by the remains of the coffin.

A second body, lying only a few feet from the first, answered the question as to how the first burial came to be disturbed, but opened a number of questions related to history. The second set of bones was laid out in a roughly northeast-southwest direction and was in perfect order, showing no previous disturbance. The skeleton was of a young man with his mouth slightly open, head turned toward the right. All bones were present and the burial appeared to be as it was when conducted long ago. The activities surrounding this burial had obviously disturbed the first burial. Those who placed the young man there appeared to have moved the other body out of the way in order to lay the man down.

There were other problems. This was not a regulation military burial and showed signs of haste in the conducting. There was no coffin for the second burial; the man appeared to have been buried with only his pants for clothing. One button and a small amount of cloth material were found in the crotch area. The button was a top pant button made of wood or bone, a common find at Fort Fillmore. The young man had also had his right hand and wrist amputated. The marks of the saw were clear. The non-regulation burial, the amputated hand, and the obvious haste in which the burial was conducted, were enlightening. He was brought straight up the hill from the Fort Fillmore hospital after his death and placed in the ground without ceremony, a court-martial offense for any officer who permitted such to happen. This burial was a violation of U.S. Army regulations.

There is only one period during Fort Fillmore history when such might have happened. Were we looking at the body of Private Lane, Private Jenkins, or Private Sherwood, mortally wounded in the Battle of Mesilla, and then buried in haste and without proper formalities on July 26, 1861, when the post was in turmoil due to the coming abandonment?

As the author looked down upon the man in preparation for the recovering, the thought came that this was but another unanswered mystery arising out of the Fort Fillmore study. Now that it is proven that bodies are still there, perhaps some security and peace will come both to them and to the ruins of their forgotten old fortress lying just to the north. That is, if the people of the future wish it to be so.

NOTES - Chapter 15

1. The court testimonial evidence provided by Jonathan Evans, U.S. Court of Claims, General Jurisdiction Case #9521, August 30, 1878, was taken from the research records developed by Dr. John Wilson in preparation for the 1966 archaeological excavation at Fort Fillmore.

2. Duchesne Testimony, August 30, 1878. This data was taken from the 1966 Fort Fillmore Archaeological Excavation records developed by Dr. John Wilson.

3. McCormick to Rigg, May 25, 1868, National Archives, RG92, Records of the Office of the Quartermaster General, Consolidated File, Fort Fillmore, New Mexico (microfilm created in 1958. Hereafter referenced as Consolidated File).

4. Consolidated File, Note to Rynerson Report, National Archives, Record Group 92, Rynerson to Enos, August 6, 1866.

5. Consolidated File, McCormick to Rigg, May 25, 1868.

6. Consolidated File, Deputy Quarter Master to Headquarters, Department of New Mexico, June 16, 1868.

7. Roscoe P. & Margaret B. Conkling, *The Butterfield Overland Mail 1857-1869*, Volume II (Glendale CA: The Arthur H. Clark Company, 1947), pp. 99, 100.

8. John P. Wilson, "Preliminary Report Submitted to the National Park Service, Southwest Region, in Partial Compliance with Contract No. 49 Stat 666, 16 USC 461-467," dated May 5, 1966, pp. 1, 2. (Hereafter cited as Wilson Report.)

9. Ibid., p. 2.

10. Ibid.

11. Ibid.

12. Dixon Stansbury Miles to Sarah Ann Briscoe Miles, October 9, 1851, Kuethe Correspondence.

13. Wilson Report, p. 9.

14. Ibid., p. 11.

15. Ibid., p. 12.

16. Edward Staski and Paul S. Johnson, "Munition Artifacts from Fort Fillmore, New Mexico," *Historical Archeology*, Vol. 26 #2 (1992).

Fort Fillmore Cemetery Memorial Ceremony,
November 18, 2001.
The author is reading the names of the known dead.
Courtesy: Author.

EPILOGUE

On November 18, 2001, a dedication ceremony was held at the Fort Fillmore Cemetery. Six known graves were marked with burial mounds and crosses. Other potential graves were left unmarked. The adobe wall surrounding the cemetery was outlined with sections from wooden telephone poles strung with wire cable. The old cemetery gateway, located with the help of the only known existing drawing of the cemetery made by a Confederate soldier, was well marked. The gateway was identified after Dr. Meade Kemrer, from New Mexico State University, located the eastern cemetery wall using a proton-magnetometer. Two new, iron flag poles were placed in the approximate center of the cemetery. A United States flag and a Confederate 1st National flag few there that day.

The author arrived at the Fort Fillmore Cemetery at about nine in the morning and, near the marked burials, raised the Fort Fillmore Project Flag, an old forty-eight-star silk flag with yellow fringe. The Project Flag has flown over many locations associated with Fort Fillmore's active period, including Fort Fillmore, Fort Fillmore Cemetery, Fort Daniel Webster, Fort Joseph Rodman West, Fort McLane, Aleman on the Jornada del Muerto, Santa Lucia Springs, San Augustine Springs, Santa Rita Copper Mines, and the Bonneville Depot. This flag-raising was symbolic—it was the first American flag to fly over all of these sites since the 1860s.

Reenactors arrived shortly thereafter dressed in Confederate and Union uniforms similar to those worn at Fort Fillmore in the early 1860s. Two cannon, one manned by soldiers dressed in Union blue and the other manned by soldiers dressed in Confederate grey, were placed near the cemetery gate, ready to fire a 21-gun salute. An unridden horse, equipped with saddle and reversed boots, was led into the cemetery accompanied by a lady dressed in a nineteenth century, all-black costume complete with parasol. She represented the wives and mothers of the dead soldiers.

After the American and Confederate flags were raised, two squads filed through the cemetery gateway and lined up in front of a wood rack displaying small blue, orange, and green pennants. These pennants contained the names of the infantry, dragoon, and Mounted Rifle regiments and companies from which soldier burials were known. An additional pennant in red-white-blue represented the Confederate dead. As the two squads of Union and Confederate representatives bowed their heads and reversed their weapons, a unique ceremony was conducted. The author, dressed in Union blue and wearing a Civil War-era kepi, read aloud the names and regiments of the dead thought to be buried there. Following the reading, the artillery teams fired their cannon twenty-one times, a fitting tribute to a forgotten fortress and to those who once served there.

APPENDIX I
Uniforms

One of the more interesting subjects to speculate about concerning the history of Fort Millard Fillmore are the types of uniforms and equipment worn or used there. Of special interest is the comparison between what the U.S. Army Regulations of 1847 said the troops should be wearing or using and what was actually available. This appendix will attempt to answer some of these questions through the use of existing regulations as well as information provided in written records.

Headgear types changed rather drastically from 1861 to 1862, the active period of the fort, but basic uniform styles worn by the soldiers remained the same. There were minor variations in cut and piping color, as well as where insignia went and didn't go, but, in general, the troops retained use of either a short jacket or a frock coat. Trousers ranged in color from light to dark blue. The infantry changed the colors of their arm (of service) in this period from white to blue. They also changed from a short light-blue jacket to a dark-blue frock coat. The dragoons changed their arm color from yellow to orange, the Mounted Rifles from yellow to green; they retained the form of their handsome short jacket throughout the period. In fact, the uniform jackets and coats, in spite of minor changes such as those just stated regarding trim colors, remained about the same, at least to the eye of the layman unfamiliar with military nuances.

When he and his soldiers marched into Fort Fillmore on September 23, 1861, Lieutenant Colonel Miles was no doubt properly configured in the uniform of the day for officers, but we cannot know the precise uniform he wore. He had several choices.

Miles may have been dressed in the frock coat specified by the 1847 Army Regulations, then still in effect on the frontier in late 1851. Although new uniform regulations, put out in June 1851, mandated a complete change in uniform style for infantry, troops on the frontier were sometimes years in making the changeover.

The dark-blue frock coat, the length of which stretched from the shoulder almost to the knee, was designed for duty wear, or for wear on journeys such as the one Miles had just completed. The 1847 Regulations prescribed that it be used for morning dress in quarters, drills, inspections, fatigue duties, and upon the march.

Regulations described the coat for his rank as being of dark-blue cloth, single-breasted, plain stand-up collar, with not less than eight nor more than ten regimental buttons down the front at equal distances. Since this was September, the regulations prescribed that the trousers worn with the coat be constructed of simple white linen, or cotton, without a white stripe down the leg as was required for the fall and winter season. White, the color used to identify United States Infantry at the time of the Mexican War, soon gave way to a light blue.[1]

Shoulder straps, similar to those familiar to American patrons of western movies, indicated rank. A silver leaf at the end of each side of the straps indicated Miles's rank of lieutenant colonel. A Miles family portrait, thought to be taken about this time, shows him wearing a double-breasted frock coat with shoulder straps of the rectangular pattern. Two rows of buttons are shown, but an exact count cannot be made. This coat was an option, being similar to the single-breasted frock coat in ease of wear but being double-breasted in cut and with up to twenty buttons in two rows on the front. This coat was only worn by colonels, lieutenant colonels, and majors.[7]

It is doubtful, though possible, that Dixon Miles wore the full-dress uniform frock coat of a United States Army lieutenant colonel. Normally used for parades or official functions, that uniform was extremely uncomfortable for a desert journey at any time of year. The 1847 Regulations describe this more formal coat as being of dark-blue cloth, double-breasted, with two rows of buttons, ten in each row. An addition is a high lace collar, something the optional double-breasted frock coat did not have. The edges closed in front with hooks and eyes, but were low enough to permit the free turning of the chin. Added to this discomfort were lace cuffs, heavy gold epaulettes on each shoulder, gold embroidery, teams of buttons, etc., etc. No doubt a thing of military beauty, it was hardly fit for a long desert trek.[3]

September 23, 1851, was on the cusp of the uniform change period from summer to fall. Miles might have worn the short white cotton or linen jacket and pants which officers were allowed to wear for field and travel when serving with a regiment. Miles no doubt had such a uniform, but wearing it would not give him the appearance of authority he would wish when bringing his command to a new post. There were other options. As regimental commander he had much leeway in such matters. He could have worn a mixture of civilian and uniform clothing. After all, uniforms were difficult to acquire on the frontier and, although forbidden by regulations during this period, civilian clothing use was not unknown.[4]

The infantry dress shako, an ungainly-looking contraption still being worn in the East for parades, would probably have been required for wear with the full dress uniform coat. According to regulations, that shako was made of black beaver fur, seven and one-half inches tall, black patent leather encircling the bottom. A silver infantry hunting horn insignia, regimental number included, was on the front with a brass eagle above that. In Miles's case, his shako would have been adorned with white cock feathers, falling from an upright stem, eight inches long, within a gilt socket. No examples of any of the infantry shako's unique insignia were encountered among the collections of Fort Fillmore artifacts examined for this work. No doubt Miles owned such a shako, but its use was probably very restricted, if he had even brought it to Fort Fillmore.[5]

Given the total lack of artifacts indicating the presence of the dress shako, no doubt only the officers were required to have it as standard equipment. Keeping the troops on the frontier equipped with the simple basics of a uniform, to include shoes and socks, was difficult enough for the wagon-borne military supply system. The frills remained with the more stable military units in the eastern part of the country, such as coastal artillery, and when recruiting unit members had to look especially brilliant to attract new recruits.

Miles most likely wore a comfortable frock coat and the Model 1839 field cap with the silver brocade officer's insignia of a hunting horn, the emblem of the United States Infantry, on the front. The regimental number '3' was located in the inner curve of the horn. The Model 1839 cap resembled the modern saucer hat the United States Army currently wears. This field cap was the headgear of choice on the frontier for much of the 1850s. Military buttons associated with this cap, unusual in design when compared to uniform buttons, were common finds in Fort Fillmore refuse dumps, indicating large numbers of the Model 39 being worn out and discarded.

To complete his uniform that day, Dixon Miles probably wore an infantry officer's sword, sword belt, and eagle buckle over a long sash of crimson silk net with silk bullion fringe ends which was wrapped twice around the waist. Being mounted he would also wear spurs of yellow metal, possibly plated silver. During the Mexican War, Miles had received a brevet for bravery at the Battle of Monterrey in Mexico. He was awarded a sword of honor as well. The sword is still in the Miles family.

The horse Miles rode, George, was his personal property, therefore not carried on the rolls as government property. An infantry officer, especially one of substantial rank, was not expected to march with the troops. Miles was allowed to own horses and wagons, and to feed the animals on government fodder, as well as use government accouterments.

Horse equipment for mounted infantry officers was specified in the 1847 Regulations. The military saddle-cloth was dark blue, two feet ten inches in length, one foot ten inches in depth, with lace five-eights of an inch in width. Since Miles was an infantry officer the lace was silver with white edging. The bridle was black leather, with gilt brass bits, stirrups, and mountings—the brass was silver plated for infantry officers. The horse collar was white leather. The front and roses were white, for infantry. The color changed to light blue after 1851 when the infantry adopted that color[6]

Brevet-Captain Barnard E. Bee may have worn the single-breasted version of the frock coat. Assistant Surgeon John Hammond is a bit more difficult to picture. The 1847 Regulations specified a full-dress uniform for medical personnel but did not specify an undress or duty uniform. Since he was probably not wearing all that frill, including the mandated Napoleonic-style, cocked hat with black silk binding and a fan not more than eleven inches nor less than nine, we will allow him to pass by without comment.[7]

We have no idea what uniform Brevet-Major Richardson was wearing, although it may have been like that worn by the staff. He might also have dressed in the casual fashion of his men. Letters, detailing critical shortages in clothing availability within the 3[d] Infantry companies at El Paso provide a glimpse at what uniforms were worn on the first day at Fort Fillmore. Although 1851 clothing change regulations were in effect, the soldiers of Company 'K' still wore the older Mexican War era uniforms.

Army uniform changes were followed by long periods of dual use when new uniform items were gradually phased in. In fact, during the 1850s, in a period of slow and cumbersome ox- and mule-hauled trains, the United States Army made major changes in the uniform three times.

The 1847 Regulations are difficult to interpret with respect to infantry enlisted men. They do not mention specific items of uniform equipment known to have been worn by Company 'K' at that time. We will diverge from the operating regulations and say what actually was there, as well as what should have been there.

The general uniform coat specified by the 1847 Regulations for infantry was similar in design to the officer frock coat and pants previously described, save for differences according to rank. In general, the coat was to be of dark-blue color, single-breasted, with one row of nine 19-20mm buttons, placed at equal distances. Smaller buttons (15mm) were worn on the cuffs. The buttons had an eagle with an 'I' for infantry on a shield on the eagle's breast. The skirts of the coat extended to within seven inches of the bend of the knee. The light-blue pants had a white stripe down the side to denote infantry. There are no indications that this coat was available, with or without trimming or epaulettes, at Fort Fillmore in September 1851.[8]

Enlisted infantry headgear was similar to the tall shako that the officers were issued. Insignia from the shako have not been identified in Fort Fillmore finds, nor were any listed in the accounts of available uniforms at El Paso in 1850. The infantry guard at Army Headquarters in New York City probably wore the shako, but very few were used in New Mexico, if any.

During the Mexican War, infantrymen were issued a short light-blue shell jacket, with a white jacket for summer use. A note in the 1847 Army Regulations states that officers and men of regiments would be provided with shell jackets to be worn in summer during the extreme heat of the season. This may be a reference to the jackets worn by the infantry at Fort Fillmore, although that is doubtful. The jackets described as being at El Paso were wool. The jackets described in the 1847 Regulations were made of white or blue cotton or linen.[9]

Pictures from the Mexican War show infantrymen wearing the light-blue wool jacket with white trim. The cross belts, waist belts, and other leather trim, were white-dyed leather. This jacket, coupled with the dark-blue Model 1839 forage cap and light-blue mixture trousers were what Company 'K' most likely wore on September 23, 1851, if they were fortunate enough to have a uniform. The infantry might also have worn their summer white cotton or linen duty jacket. This jacket, like the blue wool jacket, had a single row of nine small eagle uniform buttons down the front at equal distances. The light-weight blue or white jackets conform with the pattern of uniform button finds at Fort Fillmore. The vast majority of infantry uniform buttons identified (with an 'I' on the shield) are the small, 15mm diameter, buttons. Blouse-size buttons (approximately 19-20 mm), which would have been used on the frock coat, were very seldom found.

Although arguable, most infantrymen of Captain Richardson's Company 'K' probably arrived at Fort Fillmore wearing the light-blue shell jacket with white trim on the standup collar and shoulder boards, rather than the, as yet, unavailable frock coat. Richardson may have worn a version of the same shell jacket since there was an officer's version during the Mexican War. The walk up from El Paso would have been more comfortable in this uniform, and this was exactly the kind of service for which the shell jacket was designed.

Some contention within the expert community concerns the presence of a company letter on the front of Model 1839 field caps. Given that brass company letters from certain long-serving Fort Fillmore infantry companies of the early 1850s, specifically Company 'C,' 3^d Infantry, are nonexistent as relics at the fort, the author assumes the company letter was not used on the Model 1839 forage cap, at least not at Fort Fillmore or Fort Daniel Webster, a sub-post of Fort Fillmore. Company letters came into use in the middle 1850s on uniforms specified by the 1851 and 1854 Army regulation changes and thereafter. They did not appear at Fort Fillmore until the arrival of 7th Infantry units in 1861.

White cross-body belts with brass accouterments from the Mexican War were worn at Fort Fillmore. The three-inch diameter brass cross-belt plate with its fancy eagle has been found there, as has the miniature 1.5" x 3" belt buckle unique to infantry units during the Mexican War. The infantry had a small belt plate with the letters 'U.S.' on the front, whereas the dragoons in that period wore a larger 'U.S.' belt plate. Both have been found in refuse sites at Fort Fillmore.

While there are always arguments concerning the form and type of uniform and headgear, there is little doubt as to the weapon the infantry soldiers carried. In 1851 the infantry at Fort Fillmore was armed with the .69 Caliber, Model 1842 Musket, the same weapon they used during the Mexican War. This weapon was charged with a paper cartridge loaded most often with what was referred to as a 'buck and ball' mix. This particular wrapped paper cartridge contained a load of black gunpowder, a .69 caliber lead ball, and a group of small lead buckshot. The soldier bit, or in some manner, tore the paper open, poured the powder in first, then the buckshot, finally, ramming the large ball on top of that. The paper was then forced down the muzzle to hold the whole mix together for firing. Regulars serving in New Mexico retained this weapon as the standard until after the Navajo conflict of 1858, even though a much more effective weapon was directed by regulations in 1855.

The dragoons wore the same Model 1839 forage cap as the infantry. Some surviving artifacts from other forts show the 2^d United States Dragoons wearing a yellow band around the center of that venerable piece of headgear, but the 1st Dragoons did not adopt the alteration. The 1839 forage cap was dark blue, with the small nondescript eagle and shield button holding the chin-strap as the only addition of color. Brevet-Captain Abraham Buford probably wore the same Model 1839 forage cap as the enlisted men. He could choose to wear a large shako similar to that worn by the infantry, except for the gilt star, silver eagle, and gold chin cord. The star and eagle were worn on the front with a large, drooping, white horse-hair pompom topping it off. No insignia for such parade headgear has been identified from Fort Fillmore artifact finds. Like the elaborate infantry shako, the officers may have had one but its wear was limited.[10]

Mounted and at attention when the 3^d Infantry entered into the presence of himself and his men, Brevet-Captain Buford was no doubt dressed in his very best uniform, which may have conformed to the 1847 U.S. Army Regulations. Buford had been in the East on leave before coming to New Mexico, and may possibly have purchased a new outfit, as he was required to do. If he was wearing his best, the regulations describe it thus: The coat was of dark-blue cloth, double-breasted, similar in fashion to that of the infantry; the lace, gold; the collar, cuffs, and turn-backs, yellow. The skirt of the coat was ornamented with a star, instead of a bugle (for infantry). Gold epaulettes, with fringe, according to rank, were worn on the shoulders. The buttons were convex, with a spread-wing eagle with a 'D,' for dragoons on the shield, as opposed to the infantry letter 'I.'[11]

Buford's trousers would have been of blue-grey mixture like the infantry, with two stripes of yellow cloth running up the seam, leaving a gap of one-fourth inches between them. A Dragoon-model sword with a browned steel scabbard, the sword having a half-basket hilt, fish-skin grip, the hold of the handle bound with silver wire, and a blade with two fluted bars down each side, would have been specified. Gloves, a deep orange-colored sash worn around the waist, spurs, and a black patent leather waist belt with a rectangular brass buckle having a 'D' in a wreath in the center, were also defined by regulations.[12]

A more simple frock coat like that of the infantry could also be worn with the above equipment. In addition, dragoon officers could wear the dark-blue shell jacket so often seen in the pictures and paintings of the Mexican War era. This jacket had gold lace trimmings for an officer. As a final choice, and since it was still summer, Buford could have worn the all-white duty uniform used for stable-duty, marches, or field service.[13]

Buford's horse would have been adorned differently from that of Miles and his staff and it was probably personal property. The saddle may have been of the same military issue as his men's—a heavy brass-decorated Grimsley-model. Buford's saddle blanket would have been dark blue with a yellow cloth border, one-and-a-half inches wide. The black leather horse's bridle had a circular brass rosette near the ears on both sides of the horse's head with the number '1,' for 1st Dragoons, embossed on it. All other mountings on the bridle, as well as the saddle and other equipment, were brass, as opposed to the plated silver of the infantry. The black leather straps girding the horse's chest may have had a heart-shaped martingale device at the front, also emblazoned with the numeral '1,' although no such device has been identified from the fort.[14]

The dragoon enlisted men were colorfully attired as well, with two choices for the enlisted uniform. A very attractive waist-length dark-blue jacket with yellow trim and a stand up collar was used for both everyday and campaign duty. The jacket was virtually the same as that worn by dragoon companies during the Mexican War. The single row of brass buttons contained a 'D' on the eagle's shield. The buttons were 14-15 mm, and are often mistakenly called cuff buttons. The pants would have been the light-blue mixture similar to those worn by the infantry. In the case of the dragoons, only non-commissioned officers had yellow or orange stripes up the pant leg; sergeants had two yellow stripes, corporals, one. Dragoon enlisted men also had a lighter weight white cotton fatigue tunic which could be worn on duty during the summer. The pants may have been the same light-blue mixture. The regulations do not tell of white pants for enlisted men, although they may have existed.[15]

The dragoons had white leather cross and waist belts, similar to the infantry, adorned only with a plain open face buckle made of brass. This belt had a hook on the end to hold the long weapon they carried while mounted. An oval brass waist belt buckle, examples of which have been found at Fort Fillmore, was larger than the infantry buckle, but still retained the embossed 'US' on its face.

The weapons carried by Company 'H' in the early days of Fort Fillmore are harder to define. There were two basic choices in long arms, the Model 1847 Cavalry Musketoon, caliber .69, and the .52 caliber Hall's Carbine. Ammunition for both types has been identified in Fort Fillmore finds, although the Hall Carbine ammunition may also have served another weapon. The Hall Carbine is a little more likely for September 1851, since it was the older weapon of the two. By 1853 Company 'H,' then serving at Fort Daniel Webster on the Mimbres River, was equipped with the Musketoon. The sidearm at this point was the Model 1840 Heavy Dragoon Saber, complemented with a few revolvers. The .44 caliber Colt Dragoon Revolver was listed as available to Company 'H' in 1850 from Santa Fe stores, and no doubt a few were carried in 1851. Major Jefferson Van Horne, who commanded the 3[d] Infantry Battalion at El Paso in early 1851, mentioned a revolver in service by the infantry, but did not say what kind it was.[16]

The saddle equipment for the enlisted dragoons was almost identical to that of the officers. One difference, attested to by artifact finds, was to be found in the circular horse bridle rosettes. Enlisted versions were embossed with the company letter, 'H,' instead of the '1' reserved for the use of officers.

The bandsmen may have worn red jackets with white trim, the infantry color, while on duty as bandsmen.

When they came to New Mexico in 1856 the Regiment of Mounted Rifles' uniform trim color was green, compared to the orange of the dragoons, the yellow of the newly formed cavalry regiments, red for artillery units, and blue for infantry. In 1856 R.M.R. soldiers were probably wearing their short dark-blue Model 1854 shell jackets with green trim, with or without brass shoulder scales, the numeral '1' on the stand-up collar and a green-trimmed shako with the national eagle on the front, with no company letter. The '1' device was found in Fort Fillmore refuse sites in some quantity. The blue French-influence shako would have had a green-colored pom-pom on the top.

NOTES - Appendix I

1. *1847 General Regulations*, p 215.
2. Ibid.
3. Ibid., pp. 199, 200.
4. Ibid., pp. 214, 215.
5. Ibid., p. 200.
6. Ibid., p. 213.
7. Heitman, John Fox Hammond.
8. *1847 General Regulations*, pp. 199, 200. The coat specified for infantry in the 1847 regulations was a frock coat. No jacket, like that used by the dragoons or Mounted Rifles, was prescribed. There seems to have been a dress frock-type coat with white-colored trim and epaulettes for use on parade and formal occasion. A second frock-type coat was available with the added decoration.

9. Van Horn to McLaws, September 12, 1850, M1102, Roll 3.

10. 1847 General Regulations, p. 197.

11. Ibid., pp. 196, 197.

12. Ibid.

13. Ibid.

14. Ibid., pp. 212, 213.

15. Ibid., pp. 196, 197.

16. Joseph F. Mansfield, *Mansfield in the Condition of the Western Forts, 1853-54*, p. 223.

APPENDIX II

Officers Serving at Fort Millard Fillmore - 1851-1862

This appendix provides a listing of all officers who were stationed at Fort Millard Fillmore, or were known to have been there as part of their normal duties before 1862. The listing is divided into three parts: Those who served the Union cause during the American Civil War; those who served the Confederate cuase; and those who did not serve on either side during the Civil War. The officer's Fort Fillmore rank, as well as the highest rank attained by the individual, are also provided.

Fort Fillmore Officers Who Served the Union Cause

Major-Surgeon Eugene Hilarion Abadie	Lieutenant Colonel-Surgeon
Assistant Surgeon Charles Henry Alden	Colonel-Surgeon
	POW in New Mexico - 1861
1st Lieutenant John W. Alley	Captain - POW in Texas - 1861-62
Colonel Benjamin L.E. Bonneville	Brigadier General
Brevet-Captain Andrew Bowman	Lieutenant Colonel
Major Benjamin W. Brice	Major General
1st Lieutenant Milton Cogswell	Brevet-Colonel
Assistant Surgeon George E. Cooper	Colonel-Surgeon
2d Lieutenant Edward Cressey	Brevet-Lt. Colonel
	POW in New Mexico - 1861
2d Lieutenant Frances J. Crilly	Brevet-Colonel
	POW in New Mexico - 1861
Captain John Wynn Davidson	Major General
2d Lieutenant Benjamin Franklin Davis	Colonel
2d Lieutenant John Henry Edson	Lieutenant Colonel
Captain Washington Lafayette Elliott	Major General
2d Lieutenant Royal Thaxter Frank	Brigadier General
	POW in Texas - 1861
2d Lieutenant William Henry Freedley	Colonel
	POW in Texas - 1861
Captain Alfred Gibbs	Brevet-Major General
	POW in New Mexico - 1861
Assistant Surgeon John Fox Hammond	Colonel-Surgeon
1st Lieutenant David Porter Hancock	Brevet-Lieutenant Colonel
2d Lieutenant David H. Hastings	Major
Asst. Surgeon Thomas Charlton Henry	Brevet-Lieutenant Colonel

Fort Fillmore Officers Who Served the Union Cause, cont.

2d Lieutenant John McLean Hildt — Lieutenant Colonel
POW in Texas - 1861

1st Lieutenant George W. Howland — Brevet-Major
Fought at Valverde - 1862

1st Lieutenant William B. Lane — Brevet-Major

2d Lieutenant Richard Gregory Lay — Brevet-Lieutenant Colonel

1st Lieutenant Henry M. Lazelle — Brigadier General
POW in Texas - 1861

2d Lieutenant Richard S.C. Lord — Brevet-Lieutenant Colonel
Fought at Valverde - 1862

Major Isaac Lynde — Major
POW in New Mexico 1861

2d Lieutenant Alexander McD. McCook — Major General

Captain John Courts McFerran — Brigadier General

Asst. Surgeon James C. McKee — Brevet-Lieutenant Colonel
POW in New Mexico - 1861

Brevet-Captain Charles Hely McNally — Major
Wounded at Mesilla - 1861

Lt. Colonel Dixon Stansbury Miles — Colonel
Killed at Harper's Ferry

Colonel Joseph Fenno Mansfield — Major General
Killed at Antietam

Brevet-2d Lieutenant Lyman Mischler — 1st Lieutenant
Killed at Valverde - 1862

Captain Frederick Myers — Brevet-Brigadier General

Brevet-Major Gabriel Rene Paul — Brevet-Major General
Blinded at Gettysburg

1st Lieutenant Augustus H. Plummer — 1st Lieutenant
POW in Texas 1861-1862

Captain Joseph Haydn Potter — Brevet-Major General
POW in New Mexico 1861

Brevet-Major Israel Bush Richardson — Major General
Killed at Antietam

1st Lieutenant George Ryan — Colonel
Killed at Spottsylvania

Captain Oliver Shepherd — Brevet-Brigadier General

Brevet-Major Enoch Steen — Lieutenant Colonel

Captain Mathew Rider Stevenson — Captain
POW in New Mexico - 1861

1st Lieutenant Charles Bryant Stivers — Captain
POW in New Mexico - 1861

1st Lieutenant Samuel Davis Sturges — Brevet-Major General

Brevet-Colonel Edwin Vose Sumner — Major General

Fort Fillmore Officers Who Served the Union Cause, cont.

Asst. Surgeon Charles Sutherland	Brigadier General-Surgeon
Captain George Sykes	Brevet-Major General
1st Lt. William Dennison Whipple	Major General
1st Lieutenant Joseph Whistler	Brevet-Brigadier General
Brevet-1st Lt. John Darragh Wilkins	Colonel
1st Lieutenant William H. Wood	Colonel

Fort Fillmore Officers who Served the Confederate Cause

Brevet-Captain Barnard E. Bee	Brigadier General Killed at 1st Bull Run
2d Lieutenant Richard V. Bonneau	Major
Brevet-Captain Abraham Buford	Brigadier General
1st Lieutenant Junius Daniel	Brigadier General Killed at Spottsylvania
2d Lieutenant Nathan George Evans	Brigadier General
Captain Richard Stoddert Ewell	Lieutenant General
Captain Robert Garland	Colonel
Brigadier Gen. Albert Sydney Johnston	General (full)
Colonel Joseph Eccleston Johnston	General (full)
Captain James Longstreet	Major General
Colonel William Wing Loring	Major General
2d Lieutenant Henry C. McNeill	Colonel Fought at Valverde - 1862
2d Lt. John Sappington Marmaduke	Major General
Brevet-Major Dabney Maury	Brigadier General
1st Lieutenant Laurens O'Bannon	Major
Brevet-Captain George Pickett	Major General
2d Lieutenant Robert Ransom, Jr.	Major General
Captain Thomas Grimke Rhett	Major
2d Lt. Beverly Holcombe Robertson	Brigadier General
2d Lieutenant Charles Henry Rundell	Captain
1st Lieutenant Donald Stith	Colonel
2d Lieutenant Henry Harrison Walker	Brigadier General Wounded at Spottsylvania
2d Lieutenant Joseph Wheeler	Brigadier General, CSA - Major General USA
Captain Cadmus Wilcox	Brigadier General

Fort Fillmore Officers Who Did Not Serve in the Civil War

Major Electus Backus	Retired after surrending to Texas state forces in 1861
1st Lieutenant Edward J. Brooks	Resigned after POW in New Mexico in 1861
Brevet-Major William H. Gordon	Retired in 1862 after promotion to major
Captain William Brook Johns	Retired after surrendering to Texas state forces in 1861
Frederick H. Masten	Resigned his commission in 1857
Major Gouveneur Morris	Retired after surrendering to Texas state forces in 1861
Captain Henry Whiting Stanton	Killed by Apaches in 1855
Brevet-Major Jefferson Van Horne	Died in New Mexico in 1857
1st Lieutenant James Noble Ward	Died while on duty in Minnesota in 1858

APPENDIX III

U.S. Army Regiments and Companies Which
Served at Fort Fillmore, 1851-1862

This appendix provides a listing of all regiment and company-sized units which served at Fort Millard Fillmore or were known to have been there as part of their normal duties before 1862. The list contains the name and number of the regiments and companies within the regiments, and includes the dates of service at the fort for the companies.

U. S. Army Regiments Associated with Fort Fillmore

3d Infantry Regiment
1st Dragoon Regiment
2d Dragoon Regiment
Regiment of Mounted Rifles (R.M.R.)
U.S. Topographical Engineers
8th Infantry Regiment
7th Infantry Regiment
2d Texas Mounted Rifles (Baylor)
7th Texas Mounted Volunteers (Steele)
3d U.S. Artillery Regiment
5th California Infantry Regiment
1st Cavalry Regiment, California Volunteers
2d Cavalry Regiment, California Volunteers

U.S. Army Companies Serving at Fort Fillmore

Company 'H,' 1st Dragoon Regiment	September 1851-November 1852
	May 1854-October 1854
Company 'K,' 3d Infantry Regiment	September 1851-December 1852
	December 1852-July 1853
Company 'E,' 3d Infantry Regiment	September 1851-June 1854
Company 'D,' 2d Dragoon Regiment	February 1852-May 1852
Company 'K,' 2d Dragoon Regiment	September 1852-November 1852
Company 'C,' 3d Infantry Regiment	September 1852-January 1859
Company 'D,' 2d Dragoon Regiment	December 1852-April 1854

Company 'A,' 3d Infantry Regiment	August 1853-June 1854
	August 1854-December 1854
	February 1855-May 1855
Company 'B,' 1st Dragoon Regiment	October 1854-June 1855
Company 'G,' R.M.R.	September 1856-November 1857
Company 'C,' R.M.R.	January 1859-June 1859
	August 1859-March 1860
Company 'H,' 3d Infantry Regiment	January 1859-September 1859
Company 'D,' 1st Dragoon Regiment	April 1859-May 1860
Company 'E,' 8th Infantry Regiment	October 1859-May 1860
	October 1860-February 1861
Company 'I,' 3d Infantry Regiment	April 1860-September 1860
Company 'I,' 8th Infantry Regiment	September 1860-October 1860
Company 'A,' R.M.R.	February 1861-July 1862
Company 'D,' 7th Infantry Regiment	April 1861-July 1861
Company 'I,' 7th Infantry Regiment	April 1861-July 1861
Company 'K,' 7th Infantry Regiment	April 1861-July 1861
Company 'E,' 7th Infantry Regiment	July 1861-July 1861
Company 'A,' 7th Infantry Regiment	July 1861-July 1861
Company 'B,' 7th Infantry Regiment	July 1861-July 1861
Elements of 2d Texas Mounted Rifles	July 1861-May 1862
Company 'C,' 7th Texas Mounted Vols.	February 1862-July 1862
Company 'C,' 3d Artillery Regiment	August 1962-September 1862
Company 'A,' 1st Cav., California Vols.	August 1862-September 1862
Company 'B,' 1st Cav., California Vols.	August 1862-September 1862
Company 'B,' 2d Cav., California Vols.	August 1862-September 1862
Company 'A,' 5th Inf., California Vols.	August 1862-October 1862
Company 'B,' 5th Inf., California Vols.	August 1862-September 1862

APPENDIX IV

Fort Fillmore Cemetery - Probable Burials

1. Private Martin Butler - Co. 'E,' 3d Infantry (November 12, 1851)
2. Private Francis Clemens - Co. 'K,' 3d Infantry (November 14, 1851)
3. Private Edward Wallis - Co. 'E,' 2d Dragoons (March 1852)
4. Corporal John Montague - Co. 'K,' 2d Dragoons (November 29, 1852)
5. Private Sam H. Ray - Co. 'A,' 3d Infantry (March 8, 1853)
6. Private William Wilson - Co. 'K,' 3d Infantry (May 16, 1853)
7. Sergeant Jonathan Krollpfiffer - Co. 'D,' 2d Dragoons (May 1853)
8. Private Henry Depher - Co. 'C,' 3d Infantry (August 14, 1853)
9. Captain Henry Stanton - Co. 'B,' 1st Dragoons (January 18, 1855)
10. Private Thomas Dwyer - Co. 'B,' 1st Dragoons (January 18, 1855)
11. Private Jon Henning - Co. 'B,' 1st Dragoons (January 18, 1855)
12. Private T.L. Young - Co. 'G,' 1st Dragoons (July 15, 1855)
13. Private Darby Ryan - Co. 'E,' 8th Infantry (February 20, 1856)
14. Private Charles Spatz - Co. 'C,' 3d Infantry (August 1856)
15. Private John I. Haber - Co. 'G,' R.M.R. (May 18, 1857)
16. Private Ludwig Eppler - Co. 'C,' 3d Infantry (September 13, 1857)
17. Q.M. Sergeant John Einsedel - Q.M., 3d Infantry (October 7, 1857)
18. Private Harragan - Co. 'C,' R.M.R. (December 7, 1859)
19. Private Conher - Co. 'D,' 1st Dragoons (January 1860)
20. Private John Lane - Co. 'F,' R.M.R. (Killed at Mesilla - July 25, 1861)
21. Private Jenkins - Co. 'I,' 7th Infantry (Killed at Mesilla - July 25, 1861)
22. Private Sherwood - Co. 'G,' 7th Infantry (Killed at Mesilla - July 25, 1861)
23. Private John Poole - 7th Texas Mounted Volunteers (1861/62)
24. Private Benjamin Sellers - Co. 'C,' 7th Texas Mounted Volunteers (1861/62)

25. Private Timothy Sellers - Co. 'C,' 7th Texas Mounted Volunteers (1861/62)
26. Private George Martin - Co. 'C,' 5th California Infantry (1862)
27. Corporal Robert Welch - Co. 'A,' 5th California Infantry (1862)
28. Private Thomas J. Varner - Co. 'A,' 5th California Infantry (1862)
29-47. Nineteen soldiers from the Regular Army died from various causes while serving at Fort Fillmore. Their names are not yet known.
48. One additional Confederate Texan may be buried there.
49. The body of the Apache Leader Cuentas Azules may be buried there. (1853)
50. The sister of Brevet-Major Israel Richardson may be buried there.
51-58. At least eight Coyotero Apache women and children may be buried there. Several Apache persons were buried at the rear of the Fort Thorn Cemetery, a possible military precedent for burials at Fort Fillmore.
59. One other female, an officer's wife, arrived at Fort Fillmore in a very weakened state. She may not have survived.
60. Another woman, a company laundress, serving with the 3d Infantry died of old age and may be buried there.
61-?. Estimates in 1868 were that there were from seventy to ninety burials in the cemetery, perhaps more.

BIBLIOGRAPHY

Albert, Alphaeus H., *Record of American Uniform and Historical Buttons.* Boyertown, Pa.: Boyertown Publishing Company, 1969.

Association of Graduates, U.S.M.A., *Register of Graduates and Former Cadets of the United States Military Academy 1802-1979.* Chicago: R.R. Donnelley & Sons, 1979.

Bartlett, John R., *Personal Narrative of Explorations and Incidents in Texas, New Mexico, California, etc., Vol. II.* Chicago: The Rio Grande Press Inc., 1965.

Bennett, James A., *Forts & Forays: A Dragoon in New Mexico, 1850-1856.* Albuquerque: Univ. of New Mexico Press, 1948.

Bloom, Lansing B., *New Mexico History and Civics.* Albuquerque: The University of New Mexico Press, 1933.

Bowen, Ezra, editor, et al., *The Soldiers.* Alexandria: Time-Life Books, 1975.

Browne, J. Ross, *Adventures in the Apache Country.* New York, 1869.

Cleaveland, Agnes Morley, *Satan's Paradise.* Boston: Houghton-Mifflin Co., 1952.

Conkling, Roscoe P. & Margaret B., *The Butterfield Overland Mail 1857-1869, Volume II.* Glendale CA: The Arthur H. Clark Company, 1947.

Connelley, William Elsey, *Doniphan's Expedition and the Conquest of New Mexico and California.* Topeka: William Elsey Connelley, 1907.

Faulk, Odie B., *Crimson Desert-Indian Wars of the American Southwest.* New York: Oxford University Press, 1974.

_____, *The U.S. Camel Corps-An Army Experiment.* New York: Oxford University Press, 1976.

Flahert, Thomas H. Jr., editor, et al., *The Mexican War.* Alexandria, Virginia: Time-Life Books, 1978.

Garber, Paul Neff, *The Gadsden Treaty.* University of Pennsylvania Press, 1924.

Giese, Dale F., *Forts of New Mexico.* Silver City: Dale F. Giese, 1991.

Goetzmann, William H., *Army Explorartion in the American West 1803-1863.* Lincoln and London: University of Nebraska Press, 1979.

Griggs, George, *History of the Mesilla Valley.* Mesilla, New Mexico, 1930.

Hand, George. *The Civil War in Apacheland: Sergeant George Hand's Diary, California, Arizona, West Texas, New Mexico, 1861-1864.* Ed. Neil B. Carmony. Silver City, NM: High-Lonesome Books, 1996.

Hart, Herbert., *Old Forts of the Southwest.* Seattle: Superior Publishing Co., 1964.

Heitman, Francis B., *Historical Register and Dictionary of the United States Army, from its Organization, September 29, 1789, to March 2, 1903.* Washington: Genealogical Publishing Co., Inc., 1994.

Hinshaw, Gil, et al., *Lea, New Mexico's Last Frontier.* Hobbs: Hobbs Daily Sun News, undated.

Kupke, William A., *The Indian and the Thunderwagon: A History of the Mountain Howitzer.* Silver City, NM: privately printed, 1991

Lane, Lydia Spencer, *I Married a Soldier*. Albuquerque: Horn & Wallace, 1964.

Larson, Robert W., *New Mexico's Quest for Statehood*. Albuquerque: The University of New Mexico Press, 1968.

Leach, Colonel James B., *Report on the El Paso and Fort Yuma Wagon Road. Pacific Wagon Roads*. (U.S. Senate documents, 35th Congress, Session II, Vol. 1, 125pp., with map, February 1859.)

McCall, Colonel George Archibald, *New Mexico in 1850: A Military View*. Ed. Robert W. Frazer. Norman: University of Oklahoma Press, 1968.

McKee, James Cooper, *Narrative of the Surrender of a Command of U.S. Forces at Fort Fillmore, New Mexico in July, A. D. 1861*. Houston: Stagecoach Press, 1960.

Manion's International Auction House Inc., *U.S. Historical Collectibles, Auction #193B*. Kansas City: Manion's International Auction House, 1998.

Miller, Darlis A., *The California Column in New Mexico*. Albuquerque: University of New Mexico Press, 1982.

Moorhead, Max L., *New Mexico's Royal Road: Trade and Travel on the Chihuahua Trail*. Norman: University of Oklahoma Press, 1958.

Pierce, T.M., *New Mexico Place Names: A Geographical Dictionary*. Albuquerque: University of New Mexico, 1965.

Price, Paxton P., *Pioneers of the Mesilla Valley*. Las Cruces, NM: Yucca Tree Press, 1995.

Richardson, James D., *A Compilation of the Messages and Papers of the Presidents, Vol VI*. New York: Bureau of National Literature, Inc., 1897.

_____, *A Compilation of the Messages and Papers of the Presidents, Vol. VII*. New York: Bureau of National Literature, Inc., 1897.

Roberts, Calvin A. & Susan. *A History of New Mexico*. Albuquerque: University of New Mexico Press, 1986.

Smith, George Winston and Charles Judah, *Chronicles of the Gringos - The U.S. Army in the Mexican War, 1846-1848*. Albuquerque: University of New Mexico Press, 1968.

Sonnichsen, C.L., *Pass of the North*. El Paso: Texas Western Press, 1968.

_____, *Roy Bean, Law West of the Pecos*. New York: Devin-Adair Company, 1958.

Sweeney, Edwin R., *Cochise*. Norman and London: University of Oklahoma Press, 1991.

Taylor, John, *Bloody Valverde - A Civil War Battle on the Rio Grande, February 21, 1862*. Albuquerque: University of New Mexico Press, 1995.

Terrell, John Upton, *Apache Chronicles*. New York: World Publishing, Times Mirror, 1971.

Thomas, Alfred Barnaby, *Forgotten Frontiers: A Study of the Spanish Indian Policy of Don Juan de Anza, Governor of New Mexico, 1777-1787*. Norman: University of Oklahoma Press, 1932.

Thrapp, Dan L., *Encyclopedia of Frontier Biography*. 3 vols. Lincoln & London: Univ. of Nebraska Press, in association with Arther H. Clark Co., Spokane Washington, 1988.

Twitchell, Ralph Emerson, *The History of the Military of New Mexico from 1846 to 1851.*Chicago: The Rio Grande Press Inc., 1963.

Urwin, Gregory J.W., *The United States Cavalry - An Illustrated History.* London: Blandford Press, 1983.

_____, *The United States Infantry.* New York: Sterling Publishing Co., Inc., 1991.

Warner, Ezra J., *Generals in Blue: Lives of the Union Army Commanders.* Baton Rouge: Louisiana State University Press, 1964.

_____, *Generals in Gray: Lives of the Confederate Army Commanders* Baton Rouge: Louisiana State University Press, 1959.

Wellman, Paul I., *Death in the Desert: The Fifty Years' War for the Great Southwest.* New York: The McMillan Co., 1939.

Williams, Jerry L., et al., ed., *New Mexico in Maps.* Albuquerque: University of New Mexico Press, 1979.

Winther, Oscar O., *The Transportation Frontier.* New York: Holt, Rinehart and Winston, 1964.

Perodicals

Bloom, L.B., "Hugh Stevenson And The Brazito Grant," *New Mexico Historical Review,* Vol. 17, No. 3, 1942, p. 279.

Crimmons, M.L., "Fort Fillmore," *New Mexico Historical Review,* Vol. 6, No. 4, 1931, p. 327+.

Dinges, Bruce J, Editor-in-Chief, et al., "With the Third Infantry in New Mexico, 1851-1853: The Lost Diary of Private Sylvester W. Matson." *The Journal of Arizona History*, Volume 31, Number 4, 1990.

INDEX

Floyd, John Buchanan 293
Fort Bliss, Texas 116, 137, 155, 177, 181, 190, 192, 228-229, 261, 263, 274-276, 288-289, 311, 315, 317, 322-324, 326, 336-338, 353
Fort Breckinridge 297, 322-324, 325, 330, 345
Fort Buchanan 206, 209, 257, 264-265, 295, 296, 304, 318, 321, 323-325, 330, 337-338, 345
Fort Butler 289
Fort Conrad 24, 40, 44, 49, 63, 66, 70-71, 74, 78, 83, 96, 101-102, 105-107, 109-110, 113, 137, 219
Fort Craig 113. 137, 162, 169-170, 177-178, 181, 192, 199, 201, 228, 234, 239, 252-253, 267, 270, 286, 304, 318, 322, 326-327, 332, 337, 339-343
Fort Cummings 353
Fort Davis, Texas 339, 350
Fort Defiance 24, 52, 177, 181-182, 189, 211, 242, 244-247, 250-251, 258, 288, 292
Fort Fillmore Project Flag 375
Fort Millard Fillmore 3, 5-9, 27-28, 31-35, 37, 39-44, 46-54, 56, 58-59, 61-65, 67, 70-71, 73-85, 92-97, 100-110, 113-119, 127-130, 134, 142-143, 145-150, 152-155, 157-159, 164-167, 171, 174, 177-179, 181-182, 184-185, 187-193, 196-199, 206, 211-214, 216-222, 228-229, 231-239, 241, 243, 245, 248, 252, 254, 256, 258-259, 261-266, 268-276, 278-279, 283-284, 286, 288, 292, 296-301, 303-304, 306-319, 321-322, 324-326, 331, 334-342, 344-345, 346-360, 362-363, 365-372, 375, 377, 381-383, 389, 393, 396; *illus.* 41; *plat*

43; cemetery 51, 355-356, 358, 366, 369, 375, 396, *photos* 370, 374; Christmas Day 108, 159; excavations, 1966 360; 1986-87 363-365; farming 53-55, 75-76; hospital 158; last surviving veteran 358; 150th anniversary 357, *photo* 357; post library 85; Valentine's Day celebration 95; G. Washington birthday 96
Fort Floyd 293, 305
Fort Leavenworth, KT 2-3, 6, 8, 101, 259
Fort McLane 305, 308, 312, 317, 319, 321-322, 369, 375
Fort Massachusetts 24, 183
Fort Quitman, Texas 350
Fort Selden 355-357; Friends 369
Fort Stanton 74, 149, 151, 171, 177-178, 181, 192, 226, 308, 327-328, 350
Fort Sumter, SC 312
Fort Thorn 97, 112, 115, 118-119, 137, 157, 161-162, 166-167, 169, 174, 177, 179-181, 190, 196, 198-199, 213, 217, 228-232, 239, 245, 249, 254, 258, 260-261, 264, 285, 345, 346, 396
Fort Union 24, 26, 55, 59, 78, 130, 217, 238, 268
Fort Daniel Webster 7, 24, 31, 47-48, 56-59, 61, 64, 68, 70-75, 77, 79-83, 85-86, 88, 97, 99-101, 104-105, 107-110, 117, 118, 137, 155, 174, 266, 283-284, 293, 253, 362, 375, 383, 386; *photo* 320
Fort Joseph Rodman West 354-355, 375
.44 caliber Colt dragoon revolver 140, 364-386
Francisco Hanero 128

Morrison, Pitcairn 292, 299, 301
mountain howitzer (*see* howitzer,
   mountain)
Munroe, John 20, 79
Myers, Frederick 197, 218, 390
Munroe, John 20, 79

National Cemetery Act 355-356
Navajo Tribe 25-26, 41, 52,
   145, 199-192, 233, 238-240,
   251, 258, 266, 292
Negrito 286
New Mexico State Univ. 368
Newport Barracks, KY 50
Nichols, William Augustus 135,
   158-160, 184-185, 220-221,
   228, 235, 254-255
9th Military Department 3, 6,
   14, 16, 18, 21, 32, 34, 37, 63-
   64, 78-79, 88, 96, 107-108,
   138, 344
Northern Column, Bonneville
Campaign 200-202-204-205

O'Bannon, Laurens 58, 62, 80,
   91, 131, 132, 146, 167-169,
   181, 204, 217, 220, 391
O'Bannon, May Miles (see
   Miles, May)
Ojo del Muerto Springs 192
Organ Mts. 8, 26, 57, 178, 215,
   262, 290, 296, 327-328
Oury, Granville 285
Owings, Lewis S. 286-289, 300

Pacific Railroad Survey 154
Palanquito 127, 129, 154-155,
   178, 180
Palo Alto, battle of 68
Paso del Norte (modern Juarez,
   Mexico) 3, 11-12, 14, 19, 24,
   45, 50, 74, 81, 91, 98, 101,
   102, 278, 281
Paul, Gabriel Rene 313, 317-318,
   321, 332, 390

Paz, Nermina 359
Peña 115
Picacho Mt. 146
Pickett, George 115, 119, 391
Pierce, President Franklin 83-84,
   115, 159
Pidgeon's Ranch (*see* Glorieta Pass)
Pima Tribe 304
Pinal Tribe 182, 276-277, 281
Pinon 144, 162
Pinos Altos 219, 295, 296, 321,
   339; Mts. 25
pipes, clay, *illus*. 84
Pleasanton, Alfred 78
Plumas 154
Plummer, Augustus H. 211, 390
Plympton, Peter William Living-
   ston 341
Point of Rocks 63, 66
Polk, President James 176
Ponce 62, 72, 75, 118
Poncita 75
Pope, John 9
Poole, John 359
Potter, Joseph Haydn 321, 323,
   330, 332-333, 390
Priestley, Charlotte 366-367
Pueblo Tribes 47, 156, 191-192,
   206-207, 209
Pyron, Charles 343

Ransom, Robert 64, 110, 112,
   114, 391
Read, Benjamin 76
red-leg artillery 233
Regiment of Mounted Rifles
   (R.M.R.) 175-179, 189, 192,
   193, 199, 200-201, 205-208,
   210-212, 214, 217, 222, 233,
   239-240, 241, 246, 258-261,
   264-266, 268, 274-275, 277-
   278, 280, 283, 286, 297-304,
   306, 313, 315, 318-319, 329,
   334, 369, 377, 386, 393-394;
   illus. 186

Resaca de la Palma, battle of   68
Rhett, Thomas Grimke   179, 185,
    391
Richardson, Israel Bush   6-7, 37,
    48, 57-58, 61-63, 83, 86, 104,
    111, 130, 131, 155, 283, 381,
    383, 390, 396,
Robertson, Beverly Holcombe
    391
Robledo, Roblero [sic]   51, 130,
    193
Ruelas, Raphael   9, 284
Rundell. Charles Henry   107, 391
Ryan, George   321, 332, 390
Rynerson, W.L.   355-356, 372

saber, heavy dragoon   176, 383
Sackett, Delos   9, 11
Sacramento Mts.   58, 69, 81-82,
    106, 115, 127, 129, 139
Saige, Jerry   371
Salopek, John   360, 366-367
San Augustine Pass   328
San Augustine Springs   93, 154,
    262, 303, 327, 330-331, 335-
    336, 375
San Diego Crossing   61, 102,
    199, 346
San Elizario   3, 12, 14-16, 20,
    23, 25, 33, 45-46, 91
San Nicholas Springs   97, 216,
    262
Santa Anna, Antonio Lopez
    de   89, 98
Santa Barbara, Rancho del   62,
    109-110
Santa Lucia Springs   57, 231,
    295, 375
Santa Rita Copper Mines   13,
    15, 42, 44, 56, 58, 62, 71, 79,
    107, 146, 169-170, 219, 375
Santa Riga del Cohre (see also
Santa Rita Copper Mines)   266-
    269, 292, 295
Santo Tomás, St. Thomas   46,
    65, 98, 131-132, 134, 276,
    290, 297, 324

Santos   127, 129
Schneider, Russell   371
Scott, Winfield   12, 18, 52, 83,
    164, 174, 183
2nd Cavalry, California Volun-
    teers   348-349, 393-394
2nd Dragoon Regiment   63-64,
    66, 68, 78, 83, 86, 101, 106,
    113-114, 280, 287-288, 292,
    334, 393, 395
2nd Texas Mounted Rifles   324,
    393-394
Sellers, Benjamin   359
Sellers, Timothy   359
Sergento   144
7th Infantry Regiment   287-288,
    292, 296, 298, 310-313, 317, 322-
    323, 326, 330-331, 335, 337,
    341-342, 361-362, 393-395
7th Texas Mounted Volunteers
    393, 395-396
Sharps Carbine   224, 270, 364
Shawans (see Showano)
Shepherd, Oliver   170, 192, 390
Shoemaker, William R.   268
Showano (Shawans)   162, 174-
    175, 180
Sibley, C.C.   287, 293
Sibley, Henry Hopkins   313, 335-
    336, 339, 343-345, 352, 358
Sierra Blanca Mts.   117, 139,
    262, 339
Simonson, John   145, 199, 201
Skillman, Henry   77
Smith, James M.   108, 115
Smith, John   369, 370
Smith, Joseph   249, 350-351
Snyder, Thomas, CSA, last surviv-
    ing Fort Fillmore veteran   358
Socorro (NMT)   10, 11, 161,
    231-232
Socorro (Texas)   3, 12, 14-16,
    23, 45
Sonora, Mexican state of   253,
    257, 260, 278, 281
Soledad Canyon   206, 298

16, 19-20, 22, 24, 34, 37, 50, 59, 68, 74, 145, 179-180, 385, 388, 392

Vamer, Thomas J.   351

Venancio   264

Wadsworth, Richard, *photo*   320

Walker, Henry Harrison   131, 138, 141, 146, 239, 391

Ward, James Noble   117, 392

Warm Springs Tribe   25, 202, 260

Washington, George   85

weapons, Hall Carbine   386; Burnside Carbine   268; Maynard Carbine, 268, 270, 274; Sharps Carbine, 224, 270, 364; Model 1841 .54 caliber rifle (Mississippi Rifle)   176, 199, 202, 223, 364; Model 1842 caliber .69 infantry musket   199, 223, 244, 273, 364; Model 1847 cavalry Musketoon   364; Model 1855 caliber .58 infantry rifle/musket   244, 273, 364; .58 caliber pistol-carbine 273-274; Model 1840 heavy dragoon saber   176, 383; .44 caliber Colt dragoon revolver 140, 364-386; .36 caliber Colt Navy revolver   140, 270, 273-274

Welch, Robert   351

West, Joseph Rodman   345, 352, 354

West Point, Military Academy at 162, 164, 177, 341

Wheeler, Joseph   306, 308-309, 391

Whipple, William Dennison   78, 86, 106, 115, 188, 196, 200, 203, 206-207, 218, 220, 242, 245, 251, 391

Whistler, Joseph N.G.   288-290, 300, 391

White, C.W.   13, 26, 91

White Mts.   58, 92, 106

White Sands Missile Range, NM (WSMR)   93

Wilcox, Cadmus   313, 331, 391

Wildcat (Seminole)   69

Wilkins, John Darragh   77, 80, 82, 86, 104, 106, 112, 145, 179, 256, 278-279, 287, 300, 391

Wilson, Dr. John   360-363, 366, 373

Winston, NM   203

Wood, William H.   106, 113, 229, 391

Ysleta Pueblo   12, 14, 45, 91

Zuni Pueblo   189

Zuni Tribe   182, 246-247